Mastering Arabic Vocabulary

Mastering Arabic Vocabulary: For Beginner to Intermediate Learners of Modern Standard Arabic provides a structured vocabulary course for novice students of Arabic.

Arranged thematically, and by root, the course is a flexible resource that can be used alongside other learning materials. The unique root organisation supports students' understanding of the structure of Arabic words and of the connection between form and meaning in Arabic vocabulary. The wealth of exercises throughout are designed to reinforce learning and help students gain a solid foundation in the key vocabulary needed to reach an intermediate level.

Mastering Arabic Vocabulary is the ideal reference for building a strong foundation in Arabic vocabulary, for students from beginner level up to B1-B2 CEFR and ACTFL Intermediate-Low to Intermediate-High.

Nadia R. Sirhan has a PhD in Arabic Linguistics from SOAS, University of London.

Mastering Arabic Vocabulary
For Beginner to Intermediate Learners
of Modern Standard Arabic

Nadia R. Sirhan

LONDON AND NEW YORK

Designed cover image: proksima via Getty Images

First published 2023
by Routledge
4 Park Square, Milton Park, Abingdon, Oxon OX14 4RN

and by Routledge
605 Third Avenue, New York, NY 10158

Routledge is an imprint of the Taylor & Francis Group, an informa business

© 2023 Nadia R. Sirhan

The right of Nadia R. Sirhan to be identified as author of this work has been asserted in accordance with sections 77 and 78 of the Copyright, Designs and Patents Act 1988.

All rights reserved. No part of this book may be reprinted or reproduced or utilised in any form or by any electronic, mechanical, or other means, now known or hereafter invented, including photocopying and recording, or in any information storage or retrieval system, without permission in writing from the publishers.

Trademark notice: Product or corporate names may be trademarks or registered trademarks, and are used only for identification and explanation without intent to infringe.

British Library Cataloguing-in-Publication Data
A catalogue record for this book is available from the British Library

Library of Congress Cataloging-in-Publication Data
A catalog record for this book has been requested

ISBN: 978-1-032-16901-9 (hbk)
ISBN: 978-1-032-16900-2 (pbk)
ISBN: 978-1-003-25089-0 (ebk)

DOI: 10.4324/9781003250890

Typeset in Times New Roman
by Apex CoVantage, LLC

Contents

Introduction   1
Arabic-derived Verb Forms 3
The Participles 5
Notes on the Text 6
Use of Symbols and Abbreviations 7

1 Family and Feelings العائِلةُ والعَواطِفُ   9
Family Relations العَلاقاتُ العائلِيّةُ 9
Emotions and Feelings المشاعِرُ والعواطِفُ 16
Exercises 35

2 Health الصِّحّةُ   38
The Body الجِسمُ 38
The Senses الحَواسُّ 50
Sex and Reproduction الجِنسُ والتَّناسُلُ 52
The Mind العَقلُ 57
Ailments, Illnesses, and Disabilities الوَعكاتُ والأَمراضُ والإعاقاتُ 58
Treatments, Cures, and Death المُداواةُ والعِلاجُ والْموتُ 72
Exercises 79

3 Education التَّعليمُ   81
School المَدارسُ 81
Education التَّعليمُ 85
Performance Levels الأَداءُ التَّعليميُّ 91
University الْجامعةُ 94
Subjects المَواضيعُ 109
Extracurricular and Recreational Activities
النَّشاطاتُ اللاَّصَفِّيَّةُ والتَّرفيهِيَّةُ 110
Exercises 122

4 Politics عِلمُ السِّياسَةِ   125
Government and Politics الْحُكومَةُ والسِّياسَةُ 125

145 الأحْزابُ السِّياسِيَّةُ والايديولوجيات *Political Parties and Ideologies*
149 الإجراءاتُ الأمنِيَّةُ *Security Measures*
159 الحَربُ والسَّلامُ *War and Peace*
177 العِصيانُ المَدَنِيُّ *Civil Disobedience*
178 الانتخاباتُ والتَّصويتُ *Elections and Voting*
180 النُّزوعُ والمُساعداتُ *Displacement and Aid*
Exercises 185

5 Work, Business, and Economics العَمَلُ والتِّجارةُ والإقتِصادُ   187
187 العَمَلُ والتَّوظيفُ *Work and Employment*
196 العَمَلُ والتِّجارةُ *Business, Trade, and Commerce*
208 الإقتِصادُ والمالُ *Economics and Finance*
Exercises 225

6 Media وَسائِلُ الإعلامِ   227
227 الصَّحافَةُ والأخْبارُ *Journalism and News*
235 النَّشرُ *Publishing*
239 التَّعليقُ *Commentary*
250 رقابةُ المَطبوعاتِ *Censorship*
Exercises 252

7 Law and Order القانونُ والنِّظامُ   254
254 الإجراءاتُ القانونِيَّةُ *The Legal Process*
268 المُعاهداتُ والعُقودُ *Treaties and Contracts*
270 الجَرائِمُ *Crimes*
279 الإعتِقالُ *Under Arrest*
282 الأدِلَّةُ والبَراهينُ *Evidence and Proof*
284 أحكامُ الإدانةِ *Verdicts and Convictions*
289 السِّجنُ *Prison*
290 الإستِئنافُ والتَّسويةُ *Appeals and Settlements*
Exercises 292

8 Culture, Religion, and Society الدّينُ والثَّقافةُ والمُجتَمَعُ   294
294 الدّينُ *Religion*
319 الثَّقافةُ والمُجتَمَعُ *Culture and Society*
Exercises 335

9 Earth, Nature, and the Environment الأرضُ والطَّبيعةُ والبيئةُ   337
337 الحَيَواناتُ *Animals*
350 الطَّقسُ والمُناخُ *Weather and Climate*
356 الكَوارِثُ الطَّبيعِيَّةُ *Natural Disasters*
359 المَوارِدُ الطَّبيعِيَّةُ والطّاقةُ *Natural Resources and Energy*

The World and Beyond العالَمُ والفَضاءُ *366*
Exercises 377

10 Information Technology تِقنيَّةُ المَعلوماتِ 380
Useful Terms مُصطَلَحاتٌ مُفيدَةٌ *400*
Exercises 401

Answer Key 403
Index 415

Introduction

The Arabic language is based on a consonantal root system whereby almost every word in the language is derived from a root. Although there are exceptions, most Arabic words have a triliteral root (made up of three consonants or radicals), and it is this root that defines the underlying meaning of the word. Consequently, words which are derived from the same root will frequently have a shared basic meaning.

Using the root ك ت ب (*k t b*), we can see how the consonantal root system works:

كَتَبَ (*kataba*) he wrote
مَكْتَبٌ (*maktabun*) an office or desk
مَكْتَبَةٌ (*maktabatun*) a library or bookshop
كَاتِبٌ (*kātibun*) an author

As can be seen, words derived from this root have a meaning linked to 'writing'. By adding certain vowels and affixes to the root, particular noun or verb patterns are reproduced, which may lead to a vast number of words which are predictable in both form and meaning. When you come across a new word, assuming you recognise the root, you can approximate the word's basic meaning.

There are instances, however, where one root can have two different meanings (which might have originally been linked), and either each form applies to both meanings or each form produces a different meaning. The root س و س (*s w s*), for example, carries both the meaning 'to govern or dominate' and 'to rot or decay'.

Another difficulty arises from homonymous roots: words which share the same root letters but are different roots with different meanings. They are listed both here and in dictionaries as separate roots. An example of a homonymous root is د ي ن (*d y n*), which has one root that means 'to borrow or loan' and one root that means 'to profess or affirm one's religion'.

Since Arabic is the language of Quranic revelation, the Arabic language resists, where possible, the acceptance of loanwords. This reluctance to adopt foreign words has necessitated the practice of modernization, which involves the

DOI: 10.4324/9781003250890-1

controlled creation of new terms to fill semantic gaps and includes the following linguistic processes: extension, calques, and Arabisation. Extension is when the meaning of a word is extended to include a new term. One such example is the root د و ن (*d w n*) which gives the Form II pattern دَوَّنَ – يُدَوِّنُ (*dawwana – yudawwinu*) 'to record or write down'; its meaning has been extended to include the meaning 'to blog'. Calques are essentially the literal translations of words from foreign languages into Arabic. The word email, for example, has been translated as بَرِيدٌ إِلِكْتروني (*barīdun iliktrūniyyun*) 'electronic mail'. Another form of modernisation is Arabisation which morphologically and phonologically changes an adopted foreign word. Examples include the word for television تِلْفاز (*tilfāzun*), which has been changed to fit the Arabic morphological pattern. It has now entered the Arabic language ت ل ف ز (*t l f z*) and has a productive root. Calques and extensions tend to have roots (because they usually make use of Arabic words and roots that already exist), while only some Arabised words have roots (Versteegh 2014 (1997)).

Loanwords, however, have become more frequent as a result of the introduction of the internet and social media. Examples of these include the words email (إِيْميل – *īmayl*), computer (كومبيوتر – *kumbūtar*), and the internet (الإِنْتَرنِت – *al-internet*). Most loanwords have no roots in Arabic.

To find a root, we begin with the premise that most Arabic words are based on a triliteral root; in other words, the root we are looking for will have three consonants. (If not, the root will most likely be quadrilateral and we know to look for a root with four consonants.) The long vowels (ا و ي), which are also letters of the alphabet, are considered weak letters and they can be part of the root. However, if this is the case, it is worth remembering that they may not be present in every root pattern and they are considered irregular. They will, therefore, not follow the regular patterns provided later. If a word has only three letters then the learner can assume that those letters are the root letters. Lastly, the *tā marbūṭa* (ة) and short vowels can never be part of the root.

In learning Arabic vocabulary, understanding roots (الجِذر) is essential, if only because all Arabic dictionaries use the root system. In order to look a word up in an Arabic dictionary one must know the root of the word. The roots are listed in alphabetical order and all words derived from the root are listed under the same root. The roots of some words are inevitably harder to work out than others. However, this should not discourage the learner, because we will provide tips on how to recognise the root, and go over the root patterns so the learner can become acquainted with them. This will help the learner recognise the pattern of an unknown word, and from there work out its meaning. It is believed that in order to maximise vocabulary learning and its retention, synonymous rather than antonymous words should be learned together. As such, using root patterns when learning vocabulary can greatly enhance the learning process.

Arabic-derived Verb Forms

The derived forms are forms derived using the root in combination with affixes and vowels. Each of the following derived forms is associated with a particular meaning pattern. Knowing these patterns will aid in the retention of vocabulary. It is standard practice to convey these derived forms using the root (ف ع ل / فَعَلَ) fa'ala – 'to do' where the *f* represents the first radical, ' the second radical, and *l* the third radical.

Form	Perfect	Imperfect	Verbal Noun
		3rd person m/s	
Form I	فَعَلَ *fa'ala*	يَفْعَلُ *yaf'alu*	
Form II	فَعَّلَ *fa"ala*	يُفَعِّلُ *yufa"ilu*	تَفْعِيلٌ *taf'īlun*
			تَفْعِلَةٌ *taf'ilatun*

Form meaning: strengthening or intensification of meaning. Applying the act to a more general object. Causative action.

Examples:	عَلَّمَ to teach	يُعَلِّمُ	تَعْلِيمٌ / تَعْلِمَةٌ
Form III	فَاعَلَ *fā'ala*	يُفَاعِلُ *yufā'ilu*	فِعَالٌ *fi'ālun*
			مُفَاعَلَةٌ *mufā'alatun*

Form meaning: relation of the action to another person. Reciprocity of an action.

Examples:	كَاتَبَ to write to	يُكَاتِبُ	كِتَابٌ / مُكَاتَبَةٌ
Form IV	أَفْعَلَ *af'ala*	يُفْعِلُ *yuf'ilu*	إِفْعَالٌ *if'ālun*

Form meaning: causative of transitive verbs. Transitive of intransitive verbs. Stative verbs from derived nouns.

Examples:	أَعْلَمَ to inform	يُعْلِمُ	إِعْلَامٌ
Form V	تَفَعَّلَ *tafa"ala*	يَتَفَعَّلُ *yatafa"alu*	تَفَعُّلٌ *tafa"ulun*

Form meaning: reflexive of Form II. Can be intensive of Form I. Verbs are derived from nouns of quality or status.

Examples:	تَكَسَّرَ to break	يَتَكَسَّرُ	تَكَسُّرٌ
Form VI	تَفَاعَلَ *tafā'ala*	يَتَفَاعَلُ *yatafā'alu*	تَفَاعُلٌ *tafā'ulun*

Form meaning: the reflexive of Form III, can imply the mutual application of the action.

Examples: تَكاتَبَ to write to each other يَتَكاتَبُ تَكاتُبٌ

Form VII اِنْفَعَلَ *infaʻala* يَنْفَعِلُ *yanfaʻilu* اِنْفِعالٌ *infiʻālun*

Form meaning: renders passive or reflexive meaning of Form I.

Examples: اِنْكَسَرَ to break/be broken يَنْكَسِرُ اِنْكِسارٌ

Form VIII اِفْتَعَلَ *iftaʻala* يَفْتَعِلُ *yaftaʻilu* اِفْتِعالٌ *iftiʻālun*

Form meaning: reflexive of Form I.

Examples: اِنْتَفَعَ to profit يَنْتَفِعُ اِنْتِفاعٌ

Form IX اِفْعَلَّ *ifʻalla* يَفْعَلُّ *yafʻallu* اِفْعِلالٌ *ifʻilālun*

Form meaning: relates to colours or body defects.

Examples: اِحْمَرَّ to become red يَحْمَرُّ اِحْمِرارٌ

Form X اِسْتَفْعَلَ *istafʻala* يَسْتَفْعِلُ *yastafʻilu* اِسْتِفْعالٌ *istifʻālun*

Form meaning: thinking or attributing someone or something with the quality of the root or the Form I verb. In other words, considering someone to have the quality of the Form I verb.

Examples: اِسْتَحْسَنَ to think good يَسْتَحْسِنُ اِسْتِحْسانٌ

The verb patterns and conjugations of irregular verbs vary somewhat from the regular verb patterns shown earlier. Irregular verbs are of three types:

- Verbs with doubled consonants: these are verbs where the second and third root letters/radicals are the same. For example: تَمَّ (*tamma*) 'to end or complete' or رَدَّ (*radda*) 'to reply or restore' or دَلَّ (*dalla*) 'to guide or show'.
- Verbs where one of the three root letters is a weak letter (و or ي). These are known as weak verbs and they are of three types: assimilated verbs, hollow verbs, and defective verbs. Assimilated verbs will have the weak letter as the first radical, hollow verbs will have the weak letter as the middle radical, and defective verbs will have the weak letter as the final radical. Examples

respectively include وَصَلَ (waṣala) 'to arrive' or قَامَ بِ (qāma bi) 'to stand up or rise' and لَقِيَ (laqiya) 'to encounter or meet'.
- Verbs where one of the three root letters is a *hamza* (ء). For example, ألِفَ (alafa) 'to be acquainted or familiar with', سَأَلَ (sa'ala) 'to ask', and قرأ (qara'a) 'to read'.

The Participles

All forms of the participles are prefixed with م vowelled with *damma* ُ. The middle radical ع (') is vowelled with *kasra* ِ for the active and *fatḥa* َ for the passive.

Form	Perfect	Active Participle	Passive Participle
Form I	فَعَلَ fa'ala	فَاعِلٌ fā'ilun	مَفْعُولٌ maf'ūlun
Form II	فَعَّلَ fa''ala	مُفَعِّلٌ mufa''ilun	مُفَعَّلٌ mufa''alun
Form III	فَاعَلَ fā'ala	مُفَاعِلٌ mufā'ilun	مُفَاعَلٌ mufā'alun
Form IV	أَفْعَلَ af'ala	مُفْعِلٌ muf'ilun	مُفْعَلٌ muf'alun
Form V	تَفَعَّلَ tafa''ala	مُتَفَعِّلٌ mutafa''ilun	مُتَفَعَّلٌ mutafa''alun
Form VI	تَفَاعَلَ tafā'ala	مُتَفَاعِلٌ mutafā'ilun	مُتَفَاعَلٌ mutafā'alun
Form VII	اِنْفَعَلَ infa'ala	مُنْفَعِلٌ munfa'ilun	مُنْفَعَلٌ munfa'alun
Form VIII	اِفْتَعَلَ ifta'ala	مُفْتَعِلٌ mufta'ilun	مُفْتَعَلٌ mufta'alun
Form IX	اِفْعَلَّ if'alla	مُفْعَلٌّ muf'allun	
Form X	اِسْتَفْعَلَ istaf'ala	مُسْتَفْعِلٌ mustaf'ilun	مُسْتَفْعَلٌ mustaf'alun

Just as there are derived verb forms in Arabic, there are also derived noun patterns. A pattern (وَزن) can be applied to any root. The pattern conveys a grammatical meaning of the root. There are seven types of derived nouns.

Locative Noun/Noun of Place and Time اسْمُ المَكانِ والزمانِ / اسْمُ الظرفِ

Pattern: مَفْعَلٌ *maf'alun*

Meaning: the time when or place where the root meaning is enacted

Examples: مَطْعَمٌ restaurant, مَدْرَسَةٌ school, مَسْبَحٌ swimming pool

Active Participle اسْمُ الفاعِلِ

Pattern: فَاعِلٌ *fā'ilun*

Meaning: the one that enacts the base meaning of root

Examples: ضَارِبٌ the hitter/one who hits, شَارِبٌ the drinker/one who drinks, عَالِمٌ scholar

Hyperbolic Participle (Nouns of Intensity) اسْمُ المُبَالَغةِ

Pattern: فَعَّالٌ / فَعَّالَةٌ ‎ fa''ālun/fa''ālatun

Meaning: the one that enacts the root meaning in an exaggerated way

Examples: رَحَّالَةٌ one who travels a lot, عَلَّامَةٌ one who knows a lot

Passive Participle اسْمُ المَفْعُولِ

Pattern: مَفْعُولٌ maf'ūlun

Meaning: the one upon whom the root meaning is enacted

Examples: مَفْهُومٌ understood/concept, مَعْلُومٌ that which is known

Resembling Participle الصِّفةُ المُشَبَّهَةُ

Pattern: فَعِيلٌ fa'īlun

Meaning: the one who enacts (or upon whom is enacted) the base meaning intrinsically

Examples: عَلِيمٌ the all-knowing

Nouns of Instrument اسْمُ الآلَةِ

Pattern: مِفْعَالٌ mif'ālun

Meaning: the thing/instrument used to enact the root meaning

Examples: مِفْتَاحٌ key/the thing that is used to open

Elative اسْمُ التفضيلِ

Pattern: أَفْعَل af'al

Meaning: the one who enacts (or upon whom is enacted) the root meaning the most

Examples: أَحْلَى most beautiful, أَبْعَد furthest, أَقْصَى furthest

Notes on the Text

This book is divided into ten chapters, each covering different subject matter. Within each chapter, words have been listed by root and categorised by topic. Inevitably, some roots are relevant to more than one chapter, in which case a comprehensive treatment has been given in one chapter (as indicated), and only relevant words listed in the other. For roots which have two forms (the same root but they can be written differently), both forms have been included.

A single root can sometimes have more than one basic meaning and so the reader may find that certain words seem out of place under the chapter heading or topic. Nevertheless, words which are deemed to be part of a student's core vocabulary have been included under the appropriate root.

Under each subheading, roots have been listed alphabetically. Words with no roots have also been listed alphabetically. In some instances, a word has no root but through the process of verbing (making verbs from nouns), some foreign origin words or loanwords have become productive. These words will not have a root.

Under each root, verbs tend to be listed first (Form I–X in order, depending on which forms are relevant for each root), followed by the nouns. Nouns are given in the masculine, and only in some noteworthy instances has the feminine form been given. The Arabic plurals are given in brackets.

There are exercises at the end of each chapter to help reinforce vocabulary learning and give the student an opportunity to use the vocabulary in context.

Use of Symbols and Abbreviations

( ) Brackets are used to give the plural form.
/ A forward slash is used to separate synonyms from the same root.
– A dash is used to separate past and present verb forms.
(adj) adjective
(adv) adverb
(CA) Classical Arabic
(conj) conjunction
(esp) especially
(f) feminine
(inc) including
(lit) literally
(m) masculine
(n) noun
(pl) plural
(prep) preposition
(s) singular
(sth) something

Standard Arabic spellings have been used for common proper names as well as Arabic words found in English.

References

Abu-Chakra, F. (2007) *Arabic: An Essential Grammar*. London and New York: Routledge.

Haywood, J. A. and Nahmad, H. M. (1984 (1965)) *A New Arabic Grammar of the Written Language*. London: Lund Humphries.
Versteegh, K. (2014 (1997)) *The Arabic Language*. Second Edition. Edinburgh: Edinburgh University Press.
Wightwick, J. and Gaafar, M. (2008) *Arabic Verbs and Essentials of Grammar*. Second Edition. USA: McGraw Hill.

1 Family and Feelings العائلةُ والعواطِفُ

Family Relations العلاقاتُ العائِلِيَّةُ

No root

أبٌ (آباءٌ) father; ancestors
أُبُوَّةٌ fatherhood, paternity
أبو father of; possessor of, owner of

أ خ و

آخى – يُواخي to fraternise
تآخى – يَتآخى to act like brothers
أخٌ (إخْوَةٌ/ إخوانٌ) brother, neighbour, friend[1]
أختٌ (أخَواتٌ) sister; counterpart; cognate (grammar)
أخَوِيٌّ fraternal
أُخُوَّةٌ fraternity

No root

آدَمُ Adam
ابنُ آدَمَ human being
آدَمِيٌّ (آدَمِيّونَ / أوادِمُ) human, humane; poor, meagre
آدَمِيَّةٌ humanity

أ ه ل

أهَلَ – يأْهَلُ to get married; to be on familiar terms; to be populated (of a place)
أهَّلَ – يُؤَهِّلُ to fit; to qualify; to enable or make accessible

DOI: 10.4324/9781003250890-2

10 *Family and Feelings*

تَأَهَّلَ – يَتَأَهَّلُ to be or become fit, suitable, or qualified; to marry

اِسْتَأَهَلَ – يَسْتَأْهِلُ to deserve or merit; to be worthy

أَهْلٌ (أَهالٍ) parents, family, relatives; people, inhabitants; possessors

أَهْلُ الْبَلَدِ the native population

أَهْلِيٌّ domestic, national; of or relating to family

حَرْبٌ أَهْلِيَّةٌ civil war

أَهْلِيَّةٌ aptitude, competence; suitability

كَامِلُ الأَهْلِيَّةِ legally competent

عَديمُ الأَهْلِيَّةِ legally incompetent

آهِلٌ / مَأْهولٌ inhabited, populated

مُؤَهِّلاتٌ qualifications

الْمُؤَهِّلاتُ الأَكاديمِيَّةُ academic credentials

مُتَأَهِّلٌ qualified; married

مُسْتَأْهِلٌ worthy, deserving, entitled

أَهْلاً وسَهْلاً welcome

ب ن ن

تَبَنَّى – يَتَبَنَّى to adopt as a son; to adopt; to embrace

اِبْنٌ (أَبْناءٌ / بَنونَ) son; descendant, offspring

اِبْنَةٌ / بِنْتٌ (بَناتٌ) daughter; girl

تَبَنٍّ / التَّبَنِّي adoption (children, principles)

No root

جَدٌّ (جُدودٌ / أَجْدادٌ) grandfather; ancestors

جَدَّةٌ (جَدَّاتٌ) grandmother

No root

جيلٌ (أَجْيالٌ) generation, people; nation

ح م ى

(Full treatment in Law chapter)

حمى – يَحْمي to defend, guard, or protect[2]

حَمٌ (أَحْماءٌ) father-in-law (pl: wife's in-laws)

حماةٌ (حَمَواتٌ) mother-in-law

خ ل ف

خَلَفَ – يَخْلُفُ to be the successor; to succeed or follow; to be detained
خَلَّفَ – يُخَلِّفُ to appoint as successor; to have offspring or descendants
خالَفَ – يُخالِفُ to be contradictory or at variance; to offend
اِخْتَلَفَ – يَخْتَلِفُ to differ or vary
خَلْفَ back, behind
خَلَفٌ (أَخْلافٌ) successor, descendant; substitute
خَليفَةٌ (خُلَفاءُ) caliph; deputy, successor
خِلافَةٌ caliphate; succession, deputyship
خِلافٌ (خِلافاتٌ) difference, deviation, disparity; dispute, disagreement
مُخالَفَةٌ (مُخالَفاتٌ) contrast; inconsistency; violation; a fine
اِخْتِلافٌ (اِخْتِلافاتٌ) difference, disparity; variety; disagreement, controversy
مُخالِفٌ different; inconsistent, contradictory, conflicting; a transgressor
مُتَخَلِّفٌ residual; retarded, underdeveloped, slow
مُتَخَلِّفٌ عَقْلِياً mentally disabled
مُخْتَلِفٌ different; varied, diverse

ر ع ى

رَعى – يَرْعى to tend, guard or protect; to graze (animals); to comply
راعى – يُراعي to supervise or watch; to control or maintain; to comply; to allow
رَعْيٌ care, custody, protection
رِعايَةٌ guardianship; patronage, sponsorship; custody, charge
رِعايَةُ الطِّفْلِ childcare
مَرْعىً (مَراعٍ) pasture, grazing land
رَعِيَّةٌ (رَعايا) herd, flock; subjects (of a monarch)
مُراعاةٌ consideration, regard; deference, respect; compliance
راعٍ (رُعاةٌ) shepherd; guardian, sponsor, patron

ر م ل

رَمَّلَ – يُرَمِّلُ to sprinkle with sand
أَرْمَلَ – يُرْمِلُ to become a widow or widower
تَرَمَّلَ – يَتَرَمَّلُ to become a widow or widower
رَمْلٌ (رِمالٌ) sand
أَرْمَلُ (أَرامِلُ) widower
أَرْمَلَةٌ (أَرامِلُ) widow

Family and Feelings

ز و ج

زَوَّجَ – يُزَوِّجُ to pair, couple, or double; to marry off
تَزَوَّجَ – يَتَزَوَّجُ to get married
تَزاوَجَ – يَتَزاوَجُ to intermarry; to be double
اِزدَوَجَ – يَزدَوِجُ to pair or be in pairs; to be double
زَوجٌ (أَزواجٌ) one of a pair; husband, wife, partner
زَوجُ الأُمِّ stepfather
زَوجَةٌ (زَوجاتٌ) wife
زَوجَةُ الأَبِ stepmother
زَوجِيٌّ marital; double; in pairs; even numbers
زَواجٌ / تَزَوُّجٌ marriage, wedding
اِزدِواجٌ coupling, pairing; doubleness
مُتَزَوِّجٌ married
مُزدَوَجٌ double, twofold

س ل ف

سَلَفَ – يَسلُفُ to be over or past; to precede
سَلَّفَ – يُسَلِّفُ to lend or loan
اِستَلَفَ – يَستَلِفُ to borrow, to contract a loan
سِلفٌ (أَسلافٌ) brother-in-law
سِلفَةٌ sister-in-law
سَلَفٌ (أَسلافٌ) predecessors, ancestors, forefathers; advance payment
سَلَفاً beforehand, in advance
سُلفَةٌ (سُلَفٌ) a loan or advance; inner sole (of shoe)
تَسليفٌ credit, advance
سالِفٌ (سَلَفٌ / أَسلافٌ) predecessor; former, previous
سالِفاً previously, formerly

س م ى

سَمَّى – يُسَمِّي to name, call, or designate
أَسمى – يُسمِي to name, call, or designate
تَسَمَّى – يَتَسَمَّى to be called or named
تَسمِيَةٌ (تَسمِياتٌ) naming, appellation, designation

Family and Feelings 13

ش ب ب

شَبَّ – يَشِبُّ to become a young man; to grow up
شَبٌّ / شابٌ (شَبابٌ) youth, young man
شَبابٌ youth, youthfulness; adolescents
بيتُ الشَّبابِ youth hostel
نادي الشَّبابِ youth club

ش ق ق

شَقَّ – يَشُقُّ to split, part, tear, rip, or break
اِنْشَقَّ – يَنْشَقُّ to be split or cleft; to crack; to withdraw
اِشْتَقَّ – يَشْتَقُّ to derive (a word from)
شَقٌّ (شُقوقٌ) crack, crevice, split, gap
شِقٌّ half; side, portion; trouble, difficulty
شَقَّةٌ (شُقَقٌ) apartment, flat
شَقيقٌ (أَشِقّاءُ) full brother; a half
أَخٌ غَيْرُ شَقيقٍ stepbrother, half-brother
شَقيقةٌ (شَقيقاتٌ / شَقائِقُ) full sister
أختٌ غَيْرُ شَقيقةٍ stepsister, half-sister
مَشَقَّةٌ (مَشَقّاتٌ / مَشاقُّ) misfortune, hardship, difficulty, trouble
اِشْتِقاقٌ derivation; etymology
مُشْتَقٌّ (مُشْتَقّاتٌ) derivative

ص ب و

صَبا – يَصبو to be a child; to be childish; to bend or incline
صَباءٌ / صِبىً / صِبا childhood, youth, boyhood
صَبْوَةٌ childish manners
صَبِيٌّ (صِبيانٌ / صِبْيَةٌ) youth, boy
صَبِيَّةٌ (صَبايا) young girl

ص ه ر

صَهَرَ – يَصْهَرُ to melt or fuse
صاهَرَ – يُصاهِرُ to become related by marriage
اِنْصَهَرَ – يَنْصَهِرُ to melt or fuse; to vanish
صِهْرٌ (أَصهارٌ) son-in-law, brother-in-law; relationship by marriage

Family and Feelings

No root

عانِسٌ (عَوانِسُ) spinster

ع ز ب

عَزَبَ – يَعزُبُ to be single or unmarried; to be far or distant; to escape
عَزَبٌ (عُزّابٌ / أعزابٌ) celibate; single, unmarried; a bachelor
عُزْبَةٌ / عُزوبةٌ celibacy, bachelorhood
أعزَبُ celibate; single, unmarried; a bachelor (m)
عَزباءُ celibate, single, unmarried (f)

ع و ل

عالَ – يَعيلُ to support a family; to have a large family; to oppress or distress
أعالَ – يُعيلُ to support or provide for; to be responsible for; to have a large family
عَيِّلٌ (عِيالٌ) family, household; children, dependants
إعالةٌ sustenance, support
عالَةٌ (عالاتٌ) burden
عائِلةٌ (عائِلاتٌ / عَوائِلُ) family, household
شَجرةُ العائِلةِ family tree

ق ر ب

قَرُبَ – يَقرُبُ to be near; to approach; to approximate
قَرَّبَ – يُقَرِّبُ to bring close, to bring home; to advance; to approximate
اِقتَرَبَ – يَقتَرِبُ to approach, advance, or get close
قُرْبٌ in the vicinity of, near; towards; proximity
قِربَةٌ (قِرْباتٌ / قِرَبٌ) hot water bottle; waterskin
قَريبٌ (أقرباءُ) a relative; near, close (pl: relatives)
قَريباً soon
قَرابةٌ relation, relationship, kinship
قُربانٌ (قَرابينُ) sacrifice, offering; the Eucharist (of Christian tradition)
أقرَبُ (أقرَبونَ / أقارِبُ) nearer, nearest; more probable (pl: relations, relatives)
الأقربونَ أولى بالمَعْروفِ charity begins at home
تَقريباً approximately

ق ر ن

قَرَنَ – يَقرِنُ to join, couple, link, or connect
قارَنَ – يقارِنُ to compare; to unite or connect

Family and Feelings 15

اِقْتَرَنَ – يَقْتَرِنُ to marry; to be joined or connected to; to be interconnected
قَرْنٌ (قُرُونٌ) century; horn, tentacle
قُرْنَةٌ (قُرَنٌ) corner, nook
قَرِينٌ (أَقْرَانٌ/قُرَنَاءُ) husband, spouse; companion; connected, linked
قَرِينَةٌ (قَرِينَاتٌ) wife, spouse; consort; female demon who haunts women
قِرَانٌ marriage, wedding; close union
عَقْدُ الْقِرَانِ marriage contract
مُقَارَنَةٌ (مُقَارَنَاتٌ) comparison

ن س ب

نَسَبَ – يَنْسُبُ to relate (sth) to; to link or correlate; to attribute or ascribe; to trace
نَاسَبَ – يُنَاسِبُ to be or become related by marriage; to be of the same family; to correspond or agree
تَنَاسَبَ – يَتَنَاسَبُ to be related to one another; to be alike; to be in agreement
نَسَبٌ (أَنْسَابٌ) lineage; derivation; relationship, kinship, relationship by marriage
نِسْبَةٌ (نِسَبٌ) relationship, kinship; link, affinity; proportion, rate, percentage
بِالنِّسْبَةِ إِلَى in comparison with; in relation to, with regard
نِسْبِيٌّ relative, comparative
نَسِيبٌ (أَنْسِبَاءُ) kinsman, relative; son-in-law
مُنَاسَبَةٌ (مُنَاسَبَاتٌ) occasion, opportunity; suitability, adequacy; relationship
مُنَاسِبٌ suitable, appropriate; adequate; convenient
غَيْرُ مُنَاسِبٍ unsuitable

ن ك ح

نَكَحَ – يَنْكِحُ to marry or get married
نِكَاحٌ/عَقْدُ النِّكَاحِ marriage, marriage contract

ه ر م

هَرِمَ – يَهْرَمُ to become senile or decrepit
هَرَمٌ old age, senility
هَرَمٌ (أَهْرَامٌ/أَهْرَامَاتٌ) pyramid
هَرِمٌ senile, aged; an old man

و ل د

وَلَدَ – يَلِدُ to bear children or procreate; to generate or produce; to give birth
وَلَّدَ – يُوَلِّدُ to assist in childbirth; to bring up or raise (children); to breed

16 Family and Feelings

وَلَدٌ (أولادٌ) descendent, offspring, child, son

وِلادَةٌ childbirth, delivery, birth

وَلِيدٌ (وِلدانٌ) newborn, baby; child, boy, son (also a boy's name in the singular)

مَوْلِدٌ (مَواليدُ) birthplace; birthday, anniversary

مُعَدَّلُ المَواليدِ birth rate

المَوْلِدُ النَّبَوِيُّ الشَّريفُ Prophet Muhammad's birthday

ميلادٌ (مَواليدُ) birth, birthday, time of birth

قَبلَ الميلادِ BC (before Christ)

ميلاديٌّ AD (Anno Domini)

عيدُ ميلادٍ birthday

عيدُ الميلادِ Christmas

مَحلُّ الميلادِ / مَكانُ الميلادِ place of birth

تَوليدٌ procreation; generating (power, energy); midwifery

مُوَلِّدٌ (مُوَلِّداتٌ) generating, procreative; obstetrician (pl: generators)

والِدٌ father; parent

والِدَةٌ (والِداتٌ) mother

مَوْلودٌ (مَواليدُ) produced, born; child, baby, son

مُوَلِّدَةٌ (مُوَلِّداتٌ) midwife

ي ت م

يَتَمَ – يَيْتَمُ to be or become an orphan

تَيَتَّمَ – يَتَيَتَّمُ to be or become an orphan

يَتيمٌ (أيتامٌ / يَتامى) orphan; unique

مَيتَمٌ (مَياتِمُ) orphanage

Emotions and Feelings المشاعرُ والعواطفُ

أ س ف

أَسِفَ – يَأْسَفُ to regret, feel sorry, or be sad

تَأَسَّفَ – يَتَأَسَّفُ to regret, feel sorry, or be sad

أَسَفٌ sorrow, grief, regret

تَأَسُّفٌ regret; apology

آسِفٌ regretful, sorry, sad

مُؤْسِفٌ distressing, sad, regrettable

مُتَأَسِّفٌ sad, sorry, regretful

Family and Feelings 17

No root

أنا I
أَنانِيٌّ selfish, egotistic
أَنانِيَّةٌ selfishness, egoism

أ ن ق

أَنِقَ – يَأْنَقُ to be neat, smart, or pretty
تَأَنَّقَ – يَتَأَنَّقُ to be meticulous, to be chic or elegant
أَناقَةٌ elegance
أَنيقٌ classy, elegant, chic

No root

بَخْتٌ (بُخوتٌ) fortune, good luck
سوءُ الْبَخْتِ bad luck
قَليلُ الْبَخْتِ unlucky
بَخيتٌ / مَبْخوتٌ fortunate, lucky

ب خ ل

بَخِلَ – يَبْخَلُ to be stingy
بُخْلٌ greed, avarice
بَخيلٌ (بُخَلاءُ) greedy person, miser

ب د ه

بَدَهَ – يَبْدَهُ to surprise; to descend suddenly or befall unexpectedly
بادَهَ – يُبادِهُ to appear unexpectedly
بَداهَةُ / بَديهَةٌ spontaneity, impulse
سُرعةُ الْبَديهَةِ wit

ب ذ خ

بَذَخَ – يَبْذُخُ to be haughty or proud
بَذَخٌ luxury, pomp; pride
بَذِخٌ / باذِخٌ (بَواذِخُ) haughty, proud, lofty; lavish, extravagant

Family and Feelings

ب س ط

بَسَطَ – يَبْسُطُ to spread or flatten; to expand; to offer; to unfold
بَسَّطَ – يُبَسِّطُ to spread or flatten; to simplify or make simple
اِنْبَسَطَ – يَنْبَسِطُ to spread or extend; to be glad, delighted, or happy
بِساطٌ (بِساطاتٌ / بُسُطٌ / أَبْسِطَةٌ) carpet, rug
بَسيطٌ (بُسَطاءُ) simple, plain, uncomplicated
اِنْبِساطٌ delight, joy, happiness
مَبْسوطٌ content, happy, cheerful; spreading, extended
مُنْبَسِطٌ happy, cheerful; spreading, extended

ب س م

تَبَسَّمَ – يَتَبَسَّمُ to smile
اِبْتَسَمَ – يَبْتَسِمُ to smile
بَسْمَةٌ (بَسْماتٌ) a smile (also a girl's name in the singular)
اِبْتِسامٌ / اِبْتِسامَةٌ (اِبْتِساماتٌ) a smile

ب غ ض

بَغِضَ – يَبْغِضُ to be hated; to be hateful or odious
بَغَّضَ – يُبَغِّضُ to make hateful
أَبْغَضَ – يُبْغِضُ to loathe, detest, or hate
تَباغَضَ – يَتَباغَضُ to hate each other
بُغْضٌ / بَغْضاءُ hatred

ب ؤ س

بَؤُسَ – يَبْؤُسُ to be strong, brave, or intrepid
بَئِسَ – يَبْأَسُ to be wretched or miserable
اِبْتَأَسَ – يَبْتَئِسُ to be sad, worried, or grieved
لا بَأْسَ no problem; no objection; not bad
بُؤْسٌ misery, wretchedness, distress
بَئيسٌ / بائِسٌ (بُؤَساءُ) miserable, wretched
البُؤَساءُ Les Misérables

ت ع س

تَعَسَ – يَتْعَسُ to fall; to perish; to become wretched or miserable
أَتْعَسَ – يُتْعِسُ to make unhappy or miserable

Family and Feelings 19

تَعَسٌ / تَعاسَةٌ wretchedness, misery, misfortune
تَعِيسٌ (تُعَساءُ) wretched, miserable, unfortunate (adj, noun)
مَتعوسٌ (مَتاعيسُ) wretched, miserable, unfortunate

ج ر ؤ

جَرُؤَ – يَجرُؤُ to dare, venture, risk, or hazard
تَجَرَّأَ – يَتَجَرَّأُ to dare, risk, or hazard
جَريءٌ (جَريئونَ) brave, bold, courageous
جُرأَةٌ / جَراءةٌ bravery

ج ش ع

جَشِعَ – يَجشَعُ to be greedy or covetous
تَجَشَّعَ – يَتَجَشَّعُ to be greedy or covetous
جَشَعٌ greed

ج و د

جادَ – يَجودُ to be good; to improve; to be liberal; to donate
جَوَّدَ – يُجَوِّدُ to recite the Quran; to do well
أَجادَ – يُجيدُ to do well; to be proficient or outstanding
جَوْدَةٌ excellence
جَيِّدٌ (جِيادٌ) good, great, perfect, faultless
جَوادٌ (أَجوادٌ / أَجاويدُ) generous, magnanimous (also a boy's name in the singular)
تَجويدٌ recitation of the Quran

ح ب ب

حَبَّ – يُحِبُّ to love or like
حَبَّبَ – يُحَبِّبُ to endear or make (sth) attractive; to urge or suggest
أَحَبَّ – يُحِبُّ to love or like; to wish or want
تَحَبَّبَ – يَتَحَبَّبُ to woo, court, or ingratiate oneself
تَحابَبَ – يَتَحابَبُ to love one another
إستَحَبَّ – يَستَحِبُّ to like, to deem desirable
حُبٌّ / مَحَبَّةٌ love, affection; attachment
حَبيبٌ (أَحِبّاءُ / أَحبابٌ) friend; beloved, sweetheart
حَبيبَةٌ (حَبيباتٌ / حَبائِبُ) sweetheart, darling, beloved woman
مَحبوبٌ (مَحابيبُ) beloved

Family and Feelings

مُحَبَّبٌ likeable, pleasant, agreeable
مُستَحَبٌّ desirable; well-liked

ح ر ج

حَرَجَ – يَحرَجُ to be close or narrow; to be oppressed or anguished; to be forbidden
أحرَجَ – يُحرِجُ to embarrass; to confine or constrain
مُحرِجٌ embarrassing; disconcerting

ح ر ص

حَرَصَ – يَحرِصُ to desire or want; to strive
حِرصٌ greed; desire, aspiration
حَريصٌ (حِراصٌ / حُرصاءُ) greedy; eager

ح ز م

حَزَمَ – يَحزِمُ to tie, fasten, wrap, or pack
تَحَزَّمَ – يَتَحَزَّمُ to put on a belt
حَزمٌ determination; packaging, wrapping
حُزمَةٌ (حُزَمٌ) parcel, bundle; radiation beam
حِزامٌ (حِزاماتٌ / أحزِمَةٌ) belt, girdle, cummerbund
حِزامُ الأمانِ seat belt
حازِمٌ (حازِمونَ / حُزَماءُ) decisive, resolute; judicious, prudent (also a boy's name in the singular)

ح ز ن

حَزِنَ – يَحزَنُ to sadden; to grieve or mourn
أحزَنَ – يُحزِنُ to sadden or grieve
حُزنٌ (أحزانٌ) sadness, grief, sorrow
حَزينٌ (حَزانى / حُزَناءُ) sad, sorrowful, mournful
مُحزِنٌ sad, tragic

ح س م

حَسَمَ – يَحسِمُ to cut or sever; to complete or terminate; to settle; to deduct
انحَسَمَ – يَنحَسِمُ to be severed or cut off; to be finished; to be settled (argument)
حَسمٌ completion, termination; settlement; shutdown

Family and Feelings 21

حُسامٌ sword, sword edge (also a boy's name)
حاسِمٌ decisive, definite; conclusive

ح ش م

حَشَمَ – يَحشِمُ to shame (someone)
اِحتَشَمَ – يَحتَشِمُ to be modest or shy; to dress modestly
حِشمَةٌ shame; bashfulness, timidity, diffidence
مَحاشِمُ pubes, groin, genitals
اِحتِشامٌ / تَحَشُّمٌ shyness, modesty; decorum, decency
مُحتَشِمٌ shy, bashful, modest

ح ق د

حَقَدَ – يَحقِدُ to harbour bad feelings, to resent
أَحقَدَ – يُحقِدُ to embitter, to incite to hatred
حِقدٌ (أَحقادٌ / حُقودٌ) hatred, malice, resentment
حَقودٌ / حاقِدٌ spiteful, resentful, malicious

ح ق ر

حَقَرَ – يَحقِرُ to despise, scorn, or look down on
اِحتَقَرَ – يَحتَقِرُ to despise or scorn
حَقيرٌ (حُقَراءُ) meagre, humble; mean, contemptible; a despised person
حَقارَةٌ vulgarity, infamy, lowness; insignificance
اِحتِقارٌ contempt, disdain, scorn

ح م س

حَمِسَ – يَحمَسُ to be zealous or eager; to get excited
تَحَمَّسَ – يَتَحَمَّسُ to be zealous or overzealous; to get excited
حَماسٌ / حَماسَةٌ enthusiasm, fire, zeal; Hamas
تَحَمُّسٌ (لِ) enthusiasm (for); fanaticism
مُتَحَمِّسٌ enthusiastic; zealous, fanatical

ح ن ن

حَنَّ – يَحِنُّ to crave, long, or yearn for; to feel affection or sympathy
تَحَنَّنَ – يَتَحَنَّنُ to feel sympathy, pity, or compassion; to be tender or affectionate

Family and Feelings

حَنانٌ sympathy, compassion; love, affection (also a girl's name)

حَنينٌ nostalgia; yearning, desire (also a girl's name)

ح ي ر

حارَ – يَحارُ to be at a loss; to hesitate

حَيَّرَ – يُحَيِّرُ to confuse, baffle, or bewilder

تَحَيَّرَ – يَتَحَيَّرُ to become confused, perplexed, or at a loss; to be startled

إحتارَ – يَحتارُ to become confused, perplexed, or at a loss; to be startled

حَيْرَةٌ confusion, perplexity

حَيْرانٌ (حَيارَى) perplexed, confused

حائِرٌ / مُحتارٌ / مُتَحَيِّرٌ dismayed; confused, perplexed, uncertain

خ ب ث

خَبُثَ – يَخْبُثُ to be bad, evil, or malicious; impurities

تَخابَثَ – يَتَخابَثُ to behave viciously or with malice

خُبثٌ / خَباثَةٌ malevolence, malice, viciousness

خَبيثٌ (خُبُثٌ / خُبَثاءُ) devious, malicious, wicked, spiteful

خ ج ل

خَجِلَ – يَخجَلُ to become embarrassed or feel ashamed

خَجَّلَ – يُخَجِّلُ to shame or embarrass

خَجَلٌ shame; shyness, timidity

خَجولٌ / خَجلانٌ shy, timid

مُخجِلٌ shameful, shocking, disgraceful

ر أ ف

رَأَفَ – يَرأَفُ to show mercy, be kind, or have pity

رَأفةٌ / رآفةٌ mercy, compassion, pity

رَؤوفٌ kind, merciful, compassionate

ر د و

رَدُوَ – يَردُوُ to be bad

تَرَدَّأ – يَترَدَّأ to become bad, to be spoiled

رديءٌ (أردياءُ) bad, evil, wicked, vile

رَداءَةٌ wickedness, maliciousness

Family and Feelings 23

ر ش ق

رَشَقَ – يَرْشُقُ to throw, strike, or hurt; to be elegant or graceful
تَراشَقَ – يَتَراشَقُ to hurt one another
رَشيقٌ (رَشيقونَ) graceful, elegant; slender
رَشاقةٌ elegance, grace, agility

ر ق ق

رَقَّ – يَرِقُّ to be thin, delicate, or fine; to relent; to have sympathy
تَرَقَّقَ – يَتَرَقَّقُ to soften, relent, or sympathise
رِقَّةٌ gentleness, finesse
رَقيقٌ (أَرِقّاءُ) gentle, sensitive, soft; slaves

ز ع ج

زَعَجَ – يَزْعِجُ to disturb, harass, trouble, or inconvenience
أَزْعَجَ – يُزْعِجُ to disturb, harass, trouble, or inconvenience; to wake up
اِنْزَعَجَ – يَنْزَعِجُ to be alarmed, roused, or stirred up; to feel uneasy
إِزْعاجٌ disturbance
الرَّجاءُ عَدَمُ الإِزْعاج please do not disturb
اِنْزِعاجٌ inconvenience, discomfort, confusion
مُزْعِجٌ annoying, troublesome, unpleasant

س ع د

سَعِدَ – يَسْعَدُ to be happy, fortunate, or lucky
ساعَدَ – يُساعِدُ to help, aid, or assist; to support or encourage; to contribute
أَسْعَدَ – يُسْعِدُ to make happy; to help
سَعْدٌ (سُعودٌ) good luck, good fortune
سَعيدٌ (سُعَداءُ) lucky; happy, radiant
سَعادةٌ happiness, bliss; good fortune, success
سَعوديٌّ Saudi
سَعْدانٌ (سَعادينُ) ape
مُساعَدةٌ (مُساعداتٌ) assistance, aid, help
مُساعَداتٌ عاجِلةٌ emergency aid
ساعِدٌ (سَواعِدُ) forearm
مُساعِدٌ (مُساعِدونَ) helper, aide, assistant
مُساعِدٌ شَخْصيٌّ personal assistant

ش ج ع

شَجُعَ – يَشجُعُ to be courageous, brave, or valiant
شَجَّعَ – يُشَجِّعُ to encourage or embolden
تَشَجَّعَ – يَتَشَجَّعُ to take heart or be encouraged; to be courageous
شُجاعٌ (شُجعانٌ) courageous, brave
شَجاعَةٌ bravery, courage
تَشجيعٌ encouragement; promotion, advancement
مُشَجِّعٌ (مُشَجِّعونَ) supporter, advocate

ش ع ر

شَعَرَ – يَشعُرُ to feel, know, or perceive; to be aware
شَعرٌ (أَشعارٌ) hair; fur; bristles
شَعرَةٌ (شَعراتٌ) hair
شِعرٌ (أَشعارٌ) knowledge; poetry
شِعارٌ (شِعاراتٌ / شُعُرٌ) slogan, motto; password; sign, signal
شُعَيراتٌ دَمَوِيَّةٌ blood capillaries
شُعورٌ feeling, sensation, awareness, perception
فاقِدُ الشُعورِ unconscious
الشُعورُ مُتبادَلٌ the feeling is mutual
شُعوريٌّ emotional; conscious (adj)
لا شُعوريٌّ unconscious, subconscious (adj)
مَشاعِرُ feelings; rituals
مُثيرٌ لِلمَشاعِرِ touching, emotional
شاعِرٌ (شُعراءُ) poet

ش ف ق

أَشفَقَ – يُشفِقُ to pity or sympathise with; to shun or shirk (duties)
شَفَقٌ evening glow; twilight, dusk
شَفَقَةٌ pity, sympathy; tenderness

ش و ق

شاقَ – يَشوقُ to please, delight, or give joy
شَوَّقَ – يُشَوِّقُ to arouse longing, craving, or desire
اِشتاقَ – يَشتاقُ to long, yearn, or crave; to covet
شَوقٌ (أَشواقٌ) longing; desire, wish

تَشْوِيقٌ arousal of desire or fascination
تَشَوُّقٌ longing, yearning, desire
مُشَوِّقٌ thrilling, exciting, fascinating

ط م أ ن

طَمْأَنَ – يُطَمْئِنُ to calm, pacify, or soothe
اِطْمَأَنَّ – يَطْمَئِنُّ to feel assured or confident; to be or become quiet; to be certain
طُمَأْنِينَةٌ / اِطْمِئْنَانٌ tranquility, calm, peace
مُطْمَئِنٌّ calm, at ease; trust, reassurance

ط م ع

طَمِعَ – يَطْمَعُ to covet or desire; to be greedy or covetous
طَمَّعَ – يُطَمِّعُ to fill someone with greed; to tempt or entice
طَمَعٌ (أَطْمَاعٌ) greed, avarice
طَمَّاعٌ greedy

ط م ن

طَمَّنَ – يُطَمِّنُ to quiet, calm, or pacify
طَمْأَنَ – يُطَمْئِنُ to quiet, calm, or pacify
اِطْمِئْنَانٌ / طُمَأْنِينَةٌ reassurance, calmness, peace of mind

ط ي ش

طَاشَ – يَطِيشُ to be inconstant, undecided, or fickle; to be reckless or thoughtless
طَيْشٌ inconstancy, frivolity, fickleness
طَيَشَانٌ / طَيَاشَةٌ inconstancy; recklessness, thoughtlessness
طَائِشٌ inconstant, fickle; aimless

ظ ر ف

ظَرُفَ – يَظْرُفُ to be charming, elegant, nice, or neat
ظَرَّفَ – يُظَرِّفُ to embellish or polish; to envelop or wrap up
اِسْتَظْرَفَ – يَسْتَظْرِفُ to find something cute, charming, or witty
ظَرْفٌ (ظُرُوفٌ) envelope; condition; adverb (pl: circumstances, condition)
حَسَبَ الظُّرُوفِ according to the conditions, depending on the circumstances
ظَرِيفٌ (ظُرَفَاءُ) cute, charming, witty
ظَرَافَةٌ grace, charm

ع ش ق

عَشِقَ – يَعشَقُ to love passionately; to be passionate about
عِشقٌ love, passion, obsession
عَشيقٌ lover, sweetheart
عاشِقٌ (عاشِقونَ / عُشّاقٌ) lover or fan of

ع ط ف

عَطَفَ – يَعطِفُ to bend, incline, or lean; to awaken affection or sympathy
تَعَطَّفَ – يَتَعَطَّفُ to have compassion or sympathy
تَعاطَفَ – يَتَعاطَفُ to harbour mutual affection
اِستَعطَفَ – يَستَعطِفُ to ask for someone's compassion, to entreat or implore
عَطفٌ inclination, bending, curvature; sympathy
عِطفٌ (أَعطافٌ) side (of the body)
مِعطَفٌ (مَعاطِفُ) coat; frock
عاطِفةٌ (عَواطِفُ) sympathy, compassion; affection, emotion
تَعاطُفٌ sympathy
عاطِفِيٌّ sentimental, emotional
عاطِفيَّةٌ sentimentality

ع ن د

عَنَدَ – يَعنُدُ to swerve, deviate, diverge, or depart from
عانَدَ – يُعانِدُ to resist or oppose
عَنيدٌ (عُنُدٌ) stubborn, obstinate, opinionated
عِنادٌ / مُعانَدةٌ stubbornness, obstinacy
عِندَ (prep) at, near, with, upon
عِندَما as soon as, whenever
عِندَئِذٍ at that time, then

غ ر ر

غَرَّ – يَغُرُّ to mislead, deceive, or beguile
اِغتَرَّ – يَغتَرُّ to be conceited, deceived, or mistaken; to be fooled or misled
غَرَرٌ risk, hazard, danger
غُرورٌ conceit, arrogance; deception
مَغرورٌ deceived, deluded, fooled; arrogant, vain

Family and Feelings 27

غ ز ل

غَزَلَ – يَغْزِلُ to spin; to woo or make love to
تَغَزَّلَ – يَتَغَزَّلُ to woo or make love to; to eulogise
تَغَازَلَ – يَتَغَازَلُ to flirt (with one another)
غَزْلٌ spinning; yarn
غَزَلٌ flirtation; love
غَزَالٌ (غِزْلَانٌ) gazelle
غَزَّالَةٌ spider
تَغَزُّلٌ flirtation

غ ش م

غَشَمَ – يَغْشِمُ to treat unjustly, to wrong or oppress
غَشِمَ – يَغْشَمُ to be ignorant
اِسْتَغْشَمَ – يَسْتَغْشِمُ to regard as stupid or ignorant
غَشْمٌ oppression, repression
غَشِيمٌ (غُشَمَاءُ) ignorant, inexperienced; foolish

غ ض ب

غَضِبَ – يَغْضَبُ to be or become angry, mad, or vexed
أَغْضَبَ – يُغْضِبُ to annoy, anger, or infuriate
غَضَبٌ wrath, rage, anger
سَرِيعُ الْغَضَبِ short-tempered
غَضْبَانُ (غِضَابٌ / غَضَابَى) angry, irate, furious
غَاضِبٌ (غَاضِبُونَ) angry, annoyed, irritated

غ ف ل

غَفَلَ – يَغْفُلُ to neglect, disregard, or ignore; to be heedless
غَافَلَ – يُغَافِلُ to take advantage of another's negligence; to surprise or take unawares
تَغَفَّلَ – يَتَغَفَّلُ to take advantage of another's negligence; to surprise or take unawares
تَغَافَلَ – يَتَغَافَلُ to feign inattention; to neglect or ignore
اِسْتَغْفَلَ – يَسْتَغْفِلُ to take advantage of another's negligence; to make a fool of someone
غُفْلٌ careless, heedless; anonymous
غَفَلٌ negligence, carelessness

Family and Feelings

غَفْلَةٌ carelessness, negligence, indifference; stupidity
إِغْفالٌ / تَغافُلٌ neglect, disregard; omission
مُغَفَّلٌ indifferent; gullible, idiotic

غ ل ق

غَلَقَ – يَغْلِقُ to close, lock, or bolt
غَلَّقَ – يُغَلِّقُ to close, lock, or bolt
اِنْغَلَقَ – يَنْغَلِقُ to be closed, locked, or bolted
اِسْتَغْلَقَ – يَسْتَغْلِقُ to be dark, ambiguous, or complicated
غَلِقٌ dark, ambiguous, dubious
إِغْلاقٌ closing, locking; foreclosure (mortgage)
مُغْلَقٌ closed, locked; obscure
مُنْغَلِقٌ introvert

غ ل م

غَلِمَ – يَغْلِمُ to be seized by desire or lust
غَلِمٌ lustful, seized by desire; in heat
غُلامٌ (غِلْمانٌ / غِلْمَةٌ) boy, youth, lad; servant

غ م ر

غَمَرَ / غَمُرَ – يَغْمُرُ to be plentiful or copious; to overflow; to submerge; to lavish
غامَرَ – يُغامِرُ to venture or risk; to throw oneself into (sth)
مُغامَرَةٌ (مُغامَراتٌ) adventure, risk; hazardous
مُغامِرٌ adventurous

غ ي ر

غارَ – يَغارُ to be jealous; to vie for; to display zeal
غَيَّرَ – يُغَيِّرُ to alter, modify, or change
تَغَيَّرَ – يَتَغَيَّرُ to change, alter, or modify
غَيْرَ (prep) except, other than, different from
غَيْرَةٌ jealousy
غَيورٌ (غَيورونَ / غُيُرٌ) jealous; zealous
تَغْييرٌ (تَغْييراتٌ) change, alteration, variation

ف ر ح

فَرِحَ – يَفْرَحُ to rejoice, to be glad or delighted
فَرَّحَ – يُفَرِّحُ to gladden, delight, or cheer
فَرَحٌ (أَفْرَاحٌ) joy, rejoicing, happiness; wedding (also a girl's name in the singular)
فَرْحَةٌ joy
مُفْرِحٌ joyous, delightful

ك ب ر

كَبِرَ – يَكْبَرُ to grow older; to become or be great; to augment
كَبَّرَ – يُكَبِّرُ to make greater or bigger, to enlarge or magnify
تَكَبَّرَ – يَتَكَبَّرُ to be proud or haughty; to be overbearing
كِبْرٌ greatness, importance; pride, arrogance
كَبِيرٌ (كِبَارٌ / كُبَرَاءُ) big, great, spacious, significant; old
كَبِيرَةٌ (كَبِيرَاتٌ / كَبَائِرُ) a great sin or offence; atrocious
كِبْرِيَاءُ glory, magnificence; pride, arrogance
تَكْبِيرٌ increase, enlargement; saying اللهُ أَكْبَرُ, Allah is great
تَكَبُّرٌ / تَكَابُرٌ pride, presumption, arrogance
مُتَكَبِّرٌ proud, haughty

ك ر م

كَرُمَ – يَكْرُمُ to be noble or generous; to be precious
كَرَّمَ – يُكَرِّمُ to honour, revere, or venerate
أَكْرَمَ – يُكْرِمُ to honour, to treat with reverence; to show hospitality
تَكَرَّمَ – يَتَكَرَّمُ to feign generosity; to be noble; to be friendly; to present or bestow
كَرْمٌ (كُرُومٌ) vineyard; grapevine
كَرَمٌ nobility of nature; generosity, kindness (also a boy's name)
كَرَامَةٌ honour, dignity, nobility
كَرِيمٌ (كُرَمَاءُ / كِرَامٌ) noble, distinguished; generous, liberal (also a boy's name in the singular)
كَرِيمَةٌ (كَرَائِمُ) precious thing; valuable; daughter
تَكْرِيمٌ honouring; honour, tribute
إِكْرَامٌ honour, respect, tribute
إِكْرَامِيَّةٌ (إِكْرَامِيَّاتٌ) bonus, tip

Family and Feelings

مُكَرَّمٌ honoured, revered
مَكَّةُ الْمُكَرَّمَةُ venerable Mecca

ك ر ه

كَرِهَ – يَكْرَهُ to dislike, hate, or loathe
كَرَّهَ – يُكَرِّهُ to make someone hate; to arouse aversion
كُرْهٌ/كَرَاهِيَةٌ hatred, hate, dislike
كُرْهُ النِّسَاءِ misogyny
جَرَائِمُ الْكَرَاهِيَّةِ hate crimes
كَرِيهٌ unpleasant, disagreeable, offensive
مَكْرُوهٌ detested, odious, loathsome

ل ط ف

لَطَفَ – يَلْطُفُ to be kind or friendly; to be thin or delicate; to be graceful
لَطَّفَ – يُلَطِّفُ to make mild, soft, or gentle; to moderate; to diminish or reduce
تَلَطَّفَ – يَتَلَطَّفُ to be moderated; to be polite; to be tender or affectionate; to do in secret
اِسْتَلْطَفَ – يَسْتَلْطِفُ to find pretty, sweet, or pleasant
لُطْفٌ kindness, benevolence, gentleness
لَطَافَةٌ charm, politeness, refinement; benevolence
لَطِيفٌ (لِطَافٌ/لُطَفَاءُ) fine, delicate; agreeable, nice

م ر ح

مَرِحَ – يَمْرَحُ to be cheerful or lively
مَرَحٌ cheerful; joy, glee (also a girl's name)

م ق ت

مَقَتَ – يَمْقُتُ to detest or hate
مَقَّتَ – يُمَقِّتُ to make hateful or loathsome
مَقْتٌ hatred, aversion, disgust
مَقِيتٌ/مَمْقُوتٌ detested, odious, loathsome

م ك ر

مَكَرَ – يَمْكُرُ to deceive, delude, cheat, or dupe
مَاكَرَ – يُمَاكِرُ to try to deceive
مَكْرٌ cunning; deception, trickery

Family and Feelings 31

مَكَّارٌ cunning, sly, shrewd
ماكِر (مَكَرَة) cunning, sly, shrewd

م ل ح

مَلَحَ – يَملُحُ to be or become salty; to be beautiful, elegant, or nice
مَلَّحَ – يُمَلِّحُ to season with salt
مِلحٌ (أَملاحٌ) salt; gunpowder; wit
مالِحٌ / مِلحِيٌّ salty
مُلْحَةٌ (مُلَحٌ) anecdote, funny story, witticism
مَلاحَةٌ beauty, elegance; kindness
مِلاحَةٌ navigation
مُلوحةٌ saltiness
مَليحٌ (مِلاحٌ) handsome, beautiful, pleasant; salty
مالِحٌ salty

م ل ل

مَلَّ – يَمَلُّ to be tired of or bored; to become fed up
أَمَلَّ – يُمِلُّ to be tiresome or boring; to annoy or irritate
تَمَلَّلَ – يَتَمَلَّلُ to be bored or fed up; to embrace a religion
مِلَّةٌ (مِلَلٌ) religion, denomination, faith
مَلَلٌ (مَلالٌ) boredom, ennui
مُمِلٌّ tedious, boring

ن ب ه

نَبَهَ – يَنْبُهُ to be well-known or famous; to observe or take notice
نَبَّهَ – يُنَبِّهُ to warn; to inform or show; to waken (from sleep)
تَنَبَّهَ – يَتَنَبَّهُ to wake up; to alert; to notice or become aware
إنتَبَهَ – يَنتَبِهُ to notice or pay attention; to understand or realise
نُبْهٌ insight, perception, acumen
تَنَبُّهٌ awakening, alertness
إنتِباهٌ attention, vigilance, prudence, care
مُنَبِّهٌ (مُنَبِّهاتٌ) awakening, alerting; alarm clock; stimulant

ن ج ب

نَجَبَ – يَنجُبُ to be noble, distinguished, or generous
أَنجَبَ – يُنجِبُ to be noble, distinguished, or generous; to give birth

32 *Family and Feelings*

نَجِبٌ/نُجَبَةٌ noble, generous, magnanimous
نَجَابَةٌ nobility, excellence, superiority
نَجِيبٌ (نُجُبٌ/نُجَباءُ) noble, aristocratic, excellent (also a boy's name)

ن ذ ل

نَذُلَ – يَنذُلُ to be vile, base, or despicable
نَذْلٌ (أنذالٌ/نُذولٌ) vile, mean; simpleton; coward
نَذيلٌ (نُذَلاءُ/نِذالٌ) base, mean, vile, depraved; coward
نَذالَةٌ depravity; cowardice

ن ع م

نَعِمَ – يَنعَمُ to live in comfort; to be happy; to enjoy or savour
نَعَّمَ – يُنَعِّمُ to smooth, soften, or pamper; to pulverise or make (sth) into a powder
أنعَمَ – يُنعِمُ to make good, comfortable, or pleasant; to bestow favours
نَعَمْ yes, indeed
نَعَمٌ (أنعامٌ) livestock
نِعمةٌ (نِعَمٌ/أنعُمٌ) favour, benefit, blessing
نَعامٌ (نَعائِمُ) ostrich
نَعيمٌ comfort, ease, happiness
نُعومَةٌ softness, tenderness, fineness
ناعِمٌ gentle, soft, tender, fine

ن م م

نَمَّ – يَنُمُّ to betray, reveal, or show; to sow dissension
نَمٌّ slander, backbiting
نَمَّامٌ gossiper, slanderer; informer
نَميمَةٌ (نَمائِمُ) slander, defamation, backbiting

ه د أ

هَدَأ – يهدَأ to be calm, quiet, or tranquil
هَدَّأ – يُهَدِّئ to calm, pacify, soothe, or tranquilise
هُدوءٌ peace, calm, tranquility
هادِئٌ quiet, calm, tranquil, peaceful

Family and Feelings   33

ه ز أ

هَزَأَ – يَهْزَأُ to jeer, sneer, mock, or ridicule
تَهَزَّأَ – يَتَهَزَّأُ to deride or mock
اِسْتَهْزَأَ – يَسْتَهْزِئُ to deride or mock
اِسْتِهْزَاءٌ ridicule, derision, scorn
بِاسْتِهْزَاءٍ mockingly
هَازِئٌ / مُسْتَهْزِئٌ someone who mocks, mocker

ه ز ل

هَزَلَ – يَهْزِلُ to joke or jest; to be lean or skinny
هَزَّلَ – يُهَزِّلُ to waste away; to enervate
هَازَلَ – يُهَازِلُ to joke, mock, or jest
هَزْلٌ joking, jesting, fun
هَزِيلٌ (هَزْلَى) lean, skinny, emaciated
مَهْزَلَةٌ (مَهْزَلاتٌ / مَهَازِلُ) comedy[3]

ه ن أ

هَنَأَ – يَهْنَأُ to be beneficial, wholesome, or healthy
هَنَّأَ – يُهَنِّئُ to congratulate or felicitate; to gladden or delight
تَهَنَّأَ – يَتَهَنَّأُ to enjoy or take pleasure
هَنَاءٌ / هَنَاءَةٌ pleasure, happiness, delight
تَهْنِئَةٌ (تَهَانٍ / تَهَانِئُ / تَهْنِئَاتٌ) congratulations, felicitation

ه و ر

هَارَ – يَهُورُ to topple, demolish, or destroy; to be destroyed
هَوَّرَ – يُهَوِّرُ to endanger, jeopardise, or imperil
تَهَوَّرَ – يَتَهَوَّرُ to be destroyed; to collapse or crash down; to elapse (time)
هَوْرٌ (أَهْوَارٌ) lake
تَهَوُّرٌ carelessness, hastiness, rashness
مُتَهَوِّرٌ reckless, hasty, irresponsible
إِنْهِيَارٌ crash, collapse, breakdown

ه و ن

هَانَ – يَهُونُ to be or become easy; to be of little importance
هَوَّنَ – يُهَوِّنُ to make easy or facilitate; to minimise or belittle

34 *Family and Feelings*

أَهانَ – يُهينُ to despise; to humiliate or demean
اِستَهانَ – يَستَهينُ to consider easy; to undervalue; to misunderstand or misjudge; to disdain or despise
هَوْنٌ ease, leisure, convenience
هَيِّنٌ (هَيِّنونَ) easy; insignificant, negligible
أَهوَنُ easier; smaller; more comfortable
إهانةٌ an insult; abuse, contempt

ه ي م

هامَ – يَهيمُ to fall or be in love; to be enthusiastic or ecstatic
هَيَّمَ – يُهَيِّمُ to confuse, bewilder, or mystify; to infatuate or captivate
هُيامٌ passionate love; burning thirst
هَيْمانٌ madly in love

و د د

وَدَّ – يَوَدُّ to love or like; to want or wish
تَوَدَّدَ – يَتَوَدَّدُ to show love or affection; to flatter; to ingratiate oneself; to attract
تَوادَدَ – يَتَوادَدُ to love each other, to be on friendly terms
وُدٌّ/مَوَدَّةٌ affection, love, friendship
وُدِّيٌّ friendly, amicable
وَدادٌ love; friendship (also a girl's name)
وَدودٌ affectionate; devoted, fond, friendly

و ع ى

وَعَى – يَعي to hold, comprise, or contain; to remember; to perceive
وَعَّى – يُوَعِّي to warn or caution
تَوَعَّى – يَتَوَعَّى to act with caution or prudence
وَعْيٌ awareness, consciousness, attention
وِعاءٌ (أَوْعِيَةٌ) container, vessel
واعٍ attentive, careful, conscious

و ق ح

وَقَحَ – يَقِحُ to be shameless, impudent, or insolent
تَوَقَّحَ – يَتَوَقَّحُ to behave impudently

Family and Feelings 35

تَواقَحَ – يَتَواقَحُ to behave in an insolent way
وَقاحَةٌ impertinence, impudence, insolence
وَقِحٌ insolent, shameless, cheeky

و ل ع

وَلِعَ – يَوْلَعُ to catch fire or burn; to be madly in love; to be fond of
وَلَّعَ – يُوَلِّعُ to kindle, light, or set on fire; to enamour
تَوَلَّعَ – يَتَوَلَّعُ to catch fire or burn; to be madly in love
وَلَعٌ / وُلوعٌ passionate love, passion
وَلّاعَةٌ lighter
تَوَلُّعٌ passionate love, ardent desire, passion
مُولَعٌ in love; mad or crazy (about someone); passionate or enthusiastic about

Exercises

1) Give two derived nouns for each of these roots:

ب ن ن
خ ل ف
ر م ل
س ل ف
ع و ل
و ل د

2) Find the roots of these words:

أعزَبُ
سالِفاً
مُختَلَفٌ
مُناسَبةٌ
مُوَهِّلاتٌ

3) Give a synonym for each of the following words:

جُرأةٌ bravery
جَوادٌ generous
حِرصٌ greed
صَباءٌ youth
كُرهٌ hatred
نِكاحٌ marriage

Family and Feelings

4) Give an antonym for each of the following words:

حِقْدٌ hatred, malice, resentment

سَعيدٌ happy

كَرَمٌ generosity; nobility of nature

5) Compose three sentences using the following verbs:

اِسْتَلَفَ to borrow

اِقْتَرَبَ to approach, advance, or get close

تَبَنَّى to adopt; to embrace

تَرَمَّلَ to become a widow or widower

وَلَدَ to bear children or procreate

6) Give the plural of the following words (some may have more than one plural form):

بِساطٌ

تَعيسٌ

حِزامٌ

خَبيثٌ

قَرنٌ

مُساعِدٌ

هَرَمٌ

7) Give the Arabic words which best match these definitions:

a) a poet
b) a lover
c) a vineyard; grapevine
d) an envelope
e) an ostrich

8) Translate the following into Arabic:

- Her husband was a cunning man.
- She separated from her husband because of his miserliness.
- Her mother was delighted when she gave birth to twins.
- I became angry when I heard the disgraceful news.

9) Translate the following sentences into English:

- وَجَدَ الولدُ أهلَه وفرِحَ كثيراً.
- تَعيشُ أختي في ألمانيا مع زوجها.
- هِيَ امرأةٌ جميلةٌ وكَريمةٌ، ولكنَّ زوجَها رجلٌ كَريهةٌ وَحَقودٌ.

Notes

1 Note that إخْوان is more commonly used to refer to members of an order like the Muslim brotherhood.
2 It is worth mentioning that there is some ambiguity regarding this root. There are those that consider the in-laws and حمى 'to protect' to share the root ح م ى; others, however, believe that 'the in-laws' has no root and should be listed separately.
3 This is used in colloquial Arabic to mean 'a disaster or disgrace'.

2 Health الصِّحةُ

The Body الجِسمُ

أ ب ط

تَأَبَّطَ – يَتَأَبَّطُ to hold or carry under one's arm
إِبْطٌ (آباطٌ) armpit

أ ن ف

أَنِفَ – يَأْنَفُ to disdain or scorn
أَنْفٌ (أُنوفٌ) nose; pride
أَنَفَةٌ pride, rejection, disdain
آنِفاً previously

ب د ن

بَدَنَ – يَبْدُنُ to be fat or corpulent
بَدَنٌ (أَبدانٌ) body, trunk, torso
بَدَنِيٌّ physical, relating to the body
بَدانَةٌ obesity, corpulence, fat
بَدينٌ / بادِنٌ (بُدْنٌ) fat, obese, corpulent

ب ط ن

بَطَنَ – يَبطُنُ to hide; to be hidden or concealed
بَطْنٌ (بُطونٌ) belly, stomach, abdomen
بَطنِيٌّ abdominal
بِطنةٌ gluttony
باطِنٌ (بواطِنُ) inner, interior; intrinsic

DOI: 10.4324/9781003250890-3

Health 39

ب و ل

بالَ – يَبولُ to urinate
تَبَوَّلَ – يَتَبَوَّلُ to urinate
بَوْلٌ (أَبوالٌ) urine

ج ب ه

جَبهَةٌ (جِباهٌ / جَبهاتٌ) forehead, brow; front, façade

ج س م

جَسَّمَ – يُجَسِّمُ to shape or materialise; to enlarge; to exaggerate
تَجَسَّمَ – يَتَجَسَّمُ to materialise or take shape; to become big
جِسمٌ (أَجسامٌ) body; matter, mass; shape
جِسمِيٌّ physical, of or relating to the body
جَسيمٌ (جِسامٌ) great, big, large; corpulent

ج ل د

جَلَدَ – يَجلِدُ to whip or flog
جَلَّدَ – يُجَلِّدُ to bind (a book); to freeze
جالَدَ – يُجالِدُ to fight (an illness)
جَلدٌ flogging
جِلدٌ (جُلودٌ / أَجلادٌ) skin, hide, leather
جَلَدٌ / جَلادةٌ / جُلودةٌ endurance, patience; suffering
جَليدٌ ice

No root

جُمجُمَةٌ (جَماجِمُ) skull, cranium
جُمجُمِيٌّ cranial

ح ل ق

حَلَقَ – يَحلِقُ to shave or shave off
تَحَلَّقَ – يَتَحَلَّقُ to form a circle
حَلقٌ (حُلوقٌ) throat, gullet, pharynx; shaving
حَلَقَةٌ (حَلَقٌ / حَلَقاتٌ) ring, link, circle
حَلّاقٌ (حَلّاقونَ) barber

ح ل م

حَلَمَ – يَحْلَمُ to reach puberty; to reflect or meditate on
اِحْتَلَمَ – يَحْتَلِمُ to reach puberty
الْحُلْمُ sexual maturity, puberty
حَلَمَةٌ nipple, teat; tick, mite
حَلِيمٌ (حُلَماءُ) mild, gentle; patient

ح م ض

حَمُضَ – يَحْمُضُ to be sour
حَمَّضَ – يُحَمِّضُ to make sour or acidify; to oxidise
حَمضٌ (أَحْماضٌ) acid
الْحَمضُ النَّوَوِيُّ DNA
حُموضَةٌ heartburn, acidity, sourness

No root

حَنْجَرَةٌ / حُنْجورٌ (حَناجِرُ / حَناجيرُ) larynx, throat
عُقْدَةُ الْحُنْجَرةِ / تُفّاحَةُ آدَمَ Adam's apple

ح ن ك

حَنَّكَ – يُحَنِّكُ to sophisticate; to make experienced
حَنَكٌ (أَحْناكٌ) palate
حِنْكٌ / حُنْكَةٌ worldly experience

No root

حَوْضٌ (أَحْواضٌ) pelvis

خ د د

خَدَّ – يَخُدُّ to furrow or plough (the ground)
خَدٌّ (خُدودٌ) cheek; side
مِخَدَّة (مِخَدّاتٌ) cushion, pillow

خ ص ر

خَصِرَ – يَخْصَرُ to become cold, to suffer from the cold
اِخْتَصَرَ – يَخْتَصِرُ to shorten or condense; to summarise

Health 41

خَصْرٌ / خاصِرَةٌ (خُصورٌ / خواصِرُ) waist, hip
اِختِصارٌ (اِختِصاراتٌ) shortening, summarisation; shortcut

No root

دَمٌ (دِماءٌ) blood
دَمَوِيٌّ bloody
الفِئَةُ الدَّمَوِيَّةُ / فَصيلَةُ الدَّمِ blood type
ضَغطُ الدَّمِ blood pressure
نَقلُ الدَّمِ blood transfusion
خَفيفُ الدَّمِ amiable
ثَقيلُ الدَّمِ unpleasant, disagreeable

ذ ر ع

ذَرَعَ - يَذرَعُ to measure; to cover or cross (distance); to intervene or mediate
تَذَرَّعَ - يَتَذَرَّعُ to use or employ (excuse or pretext)
ذَرعٌ power, ability, capability
ذِراعٌ (أَذرُعٌ / ذُرعانٌ) arm, forearm
ذَريعَةٌ excuse, pretext

No root

ذَقَنٌ (أَذقانٌ / ذُقونٌ) chin

No root

رِئَةٌ (رِئاتٌ) lung
رِئَوِيٌّ pulmonary, pulmonic
اِلتِهابٌ رِئَوِيٌّ pneumonia

ر أ س

(Full treatment in Politics chapter)

رَأسٌ (رُؤوسٌ) head; chief, leader

No root

رَبلَةُ السّاقِ calf (leg)

42 Health

ر ج ل

رَجَلَ – يَرجُلُ to walk or go on foot
تَرَجَّلَ – يَتَرَجَّلُ to assume masculine manners, to behave like a man
رِجلٌ (أَرجُلٌ) leg, foot
رَجُلٌ (رِجالٌ) an important man[1]
رُجولَةٌ/رُجولِيَّةٌ masculinity, virility

ر د ف

رَدَفَ – يَردَفُ to follow or succeed
تَرادَفَ – يَتَرادَفُ to come in succession; to be synonymous
رِدفٌ (أَردافٌ) bottom, backside, rear
مُرادِفٌ (مُرادِفاتٌ) synonym; synonymous, analogous

No root

رُضابٌ/لُعابٌ saliva

ر ف ق

(Full treatment in Education chapter)

مَرفِقٌ (مَرافِقُ) elbow

ر ك ب

رَكِبَ – يَركَبُ to mount or ride; to go or travel
اِرتَكَبَ – يرتَكِبُ to commit (crime); to pursue (sth)
رُكبَةٌ (رُكَبٌ) knee
مَركَبٌ (مَراكِبُ) boat, ship
اِرتِكابٌ perpetuation (of a crime or sin)

No root

شِريانٌ (شَرايينُ) artery

No root

شَفَةٌ (شِفاةٌ/شَفَواتٌ) lip; edge
شَفائِفُ/شَفايِفُ lips

Health 43

ص ب ع

صَبَعَ – يَصبَعُ to point with the finger
إِصْبَعٌ (أَصابِعُ) a finger or toe
إِصبعُ اليَدِ finger

ص د ر

(Full treatment in Work chapter)

صَدرٌ (صُدورٌ) chest, breast, bust, bosom
عَظمُ الصَّدرِ sternum, breastbone

No root

صُدْغٌ (أَصداغٌ) temple

ض ل ع

ضَلَعَ – يَضلَعُ to be strong or sturdy; to be crooked or bent
ضِلْعٌ (ضُلوعٌ / أَضلاعٌ) ribs (body); cutlet, chops
مُضَلَّعٌ ribbed; polygon

ظ ف ر

ظَفِرَ – يَظفَرُ to be successful or triumphant; to defeat or conquer
ظُفرٌ (أَظافِرُ) fingernail, nail, toenail; claw, talon
ظافِرٌ victor, conqueror (also a boy's name)

ظ ه ر

(Full treatment in Politics chapter)

ظَهْرٌ (ظُهورٌ) back; rear side, reverse; surface

ع ت ق

عَتَقَ – يَعتُقُ to grow old, age, or mature; to be free (of a slave)
عَتيقٌ old, ancient, antique; noble
عاتِقٌ (عَواتِقُ) shoulder

ع ر ق

عَرَّقَ – يُعَرِّقُ to take root; to sweat

ع ص ب

عَصَبَ – يَعصِبُ to tie or bind; to wrap or bandage
تَعَصَّبَ – يتَعَصَّبُ to bandage; to be a fanatic; to plot or conspire
عَصَبٌ (أَعصابٌ) nerves
عَصَبِيٌّ nervous
الجِهازُ العَصَبِيُّ the nervous system
عَصَبِيَّةٌ (عَصَبِيّاتٌ) nervousness; fanaticism, religious bigotry
عِصابةٌ (عِصاباتٌ) gang, group; league, federation
تَعَصُّبٌ fanaticism
مُتَعَصِّبٌ fanatic, extremist

ع ض ل

عَضَلَ – يَعضُلُ to be muscular; to prevent (a woman) from marrying
عَضِلٌ muscular, brawny
عَضَلَةٌ (عَضَلاتٌ / عَضَلٌ) muscle
عُضالٌ chronic, incurable (of a disease)

ع ظ م

عَظُمَ – يَعظُمُ to be or become large or great; to be distressing or painful
عَظَّمَ – يُعَظِّمُ to make greater or more powerful; to enlarge
عَظمٌ (أَعظامٌ / عِظامٌ) bone
عُظمٌ greatness, power, might
عَظيمٌ (عُظماءُ) great, big, significant; powerful; sublime
مُعظَمُ (النَّاسِ) most of (them), the majority of (people)

ع ي ن

عَيَّنَ – يُعَيِّنُ to specify or determine; to nominate or appoint
عايَنَ – يُعايِنُ to see, examine, or inspect; to be appointed
عَينٌ (عُيونٌ) eye; the evil eye; spring, fountain
عَيِّنَةٌ (عَيِّناتٌ) sample, specimen
عُوَيناتٌ glasses, spectacles

مُعَيَّنٌ fixed, determined; nominated, appointed
مُعايَنَةُ المريضِ patient observation

No root

غُدَّةٌ (غُدَدٌ) gland
الْغُدّة الدُّرَقِيَّةُ thyroid gland

No root

فُؤادٌ (أَفْئِدَةٌ) heart

ف خ ذ

فَخِذٌ (أَفْخاذٌ) thigh; leg (of meat)

ف ق ر

فَقَرَ – يَفْقُرُ to pierce or perforate; to be or become poor
فَقْرٌ poverty, need, lack
فَقَرَةٌ (فقَراتٌ) vertebra; section, paragraph, passage
الْعَمودُ الفِقَرِيُّ spine
حَيوانات فِقَرِيَّةٌ / الفَقارِيّاتُ vertebrates
فَقيرٌ (فُقَراءُ) poor, poverty-stricken; a pauper

ف ك ك

فَكَّ – يَفُكُّ to dislocate or separate; to break up or disintegrate
فَكٌّ (فُكوكٌ) jaw, jawbone; redemption (of a pledge)
فَكَّةٌ small change (money)

No root

فَمٌ (أَفواهٌ / أَفمامٌ) mouth; orifice, aperture, hole

ق د م

قَدَمٌ (أَقْدامٌ) foot, step
إِصبعُ الْقَدَمِ toe

Health

ق ص ب

قَصَبَ – يَقصِبُ to cut up
قَصَبٌ cane, reed; sugar cane; brocade
قَصَبَةٌ (قَصَبَاتٌ) windpipe, trachea; cane, reed
قَصَبَةُ الرِّئَةِ windpipe, trachea
قَصَبَةُ المَرِيءِ oesophagus

ق ص ص

(Full treatment in Media chapter)

قَصٌّ sternum, breastbone; clippings, cuttings

ق ض ب

قَضَبَ – يَقضِبُ to prune or trim; to cut off
قَضِيبٌ (قُضبَانٌ) penis; twig, stick

ق ف و

قَفَا – يَقفُو to follow
قَفاً (أَقفِيَةٌ) nape; back of the head; posterior (colloquial)
قَفَاءٌ nape; back of the head

ق ل ب

قَلَبَ – يَقلِبُ to turn around; to topple or reverse
اِنقَلَبَ – يَنقَلِبُ to be reversed; to be overthrown
قَلبٌ reversal; upheaval; overthrow (of government)
قَلبٌ (قُلوبٌ) heart; centre, core
دَقَّاتُ القَلبِ heartbeat
طَيِّبُ القَلبِ kind-hearted
أَزمَةٌ/نَوبَةٌ قَلبِيَّةٌ heart attack
اِنقِلابٌ (اِنقِلاباتٌ) coup, revolution; change, alteration

ك ب د

كَبَدَ – يَكبُدُ to affect severely; to wear out or wear down
تَكَبَّدَ – يَتَكَبَّدُ to endure, bear, or suffer
كَبِدٌ (أَكبادٌ/كُبودٌ) liver; interior, heart (i.e. essence)

Health 47

ك ت ف

كَنَفَ – يَكْتِفُ to shackle, bind, or tie (hands) behind the back
تَكَنَّفَ – يَتَكَنَّفُ to cross or fold one's arms
تَكَاتَفَ – يَتَكَاتَفُ to stand shoulder to shoulder, to stand together and united
كَتِفٌ (أَكْتَافٌ) shoulder, scapula, shoulder blade

ك ح ل

كَحَلَ – يَكْحَلُ to rub kohl on eyes
تَكَحَّلَ – يَتَكَحَّلُ to colour the eye with kohl
كُحْلٌ (أَكْحَالٌ) antimony, kohl
كَحِيلٌ (كَحَائِلُ) black
كُحُولٌ alcohol
كَاحِلٌ (كَوَاحِلُ) ankle, ankle bone

ك ع ب

كَعَبَ – يَكْعُبُ to be full and round; to be swelling (of breasts)
كَعْبٌ (كِعَابٌ/كُعُوبٌ) heel; joint; cube
كَعْبَةٌ (كَعَبَاتٌ) cube; cubic; structure
الكَعْبَةُ المُشَرَّفَةُ the Kaaba in Mecca

No root

كُلْيَةٌ/كُلْوَةٌ (كُلًى) kidneys
غَسْلُ الكُلَى dialysis

ك ه ل

كَهَلَ – يَكْهَلُ to be in middle age
كُهُولَةٌ middle-aged, mature
كَاهِلٌ (كَوَاهِلُ) shoulders, upper back

No root

لِثَّةٌ (لِثَاتٌ/لِثًى) gum

ل س ن

لَسِنَ – يَلْسَنُ to be eloquent

48   Health

لَسِنٌ / أَلْسَنُ (لُسْنٌ) eloquent
لِسانٌ (أَلْسِنةٌ) tongue, mouthpiece; language

No root

مَثانةٌ (مَثاناتٌ) bladder

No root

مُخٌّ (مِخاخٌ) brain; marrow, core
مُخِّيٌّ cerebral

م ر ر

مَرَّ – يَمُرُّ to be or become bitter
مُرٌّ (أَمرارٌ) bitter; severe, painful
مَرارةٌ (مَراراتٌ) gall bladder; bitterness, rancour

م ع د

مَعِدةٌ (مِعَدٌ) stomach

No root

مِعىً / مِعاءٌ (أَمعاءٌ / أَمعيَةٌ) intestines, bowels, gut
الأَمعاءُ الدَّقيقةُ small intestines
الأَمعاءُ الغَليظةُ large intestines

ن ب ض

نَبَضَ – يَنبِضُ to beat, throb, or pulse
نبضٌ (أَنباضٌ) pulse
نَبْضةٌ (نَبْضاتٌ) a pulse or beat

ن س ل

نَسَلَ – يَنسُلُ to beget or father; to unravel or fall out
نَسلٌ progeny, descendants; procreation
تَحديدُ النَّسلِ birth control
تَناسُلٌ reproduction, procreation

Health 49

الأَعْضاءُ التَّناسُليَّةُ genitals
مَرَضٌ تَناسُليٌّ venereal disease
الجِهازُ التَّناسُليُّ the reproductive system
تَناسُليّاتٌ / أَعضاءٌ تَناسُليَّةٌ sexual organs

ن ش ق

نَشِقَ – يَنشَقُ to smell, sniff, or inhale
اِنتَشَقَ – يَنتَشِقُ to inhale or breathe in
نَشْقٌ / تَنَشُّقٌ / اِستِنشاقٌ inhaling, inhalation, breathing

ن م ل

نَمِلَ – يَنمَلُ to tingle or be numb
نَملٌ (نِمالٌ) ants
نَمَلٌ / تَنميلٌ tingling, itching, pins and needles
أُنمُلَةٌ (أَنامِلُ) fingertips

ن ه د

نَهَدَ – يَنهَدُ to become round and full; to swell (of breasts)
تَنَهَّدَ – يَتَنَهَّدُ to sigh
نَهدٌ (نُهودٌ) breast, bosom; elevation, rise
تَنَهُّدٌ (تَنَهُّداتٌ) sigh

ه ب ل

هَبِلَ – يَهبَلُ to be bereaved of a son (as a mother)
هَبيلٌ / مَهْبولٌ a fool or simple person
أَهبَلُ (هُبْلٌ) idiotic, dim-witted, weak-minded
مَهْبَلٌ (مَهابِلُ) vagina

ه ض م

هَضَمَ – يَهضِمُ to digest (food); to oppress or terrorise
هَضمٌ digestion
عُسرُ الهَضمِ indigestion
الجِهازُ الهَضميُّ the digestive system

50   Health

No root

هَيْكَلٌ (هَياكِلُ) skeleton, frame; temple, altar

No root

وَجْنَةٌ (وَجَناتٌ) cheek

و ج ه

(Full treatment in Media chapter)

وَجْهٌ (وُجوهٌ) face

No root

وِداجٌ jugular vein

و ر د

وَريدٌ (أَوْرِدَةٌ) vein, jugular vein

No root

وِرْكٌ (أَوْراكٌ) hip, thigh

No root

يَدٌ (أَيْدٍ / أَيادٍ) hand; control, authority; assistance, help
يَدَوِيٌّ manual

The Senses الحَواسُّ

ب ص ر

بَصَرَ – يَبْصُرُ to look or see; to understand or realise
تَبَصَّرَ – يَتَبَصَّرُ to look or regard; to ponder
بَصَرٌ (أَبْصارٌ) gaze, vision, eyesight; insight

ح س س

حَسَّ – يَحُسُّ to feel or sense; to sympathise

Health 51

حَسَّسَ – يُحَسِّسُ to grope or feel
حَسَّاسٌ sensitive; sensible; sensual
حَسَاسِيَّةٌ sensitivity
حِسٌّ feeling, sensation; sense; voice
إِحْسَاسٌ (إِحْسَاسَاتٌ / أَحَاسِيسُ) feelings, sensation, emotion
حَاسَّةٌ (حَوَاسُّ) sense
الْحَوَاسُّ الْخَمْسُ the five senses

ذ و ق

ذَاقَ – يَذُوقُ to taste or sample (food); to test or try out
تَذَوَّقَ – يَتَذَوَّقُ to savour or relish; to sense or perceive
ذَوْقٌ (أَذْوَاقٌ) taste; inclination; sensitivity
حَاسَّةُ الذَّوَاقِ / الذَّوْقُ sense of taste

س م ع

سَمِعَ – يَسْمَعُ to hear or listen; to pay attention
اِسْتَمَعَ – يَسْتَمِعُ to hear or listen; to overhear or eavesdrop
سَمْعٌ (أَسْمَاعٌ) hearing, sense of hearing
سَمْعِيٌّ auditory
سُمْعَةٌ reputation, standing
سَمَّاعَةٌ (سَمَّاعَاتٌ) earphone, earpiece; stethoscope
الْمُسْتَمِعُونَ the audience

ش م م

شَمَّ – يَشُمُّ to smell or sniff
حَاسَّةُ الشَّمِّ sense of smell

ل م س

لَمَسَ – يَلْمِسُ to touch or handle; to perceive; to search for
لَامَسَ – يُلَامِسُ to be in touch or contact; to have sex with
لَمْسٌ feeling, touching
لَمْسِيٌّ tactile
لَمْسَةٌ (لَمْسَاتٌ) touch, retouch
لَمِيسٌ soft to the touch (also a girl's name)

مَلْمَسٌ (مَلامِسُ) point of contact; tentacle, feeler
مُلامَسَةٌ touching; sexual intercourse

Sex and Reproduction الجِنسُ والتَّناسُلُ

ب ل غ

بَلَغَ – يَبْلُغُ to reach or arrive; to come of age or reach puberty
بَلَّغَ – يُبَلِّغُ to make (someone) reach; to inform, convey, or notify
بالَغَ – يُبالِغُ to exaggerate, overdo, or to go to great lengths
بَليغٌ (بُلَغاءُ) eloquent; intense, serious
بُلوغٌ maturity, legal majority
سِنُّ البُلوغِ puberty
بَلاغَةٌ eloquence; literature
مَبْلَغٌ (مَبالِغُ) a sum of money, an amount; scope, range
تَبْليغٌ (تَبْليغاتٌ) a communication, announcement, or report; transmission, delivery
مُبالَغَةٌ (مُبالَغاتٌ) exaggeration
بالِغٌ (بالِغونَ) excessive, considerable; serious; mature (of age) (pl: adults)

ج ذ ب

جَذَبَ – يَجْذِبُ to attract, pull or draw
اِنْجَذَبَ – يَنْجَذِبُ to be attracted or gravitate towards
جَذْبٌ attraction, appeal; gravitation
جَذّابٌ attractive, magnetic
جاذِبِيَّةٌ attraction, gravitation

ج ن س

جَنَّسَ – يُجَنِّسُ to make similar or assimilate; to classify or sort
تَجَنَّسَ – يَتَجَنَّسُ to become naturalised or receive citizenship
جِنْسٌ (أَجْناسٌ) sexual intercourse; kind, sort, category
جِنْسِيٌّ sexual; generic
لا جِنْسِيٌّ asexual
شُذوذٌ جِنْسِيٌّ homosexuality
جِنْسِيَّةٌ (جِنْسِيَّاتٌ) nationality, citizenship
جِناسٌ a pun; assonance; rhetoric

ج ن ن

جَنَّ – يَجِنُّ to cover, hide, or conceal
جَنَّنَ – يُجَنِّنُ to craze, madden, or enrage
تَجَنَّنَ – يَتَجَنَّنُ to go mad or become crazy
جِنٌّ jinn, demons
جَنَّةٌ (جَنَّاتٌ) paradise, heaven
جُنَيْنَةٌ (جُنيناتٌ / جَنائِنُ) little garden
جَنانٌ (أَجنانٌ) heart, soul
جَنينٌ (أَجِنَّةٌ) embryo, foetus; a seed or bud
جُنونٌ possession (by jinn); madness, obsession
جانٌّ jinn, demons
مَجنونٌ (مَجانينُ) obsessed; possessed; mad

ج ه ض

أَجهَضَ – يُجهِضُ to have a miscarriage; to have a litter
إِجهاضٌ abortion, miscarriage

ح ب ل

حَبِلَ – يَحبَلُ to conceive or be pregnant
حَبَّلَ – يُحَبِّلُ to impregnate
حَبَلٌ conception; pregnancy
حُبلى (حَبالى) pregnant

ح م ل

حَمَلَ – يَحمِلُ to carry or lift; to bear (a child)
حَمَّلَ – يُحَمِّلُ to load or burden; to charge or task; to upload (file)
تَحَمَّلَ – يَتَحَمَّلُ to endure or tolerate; to assume (responsibilities)
حَمْلٌ pregnancy; carrying, bearing
حُبوبُ مَنعِ الحَملِ contraceptive pills
حِملٌ (أَحمالٌ) load, burden; cargo
حَمْلَةٌ (حَمَلاتٌ) a campaign; an attack or offensive
تَحامُلٌ prejudice, bias; intolerance
مُحتَمَلٌ bearable; likely, probable

ح ي ض

حاضَتْ – تَحيضُ to menstruate
حَيْضٌ / حِياضٌ menstruation

خ ص ب

خَصَبَ – يَخصِبُ to be fertile
أخصَبَ – يُخصِبُ to fertilise or make fertile
خَصِبٌ / خَصيبٌ fertile
خُصوبةٌ / إخصابٌ fertility
تَخصيبٌ fertilisation

خ ل ط

خَلَطَ – يَخلِطُ to mix or mingle; to confuse
خَلَّطَ – يُخَلِّطُ to mix or mingle; to cause confusion
اِختَلَطَ – يَختَلِطُ to be mixed; to be promiscuous; to be on intimate terms
خَلْطٌ a combination; mingling
خَلْطةٌ a mixture or blend
مُختَلِطٌ mixed

ر ض ع

رَضِعَ – يَرضَعُ to suckle or suck
رَضَّعَ – يُرَضِّعُ to nurse, breastfeed, or suckle
رَضيعٌ / راضِعٌ (رُضعاءُ / رُضَّعٌ) baby or infant

ر ه ق

رَهِقَ – يَرهَقُ to overtake; to begin to affect (someone)
راهَقَ – يُراهِقُ to be adolescent or to reach the age of sexual maturity
مُراهَقةٌ puberty
سِنُّ المُراهَقةِ adolescence
إرهاقٌ fatigue
مُراهِقٌ (مُراهِقونَ) adolescent, teenager

س ق ط

سَقَطَ – يَسقُطُ to fall, drop, or tumble
أسقَطَ – يُسقِطُ to miscarry; to drop or let fall

Health 55

سِقْطٌ a miscarried foetus
مَسْقَطٌ (مَساقِطُ) a place where something falls
مَسْقَطُ الرَّأْسِ birthplace
مَسْقَطٌ Muscat (capital of Oman)
إسْقاطٌ an abortion

ش ب ق

شَبِقَ – يَشْبَقُ to be lustful; to be lewd or lecherous
شَبَقٌ lust; lewdness
مَناطِقُ شَبَقِيَّةٌ erogenous zones

ش ذ ذ

شَذَّ – يَشِذُّ to segregate, separate, or isolate; to be lacking
شَذٌّ (شُذوذٌ) deviation, irregularity, anomaly; sexual deviance
شاذٌّ (شَوَاذٌّ) irregular, peculiar; isolated

ش ه و / ش ه ى

شَها – يَشْهو to desire, crave, or long for
اِشْتَهى – يَشْتَهي to crave, desire, or wish; to be covetous or greedy
شَهْوَةٌ (شَهَواتٌ) a craving or desire; pleasure, indulgence
شَهِيٌّ pleasant, delicious
شَهِيَّةٌ appetite

ط م ث

طَمَثَ – يَطْمُثُ to menstruate; to deflower
طَمَثٌ menstruation, period
اِنْقِطاعُ الطَّمَثِ menopause

ع ر ي

عَرِيَ – يَعْرى to be naked or nude
عَرَّى – يُعَرِّي to undress or strip; to deprive
عُرْيٌ / عَراءٌ nakedness, nudity
عُرْيانٌ (عَرايا) naked, bare

ع ق ر

عَقَرَ – يَعقِرُ to wound; to be barren or sterile
الْعُقرُ sterility
عَقارٌ (عَقاراتٌ) real estate
عقاقيرُ طِبّيَّةٌ medical drugs
عاقِرٌ (عَواقِرُ) barren, sterile

ع ق م

عَقَمَ – يَعقُمُ to be barren or sterile; to render barren
تَعَقَّمَ – يَتَعَقَّمُ to be sterilised (person / thing)
عُقْمٌ infertility
عَقيمٌ (عُقْمٌ / عِقامٌ) sterile; infertile; ineffective
تَعقيمٌ sterilisation, disinfection, pasteurisation
مُعَقَّمٌ sterilised, pasteurised, disinfected

م ن و / م ن ي

مَنا – يَمنو to put to the test; to afflict; to tempt
مَنَّى – يُمَنِّي to wish; to promise; to awaken the desire (in someone for sth)
أمنى – يُمني to shed (blood); to emit or ejaculate
تَمَنَّى – يَتَمَنَّى to desire
إستَمنى – يَستَمني to masturbate
مِنيَّ sperm
أُمنِيَةٌ (أَمانٍ) a wish or desire; a demand
تَمَنٍ (تَمَنِّياتٌ) a wish or desire; a request

ن ص ب

إنتِصابٌ erection
ضعفُ الإنتِصابِ erectile dysfunction

و م ض

وَمَضَ – يَمِضُ to flash or flush
أومَضَ – يومِضُ to glance furtively; to wink
وَمضَةٌ حَرارِيَّةٌ hot flushes; menopause

Health 57

ع ف ي

يَفَعَ – يَيْفَعُ to reach adolescence or puberty
يَفَعٌ adolescence, puberty
يافِعٌ an adolescent; a grown-up

The Mind العَقْلُ

No root

بالٌ mind; state, condition
فراغُ البالِ leisure; being stress-free
مَشغولُ البالِ anxious, worried

No root

ذِهنٌ (أَذهانٌ) mind, intellect

ص و ب

صابَ – يَصوبُ to hit (a target); to be right or hold true
صَوَّبَ – يُصَوِّبُ to aim or point; to agree, approve, or assent
صَوابٌ that which is proper or correct; reason, intellect
فَقَدَ صَوابَهُ he lost his mind
إِصابَةٌ (إِصاباتٌ) an injury or wound; a goal
مُصيبَةٌ (مَصائِبُ / مُصيباتٌ) a misfortune, calamity, or disaster

ف ص م

فَصَمَ – يَفصِمُ to split or crack; to cause to crack
اِنفَصَمَ – يَنفَصِمُ to be split, cleft, or cracked
اِنفِصامٌ a split; schizophrenia
اِنفِصامُ الشَّخصِيَّةِ schizophrenia, split personality

م ز ج

مَزَجَ – يَمزُجُ to mix, mingle, or blend
مَزجٌ blending, mixing
مِزاجٌ (أَمزِجَةٌ) mood, temper; physical constitution; mixture

ن ف س

نَفَسَ – يَنْفُسُ to be precious, priceless, or valuable
تَنَفَّسَ – يَتَنَفَّسُ to breathe; to rest or have a break
تَنافَسَ – يَتَنافَسُ to rival, compete, or contend
نَفَسٌ (أَنْفاسٌ) breath
نَفْسٌ (نُفوسٌ) soul, self; a person
الثِّقَةُ بِالنَّفْسِ self-confidence
نَفْسِيٌّ spiritual, mental, psychological
تَحْليلٌ نَفْسِيٌّ psychoanalysis
نَفْسِيَّةٌ psyche, mentality; psychology
الطِّبُّ النَفْسانِيُّ psychiatry
طَبيبٌ نَفْسانِيٌّ psychiatrist
عالِمٌ نَفْسانِيٌّ psychologist
نَفيسٌ precious, costly
مُنافَسَةٌ (مُنافَساتٌ) competition, rivalry
تَنَفُّسٌ respiration

Ailments, Illnesses, and Disabilities الوَعَكاتُ والأَمْراضُ والإعاقاتُ

أ ر ق

أَرِقَ – يَأْرَقُ to be unable to sleep
أَرَّقَ – يُؤَرِّقُ to make sleepless or to prevent (someone) from sleeping
أَرَقٌ insomnia, sleeplessness

أ ز م

تَأَزَّمَ – يَتَأَزَّمُ to be critical; to come to a head
أَزْمَةٌ (أَزَماتٌ) emergency, crisis; asthma

No root

الكُولِسْتِرولُ cholesterol

أ ل م

أَلِمَ – يَأْلَمُ to suffer or feel pain; to be in pain
تَأَلَّمَ – يَتَأَلَّمُ to suffer or feel pain

Health 59

أَلَمٌ (آلامٌ) pain, ache; grief
مُؤلِمٌ aching, painful; sad, distressing
مُتَألِّمٌ aching, painful; suffering, in pain

أ ن ن

أَنَّ – يَئِنُّ to groan or moan
أَنَّةٌ (أَناتٌ) a groan or moan

ب ث ر

بَثَرَ – يَبْثُرُ to break out in spots
بَثْرٌ (بُثورٌ) a spot or pimple; a blister
بَثْرَةٌ (بَثَراتٌ) a spot or pimple; a blister

ب ر د

بَرَدَ – يَبْرُدُ to be or feel cold; to soothe
بَرَّدَ – يُبَرِّدُ to cool or refrigerate; to soothe
بَرْدٌ cold, catarrh; coldness, chilliness
بَرَدٌ hail
بُرودَةٌ / بُرودٌ coldness; emotional coldness, frigidity
بَرّادَةٌ / بَرّادٌ fridge
بارِدٌ cold, chilly; silly

No root

بكتيريا bacteria

ب ك م

بَكِمَ – يَبْكَمُ to be dumb; to hold one's tongue or be silent
بُكْمٌ dumbness
أَبْكَمُ (بُكْمٌ) dumb (m)
بَكْماءُ (بَكْماواتٌ / بُكْمٌ) dumb (f)

ت ع ب

تَعِبَ – يَتْعَبُ to work hard, toil, wear oneself out, be or become tired
أَتْعَبَ – يُتْعِبُ to trouble or inconvenience; to fatigue

Health

تَعَبٌ exertion, fatigue; inconvenience, burden, nuisance
تَعِبٌ / مُتْعَبٌ / تَعْبانٌ tired, exhausted

ت م ت م

تَمْتَمَ – يُتَمْتِمُ to stammer; to mumble or mutter

ج د ر

جَدِرَ – يَجْدَرُ to have smallpox
جَدَرِيٌّ smallpox
مَجْدورٌ infected with smallpox; pockmarked

No root

جُرثومٌ / جُرثومَةٌ (جَراثيمُ) germ, microbe

ح د ب

حَدِبَ – يَحْدَبُ to be hunchbacked; to be nice or kind
حَدَبٌ fondness, love
أَحْدَبُ (حُدْبٌ) hunchbacked

ح ص ب

حَصِبَ – يَحْصَبُ to have measles
حَصْبَةٌ measles

ح م م

حَمَّ – يَحَمُّ to be feverish; to make hot
حَمَّمَ – يُحَمِّمُ to heat; to bathe or wash
اِسْتَحَمَّ – يَسْتَحِمُّ to bathe
حُمَّى (حُمَّياتٌ) fever
حُمَّى الدَّريسِ hay fever
حَمامَةٌ / حَمامٌ (حَماماتٌ) pigeon
حَمَّامٌ (حَمَّاماتٌ) bathroom; spa, hammam

خ د ش

خَدَشَ – يَخْدِشُ to scratch; to violate; to ruin (reputation)
خَدْشٌ (خُدوشٌ / أَخْداشٌ) bruise, scratch, mark

Health 61

خ ر س

خَرِسَ – يَخرَسُ to be dumb or mute; to be silent
أخرَسَ – يُخرِسُ to silence or gag
أخرَسُ (خُرسٌ/خُرسانٌ) dumb

خ ط ر

خَطَرَ – يَخطُرُ to shake, tremble, or vibrate; to swing or wave
خَطُرَ – يَخطُرُ to become dangerous
خَطَرٌ (أخطارٌ) danger, peril
خَطيرٌ (خُطُرٌ) weighty, momentous; dangerous, perilous; grave
خُطورَةٌ importance, significance; danger; gravity
مَخاطِرُ dangers
مُخطِرٌ critical; perilous, risky

د م ن

دَمِنَ – يَدمَنُ to fertilise (soil)
أدمَنَ – يُدمِنُ to be addicted; to give or devote oneself
دِمنٌ (دِمَنٌ) fertiliser, manure
الإدمانُ addiction; excess; mania
إدمانُ الكُحولِ alcoholism
إدمانُ المُخَدِّراتِ drug addiction
مُدمِنٌ addicted; an addict

د و ء

داءٌ illness, disease

ر ج ج

رَجَّ – يَرُجُّ to convulse or shake
رَجٌّ shaking, convulsion
رَجَّةٌ/ارتِجاجٌ convulsion; concussion

ر م د

رَمِدَ – يَرمَدُ to have sore eyes; to be inflamed (of eyes)
رَمَّدَ – يُرَمِّدُ to burn to ashes or incinerate

62 *Health*

رَمَدٌ inflammation of the eyes
رَمِدٌ sore-eyed
رَمادٌ (أَرمِدَةٌ) ashes
رَمادِيٌّ ashen, grey
تَرميدٌ cremation

No root

روماتِزمٌ rheumatism

ز ك م

زَكَمَ – يَزكُمُ to catch a cold
زُكامٌ cold, catarrh

ز م ن

زَمِنَ – يَزمَنُ to be chronically ill
أَزمَنَ – يُزمِنُ to be chronic (disease); to remain or stay (for a long time)
زَمَنٌ (أَزمانٌ) time, period, duration
زَمانٌ (أَزمِنَةٌ) time, duration; fortune, fate
مُزمِنٌ chronic (illness); enduring
مَرَضٌ مُزمِنٌ terminal or chronic illness

س ر ط

سَرَطَ – يَسرُطُ to swallow or gulp
سَرَطانٌ (سَرَطاناتٌ) crayfish; cancer; Cancer
سَرَطانٌ بَحرِيٌّ lobster
السَّرَطانُ / المَرَضُ الخَبيثُ cancer

س ع ل

سَعَلَ – يَسعُلُ to cough
سُعلَةٌ / سُعالٌ cough

س ق م

سَقِمَ – يَسقَمُ to be ill; to become thin; to be poor
سَقَمٌ / سُقمٌ (أَسقامٌ) illness; thinness
سَقيمٌ (سِقامٌ / سُقَماءُ) ill, unwell

Health 63

س م م

سَمَّ – يَسُمُّ to poison
سَمَّمَ – يُسَمِّمُ to poison oneself or to be poisoned
سَمٌّ (سُمومٌ / سِمامٌ) poison, toxin, venom; eye of a needle
مَسامٌّ (مَساماتٌ) pores (of the skin)
سَمومٌ (سَمائِمُ) hot wind or sandstorm, simoom
تَسَمُّمٌ poisoning
سامٌّ / مُسِمٌّ poisonous, toxic

س م ن

سَمِنَ – يَسمَنُ to be fat or obese
سَمَّنَ – يُسَمِّنُ to fatten or make plump
سَمنٌ cooking butter, ghee
سِمنَةٌ / سُمنَةٌ corpulence, obesity
سَمينٌ (سِمانٌ) overweight, fat, obese

س ه ل

سَهَلَ – يَسهُلُ to be smooth, even, or easy
سَهَّلَ – يُسَهِّلُ to smooth or level; to facilitate
أَسهَلَ – يُسهِلُ to purge or relieve; to have diarrhoea
سَهلٌ easy, convenient; level, smooth
بِسهولةٍ easily
إِسهالٌ diarrhoea
مُسَهِّلٌ (مُسَهِّلاتٌ) laxative
تسهيلاتٌ facilities

ش ح ب

شَحَبَ – يَشحُبُ to be or become pale; to be lean or emaciated; to look ill
شُحوبٌ pallor, emaciation
شاحِبٌ (شواحِبُ) pale, dull; haggard; emaciated

ش ل ل

شَلَّ – يَشِلُّ to be lame or paralysed; to dry up or wither
اِنشَلَّ – يَنشَلُّ to be paralysed
شَلَلٌ paralysis

شَلّالٌ (شَلّالاتٌ) waterfall; cataract
مَشلولٌ paralysed, lame

ش ن ج

شَنَجَ – يَشنُجُ to contract or shrink
تَشَنَّجَ – يَتَشَنَّجُ to contract or shrink; to suffer convulsions
تَشَنُّجٌ contraction, shriveling, shrinking; convulsions, cramps
تَشَنُّجاتٌ cramps, seizures

ش و ه

شَوِهَ – يَشْوَهُ to be or become deformed or disfigured
شَوَّهَ – يُشَوِّهُ to disfigure, deface, or mutilate; to slander
شَوَهٌ/تَشويهٌ deformity, malformation
تَشَوُّهٌ (تَشَوُّهاتٌ) deformity, malformation
مُشَوَّهٌ disfigured, deformed

ش ي خ

شاخَ – يَشيخُ to age or grow old
شَيخٌ (شُيوخٌ/أَشياخٌ) old man, venerable person, elder; sheikh
شَيخَةٌ (شَيخاتٌ) old or elderly woman
الشَّيخوخَةُ old age, senility

ص د ع

صَدَّعَ – يُصَدِّعُ to cause a headache; to molest, harass, or trouble
صُداعٌ headache

ص د ف

صَدَفَ – يَصْدِفُ to avoid, shun, or turn away
تَصادَفَ – يَتَصادَفُ to happen by chance
صَدَفٌ (أَصدافٌ) pearl oyster, sea shell
الصَّدَفِيَّةُ psoriasis
صُدفَةٌ (صُدَفٌ) chance, coincidence

ص م م

صَمَّ – يَصَمُّ to be or become deaf; to cork or plug
صَمَّمَ – يُصَمِّمُ to deafen; to decide; to design or plan

Health 65

صَمَمٌ deafness
صَمِيمٌ heart, core, essence; true, sincere
تَصْمِيمٌ determination, resolve; plan, design, sketch
أَصَمُّ (صُمٌّ) deaf (m)
صَمَّاءُ (صَمَاواتٌ/صُمٌّ) deaf (f)

ض ر ر

ضَرَّ – يَضُرُّ to injure, harm, hurt, or damage
إنْضَرَّ – يَنْضَرُّ to be damaged, injured, or harmed
اضْطَرَّ – يَضْطَرُّ to force, compel, or coerce
ضُرٌّ damage, harm
ضَرِيرٌ (أَضِرَّاءٌ) blind
ضَرُورَةٌ (ضَرُوراتٌ) necessity, need; stress, distress
ضَرُورِيٌّ necessary
ضَارٌّ/مُضِرٌّ harmful, injurious, detrimental; disadvantageous

ض غ ط

ضَغَطَ – يَضْغَطُ to press, squeeze, oppress, or compress
ضَغْطٌ (ضُغُوطٌ) pressure, stress, tension
مَضْغُوطٌ compressed, under pressure, stressed

ض م ر

ضَمَرَ – يَضْمُرُ to be or become emaciated or skinny; to contract or shrink
ضَمَّرَ – يُضَمِّرُ to make thin or lean; to conceal or hide
ضُمُورٌ emaciation, leanness, skinniness
ضَمِيرٌ (ضَمَائِرُ) heart, mind, conscience; pronoun (grammar)

ط ر أ

طَرَأَ – يَطْرَأُ to descend; to occur or happen unexpectedly
طَارِئَةٌ (طَوارِئُ) accident, unforeseen event
قِسْمُ الطَّوارِئِ accident and emergency
حَالَةٌ طَارِئَةٌ emergency

ط ر ش

طَرِشَ – يَطْرَشُ to be or become deaf
طَرَشٌ deafness

أَطرَشُ (طُرشٌ) deaf (m)
طَرشاءُ (طَرشاواتٌ/طُرشٌ) deaf (f)

ط ف ل

طَفَّلَ – يُطَفِّلُ to intrude or impose; to sponge off other people
طَفلٌ soft, tender
طِفلٌ (أَطفالٌ) infant, baby, child
طِبُّ الأَطفالِ paediatrics
طُفولَةٌ/طُفولِيَّةٌ infancy, childhood; childishness

ع ر ج

عَرَجَ – يَعرُجُ to ascend or mount; to be lame or to walk with a limp
أَعرَجُ (عُرجٌ) lame, limping; the jack in a deck of cards
عَرجاءُ (عَرجاواتٌ/عُرجٌ) lame, limping

ع ط س

عَطَسَ – يَعطِسُ to sneeze
عُطاسٌ/عَطسٌ sneezing

ع ل ل

عَلَّ – يَعِلُّ to be or fall ill
اِعتَلَّ – يَعتَلُّ to be weak or fall ill; to pretend or allege
عِلَّةٌ (عِلّاتٌ) illness, disease, malady
عِلَّةٌ (عِلَلٌ) cause, reason; excuse, pretext, plea
عَليلٌ (أَعِلّاءُ) a sick or ill person, a patient
إِعتِلالٌ illness, sickness, disease, malady

ع م ى

عَمِيَ – يَعمى to lose one's eyesight or to be blind
أَعمى (عُمْيٌ/عُميانٌ) blind (m)
عَمياءُ (عَمياواتٌ/عُمْيٌ) blind (f)
عَمىً blindness

ع ي ي

عَيَّ/عَيِيَ – يَعيا to fall ill; to lack strength or be incapable; to be unable to express

Health 67

عَيٌّ (أَعْياءٌ) weak, impotent; unable to express oneself
عَيَّانٌ sick, ill; tired, fatigued

غ ث ى

غَثى – يَغْثي to confuse, muddle, or jumble
غَثَيانٌ / غَثْيٌ nausea, sickness

غ و ط

غَوَّطَ – يُغَوِّطُ to deepen or make deep
تَغَوَّطَ – يَتَغَوَّطُ to relieve nature, to evacuate the bowels
غَوْطٌ (غُوطٌ/أَغْواطٌ) cavity, depression
غَويطٌ deep
غائِطٌ human faeces

No root

فَأْفَأٌ stuttering

ف ت ك

فَتَكَ – يَفْتِكُ to destroy; to assassinate or murder
فَتَّاكٌ deadly (illness), lethal, fatal; murderous
مرضٌ فَتَّاكٌ deadly illness

ف ح ص

فَحَصَ – يَفْحَصُ to inspect, scrutinise, or examine; to search
فَحْصٌ (فُحوصٌ) check-up, examination; investigation; search

ف ح ل

اِسْتَفْحَلَ – يَسْتَفْحِلُ to become dreadful or serious; to get out of control
فَحْلٌ (فُحولٌ) stallion; a star or celebrity; a master
فُحولَةٌ virility; excellence, perfection
اِسْتِفْحالٌ gravity, seriousness; difficulty
اِسْتَفْحَلَ الْمَرَضُ the illness spread

ف ش و

فَشا – يَفْشو to spread, diffuse, or circulate

68 Health

تَفَشَّى – يَتَفَشَّى to spread, gain ground, or rage
تَفَشَّى بِهِ المَرَضُ the illness spread in his body
تَفَشٍّ spreading, outbreak

No root

فَيْروسٌ (فَيْروساتٌ) viruses

ق ل ص

قَلَصَ – يَقْلِصُ to contract, shrink, or decrease
تَقَلُّصٌ contraction, shrinking, shrinkage
تَقَلُّصاتٌ cramps

ك د م

كَدَمَ – يَكْدِمُ to bruise; to bite (with front teeth)
كَدْمَةٌ (كدمَاتٌ) a bruise; a bite or wound

ك س ر

كَسَرَ – يَكْسِرُ to break, shatter, or fracture; to destroy or defeat (an army)
اِنْكَسَرَ – يَنْكَسِرُ to break or be broken; to be defeated
كَسْرٌ (كُسورٌ) breaking, fracturing, shattering
كَسْرَةٌ defeat; breakdown; vowel (i) ِ in Arabic grammar
مَكْسورٌ broken, fractured

ك ئ ب

كَئِبَ – يَكْأَبُ to be dejected, dispirited, or sad
اِكْتَأَبَ – يَكْتَئِبُ to be depressed or sad; to be worried
اِكْتِئابٌ / كَآبةٌ depression, sadness, sorrow, grief
كَئيبٌ / مُكْتَئِبٌ sad, dejected, depressed, melancholy

ل ه ب

لَهَبَ – يَلْهَبُ to flame, burn, or blaze
اِلْتَهَبَ – يَلْتَهِبُ to flare up or to be inflamed; to catch fire
لَهَبٌ / لَهيبٌ flame, blaze

مُلْتَهِبٌ inflamed, burning
اِلْتِهابٌ / إِلْهابٌ inflammation, burning
اِلْتِهابُ المَفاصِلِ arthritis, inflammation of the joints

م ر ض

مَرِضَ – يَمْرَضُ to fall ill or to be sick
مَرَّضَ – يُمَرِّضُ to make ill or sick; to nurse
مَرَضٌ (أَمْراضٌ) disease, ailment, illness
أَعْراضُ المَرَضِ symptoms (of illness)
تَشْخيصُ المَرَضِ diagnosis
مَرَضٌ عَقْلِيٌّ mental illness
مَريضٌ (مَرْضى) sick; a patient, an ill person
مُمَرِّضٌ (مُمَرِّضونَ) nurse, hospital attendant
مُمَرِّضَةٌ (مُمَرِّضاتٌ) female nurse

م س ك

مَسَكَ – يَمْسِكُ to grab, grasp, seize, or hold
تَمَسَّكَ – يَتَمَسَّكُ to hold on, persist, or adhere
مَسْكٌ seizure; grip, hold
مِسْكٌ musk
إِمْساكٌ constipation; restraint

م ن ع

(Full treatment in Law chapter)

مَنَعَ – يَمْنَعُ to defend, protect, or guard; to detain or prevent from entering
اِمْتِناعٌ abstention; refusal
مَناعَةٌ immunity, strength, impenetrability
الجِهازُ المَناعِيُّ الإِنْسانِيُّ human immune system
الإيدز / مرضُ فُقْدانِ المَناعَةِ AIDS

ن ح ف

نَحُفَ – يَنْحَفُ to be thin, slim, or slender; to lose weight
نَحافَةٌ leanness, thinness, slenderness
نَحيفٌ (نِحافٌ / نُحَفاءُ) thin, slim, slender; delicate

ن ز ف

نَزَفَ – يَنزِفُ to bleed; to drain, exhaust, or empty
نَزْفٌ/نَزِيفٌ haemorrhage, bleeding, loss of blood

ن س ي

نَسِيَ – يَنسى to forget
أَنْسى – يُنسي to make (someone) forget
نِسيانٌ forgetfulness, forgetting; oblivion

ن ف خ

نَفَخَ – يَنفُخُ to blow or puff; to breathe; to inflate
اِنتَفَخَ – يَنتَفِخُ to be inflated; to swell or puff up
نَفْخٌ blowing, inflation, filling with air
اِنتِفاخٌ swelling; bloating, flatulence
مَنفوخٌ blown up; flatulent; conceited

ه ش ش

هَشَّ – يَهِشُّ to be crisp (bread); to smile; to be in good spirits
هَشٌّ delicate, fragile; crisp, brittle
هَشاشَةٌ softness; happiness
هَشاشَةُ الْعِظامِ osteoporosis

ه و ر

هارَ – يَهورُ to be destroyed; to fall down or collapse
اِنهارَ – يَنهارُ to collapse or break down
تَهَوُّرٌ light-headedness; carelessness, hastiness
اِنهِيارٌ a collapse or breakdown
مُتَهَوِّرٌ hasty, rash; frivolous

و ب ئ

وَبِئَ – يَوْبَأُ to be plague-stricken; to be infected or poisoned
وَباءٌ (أَوْبِئَةٌ) epidemic, plague
مَوْبوءٌ poisoned; contaminated, infested, infected

Health 71

و ت ر

وَتَرَ – يَتِرُ to wrong, cheat, or dupe; to stretch; to string (instrument)
وتَّرَ – يُوَتِّرُ to stretch or strain; to tighten or pull taut (rope, string)
وِتْرٌ odd (number)
وَتَرٌ (أَوْتَارٌ) tendon, chord; string (of instrument)
تَوَتُّرٌ (تَوَتُّراتٌ) tension; instability
مُتَوَتِّرٌ stressed; tight, tense

و ج ع

وَجِعَ – يَوْجِعُ to feel pain; to hurt or cause pain
تَوَجَّعَ – يَتَوَجَّعُ to suffer pain; to lament; to feel sorrow or compassion
وَجَعٌ (أوجاعٌ) pain, ache, ailment
مَوجوعٌ feeling pain; in pain, suffering

و ر ث

وَرِثَ – يَرِثُ to inherit or be heir to
إرْثٌ / وِرْثٌ inheritance; heritage
وِراثَةٌ hereditary; inheritance, legacy
وِراثِيٌّ hereditary
عَوامِلُ وِراثِيَّةٌ genetic factors

و ر م

وَرَمَ – يَرِمُ to swell or be swollen
تَوَرَّمَ – يَتَوَرَّمُ to swell or be swollen
وَرَمٌ (أَورامٌ) a swelling or tumour
وَرَمٌ خَبيثٌ malignant tumour
وَرَمٌ حَميدٌ benign tumour
وارِمٌ swollen

و ع ك

تَوَعَّكَ – يَتَوَعَّكُ to be indisposed or unwell
وَعْكَةٌ illness, indisposition
مُتَوَعِّكٌ / وَعِكٌ indisposed, unwell, ill

72 Health

و ه ن

وَهَنَ – يَهِنُ to be weak or feeble, to lack strength
أَوْهَنَ – يوهِنُ to weaken; to discourage
وَهْنٌ weakness
وَهْنُ الْقَلْبِ heart failure
واهِنٌ (وُهْنٌ) weak, feeble, debilitated; unnerved

Treatment, Cures, and Death الْمُداواةُ والعِلاجُ والْموتُ

ب ت ر

بَتَرَ – يَبْتُرُ to cut off, sever, or amputate; to mutilate
اِنْبَتَرَ – يَنْبَتِرُ to be cut or severed
بَتْرٌ amputation, severance
أَبْتَرُ / مَبتورٌ cut off; isolated; childless

ب ك ى

بَكى – يَبْكي to weep or cry; to lament or mourn
أَبْكى – يُبْكي to make (someone) cry
بَكّاءٌ tearful
باكٍ (بُكاةٌ) weeping, crying; a mourner

ج ث ث

جَثَّ – يَجُثُّ to uproot
جُثَّةٌ (جُثَثٌ / أَجْثاثٌ) corpse, body

ج ر ح

جَرَحَ – يَجرَحُ to hurt, wound, or injure
جُرْحٌ (جُروحٌ) a wound, cut, or injury
جُروحٌ خَطيرَةٌ serious injuries
جُروحٌ طَفيفَةٌ minor injuries
جَرّاحٌ (جَرّاحونَ) surgeon
مَجروحٌ (مَجاريحُ) wounded, injured, hurt

ج ر ع

جَرَعَ – يجرَعُ to swallow, gulp, or devour
جُرْعَةٌ (جُرَعٌ / جُرْعاتٌ) a dose, gulp, or mouthful

Health 73

ح ق ن

حَقَنَ – يَحقِنُ to give (someone) an injection; to hold back or detain
اِحتَقَنَ – يَحتَقِنُ to be injected; to become congested; to take an enema
حَقنٌ injection
حُقنَةٌ (حُقَنٌ) an injection; an enema
مِحقَنَةٌ (مَحاقِنُ) syringe

ح ي و / ح ي ي

(Full treatment in Earth chapter)

حَيَّ – يَحيا to live, experience, or witness
حَيَّا – يُحَيِّي to keep alive; to grant (someone) long life
اِستَحى – يَستَحي to be ashamed; to feel or become embarrassed
حَياءٌ shyness; shame, diffidence
حَياةٌ (حَيَواتٌ) life; liveliness, animation
مُضادٌّ حَيَوِيٌّ antibiotics
حَيوانٌ (حَيواناتٌ) animal, beast, living creature

خ د ر

خَدِرَ – يَخدَرُ to be numb or paralysed; to tingle
خَدَّرَ – يُخَدِّرُ to anaesthetise or numb, to put to sleep
خَدَرٌ numbness, insensibility; daze
تَخديرٌ anaesthetisation, numbing
مُخَدِّرٌ (مُخَدِّراتٌ) anaesthetic, tranquiliser; narcotics, drug

د و ى

دَوى – يَدوي to echo, reverberate; to sound
داوى – يُداوي to treat (a patient or disease)
تَداوى – يَتَداوى to treat or medicate oneself; to be cured
دوىً (أدواءٌ) disease, sickness, illness
دَواءٌ (أدوِيَةٌ) medicine, remedy, drug
تَناوُلُ الدَّواءِ taking medicine
مُداواةٌ treatment, therapy

س ع ف

ساعَفَ – يُساعِفُ to help or support
أسعَفَ – يُسعِفُ to help or assist; to comply with someone's wishes

74 *Health*

إِسْعَافٌ (إِسْعَافَاتٌ) medical aid; relief, help, assistance
الإِسْعَافُ ambulance
إِسْعَافٌ أَوَّلِيٌّ first aid

ش ف ى

شَفَى – يَشْفِي to cure or heal
شَفِيَ – يَشْفَى to be healed or cured
شِفَاءٌ cure, recovery, healing
بِالهَنا والشِّفا / صَحتين bon appetit
مَشْفًى / مُسْتَشْفًى (مَشافٍ / مُسْتَشْفَيَاتٌ) hospital

ص ح ح

صَحَّ – يَصِحُّ to be healthy; to recover or recuperate
صَحَّحَ – يُصَحِّحُ to cure or restore to health; to correct or rectify
صِحَّةٌ health; hygiene; correctness
الصِّحَّةُ والأَمانُ health and safety
التَّأْمِينُ الصِّحِّيُّ health insurance
حَجْرٌ صِحِّيٌّ quarantine
الخَدَماتُ الصِّحِّيَّةُ الوَطَنِيَّةُ national health services
صَحِيحٌ (صِحاحٌ / أَصِحَّاءُ) healthy, well, sound; genuine, authentic
تَصْحِيحٌ correction, rectification

ص و ن

صَانَ – يَصُونُ to preserve or conserve; to retain or maintain
صَوْنٌ protection; preservation, conservation; maintenance
مَصُونٌ immune; well-protected, sheltered

No root

صَيْدَلَةٌ pharmacy; pharmacology
صَيْدَلِيٌّ (صَيادِلَةٌ) chemist, pharmacist; pharmacy
صَيْدَلِيَّةٌ (صَيْدَلِيَّاتٌ) pharmacy; chemist

ض ع ف

ضَعَّفَ – يُضَعِّفُ to double or multiply
ضَاعَفَ – يُضَاعِفُ to double or multiply

Health

ضِعفٌ (أَضعافٌ) double, multiple
مُضاعَفةٌ (مُضاعَفاتٌ) complications (disease); side effects; doubling, multiplying
مُضاعَفاتٌ / آثارٌ جانبِيّةٌ side effects, complications

ط ب ب

طَبَّ – يَطُبُّ to treat medically or to give treatment
تَطَبَّبَ – يَتَطَبَّبُ to receive medical treatment; to practise medicine
طِبٌّ medicine, medical treatment
طَبيبٌ (أَطِبّاءُ) doctor, physician
طَبيبٌ عامٌّ general practitioner
الطِّبُّ البَديلُ alternative medicine

ع ص م

عَصَمَ – يَعصِمُ to immunise or guard; to preserve; to restrain or check
عِصمَةٌ safeguarding, protection, defence
عاصِمٌ immune, protected; guardian
عاصِمَةٌ (عَواصِمُ) capital city, metropolis
مِعصَمٌ (مَعاصِمُ) wrist
إعتِصامٌ (إعتِصاماتٌ) a vigil; maintenance, preservation

ع ل ج

عالَجَ – يُعالِجُ to attend to or treat
تَعالَجَ – يَتَعالَجُ to receive medical treatment
مُعالَجَةٌ / عِلاجٌ medical treatment, nursing; manipulation
عِلاجٌ طَبيعِيٌّ natural treatment; physiotherapy

ع ن ى

عَنِيَ – يَعنى to worry or discomfort; to be worried or anxious
عانى – يُعاني to suffer or endure
إعتَنى – يَعتَني to take care (of); to provide; to be concerned
عَناءٌ trouble, pains, difficulty
عِنايَةٌ care, concern, attention (also a girl's name)
قِسمُ العِنايَةِ المُرَكَّزَةِ intensive care unit
مَعنىً (مَعانٍ) sense, meaning, signification; concept, idea
مُعاناةٌ suffering

76   *Health*

ع و ق

عاقَ – يَعوقُ to hinder, delay, prevent, or restrain; to withhold or defer
تَعَوَّقَ – يَتَعَوَّقُ to be hindered, delayed, prevented, or restrained
عَوْقٌ / إعاقةٌ retardation; hindering, restraining
إعاقةٌ disability, hindrance; delaying
عائِقٌ / عائقةٌ (عَوائِقُ) obstacle, barrier, impediment, hindrance
مُعاقٌ (مُعاقونَ) disabled

ع ي ش

عاشَ – يَعيشُ to live or be alive
أعاشَ – يُعيشُ to keep alive; to feed or provide for
تَعايَشَ – يَتَعايَشُ to live together
عيشةٌ / عَيْشٌ life; way of life; livelihood
مَعاشٌ (مَعاشاتٌ) life; subsistence; livelihood, income
مُعايَشةٌ / تَعايُشٌ co-existence

غ ش و / غ ش ي

غَشِيَ – يَغْشى to cover, wrap, or conceal
غُشِيَ عَلَيهِ – يُغْشى عَلَيهِ to faint or lose consciousness
غَشْيٌ fainting, swooning; unconsciousness
غِشاءٌ (أغْشِيَةٌ) cover, wrap, envelope

ف ق د

فَقَدَ – يَفْقِدُ to lose, miss, or be deprived
أفْقَدَ – يُفْقِدُ to bereave, deprive, dispossess, or rob
إفْتَقَدَ – يَفْتَقِدُ to seek; to miss
فَقْدٌ loss; bereavement
فَقيدٌ (فُقَداءُ) deceased; lost, missing

ك ر ب

كَرَبَ – يَكْرُبُ to oppress, distress, grieve, or worry
إكْتَرَبَ – يَكْتَرِبُ to be concerned, worried, or distressed
كَرْبٌ (كُروبٌ) grief, sorrow, sadness
مُكْتَرِبٌ sad, worried, grieved; apprehensive, fearful

Health 77

ك م ل

كَمَلَ – يَكْمُلُ to be whole, entire, or integral; to be completed or finished
كَمَّلَ – يُكَمِّلُ to finish, complete, or conclude
اِستَكمَلَ – يَستَكمِلُ to perfect; to complete or fulfil; to complement or supplement
كَمالٌ (كَمالاتٌ) perfection; completeness; termination
مُكَمِّلاتٌ supplements, complements
مُكَمِّلاتُ الفيتاميناتِ vitamin supplements

م ر أ

مَرَأَ – يَمْرُؤُ to be palatable (of food); to be wholesome or healthful
اِستَمرَأَ – يَستَمرِئُ to enjoy, savour, or derive pleasure from
إمرُؤٌ / إمرَأً / إمرِئٍ person (nominative, accusative, genitive); man; human being
هَنيئاً مَريئاً bon appetit
المَرْءُ a person, a human being
اِمْرَأَةٌ (نِساءٌ / نِسوَةٌ) woman
النِّساءُ والوِلادَةُ gynaecology
مُروءَةٌ / مُرُوَّةٌ honour
المَرأَةُ the woman (note with definite article, initial alif is dropped)
نِسائِيٌّ feminine, womanly, relating to women
النِسَّوِيَّةُ feminism

م و ت

ماتَ – يَموتُ to die or perish
مَوْتٌ / مَوْتَةٌ death, demise
مَوْتُ المَهدِ cot death
مَيِّتٌ (أَمواتٌ / مَوْتى) dead, lifeless, deceased; inanimate

ن و م

نامَ – يَنامُ to sleep; to be inactive; to be numb; to neglect or overlook
نَوَّمَ – يُنَوِّمُ to put to bed or lull to sleep; to anaesthetise
نَوْمٌ sleep, slumber
مَنامٌ (مَناماتٌ) dream, sleep
المَنامَةُ Manama (Bahrain)

تَنويمٌ drugging, anaesthetisation; hypnosis
مُنَوِّمٌ (مُنَوِّماتٌ) sleep-inducing, soporific; sleeping pills

و ص ف

وَصَفَ – يَصِفُ to describe, depict, characterise, or picture
اِستَوصَفَ – يَستَوصِفُ to consult (a doctor)
صِفَةٌ (صِفاتٌ) trait, quality, characteristic
صِفاتٌ سائِدَةٌ dominant characteristics
صِفاتٌ مُتَنَحِّيَةٌ recessive characteristics
وَصفٌ (أَوصافٌ) description, portrayal, characterisation
وَصفَةٌ description; medical prescription
مُستَوصَفٌ (مُستَوصَفاتٌ) clinic

و ف ى

وَفَى – يَفي to be complete or perfect; to fulfil or satisfy; to pay; to suffice
تُوُفِّيَ – يُتَوَفَّى to die; to take one's full share
وَفاءٌ loyalty; fulfilment (of a promise); payment (of a debt); (also a girl's name)
وَفاةٌ (وَفَيَاتٌ) death, demise
مُعَدَّل الوَفَياتِ mortality rate
وَفِيٌّ (أَوفِياءُ) faithful, reliable, trustworthy
مُتَوَفَّى deceased, dead
تُوُفِّيَ he died

و ق ى

وَقَى – يَقي to protect, preserve, shield, or safeguard
اِتَّقَى – يَتَّقي to fear (God); to protect oneself; to be wary or on one's guard
وِقاء / وِقاية protection; prevention
وِقائِيٌّ prevention, protection, defence
إِجراءاتٌ وِقائِيَّةٌ preventive measures
تَقوىً / تُقىً devotion, piety, godliness

ي ئ س

يَئِسَ – يَيأَسُ to despair or give up all hope
اِستَيأَسَ – يَستَيئِسُ to despair or give up all hope

Health 79

يَأْسٌ desperation, hopelessness, resignation
يائِسٌ / يَؤوسٌ / مُسْتَيْئِسٌ desperate, hopeless

Exercises

1) Give two derived nouns for each of the following roots:

ب د ن
ج ل د
ل ج ر
ع م س
ع ص ب
ق ل ب

2) Find the roots of the following words:

إرهاقٌ
إصابَةٌ
اِكتِئابٌ
اِنهيارٌ
بارِدٌ
جِنسيَّةٌ
حَمامَةٌ
ضَرورةٌ
عاقِرٌ
مَجنونٌ

3) Give a synonym for each of the following words:

حَلْقٌ
ضَريرٌ
عَيَّانُ
فؤادٌ
مُزمِنٌ
وَجَعٌ

4) Give the plural of these words (some may have more than one plural):

جُنَيْنَةٌ
حُقْنَةٌ
زَمانٌ

Health

سَمٌّ
ضَمِيرٌ
مُسْهِلٌ
وَباءٌ

5) Translate the following sentences into Arabic:

   a) She injured her leg playing football.
   b) He suffers from bad headaches.
   c) Their daughter died.
   d) She divorced her husband when she found out that he was infertile.

6) Translate the following into English:

- زارتْ سارة الطَّبيبَ لأنها تَشعرُ بألمٍ في ظَهرها.
- ماتَ والِدهُم بعدَ يومين في المُستشفى.
- أُحسُّ بِوَجعٍ شَديدٍ في كتفي عِندَما أستَخدِمُ الحاسوبَ.
- أصبَحت ظاهرةُ البَدانةِ مشكلةً كبيرةً في دُوَل الْخَليج.
- بعدَ الفَحصِّ أخبَرَهُ الطبيبُ بأنَّ السَّرطانَ قد انتَشَرَ في جسمِهِ.

Note

1 In the Levantine dialects, this is used to mean 'a man' and not necessarily a distinguished one.

3 Education التَّعليمُ

School المَدارِسُ

ب د أ

بَدَأَ – يَبدَأُ to begin or start
بَدَّأَ – يُبَدِّئُ to give precedence or priority
أَبدأَ – يُبدِئُ to produce; to bring out
اِبتَدَأَ – يَبْتدِئُ to begin or start
بَدْءٌ / بِدايَةٌ beginning, start
بدائيٌّ primitive
مَبْدَأٌ (مَبادِئُ) principle, basis; concept; start
اِبتِداءٌ beginning, start
اِبتِدائيٌّ primary, elementary, original
مُبتَدِئٌ (مُبتَدِئونَ) beginner; apprentice, novice; beginning
مُبتَدَأٌ subject (Arabic grammar); beginning

ت ل م ذ

تَلْمَذَ – يُتَلْمِذُ to take on as a pupil; to be or become a pupil
تَلْمَذَةٌ school days; college years; working as an apprentice
تِلميذٌ (تَلاميذُ) school student, pupil, apprentice

ث ن ى

ثَنَى – يَثْني to double; to fold or bend
ثَنَّى – يُثَنِّي to double or repeat; to form the dual (grammar)
أَثنى – يُثْني to commend or praise
اِستَثنى – يَستَثني to exclude
ثَنْيٌ bending, folding, turning away

82 *Education*

أَثْناءَ (prep) during, while
ثَنْيَةٌ (ثَنْياتٌ) fold, pleat
ثَناءٌ commendation; eulogy
ثُنائِيٌّ twofold, double, dual
اثْنانِ two (m)
اثْنَتانِ two (f)
اثْنا عَشَرَ 12 (m)
اثْنَتا عَشرَةَ 12 (f)
يَوْمُ الإثْنين / الإثْنين Monday
الثّاني the second
ثانِيَة (ثَوانٍ) a second (unit of time)
ثانَوِيٌّ secondary; minor
المَدرَسَةُ الثّانَوِيَّة secondary school
اِسْتِثْناءٌ exception, exclusion
اِسْتِثْنائِيٌّ exceptional
مَثْنِيٌّ folded; doubled
المُثَنَّى dual

ح ص ص

حَصَّ – يَحُصُّ to fall as a share
حِصَّةٌ (حِصَصٌ) class, lesson; share, portion

ح ض ن

حَضَنَ – يَحضُنُ to embrace; to nurse; to raise
اِحْتَضَنَ – يَحْتَضِنُ to embrace; to raise (child); to concoct or contrive
حِضْنٌ (أَحضانٌ) breast, bosom; armful
حَضانَةٌ (حَضاناتٌ) a nursery; raising, bringing up
دارُ الحَضانَة nursery, crèche
حاضِنَةٌ (حَواضِنُ) nursemaid; incubator

د ر س

دَرَسَ – يَدرُسُ to study or learn; to obliterate or extinguish
دَرَّسَ – يُدَرِّسُ to teach or instruct
دَرْسٌ (دُروسٌ) lesson, chapter, lecture; study; obliteration
دُروسٌ خُصوصِيَّةٌ private lessons

Education

دِراسةٌ (دِراساتٌ) study
فصلٌ دِراسِيٌّ term, semester
سَنةٌ دِراسيّةٌ academic year
المَراحِلُ الدِّراسيّةُ educational stages
دِراساتُ التَّعليمِ العالي higher education studies
الدِّراساتُ الدِّينيّةُ religious studies
الدِّراساتُ الحَضاريّةُ cultural studies
مَدرَسةٌ (مَدارسُ) school; religious school
مُديرُ مَدرَسة head teacher
مَدرَسةٌ ابتدائيةٌ primary school
مَدرَسةٌ إعداديّةٌ secondary school
مَدرَسةٌ ثانويّةٌ high school
مَدرَسةٌ خاصّةٌ private school
مَدرَسةٌ حُكوميّةٌ public or state school
مدارسُ تَعليمِ الكِبارِ adult educational schools
مَدرَسِيٌّ scholastic, of or relating to school
تَقريرٌ مَدرَسِيٌّ school report
واجبٌ مدرسيٌّ homework
تَدريسٌ teaching, tuition, instruction
مُدَرِّسٌ (مُدَرِّسونَ) teacher, lecturer

ر و ض

راضَ – يَروضُ to tame or domesticate; to train; to placate
تَرَوَّضَ – يَتَرَوَّضُ to practise; to exercise
رَوْضةٌ (رَوْضاتٌ/رِياضٌ) nursery, kindergarten; garden
رَوْضةُ الأطفالِ kindergarten
رياضةٌ (رياضاتٌ) sport, practice, exercise; walk, promenade
التَّربيةُ الرِّياضيّةُ / التَّربيةُ البَدنيّةُ physical education
الألعابُ الرِّياضيّةُ sports
رياضِيٌّ sporty
نادٍ رياضيٌّ sports club
رياضيّاتٌ mathematics

س ب ر

سَبَرَ – يَسبُرُ to examine or explore
سَبْرٌ exploring, examination

84   *Education*

مِسبارٌ (مَسابيرُ) a medical probe
سَبّورَةٌ blackboard
سَبّورَةٌ تَفاعُلِيَّةٌ interactive whiteboard

ص ف ف

صَفَّ – يَصُفُّ to set; to arrange or line up; to park a car (colloquial)
صَفٌّ (صُفوفٌ) classroom; line, queue
مَصَفٌّ (مَصافٌّ) position, rank (army); row, line; parking space (colloquial)

ط ل ب

طَلَبَ – يَطلُبُ to demand or ask for; to seek
طالَبَ – يُطالِبُ to demand, claim, or reclaim
تَطَلَّبَ – يَتَطَلَّبُ to require or necessitate
طَلَبٌ (طَلَباتٌ) search; request, demand; form; application; petition
العرضُ والطَّلَبُ supply and demand
طلبُ التحاقٍ / استِمارةُ طَلَبٍ application form
طَلَبِيَّةٌ (طَلَبِيّاتٌ) order, commission
طالِبٌ (طُلّابٌ / طَلَبَةٌ) seeker, claimant; student, scholar
الطّالِبانِ the Taliban (literally 'seekers of knowledge', dual form)
مَطلوبٌ (مَطلوباتٌ / مَطاليبُ) liabilities; wanted; debts; requested, required
مُطالِبٌ (مُطالِبونَ) claimant
مُتَطَلَّباتٌ requirements

غ ي ب

غابَ – يَغيبُ to be or remain absent; to withdraw or leave; to disappear
تَغَيَّبَ – يَتَغَيَّبُ to be absent; to play truant
اِغتابَ – يَغتابُ to backbite
غَيْبٌ (غُيوبٌ) absence; concealed, invisible
غابَةٌ (غاباتٌ) forest, jungle
غِيبَةٌ slander
غِيابٌ absence
غَيْبوبَةٌ loss of consciousness; coma
تَغَيُّبٌ / التَّغَيُّبُ الدِّراسِيُّ truancy
اِغتِيابٌ gossip, defamation, backbiting
غائِبٌ (غائِبونَ) absent, concealed, invisible

م ه د

مَهَّدَ – يُمَهِّدُ to smooth, facilitate, or prepare; to arrange
تَمَهَّدَ – يَتَمَهَّدُ to be paved; to go smoothly; to put in order
مَهَّدَ الطَّريق to pave the way
مَهْدٌ (مُهودٌ) cradle, bed
تَمهيدٌ facilitation; preparation; levelling; foreword
تَمهيديٌّ introductory, preparatory

التَّعليمُ Education

No root

أُسْتاذٌ (أَساتِذَةٌ) professor, teacher

ج م ل

جَمَلَ – يَجمُلُ to sum up or summarise; to be beautiful; to be proper
جَمَّلَ – يُجَمِّلُ to beautify or embellish
جامَلَ – يُجامِلُ to be polite or amiable
جُملةٌ (جُمَلٌ) sentence or clause (grammar); totality, sum; group
جُملةٌ اسميَّةٌ nominal clause
جُملةٌ فِعليَّةٌ verbal clause
جُملةٌ شَرطيَّةٌ conditional clause
جَمالٌ beauty (also a boy's name)
عِلمُ الجَمالِ aesthetics
جَميلٌ beautiful, lovely
عِرفانٌ بِالجَميلِ gratitude
تَجميلٌ beautification; cosmetics
عَمَليَّةُ تَجميلٍ plastic surgery
مُجامَلَةٌ (مُجامَلاتٌ) flattery; amiability, civility
إجمالاً on the whole, in general
مُجمَلٌ summary; sum, total

د ر ى

دَرى – يَدري to know; to understand or comprehend
أَدرى – يُدري to inform or notify
دارٍ aware, knowing
لا أدري I don't know

ذ ك ر

ذَكَرَ – يَذكُرُ to mention; to remember
ذاكَرَ – يُذاكِرُ to negotiate or confer; to memorise, learn, or study
ذِكرٌ memory, remembrance; quoting
الجَديرُ بِالذِّكرِ أنَّ مِن it is worth mentioning that
ذَكَرٌ (ذُكورٌ) male
ذِكرى (ذِكرَياتٌ) memory; reminder
تِذكارٌ memento, reminder
تَذكِرةٌ (تَذاكِرُ) ticket
مُذاكَرَةٌ (مُذاكَراتٌ) studying; negotiation; decree; memoirs
ذاكِرةٌ memory
مُذَكَّرٌ masculine (grammar)
مُذَكِّراتٌ memoirs; notes

ر ب و

رَبا – يَربو to increase or grow; to exceed
رَبَّى – يُرَبِّي to raise or breed; to educate or instruct; to develop
رابى – يُرابي to practise usury
تَرَبَّى – يَتَرَبَّى to be brought up or educated
رَبوٌ asthma
رَبوَةٌ (رُبىً/رَبواتٌ) hill
رِباً usury, interest
تَربِيَةٌ education, instruction; breeding
قَليلُ التَّربِيَةِ ill-bred
التَّربِيَةُ البَدَنِيَّةُ/التَّربِيَةُ البَدَنِيَّةُ والرِّياضِيَّةُ physical education
تَربَوِيٌّ pedagogic
مُرَبٍّ (مُرَبُّونَ) educator, teacher; breeder
مُرَبِّيَةُ أطفالٍ nanny, childminder
مُرَبّىً (مُرَبَّياتٌ) jam, preserves
مُتَرَبٍّ/مُرَبّىً well mannered, well bred
التَّربِيَةُ والتَّعليمُ education[1]
وزارةُ التَّربِيَةِ والتَّعليمِ Ministry of Education

ر ج ع

رَجَعَ – يَرجِعُ to return or come back; to consult

Education 87

رَجَّعَ – يُرَجِّعُ to cause to return, to give or send back
راجَعَ – يُراجِعُ to revise; to return; to reiterate
تَراجَعَ – يَتَراجَعُ to withdraw or retreat; to diminish
رَجْعٌ (رُجوعٌ) a return; coming back
رَجْعُ الصَّوتِ/ الصَّدى echo
رَجْعِيٌّ reactionary
مَرْجِعٌ (مَراجِعُ) an authority or expert; reference books; a return or retreat
مُراجَعَةٌ revision, repetition; examination
تَراجُعٌ withdrawal, retreat

ر ش د

رَشَدَ – يرشُدُ to be well guided or on the right path
أرْشَدَ – يُرشِدُ to lead on the right path; to direct; to inform
اِسْتَرْشَدَ – يَسْتَرشِدُ to ask (someone) for guidance, to consult
رُشْدٌ proper, sensible; reason, maturity (of the mind)
سِنُّ الرُّشدِ majority, full legal age
إرشادٌ guidance, instruction
راشِدٌ (راشِدونَ) rightly guided, reasonable; adult; (also a boy's name in the singular)
مُرْشِدٌ (مُرْشِدونَ) advisor, spiritual guide, instructor

ص ف ح

صَفَحَ – يَصفَحُ to widen or flatten; to pardon or forgive
صافَحَ – يُصافِحُ to shake hands or greet; to touch
تَصَفَّحَ – يَتَصَفَّحُ to leaf through a book; to examine or scrutinise; to browse
اِسْتَصفَحَ – يَسْتَصفِحُ to apologise or ask someone's forgiveness
صَفْحٌ forgiveness; side, surface
صَفْحَةٌ (صَفَحاتٌ) page, sheet; surface
تَصَفُّحٌ examination, scrutiny; browsing

ط ر ق

طَرَقَ – يَطرُقُ to bang or hammer; to reach; to touch upon a topic
طَرْقَةٌ (طَرْقاتٌ) a knock; banging
طَريقٌ (طُرُقٌ/ طُرُقاتٌ) way, road, path; way, method
طَريقَةٌ (طُرُقٌ) method, manner, mode; system
مِطرَقَةٌ (مَطارِقُ) hammer

ع ل م

عَلِمَ – يَعْلَمُ to know; to be aware, familiar, or acquainted; to learn
عَلَّمَ – يُعَلِّمُ to teach, instruct, or train; to designate; to mark
تَعَلَّمَ – يَتَعَلَّمُ to learn or study; to know
اِسْتَعْلَمَ – يَسْتَعْلِمُ to inquire or ask; to gather information
عِلْمٌ (عُلُومٌ) science, knowledge of (with subject, corresponds to -ology suffix)
عِلْمُ الأَحْياءِ biology
عِلْمُ الآثارِ archaeology
عِلْمُ الإِجْتِماعِ sociology
عِلْمُ الإِحْصاءِ statistics
عِلْمُ الإِقْتِصادِ economics
عِلْمُ الكيمياءِ chemistry
عِلْمُ الفَلْسَفَةِ / فَلْسَفَةٌ philosophy
عِلْمُ النَّفْسِ psychology
العُلُومُ الإنْسانِيَّةُ humanities
عِلْمُ الإِقْتِصادِ economics
عِلْمِيٌّ scientific
عَلَمٌ (أَعْلامٌ) sign or token; flag or banner
عالَمٌ (عَوالِمُ) world; universe, cosmos
عالَمِيٌّ worldly, secular; global
عَوْلَمَةٌ globalisation
عِلْمانِيٌّ / عِلْمانِيَّةٌ layman; secular
عَلِيمٌ (عُلَماءُ) learned, erudite; knowing
عَلامَةٌ (عَلاماتٌ) mark, sign, characteristic; badge, emblem
مَعْلَمٌ (مَعالِمُ) place, landmark; sign
تَعْليمٌ (تَعْليماتٌ / تَعاليمُ) teaching, education; information, instructions; doctrines
التَّعْليمُ الإِبْتِدائِيُّ primary education
التَّعْليمُ الثَّانَوِيُّ secondary education
التَّعْليمُ العالي higher education
تَعْليمٌ مُخْتَلَطٌ co-education
تَعْليمٌ عَبْرَ الإِنْتَرْنِت / التَّعْليمُ الإِلِكْتْرُوني e-learning
تَعْليمٌ إِفْتِراضِيٌّ virtual learning
نَشْرَةُ التَّعْليماتِ instructions
تَعَلُّمٌ learning, education; studying
اِسْتِعْلامٌ (اِسْتِعْلاماتٌ) inquiry; information
مَعلومَةٌ (مَعلوماتٌ) information, data; instructions

Education 89

مُعَلِّمٌ (مُعَلِّمونَ) teacher, instructor, master
مُتَعَلِّمٌ (مُتَعَلِّمونَ) educated person

ف ك ر

فَكَّرَ – يُفَكِّرُ to think or reflect; to remind
اِفتَكَرَ – يَفتَكِرُ to remember or recall
فِكرٌ (أَفكارٌ) thinking, reflection; cognition; thought, notion
فِكرَةٌ (فِكراتٌ / فِكَرٌ) thought, idea, concept; hesitation
فِكرِيٌّ intellectual
التَّطَوُّرُ الفِكرِيُّ intellectual growth
تَفكيرٌ thinking; cognition; thought
مُفَكِّرٌ (مُفَكِّرونَ) thinkers

ف ه م

فَهِمَ – يَفهَمُ to understand or comprehend; to realise
فَهَّمَ – يُفَهِّمُ to instruct or make (someone) understand
تَفاهَمَ – يَتَفاهَمُ to agree; to understand
فَهمٌ (أَفهامٌ) understanding, comprehension
سوءُ الفَهمِ misunderstanding
فَهيمٌ (فُهَماءُ) sensible, intelligent
تَفاهُمٌ / التَّفاهُمُ المُتَبادَلُ mutual understanding or agreement
سوءُ تَفاهُمٍ misunderstanding
عَلامةُ الاِستِفهامِ question mark
اِستِفهامِيٌّ interrogative (grammar)
مَفهومٌ (مَفاهيمُ) concept, notion; understood; comprehensible

ل و ح

لاحَ – يَلوحُ to appear or emerge; to show or seem
لَوَّحَ – يُلَوِّحُ to signal or beckon; to hint
لَوحٌ (أَلواحٌ) board, blackboard, slab; shoulder blade
لَوحَةٌ (لَوحاتٌ) board, blackboard, tablet, slab
لَوحَةُ إِعلاناتٍ notice board
لائِحَةٌ (لائِحاتٌ) project; bill, motion; decree
لائِحَةٌ قانونِيَّةٌ bill, draft law
لائِحَةُ الطَّعامِ menu

م ح ن

مَحَنَ – يَمْحَنُ to try out; to examine; to afflict
اِمْتَحَنَ – يَمتَحِنُ to try out or test; to examine; to afflict
مِحْنَةٌ (مِحَنٌ) affliction, misfortune, hardship
اِمتِحانٌ (اِمتِحاناتٌ) exam, test; experiment
اِمْتِحانُ الدُّخولِ entrance exam
اِمْتِحانٌ نِهائِيٌّ final exam
مُمْتَحِنٌ examiner

م ن ح

مَنَحَ – يَمنَحُ to grant, give, or bestow
مِنحَةٌ (مِنَحٌ) scholarship, grant; gift, present; stipend
مانِحٌ donor, giver

ن ه ج

نَهَجَ – يَنهَجُ to proceed; to pursue a plan; to follow; to be out of breath
نَهَّجَ – يُنَهِّجُ to clarify or explain; to make breathless
نَهجٌ (نُهوجٌ) open way; method, procedure; road
مَنهَجٌ / مِنهاجٌ (مَناهِجُ) method, procedure; course; syllabus, curriculum
المِنهاجُ اليَومِيُّ routine

ه ذ ب

هذَبَ – يَهذِبُ to prune or trim; to clean or purify; to smooth
هَذَّبَ – يُهَذِّبُ to improve or refine; to educate or instruct
تَهذيبٌ correction; refinement, culture, education
تَهَذُّبٌ manners; education
مُهَذِّبٌ educator, teacher
مُهَذَّبٌ / مُتَهَذِّبٌ well behaved, courteous; refined, polished

و ج ب

وَجبَ – يَجِبُ to be necessary or obligatory
وَجَّبَ – يُوَجِّبُ to impose; to enjoin or obligate
اِستَوجَبَ – يَستَوجِبُ to deserve or merit; to be worthy or entitled
كَما يَجِبُ as it should be

وَجْبَةٌ (وَجَباتٌ) meal
إيجابٌ obligation, commitment; positive
إيجابِيٌّ positive, affirmative
واجِبٌ (واجِباتٌ) necessary, essential; duty, homework
واجِبٌ مَنزِلِيٌّ homework

و ع ب

إستَوعَبَ – يَستَوعِبُ to absorb or comprehend; to study; to uproot
إستيعابٌ understanding, comprehension; study; capacity

الأَداءُ التَّعليمِيُّ Performance Levels

ب ر ع

بَرَعَ – يَبرَعُ to surpass or excel; to distinguish oneself; to be skilful
تَبَرَّعَ – يَتَبَرَّعُ to donate or contribute; to undertake or volunteer
بَراعَةٌ/بُروعَةٌ skill, proficiency; capacity
تَبَرُّعٌ (تَبَرُّعاتٌ) donation, contribution

ج ه ل

جَهِلَ – يَجهَلُ to be ignorant; to be irrational or foolish
تَجاهَلَ – يَتَجاهَلُ to ignore or disregard; to feign ignorance
إستَجهَلَ – يَستَجهِلُ to consider ignorant
جَهلٌ/جَهالَةٌ ignorance, foolishness, stupidity
تَجاهُلٌ ignoring, disregarding
جاهِلٌ (جَهَلَةٌ/جُهلاءُ) ignorant, illiterate, uneducated
جاهِلِيٌّ pagan
الجاهِلِيَّةُ Days of Ignorance (i.e. days before Islam)
مَجهولٌ unknown (passive form in grammar)

د ق ق

دَقَّ – يَدِقُّ to be fine or fragile; to be insignificant; to grind or pound
دَقَّقَ – يُدَقِّقُ to be precise or exact; to scrutinise; to pulverise
دَقٌّ crushing; knocking; ringing (bell)
دِقٌّ/دِقَّةٌ fine, delicate, fragile; precision
دَقَّةٌ (دَقَّاتٌ) a bang, knock, beat, or stroke

دَقيقٌ (دِقاقٌ) precise, meticulous; delicate, little
دَقيقةٌ (دَقائِقُ) minute (time); detail
تَدقيقٌ precision, exactitude

ذ ك و / ذ ك ى

ذَكا – يَذكو to blaze or flare up (of fire)
ذَكى – يَذكي to be sharp-witted or intelligent
ذَكاءٌ intelligence, acumen
ذَكِيٌّ (أَذكياءُ) intelligent, sharp-witted

No root

عَبقَريٌّ (عَباقِرةٌ / عَبقَريونَ) genius, a genius (noun, adj)
عَبقَريَّةٌ genius (noun)

ع ز م

عَزَمَ – يَعزِمُ to decide; to be determined
اِعتَزَمَ – يَعتَزِمُ to decide or resolve
عَزمٌ determination, firm will, decisiveness
عُزومَةٌ invitation
عازِمٌ (على) determined (to do)

غ ب و / غ ب ي

غَبِيَ – يَغبى to not understand, to be ignorant or unfamiliar
تَغابى – يَتَغابى to be unaware; to feign stupidity
غَبِيٌّ (أَغبياءُ) ignorant, stupid, foolish
غَباءٌ / غَباوَةٌ ignorance, stupidity

ل ح ح

لَحَّ – يَلِحُّ to be close (of relationships)
أَلَحَّ – يُلِحُّ to implore or beseech; to pester
لَحوحٌ stubborn, persistent
إلحاحٌ insistence, emphasis
مُلِحٌّ pressing, urgent, persistent

Education 93

م ط ل

مَطَلَ – يَمْطُلُ to postpone or delay; to draw out; to strengthen; to hammer or shape
ماطَلَ – يُماطِلُ to take one's time; to put off or delay
مُماطَلَةٌ procrastination, postponement
مُماطِلٌ procrastinator

ن ب غ

نَبَغَ – يَنْبَغُ to arise or emerge; to excel or be distinguished; to be a genius
نُبوغٌ eminence; gifted, genius
نابِغٌ outstanding, talented; man of genius
نابِغَةٌ (نوابِغُ) a genius;[2] distinguished person

ن ش ط

نَشِطَ – يَنْشَطُ to be lively, eager, or zealous
نَشَّطَ – يُنَشِّطُ to incite or spur on; to stimulate or energise
تَنَشَّطَ – يَتَنَشَّطُ to be lively, energetic, or active
نَشاطٌ activity, animation; energy
نَشيطٌ (نِشاطٌ/نُشطاءُ) active, lively, energetic
تَنْشيطٌ encouragement, incitement; animation
ناشِطٌ (ناشِطونَ) activist

ه م ل

هَمَلَ – يَهْمُلُ to shed tears
أَهْمَلَ – يُهْمِلُ to neglect or omit; to overlook
إهمالٌ neglect, disregard; negligence
هامِلٌ (هُمَّلٌ) roaming; vagabond
مُهْمِلٌ inattentive, careless
مُهْمَلٌ neglected, omitted; lacking, devoid
سَلَّةُ المُهْمَلاتِ wastebasket

و ظ ب

وَظَبَ – يَظِبُ to do persistently or practise constantly
واظَبَ – يُواظِبُ to persevere or to apply oneself assiduously
مُواظَبَةٌ diligence, perseverance, persistence
مُواظِبٌ diligent, persevering, persistent

الْجامعةُ University

أ ب ى

أَبَى – يَأْبَى to refuse, reject, or deny
إِباءٌ rejection, disdain; pride
أَبِيٌّ proud, lofty, disdainful

أ ث ر

أَثَرَ – يَأْثُرُ to transmit, relate, or report
أَثَّرَ – يُؤَثِّرُ to affect or influence; to produce an effect
تَأَثَّرَ – يَتَأَثَّرُ to be impressed or influenced; to be moved or touched
أَثَرٌ (آثارٌ) trace, impression, mark; remnants; ruins; antiquities
أَثَرَةٌ selfishness (noun)
تَأْثيرٌ influence, effect; action
تَأَثُّرٌ (تَأَثُّراتٌ) feeling, emotion; sensation, perception; influence
مُؤَثِّرٌ (مُؤَثِّراتٌ) influencing factor, influence; moving, touching (pl: effects)
مُؤَثِّراتٌ تِقَنيَّةٌ special effects (technological)
مُؤَثِّراتٌ صَوْتِيَّةٌ sound effects

أ د ب

أَدُبَ – يَأْدُبُ to be well-bred, well mannered, or cultured
أَدَّبَ – يُؤَدِّبُ to discipline, punish, or chastise; to refine or educate
أَدَبٌ (آدابٌ) culture, refinement, good manners; literature
الأَدَبُ المُقارَنُ comparative literature
قَليلُ الأَدَبِ ill-mannered
آدابُ السُّلوكِ etiquette
الآدابُ morals
أَدَبِيٌّ literary; ethical, moral
الفَلْسَفةُ الأَدَبِيَّةُ ethics
أَديبٌ (أُدَباءُ) cultured, refined, educated; writer, author
تَأْديبٌ education; discipline, punishment
تَأَدُّبٌ good manners, courteousness
مُؤَدَّبٌ (مُؤَدَّبونَ) polite, well-bred

أ ل ف

أَلِفَ – يَأْلَفُ to be acquainted, familiar, or conversant; to be habituated

Education 95

أَلَّفَ – يُؤَلِّفُ to compile, compose, or write; to habituate; to tame or domesticate
تَأَلَّفَ – يَتَأَلَّفُ to be composed of; to be united
أُلْفَةٌ affection, intimacy, familiarity
أَلِيفٌ tame, domesticated; familiar, intimate
تَأْلِيفٌ formation; literary works
تَأَلُّفٌ harmony; familiarity, intimacy
اِئْتِلافٌ concord, harmony; union, coalition
اِئْتِلافِيٌّ coalition (adj)
مَأْلُوفٌ familiar, accustomed; customary
مُؤَلِّفٌ (مُؤَلِّفُونَ) author, writer

ب ح ث

بَحَثَ – يَبْحَثُ to search, examine, or study; to investigate or research
باحَثَ – يُباحِثُ to discuss
بَحْثٌ (بُحوثٌ / أَبحاثٌ) search, study, research, investigation
مَبْحَثٌ (مَباحِثُ) subject, theme, research, examination, investigation
مُباحَثَةٌ (مُباحَثاتٌ) negotiation, talk, discussion; research
باحِثٌ (باحِثونَ / بُحّاثٌ) scholar; researcher, examiner, investigator

ب ي ت

باتَ – يَبيتُ to spend the night
بَيَّتَ – يُبَيِّتُ to brood; to plot; to put up for the night
بَيْتٌ (بُيوتٌ) house, building; tent; room
بَيْتٌ (أَبْياتٌ) line, verse (poetry)
بَيْتِيٌّ domestic
بائِتٌ stale, old

ت ر ج م

تَرْجَمَ – يُتَرْجِمُ to translate; to interpret; to write a biography
تَرْجَمَةٌ (تَراجِمُ) translation; interpretation; biography
خَدَماتُ التَّرْجَمَةِ translation services
تَرْجَمَةٌ مَطْبوعَةٌ subtitles
تَرْجَمَةٌ فَوْرِيَّةٌ simultaneous translation
مُتَرْجِمٌ (مُتَرْجِمونَ) translator, interpreter; biographer
مُتَرْجَمٌ translated

96 *Education*

ت م م

تَمَّ – يَتِمُّ to be or become complete or finished

أَتَمَّ – يُتِمُّ to complete or finish; to execute or perform

تَمامٌ completeness, entirety; perfection

تَماماً exactly, perfectly, completely

تَميمَةٌ (تَمائِمُ) talisman, amulet

إِتمامٌ completion, fulfilment; perfection

تامٌّ complete, perfect, entire

ج ر ر

جَرَّ – يَجُرُّ to pull or drag; to put a word in the genitive case, to pronounce the final consonant with *i* ◌ (kasra)

اِنجَرَّ – يَنجَرُّ to be pulled or dragged; to have put a word in the genitive case

جَرٌّ dragging; causing; genitive case

جَرَّةٌ (جِرارٌ) jar, urn

جَرّارٌ (جَرّاراتٌ) tractor

مَجَرَّةٌ galaxy

جارورٌ (جَواريرُ) drawer

اَلْمجرورُ genitive case

ج ز م

جَزَمَ – يَجزِمُ to cut off; to judge or settle; to pronounce the final consonant of a word without a vowel

جَزْمٌ cutting off; resolve; jussive form

جازِمٌ decisive, definite; final

مَجْزومٌ vowelless (final consonant); cut off, clipped

اَلْمَجزومُ jussive mood (for verbs)

ج م ع

جَمَعَ – يَجمَعُ to gather, unite, or bring together; to summarise; to convene

جَمَّعَ – يُجَمِّعُ to amass, accumulate, or assemble

جامَعَ – يُجامِعُ to have sexual intercourse

تَجَمَّعَ – يَتَجَمَّعُ to gather or congregate; to rally together

اِجتَمَعَ – يَجتَمِعُ to join or get together

جَمْعٌ (جُموعٌ) gathering, crowd; collection

Education 97

جُمْعَةٌ (جُمعاتٌ) week; Friday
جُمْعَةُ الآلامِ / الجُمْعَةُ العَظيمَةُ Good Friday
جَمعيَّةٌ (جَمعيَّاتٌ) assembly; society, club, organisation
جَماعَةٌ (جَماعاتٌ) community, group, party
جِماعٌ sexual intercourse
تَجَمُّعٌ (تَجَمُّعاتٌ) meeting, gathering; crowd, mob
اِجتِماعٌ (اِجتِماعاتٌ) meeting, gathering; assembly; rally
عِلمُ الإِجتِماعِ sociology
إِجتِماعيٌّ social, community related; socialist
الحالةُ الإِجتِماعيَّةُ social status
المَعاييرُ الإِجتِماعيَّةُ social norms
الخَدماتُ الإِجتِماعيَّةُ social services
جامِعٌ comprehensive, extensive; general
جامِعٌ (جَوامِعُ) mosque
جامِعةٌ (جامِعاتٌ) university; league, union
الحَرَمُ الجامِعيُّ university campus
جامِعيٌّ academic; university related
مَجموعَةٌ (مَجموعاتٌ) group
مُجتَمَعٌ (مُجتَمَعاتٌ) society, community

ج ي ء

جاءَ – يَجيءُ to come or arrive; to perpetuate
مَجيءٌ coming, arrival, advent

ح ب ط

حَبَطَ – يَحبِطُ to be futile; to fail or miscarry
أَحبَطَ – يُحبِطُ to frustrate, thwart, or foil
حُبوطٌ futility, failure
إِحباطٌ depression, decline; lack of motion; frustration

ح ض ر

حَضَرَ – يَحضُرُ to be present or appear; to participate or attend; to be sedentary (as opposed to nomadic)
حَضَّرَ – يُحَضِّرُ to ready or prepare; to study; to civilise
حاضَرَ – يُحاضِرُ to lecture

98 Education

أَحْضَرَ – يُحْضِرُ to fetch or get; to supply
تَحَضَّرَ – يَتَحَضَّرُ to prepare oneself; to become urbanised
حَضَرٌ civilised or settled region; town dwellers
حَضَرِيٌّ / حَضارِيٌّ settled, resident; non-Bedouin
حُضورٌ attendance, presence
حُضورٌ إِجْبارِيٌّ compulsory attendance
حَضارَةٌ (حَضاراتٌ) civilisation, culture
تَحْضيرٌ (تَحْضيراتٌ) preparing, making ready
تَحْضيرِيٌّ preparatory
مُحاضَرَةٌ (مُحاضَراتٌ) a lecture
قاعَةُ المُحاضَراتِ lecture hall
حاضِرٌ (حُضورٌ) present; attending
مُحاضِرٌ (مُحاضِرونَ) lecturer, speaker
مُتَحَضِّرٌ civilised

ح ك ى

حَكى – يَحْكي to speak or relate; to imitate
حَكْيٌ speech
حِكايَةٌ (حِكاياتٌ) story, tale, narrative
حاكٍ narrator, storyteller

ح و ج

أَحْوَجَ – يُحْوِجُ to need or require; to compel; to impoverish
اِحْتاجَ – يَحْتاجُ to be in want; to require
حَوْجٌ need, want, lack
حاجَةٌ (حاجاتٌ) need, requirement; an object
حاجَةٌ (حَوائِجُ / حاجِياتٌ) need, necessities; belongings, stuff
اِحْتِياجٌ (اِحْتِياجاتٌ) needs, wants, requirements, necessities
مُحْتاجٌ in need, poor

ح و ى

حَوى – يَحوي to gather, collect, or unite; to include or comprise
اِحْتَوى – يَحْتَوي to encompass or embrace; to possess
مُحْتَوَياتٌ contents (of a book)

خ ر ج

خَرَجَ – يَخرُجُ to go out; to depart
أَخرَجَ – يُخرِجُ to bring (sth) out; to evict; to dislodge; to unload or disembark
تَخَرَّجَ – يَتَخَرَّجُ to be educated; to graduate
خُروجٌ exit, departure, emigration, exodus
خِرِّيجٌ / مُتَخَرِّجٌ (خِرِّيجونَ / مُتَخَرِّجونَ) graduate
مَخرَجٌ (مَخارِجُ) exit, way out, escape
تَخريجٌ / تَخَرُّجٌ graduation
حفلُ تَخَرُّج graduation ceremony
اِستِخراجٌ removal, extraction; derivation
خارِجٌ outer, exterior; foreign; outside
مُخرِجٌ (مُخرِجونَ) director

خ ط ئ

خَطِئَ – يُخطَأُ to be mistaken
خَطَّأَ – يُخَطِّئُ to charge with an offence; to declare guilty
خَطَأٌ (أَخطاءٌ) mistake, fault
خَطيئَةٌ (خَطيئاتٌ / خَطايا) mistake, lapse; fault, crime, sin
خاطِئٌ (خَواطِئُ / خُطاةٌ) wrong, incorrect
مُخطِئٌ mistaken, wrong, at fault

خ ي ب

خابَ – يَخيبُ to fail or miscarry
خَيَّبَ – يُخَيِّبُ to thwart or frustrate; to disappoint; to defeat
خَيبَةٌ failure, defeat; disappointment
خَيبَةُ أَمَلٍ disappointment
خائِبٌ failing, unsuccessful; disappointed

خ ي ل

خالَ – يَخالُ to imagine, think, or believe
خَيَّلَ – يُخَيِّلُ to suggest; to make someone believe; to gallop on a horse
تَخَيَّلَ – يَتَخَيَّلُ to imagine or fancy
خَيالٌ (أَخيِلَةٌ) imagination, fantasy; vision; ghost
خَيالٌ عِلمِيٌّ science fiction

Education

خَيالَةٌ (خَيالاتٌ) ghost, spirit
خَيالِيٌّ amazing, unreal; fictitious
تَخَيُّلٌ (تَخَيُّلاتٌ) imagination, fantasy; delusion
اِختِيالٌ / خُيَلاءُ pride, arrogance
مُخَيِّلَةٌ imagination, fantasy; vision

No root

دُكْتورٌ (دَكاتِرَةٌ) doctors
دُكْتوراةٌ doctorate
رِسالَةُ الدَكْتوراةِ / أُطروحَةٌ PhD thesis

ر س ب

رَسَبَ – يَرسُبُ to fail an examination; to sink, settle, or subside
رَسَّبَ – يُرَسِّبُ to cause to settle (sth in liquid); to deposit (sediment)
رُسوبٌ sediment; failure (exam)

ر ط ن

رَطَنَ – يَرطُنُ to talk gibberish
رَطانَةٌ gibberish; lingo
رَطْنٌ gibberish; foreign language

ر ف ض

رَفَضَ – يَرفُضُ to refuse or reject; to abandon or leave
رَفْضٌ rejection, refusal
مَرفوضٌ rejected

ر ف ع

رَفَعَ – يَرفَعُ to lift; to put a word in the nominative or indicative case; to pronounce the final consonant with *u* ُ (damma)
رَفَّعَ – يُرَفِّعُ to raise or lift
اِرتَفَعَ – يَرتَفِعُ to rise or lift; to become higher
رَفْعٌ lifting; elevation; pronunciation of the final consonant with *u* ُ
رَفيعٌ thin, fine; high, lofty
اِرتِفاعٌ elevation; increase
مُرتَفَعٌ (مُرتَفَعاتٌ) height, altitude; elevated place

Education 101

مُرتَفَعاتُ الْجولانِ the Golan Heights
الْمَرفوعُ indicative mood (verbs), nominative case (nouns)

س ج ل

سَجَّلَ – يُسَجِّلُ to register, document, or record; to give evidence
سِجِلٌّ (سِجِلّاتٌ) record, register, list; archives
تَسجيلٌ (تَسجيلاتٌ) registration; documentation, recording
مُسَجِّلٌ (مُسَجِّلونَ) registrar; notary public; tape recorder
مُسَجِّلٌ (مُسَجِّلاتٌ) tape recorder
مُسَجَّلٌ recorded

س ع ى

سعى – يَسعى to strive; to attempt; to achieve
سَعيٌ course; effort
مَسعىً (مَساعٍ) effort, endeavour
ساعٍ (سُعاةٌ/ساعونَ) messenger; delivery boy
ساعي الْبَريدِ postman

س ك ن

سَكَنَ – يَسكُنُ to live or inhabit; to be tranquil; to be vowelless (grammar)
سَكَّنَ – يُسَكِّنُ to reassure, or soothe
أَسكَنَ – يُسكِنُ to provide living quarters (for someone)
سَكَنٌ dwelling, abode, habitation
قاعةُ السَّكَنِ الداخِليِّ dormitory
سُكونٌ calm, tranquility, peace; silence; symbol for vowellessness
سِكّينٌ (سَكاكينُ) knife
سِكّينةٌ knife
سَكينةٌ presence of God; calm, tranquility
مَسكَنٌ (مَساكِنُ) home, dwelling
إِسكانٌ settling; settlement
ساكِنٌ (سُكّانٌ/ساكِنونَ) inhabitant, resident (pl: population)
تَعدادُ السُّكّانِ population
ساكِنٌ (سَواكِنُ) calm, motionless; vowelless
مَسكونٌ populated, inhabited; possessed (by demons or jinn)
مُسَكِّنٌ (مُسَكِّناتٌ) sedative, pacifier

102 *Education*

س ل ب

سَلَبَ – يَسْلُبُ to take or snatch away; to deny; to be in mourning
تَسَلَّبَ – يَتَسَلَّبُ to be in mourning
سَلْبِيٌّ / سالِبٌ negative
سَلْبِيَّةٌ negativity
سَلْبٌ (أَسْلابٌ) loot, booty
أُسْلوبٌ (أَساليبُ) style (especially literary); method, way, manner

ش خ ص

شَخَصَ – يَشْخَصُ to rise, ascend, or appear; to stare
شَخَّصَ – يُشَخِّصُ to personify; to specify; to identify; to act or play
شَخْصٌ (أَشْخاصٌ) person, individual, character
شَخْصِيٌّ personal, private
شَخْصِيَّةٌ (شَخْصِيَّاتٌ) personality, individuality
بِطاقَةٌ شَخْصِيَّةٌ ID card
مَعلوماتٌ شَخْصِيَّةٌ personal information
تَشْخيصٌ personification; diagnosis; performance, acting

ص د ق

صَدَقَ – يَصْدُقُ to speak the truth, to be right; to be sincere
صَدَّقَ – يُصَدِّقُ to believe; to give credence to
صادَقَ – يُصادِقُ to treat as a friend; to agree, approve, or grant
تَصَدَّقَ – يَتَصَدَّقُ to give alms; to donate
صِدْقٌ truth, sincerity
صَدَقَةٌ (صَدَقاتٌ) charity
صَداقَةٌ (صَداقاتٌ) friendship
صَديقٌ (أَصْدِقاءُ) friend, friendly
صادِقٌ true; truthful (also a boy's name)
مِصْداقٌ / مِصْداقِيَّةٌ credibility; confirmation

ض ر ع

ضَرَعَ – يَضْرَعُ to be humble or submissive; to implore
ضارَعَ – يُضارِعُ to be similar or equal, to resemble
ضَراعَةٌ submissiveness; humility; begging; entreaty
المُضارِعُ imperfect tense

ط م ح

طَمَحَ – يَطْمَحُ to turn or be directed; to strive; to aspire or yearn
طُموحٌ (طُموحاتٌ) ambitions, aspirations; endeavour; striving
طامِحٌ ambitious, eager; yearning

ع ج ب

عَجِبَ – يَعجَبُ to wonder at; to be astonished
عَجَّبَ – يُعَجِّبُ to amaze, surprise, or delight
تَعَجَّبَ – يَتَعَجَّبُ to wonder or marvel
عَجَبٌ (أعجابٌ) amazement; marvel, wonder
عَجيبٌ wonderful, remarkable, strange, odd
عَجيبَةٌ (عَجائِبُ) wondrous or strange things; curiosities
أعجوبةٌ (أعاجيبُ) wondrous thing, miracle, prodigy
إعجابٌ admiration; pleasure, satisfaction
تَعَجُّبٌ / إستِعجابٌ astonishment, amazement
مُعْجَبٌ admirer

ع ج م

عَجَمَ – يَعجُمُ to try or test
أعجمَ – يَعْجُمُ to provide a letter with a diacritical point
إنعَجَمَ – يَنعَجِمُ to be incomprehensible or unintelligible
إستَعجَمَ – يَستَعجِمُ to become un-Arabic
عَجَمٌ barbarians, non-Arabs; Persians
العَجَمُ Persians
عَجَميٌّ (أعجامٌ) barbarian, non-Arab
عَجماءُ (عَجمَاواتٌ) beast
أعجمُ (أعاجِمُ) speaking incorrect Arabic; barbarian; non-Arab; a Persian
أعجَميٌّ foreigner, alien, non-Arabic; non-Arab, Persian
مُعْجَمٌ (مَعاجِمُ) incomprehensible; dictionary, lexicon; provided with a diacritical point

ع م د

عَمَدَ – يَعمَدُ to support or prop; to intend; to approach; to undertake; to baptise
عَمَّدَ – يَعمِّدُ to baptise or christen
تَعَمَّدَ – يَتَعَمَّدُ to intend or do intentionally; to approach; to be baptised

104 *Education*

عَمْدٌ intention, premeditation, purpose
عَمْدِيٌّ / مُتَعَمَّدٌ deliberate
عُمْدَةٌ (عُمَدٌ) magistrate
عِمادٌ (عَمَدٌ) support, pillar
عَميدٌ (عُمَداءُ) dean, headmaster, head, chief; support
عَمودٌ / عامودٌ (أَعْمِدَةٌ / عَواميدُ) flagpole, pillar, column
تَعَمُّدٌ intention, determination, design
تَعْميدٌ baptism
مُتَعَمَّدٌ deliberate
مُعْتَمَدٌ reliable; approved

ف ر د

فَرَدَ – يَفْرُدُ to be single or alone; singular, unique
اِنْفَرَدَ – يَنْفَرِدُ to stand alone; to be without parallel; to withdraw
فَرْدٌ (أَفْرادٌ) singular (grammar); an individual; single, only
فَرْدٌ (فُرودٌ) gun
فَرْدَةٌ one of a pair
فَرْدِيَّةٌ individuality
فَريدٌ unique; alone, solitary (also a boy's name)
فَريدَةٌ (فَرائِدُ) precious gem, solitaire (also a girl's name)
اِنْفِرادٌ seclusion, solitude, loneliness
مُفْرَدٌ singular (grammar); solitary, lone
مُفْرَداتٌ vocabulary, words, terms
قائِمَةُ المُفْرَداتِ lexicon
مُنْفَرِدٌ isolated, detached, solitary

ف ش ل

فَشِلَ – يَفْشَلُ to fail; to lose courage
فاشِلٌ unsuccessful, futile, worthless

ف ص ح

فَصُحَ – يَفْصُحُ to be eloquent
فَصَّحَ – يُفَصِّحُ to use correct Arabic
أَفْصَحَ – يُفْصِحُ to express oneself in flawless Arabic; to speak clearly
فَصيحٌ (فُصَحاءُ / فُصُحٌ) pure Arabic; fluent, eloquent; clear, distinct (language)

فَصاحَةٌ eloquence, fluency; purity of language
إِفصاحٌ flawless literary Arabic; an open declaration

ف ن ن

فَنَّنَ – يُفَنِّنُ to diversify or vary; to mingle or jumble
تَفَنَّنَ – يَتَفَنَّنُ to be versatile; to be a specialist; to do something in an artistic way
فَنٌّ (فُنونٌ) art; field, discipline
فَنُّ الخَطِّ calligraphy
الفُنونُ الجَميلَةُ fine arts
الفُنونُ العَسكَرِيَّةُ martial arts
قاعَةُ الفُنونِ art gallery
فَنِّيٌّ artistic; technical; professional
فَنَّانٌ (فَنَّانونَ) artist, craftsman
تَفَنُّنٌ diversity, variety; versatility; skill

ق ب س

قَبَسَ – يَقبِسُ to derive; to loan or borrow; to acquire
اِقتَبَسَ – يَقتَبِسُ to take; to learn; to loan or borrow
قابوسٌ nightmare
اِقتِباسٌ adaptation (text); loaning, borrowing (words); quotation
مُقتَبَساتٌ loans, borrowings; quotations

ق م س

قَمَسَ – يَقمِسُ to dip, immerse, or soak
قاموسٌ (قَواميسُ) dictionary, lexicon; ocean

ك ر ر

كَرَّ – يَكُرُّ to turn around and attack; to return; to withdraw or retreat
كَرَّرَ – يُكَرِّرُ to repeat; to ask repeatedly; to clarify
تَكَرَّرَ – يَتَكَرَّرُ to be repeated; to be refined or purified
كَرٌّ attack
كَرَّةٌ (كَرَّاتٌ) attack; return, comeback, recurrence; one time
تَكريرٌ / تَكرارٌ repetition, reiteration
مِراراً وتَكراراً repeatedly
مُكَرَّرٌ / مُتَكَرِّرٌ repeated, reiterated

No root

كُلُّ (followed by a definite noun) all, entire, whole; (followed by an indefinite noun) every

كُلَّما whenever

كُلِّيٌّ complete, absolute, total

كُلِّيَّةٌ (كُلِّيَّاتٌ) totality (pl: college, university faculty)

كُلِّيَّةُ الْفنونِ الْجميلَةِ department of fine arts

كُلِّيَّةُ التِّجارَةِ faculty of trade and commerce

كُلِّيَّةُ الْحُقوقِ faculty of law

ل ح ظ

لَحَظَ – يَلْحَظُ to observe, look, or view; to notice

لاحظَ – يُلاحِظُ to view, observe, see, or notice; to perceive or notice

لَحظٌ (ألْحاظٌ) look, glance

لَحظَةٌ (لَحظاتٌ) look, glance, glimpse; moment

مُلاحَظَةٌ (مُلاحَظاتٌ) remark, comment, note; observation

مَلحوظٌ noteworthy, remarkable

مَلحوظَةٌ (مَلحوظاتٌ) observation, remark, note; seeing, perception

ل ف ظ

لَفَظَ – يلفِظُ to pronounce, enunciate, or articulate; to emit; to spit out

تَلَفَّظَ – يَتَلَفَّظُ to pronounce, enunciate, or articulate

لَفظٌ (ألفاظٌ) expression, term; articulation, pronunciation

ألفاظٌ نابِيَةٌ rude words, swear words

لَفظيٌّ verbal; literary; oral

لَفظَةٌ (لَفظاتٌ) word; utterance

تَلَفُّظٌ pronunciation, articulation

مَلفوظٌ pronounced

ل ك ن

لَكِنَ – يَلكَنُ to speak incorrectly; to stammer

لُكنَةٌ stutter, stammer; incorrect pronunciation; ungrammatical language

لَكانَةٌ speech defect

ل ه ج

لَهِجَ – يَلهَجُ to be devoted or dedicated; to be in love

لَهجَةٌ (لَهجاتٌ) dialect, vernacular; tongue; manner of speaking; tone

م د ح

مَدَحَ – يَمدَحُ to praise or commend; to eulogise
مَدْحٌ commendation, praise, glorification
مَديحٌ (مَدائِحُ) praise, commendation; eulogy

م د د

(Full treatment in Politics chapter)

مَدَّ – يُمدُّ to extend or spread out; to help or assist; to supply or provide; to reinforce (army)
مَدٌّ (مُدودٌ) stretching, lengthening; extension
مَدَّةٌ long sign over *alif* (آ)
مُدَّةٌ (مُدَدٌ) period; interval; duration
مادَّةٌ (مَوادُّ) subject, topic, theme; chemical element; component; material
مَوادُّ اِختِيارِيَّةٌ optional subjects

ن ج ح

نَجَحَ – يَنجَحُ to succeed or progress well; to pass (exam)
نَجَّحَ – يُنَجِّحُ to let or make someone succeed
نَجاحٌ success; passing (an exam) (also a girl's name)
ناجِحٌ successful; having passed (exam)

ن ج ز

نَجَزَ – يَنجُزُ to carry out or execute; to fulfil or accomplish
أَنجَزَ – يُنجِزُ to carry out, execute, or implement; to accomplish or complete
نَجزٌ / إنجازٌ / تَنجيزٌ / نَجازٌ achievement; performance; execution, implementation
ناجِزٌ completed; entire, complete, total

ن ح و

نَحا – يَنحو to wend one's way; to go, walk, or move
نَحَّى – يُنَحِّي to remove; to put aside or push away
نَحوٌ (أنحاءٌ) direction; side; course, method
النَّحوُ Arabic grammar; grammar
نَحوَ (prep) in the direction of, towards; according to; similar to
ناحِيَةٌ (نَواحٍ) side, direction; viewpoint; domain
مِن ناحِيَةٍ... وَمِن ناحِيَةٍ أُخرى on the one hand ... on the other hand

Education

ن س خ

نَسَخَ - يَنْسَخُ to transcribe or copy; to delete, abolish, invalidate, or repeal
اِسْتَنْسَخَ - يَسْتَنْسِخُ to transcribe or copy; to demand the abolition of
نَسْخٌ abolition, cancellation; copying, transcription
نَسْخِيٌّ ordinary Arabic cursive script
نُسْخَةٌ (نُسَخٌ) a copy or transcript
تَنَاسُخٌ succession
اِسْتِنْسَاخٌ cloning; copying, transcription
نَاسِخٌ (نُسَّاخٌ) transcriber, copyist

ن ص ح

نَصَحَ - يَنْصَحُ to advise or counsel; to be sincere or act in good faith
نَاصَحَ - يُنَاصِحُ to give someone sincere advice; to be sincere in one's intentions
اِسْتَنْصَحَ - يَسْتَنْصِحُ to ask someone for advice
نُصْحٌ good advice, counsel, guidance
نَصِيحٌ sincere and faithful advisor
نَصِيحَةٌ (نَصَائِحُ) advice, friendly advice
نَاصِحٌ (نُصَّاحٌ) sincere; good counsellor or advisor[3]

ن ص ص

نَصَّ - يَنُصُّ to fix, determine, or compose; to state in writing
نَصٌّ (نُصُوصٌ) text, wording; version; sentence, clause, passage
النَّصُّ الإِبْدَاعِيُّ creative text
بِنَصِّهِ verbatim
تَنْصِيصٌ quotation
عَلَامَاتُ التَّنْصِيصِ quotation marks
مِنَصَّةٌ (مِنَصَّاتٌ) raised platform, podium

ن و ن

نَوَّنَ - يُنَوِّنُ to add a final *nūn* to a noun, to provide with nunnation
تَنْوِينٌ nunnation (grammar)

No root

هُوَ he, it
هُوِيَّةٌ ID card; identity; essence, nature

Education 109

و ج د

وَجَدَ – يَجِدُ to find or come across; to invent; to experience or feel
أوجَدَ – يوجِدُ to produce; to provoke or cause; to create or invent
وَجْدٌ strong emotion, passion, ardour
وُجودٌ existence, presence; finding, discovery
وُجودِيٌّ existential
إيجادٌ creation, origination, production
مَوجودٌ present, existent, available, found

و س ع

وَسِعَ – يَوْسِعُ / يَسَعُ to be wide, spacious, or extensive; to include; to accommodate
وَسَّعَ – يُوَسِّعُ to widen or expand
تَوَسَّعَ – يَتَوَسَّعُ to be extended, expanded, or widened
سَعَةٌ wideness, roominess, capacity; ability
ذو سَعَةٍ wealthy
وُسْعٌ capability, ability, capacity, power
وُسعَةٌ wideness, spaciousness; extent, range
وَسيعٌ (وِساعٌ) wide, vast, roomy
تَوسيعٌ / تَوَسُّعٌ extension, expansion, widening, increase
تَوَسُّعِيٌّ expansionist
إتِّساعٌ vastness, spaciousness
واسِعٌ wide, broad, spacious, roomy
مَوْسوعَةٌ (مَوْسوعاتٌ) encyclopaedia, thesaurus

و ض ع

(Full treatment in Media chapter)

وَضَعَ – يَضَعُ to put down, place or lay; to set up; to bear (children)
مَوْضوعٌ (مَواضيعُ) subject, theme, topic; issue, question
المَواضيعُ الدِّراسِيَّةُ subjects
مَواضيعُ ذاتُ صِلَةٍ related topics

Subjects المَواضيعُ

أ ر خ

أَرَّخَ – يُؤَرِّخُ to date (a letter etc.); to write the history of something

110 *Education*

تَارِيخٌ (تَوَارِيخُ) date; time; history
التَّارِيخُ history
مُؤَرِّخٌ (مُؤَرِّخُونَ) historian

ل غ و

لَغَا - يَلْغُو to speak; to talk nonsense or make mistakes in speech; to be null
أَلْغَى - يُلْغِي to cancel or nullify; to withdraw; to render ineffectual
لَغْوٌ foolish talk, nonsense; ungrammatical language
لُغَةٌ (لُغَاتٌ) language, dialect, idiom, vernacular
اللُّغَةُ العَامِّيَّةُ colloquial language
عِلْمُ اللُّغَةِ linguistics
قَوَاعِدُ اللُّغَةِ grammar
اللُّغَةُ العَرَبِيَّةُ / لُغَةُ الضَّادِ Arabic language
اللُّغَةُ الأُمُّ mother tongue
اللُّغَةُ الإنجليزِيَّةُ English language
اللُّغَةُ الفَرَنسِيَّةُ French
لُغَةُ الإشَارَةِ sign language
لُغَوِيٌّ linguistic
ثُنَائِيَّةٌ لُغَوِيَّةٌ bilingualism
لَغْوَةٌ dialect, idiom, vernacular
إِلْغَاءٌ abolition, elimination, cancellation
مُلْغَى invalid; abolished, annulled

المَوَاضِيعُ الأُخرى Other Subjects

إدَارَةُ الأَعْمَالِ business administration
الأَنثروبولوجيا / عِلْمُ الإنسَانِ anthropology
التِّجَارَةُ trade, business
التَّدبيرُ المَنزِلِيُّ home economics
التَّصَامِيمُ والتِّكنولوجيا design and technology
الصَّحَافَةُ journalism
الْجُغرافيا geography
الْموسيقى music
دِرَاسَاتُ الإعلامِ media studies

Extracurricular and Recreational Activities
النَّشَاطَاتُ اللّاصَفِّيَّةُ والتَّرفيهِيَّةُ

أ ن س

أَنِسَ – يَأْنَسُ to be sociable, friendly, or nice
آنَسَ – يُؤنِسُ to keep someone company; to entertain or amuse
أُنْسٌ intimacy; sociability
إِنْسٌ man, human, mankind
ناسٌ (أَناسٌ) people
أَنيسٌ close friend (also a boy's name)
إِنْسانٌ human, man
إِنْسانِيٌّ human, humane
لا إِنْسانِيٌّ inhumane
إِنْسانِيَّةٌ humanity; kindness, politeness
إيناسٌ intimacy; friendliness, sociability (also a girl's name)
آنِسَةٌ (آنِساتٌ) Miss; a young lady

ب ر ى

بَرى – يَبري to trim or shape; to exhaust or wear out
تَبارى – يَتَبارى to vie, compete, or contend
اِنْبَرى – يَنْبَري to be sharpened or trimmed; to defy or oppose; to undertake
بَرّايَةٌ pencil sharpener
مُباراةٌ (مُبارياتٌ) competition, match, tournament
مُتَبارٍ contestant, competitor, rival

ب ط ل

بَطَلَ – يَبطُلُ to be brave or heroic, to be a hero
بَطَلٌ (أَبطالٌ) champion, hero, protagonist; brave, heroic
بُطولَةٌ (بُطولاتٌ) championship, tournament; bravery, heroism; leading role

ب ن ى

بَنى – يَبْني to build, erect, or establish
بِناءٌ (أَبنِيَةٌ) building, construction, structure
بُنْيَةٌ (بُنىً) structure; build, frame
بَنّاءٌ (بَنّاءونَ) constructive; builder (pl: builders)
غَيرُ بَنّاءٍ / غَيرُ بَنّاءةٍ unconstructive
بِنايَةٌ (بِناياتٌ) building, structure, edifice
مَبنىً (مَبانٍ) building, construction, structure

Education

No root

تِبغٌ (تُبوغٌ) tobacco

No root

جَوْقٌ / جَوقَةٌ (أجواقٌ / جَوقاتٌ) troop, group, choir, theatrical group
مُديرُ الجَوْق conductor
جَوقةٌ موسيقيّةٌ orchestra

ح ش ش

حَشَّ – يَحِشُّ to mow grass
حَشَّشَ – يُحَشِّشُ to smoke hashish
حَشيشٌ grass, cannabis, weed, hashish
حَشّاشٌ (حَشّاشونَ) hashish smoker

ح ط ط

حَطَّ – يَحُطُّ to put or place; to lower or dismount
حِطّةٌ relief; abasement, humiliation, insult, indignity
مَحَطّةٌ (مَحَطّاتٌ) stopping place, station, post; broadcasting station
مَحَطّةُ الحافِلاتِ / مَحَطّةُ الباصاتِ coach or bus station

ح ي ن

حانَ – يَحينُ to draw near or approach
حَيَّنَ – يُحَيِّنُ to set a time
حانَ الوقتُ the time has come, it is the right time
حانةٌ (حاناتٌ) bar, pub, tavern
حينٌ (أحيانٌ) time, opportunity
أحياناً occasionally
بَعضُ الأحيانِ sometimes
حينئِذٍ at that time, that day
حينَما (conj) while, when, as

خ ل ل

خَلَّ – يَخِلُّ to pierce; to transfix
خالَلَ – يُخالِلُ to treat as a friend

Education 113

اِخْتَلَّ – يَخْتَلُّ to be defective, faulty, or imperfect; to be upset or unbalanced
اِخْتَلَّ تَوازُنُهُ to lose one's balance
خِلٌّ (أَخْلالٌ) friend, buddy
خَلَلٌ (خِلالٌ) rupture; imbalance; defectiveness, damage
خَليلٌ (أَخِلاءُ) friend, companion; lover
الْخَليلُ Hebron in Palestine
إِخْلالٌ (إِخْلالاتٌ) violation (of law), offence, transgression; harm
اِخْتِلالٌ disorder, confusion; imperfection, deficiency

د خ ن

دَخَنَ – يَدْخَنُ to smoke (food, cigarette)
دَخَّنَ – يُدَخِّنُ to smoke (food, cigarette); to fumigate
دُخانٌ (أَدْخِنَةٌ) smoke, tobacco, fumes, vapour
مَدْخَنَةٌ (مَداخِنُ) chimney; chain smoker
تَدْخينٌ smoking
الإقْلاعُ عَنِ التَّدْخينِ giving up smoking
مُدَخِّنٌ smoker

د ر ب

دَرِبَ – يَدْرَبُ to be accustomed; to be trained or skilled
دَرَّبَ – يُدَرِّبُ to practise; to habituate or accustom; to train or coach
تَدَرَّبَ – يَتَدَرَّبُ to be accustomed; to be trained
تَدْريبٌ training, practice, habituation
مُدَرِّبٌ (مُدَرِّبونَ) trainer, coach, instructor

د ر ج

دَرَجَ – يَدْرُجُ to go or depart; to walk, proceed, or advance
دَرَّجَ – يُدَرِّجُ to advance by steps; to approximate; to circulate; to grade
تَدَرَّجَ – يَتَدَرَّجُ to progress by steps, to advance gradually
دُرْجٌ (أَدْراجٌ) drawer; desk
دَرَجٌ (أَدْراجٌ) stairs, steps; route
دَرَجَةٌ (دَرَجاتٌ) step, degree, grade, class; stairs
دَرَجَةٌ أولى first class
الدَّرَجَةُ الثّانِيَةُ second class
دَرَجَةُ رِجالِ الأَعْمالِ business class

Education

دَرَّاجَةٌ (دَرَّاجاتٌ) bicycle
دَرَّاجَةٌ ناريَّةٌ motorcycle
تَدريجِيٌّ gradual
دارِجٌ current; widespread, common
اللُّغَةُ الدّارِجَةُ colloquial, spoken language
مُدَرَّجٌ (مُدَرَّجاتٌ) open staircase; amphitheatre; graduated
المُدَرَّجُ الرِّياضِيُّ / الإِسْتادُ stadium

د ع ب

دَعَبَ – يَدعَبُ to joke, jest, or make fun
داعَبَ – يُداعِبُ to play, joke, or jest
دَعِبٌ joking, playful, funny
دُعابَةٌ (دُعاباتٌ) joking, jesting

ر ف ق

رَفَقَ – يرفِقُ to be kind, friendly, or courteous
رافَقَ – يُرافِقُ to be a companion or friend; to accompany or escort
رِفقٌ friendliness, kindness
جمعيَّةُ الرِّفقِ بالحيوانِ Society for the Prevention of Cruelty to Animals
رِفقَةٌ (رِفاقٌ) group, troop, company
رَفيقٌ / مُرافِقٌ (رُفَقاءُ / مُرافِقونَ) friend, companion, escort
مَرفِقٌ (مَرافِقُ) elbow; utilities, conveniences, facilities
مَرافِقُ عامَّةٌ public utilities
مَرافِقُ صِحِّيَّةٌ عامَّةٌ public toilets
مُرافَقَةٌ accompaniment; association

ر ف ه

رَفَهَ – يَرفِهُ to be comfortable; to be pleasant
رَفَّهَ – يُرَفِّهُ to make pleasant and comfortable; to live in comfort; to relax
رَفهٌ / رَفاةٌ well-being, welfare; good living
رَفاهَةٌ / رَفاهِيَّةٌ luxurious life; comfort
تَرفيهٌ recreation, relaxation
تَرفيهِيٌّ recreational
مَركَزٌ تَرفيهِيٌّ / مَركَزُ التَّرفيهِ والتَّسلِيَةِ recreational centre

ر ق ص

رَقَصَ – يَرقُصُ to dance or prance
رَقَّصَ – يُرَقِّصُ to make someone dance; to make the heart tremble
رَقصٌ dancing, dance
رَقصٌ شَعْبِيٌّ folk dancing
رَقصٌ شَرقِيٌّ belly dancing
حَلَبَةُ الرَّقصِ dance floor
رَقْصَةٌ (رَقْصاتٌ) dance

ر ك ز

رَكَزَ – يركِزُ to plant in the ground; to fix or embed firmly
تَرَكَّزَ – يَتَرَكَّزُ to concentrate
رَكيزَةٌ (رَكائزُ) treasure; support, post, pillar
مَركَزٌ (مَراكِزُ) centre, office; station, post; basis
مَركَزٌ رياضِيٌّ sports centre

س ل و

سلا – يسلو to forget
سَلَّى – يُسَلِّي to comfort, console, or cheer someone up; to distract
تَسَلَّى – يَتَسَلَّى to delight in or have fun; to find comfort
تَسْلِيَةٌ (تَسالٍ) consolation; amusement, fun, distraction
مُسَلٍّ amusing, entertaining

ص ح ب

صَحِبَ – يَصحَبُ to be a companion, associate, or friend
صاحَبَ – يُصاحِبُ to keep company
اِصطَحَبَ – يَصطَحِبُ to accompany or escort
صُحبَةٌ friendship, company; companions, associates
الصَّحابَةُ companions of the Prophet Mohammad
مُصاحَبَةٌ company; companionship, escort
صاحِبٌ (أَصحابٌ) friend, companion; adherent, follower

ط ر ب

طَرِبَ – يَطرَبُ to be moved, delighted, or overjoyed

116 Education

طَرَبٌ (أَطْرابٌ) joy, pleasure, amusement
آلةُ الطَّرَبِ musical instrument
مُطرِبٌ musician, singer; delightful, amusing, charming

ط ل ع

طَلَعَ – يَطلُعُ to rise or ascend; to appear or emerge
طالَعَ – يُطالِعُ to read (as a hobby), peruse, or study; to elucidate
تَطَلَّعَ – يَتَطَلَّعُ to have an eye on something; to look out for
مُطالَعةٌ (مُطالَعاتٌ) reading, perusal, study (pl: announcements)

ع ز ف

عَزَفَ – يَعزِفُ to play (an instrument); to make music; to avoid or refrain from
مِعزَفٌ (مَعازِفٌ) stringed instrument, piano
عازِفٌ performer, musician

ف ر غ

فَرَغَ – يَفرُغُ to be empty or void; to finish or terminate
فَرَّغَ – يُفَرِّغُ to empty, discharge, or unload
تَفَرَّغَ – يَتَفَرَّغُ to have leisure, to be free from work; to be idle
اِستَفرَغَ – يَستَفرِغُ to empty; to vomit; to make every effort
فَراغٌ void, empty space, gap
وقتُ الفَراغِ free time
اِستِفراغٌ vomiting; emptying
فارِغٌ empty, void, vacant

ف ك ه

فَكِهَ – يَفكَهُ to be cheerful or humorous
فَكَّهَ – يُفَكِّهُ to amuse with jokes
فُكاهةٌ joking, jesting
مُفاكَهةٌ joking, banter, kidding
فاكِهةٌ (فَواكِهُ) fruit

No root

كُرةٌ (كُراتٌ) ball
كُرةُ القَدَمِ football

Education 117

كُرَةُ السَّلَّةِ basketball
الكُرةُ الطَّائِرَةُ volleyball
الاتِّحادُ الدُّوَلِيُّ لِكُرَةِ القَدَمِ FIFA

ك ي ف

كَيَّفَ – يُكَيِّفُ to form, shape, or fashion; to adjust or regulate; to dope (drugs)
تَكَيَّفَ – يَتَكَيَّفُ to be shaped or formed; to amuse oneself; to be tipsy; to smoke (tobacco)
كَيْفَ؟ how?
كَيْفَما however
كَيْفٌ (كُيوفٌ) state, condition, mood; well-being, good humour, will (pl: narcotics)
كَيْفِيَّةٌ manner, mode, fashion; nature, state
مُكَيِّفٌ (مُكَيِّفاتٌ) air conditioning

ل ح ن

لَحَنَ – يَلْحَنُ to speak ungrammatical Arabic; to be intelligent
لَحَّنَ – يُلَحِّنُ to chant; to compose
لَحْنٌ (أَلْحانٌ / لُحونٌ) tune, melody; grammatical mistake
لَحِنٌ intelligent; sensible
تَلْحينٌ (تَلاحينُ) musical composition
مَلْحونٌ ungrammatical (language)

ل ع ب

لَعِبَ – يَلْعَبُ to drool; to play; to trick or cheat
لَعَّبَ – يُلَعِّبُ to make someone play; to wag (tail)
لاعَبَ – يُلاعِبُ to play with someone; to have fun; to jest
لَعِبٌ (أَلْعابٌ) play, game, joke, jest, fun
لَعِبُ الأَلْواحِ board game
أَلْعابٌ رِياضِيَّةٌ / أَلْعابُ القُوى / أَلْعابُ السّاحَةِ والمَيدانِ athletics
ساحَةُ الأَلْعابِ sports field, athletics field
أَلْعابُ القِتالِ martial arts
الأَلْعابُ الأُولمبِيَّةُ / الأُولمبِيادُ Olympic games
أَلْعابٌ نارِيَّةٌ fireworks
لُعْبَةٌ (لُعَبٌ) toy, doll; sport
لُعْبَةُ تِنِسِ الطّاوِلَةِ table tennis
لُعْبَةُ الرّاغبي rugby

118 Education

لُعبةُ السكواش squash
لُعابٌ saliva
أُلعوبةٌ (أَلاعيبُ) toy; play, sport
مَلعَبٌ (مَلاعِبُ) playground, stadium, theatre
لاعِبٌ player, sportsman

ل ه و / ل ه ى

لَها – يَلهو to amuse oneself or have fun; to pass time
لَهَّى – يُلهِّي to delight or amuse; to distract or divert
لَهوٌ pleasure, amusement, entertainment
لَهَوِيٌّ velar (adj)
مَلهىً (مَلاهٍ) amusement centre; fun, diversion
مَدينةُ المَلاهي fairground, amusement park
تَلهِيَةٌ distraction, diversion, amusement

ل ي ق

لاقَ – يَليقُ to be suitable, worthy, or fit
لِياقَةٌ propriety, decency; worthiness; competence, efficiency
اللِّياقَةُ البَدَنِيَّةُ physical fitness
لائِقٌ suitable, appropriate, proper
غَيْرُ لائِقٍ unsuitable

م ت ع

مَتَعَ – يَمتَعُ to carry or take away; to be strong or firm
مَتَّعَ – يُمتِّعُ to make someone enjoy; to equip, or supply
اِستَمتَعَ – يَستَمتِعُ to enjoy, savour, or relish
مُتعَةٌ (مُتَعٌ) enjoyment, pleasure, gratification
مَتاعٌ (أَمتِعَةٌ) pleasure, gratification; an object of delight; goods, luggage, gear
أَمتِعَةُ السَّفَرِ luggage
اِستِمتاعٌ / تَمَتُّعٌ enjoyment
مُمتِعٌ pleasant, enjoyable

م ر س

مارَسَ – يُمارِسُ to exercise; to pursue or practise
مُمارَسَةٌ pursuit; exercise, execution, implementation
تَمَرُّسٌ practising

م ر ن

مَرَنَ – يَمرُنُ to be flexible or elastic; to be accustomed
مَرَّنَ – يُمَرِّنُ to train; to accustom; to get used to
تَمَرَّنَ – يَتَمَرَّنُ to become accustomed; to exercise or practise; to be trained
مَرِنٌ flexible, elastic, supple
مُرونَةٌ flexibility, elasticity, plasticity, agility
تَمْرينٌ (تَمْريناتٌ/تَمارينُ) practice, training, exercise, drills
تَمَرُّنٌ exercise, practice

م ز ح

مَزَحَ – يَمزَحُ to joke or make fun
مَزْحٌ/مُزاحٌ/مُزاحَةٌ joking; joke, jest, fun
مَزَّاحٌ joker

م ض ى

مَضى – يَمضي to leave; to pass or elapse; to terminate; to carry out
أمضى – يُمضي to spend time; to perform or accomplish; to terminate
مَضاءٌ sharpness; wisdom
تَمضِيَةٌ completion; accomplishment; passing of time
ماضٍ sharp, cutting, acute; effective; past, bygone
الماضي the past tense, the perfect tense

ن د و

نَدى – يَندَى to call or summon; to assemble or convene; to be moist
نَدّى – يُنَدّي to moisten
نادى – يُنادي to exclaim, shout, or call out; to announce; to summon
تنادى – يَتَنادى to get together, meet, or assemble; to form a club
نَدْوَةٌ seminar; council; club, group
نَدىً (أنداءٌ) dew; moisture; generosity, liberality (also a girl's name in the singular)
نِداءٌ (نِداءاتٌ) shout, call, exclamation; summons, appeal
مُناداةٌ calling, shouting; announcement
نادٍ (أنديَةٌ/نَوادٍ) club, centre, association; vocative (grammar)
نادٍ رياضيٌّ sports centre
مُنادٍ caller, crier

ن ز ه

نَزُهَ – يَنْزُهُ to be far; to be untouched or unblemished; to be free
تَنَزَّهَ – يَتَنَزَّهُ to go for a walk or stroll; to enjoy oneself
نَزِيهٌ (نُزَهاءُ) pure, blameless, decent, honourable
نُزْهَةٌ (نُزْهاتٌ) amusement, pleasure, recreation; a walk or stroll; excursion
مُتَنَزَّهٌ (مُتَنَزَّهاتٌ) recreation ground, a park; a walk or stroll

ن غ م

نَغَمَ – يَنْغَمُ to hum or sing a tune
نَغَمَةٌ (نَغَماتٌ) melody, song; inflection, intonation; musical note
نَغَمٌ (أَنْغامٌ) melody, tune; voice; sound, tone (also girl's name in the singular)

ن ك ت

نَكَتَ – يَنْكُتُ to scratch up (the ground); to think deeply
نَكَّتَ – يُنَكِّتُ to crack jokes, poke fun, or ridicule
نُكْتَةٌ (نُكَتٌ/نِكاتٌ) joke, witticism; anecdote
حاضِرُ النُّكْتَةِ quick-witted
نَكَّاتٌ/مُنَكِّتٌ witty, humorous; joker

ه ر ج

هَرَجَ – يَهْرِجُ to be excited or agitated
هَرَّجَ – يُهَرِّجُ to make someone drunk; to joke or make fun
هَرْجٌ excitement, agitation; disorder, confusion
مُهَرِّجٌ jester, clown
هَرْجٌ وَمَرْجٌ confusion, turmoil

ه و ى

هَوى – يَهْوي to drop, fall, or topple; to love or like; to take up as a hobby
هَوَّى – يُهَوِّي to air or ventilate; to expose to the wind
هاوى – يُهاوي to humour; to flatter
اسْتَهْوى – يَسْتَهْوي to attract someone, to seduce, tempt, or entice
هُوَّةٌ (هُوىً/هُوَّاتٌ) gap; abyss, hole; pit, ditch
هَوىً (أَهْواءٌ) love, affection, passion; wish, desire
هَواءٌ (أَهْواءٌ) air, atmosphere; wind; weather, climate

Education 121

هِوَايَةٌ (هِوَايَاتٌ) hobby; amateur sport or art
مَارَسَ هِوَايَةً to pursue a hobby
هَوَّايَةٌ (هَوَّايَاتٌ) fan, ventilator
اِسْتِهْوَاءٌ fascination, captivation; temptation
هَاوٍ (هُوَاةٌ) sinking; in love; lover

و ل ي

وَلِيَ – يَلِي to be near someone, to border or be adjacent to; to be friends with
وَلَّى – يُوَلِّي to turn, avoid, or shun; to appoint as governor or ruler; to entrust
وَالَى – يُوَالِي to be a friend, helper, or patron
تَوَلَّى – يَتَوَلَّى to occupy, seize, or control; to be entrusted or to take charge
اِسْتَوْلَى – يَسْتَوْلِي to take possession, capture, or confiscate; to overpower
وَلِيٌّ (أَوْلِيَاءُ) near, close; sponsor, legal guardian, patron, next of kin
وَلِيُّ الْعَهْدِ heir, crown prince
وَلِيُّ الأَمْرِ legal guardian, ruler
وَلَاءٌ friendship, amity, fidelity, good will
وِلَايَةٌ (وِلَايَاتٌ) sovereign power, rule, government; state, province
أَوْلَوِيَّةٌ (أَوْلَوِيَّاتٌ) priority; essential component or element
عَلَى التَّوَالِي consecutively, continuously
وَالٍ (وُلَاةٌ) ruler, governor, executive; leading, managing
اِسْتِيلَاءٌ appropriation, capture
مُتَوَالٍ successive, consecutive

Words with roots that are uncommon, less frequently used, or have no root:

الْبَالِيه ballet
الْبُوقُ trumpet
الْبِيَانُو piano
الْبِيسْبُول baseball
التَّجْذِيفُ rowing
التَّرَحْلُقُ skateboarding
التَّزَلُّجُ skiing, skating
التَّزَلُّجُ الْمَائِيُّ jet skiing
التَّسَلُّقُ climbing
التَّصْوِيرُ photography
التِّنِسُ tennis

Education

الْجَرْيُ / الْعَدْوُ / الرَّكْضُ running
الْجُمْبازُ gymnastics, calisthenics, athletics
الْجُولْفُ golf
الرَّسْمُ drawing
الرَّقْصُ dancing
الرَّمايَةُ archery, shooting
الزُّمَّارَةُ clarinet
السِّباحَةُ / الْعَوْمُ swimming
السّينما cinema
الشَّطْرَنْجُ chess
الْعَدْوُ الْبَطيءُ / الْهَرْوَلَةُ jogging
الْعودُ lute
الْغَطْسُ diving
الْغِناءُ singing
الْفُروسِيَّةُ horsemanship, equitation
الْقيثارَةُ guitar
الْكَمانُ violin
الْمُبارَزَةُ fencing
الْمَسْرَحُ theatre
الْمُصارَعَةُ wrestling
الْمُلاكَمَةُ boxing
الموسيقى music
النَّايُ flute
تَسَلُّقُ الْجِبالِ mountain climbing
تَنِسُ الطَّاوِلَةِ table tennis
رَفْعُ الأَثْقالِ weightlifting
رُكوبُ الأَمْواجِ surfing
رُكوبُ الدَّرَّاجاتِ cycling

Exercises

1) Give two derived nouns for each of the following roots:

ب د أ
ج م ل
د ر س
س ك ن
ع ل م

Education 123

2) Find the roots of these words:

اِبتِدائِيٌّ
اِمتِحانٌ
تَعليمٌ
ذاكِرَةٌ
صَداقَةٌ
غابَةٌ
مُراجَعَةٌ
مُفرَداتٌ
ناجِحٌ

3) Give the singular of the following words (some may have more than one):

اِجتِماعاتٌ
أَساليبُ
بُيوتٌ
تَخَيُّلاتٌ
حِكاياتٌ
صَفحاتٌ
صُفوفٌ
لَوْحاتٌ
مَدارِسُ

4) Translate the following sentences into Arabic:

a) Students must register for ID cards at the start of the academic year.
b) I don't know where the teacher is.
c) The entrance exam is in March, but the final exam is in July.
d) My sister is a genius.
e) They neglected their duties.

5) Translate the following sentences into English:

- أَبَى الطّالِبُ أَنْ يَدرُسَ.
- تَدرُسُ أُختي الأَدَبَ المُقارنَ في جامِعَةِ باريس.
- أَصبَحَ المُؤَلِّفُ مَشهوراً جِدّاً.
- هُوَ وَلَدٌ مُهمِلٌ.
- تَرجَمَت البِنتُ المُحاضَرةَ لِلتِلميذِ العَرَبيِّ الجَديدِ.
- مَمنوع التَّدخين في الحَرَمِ الجامِعِيِّ.

6) Give synonyms of the following words:

تَفَنُّنٌ skill
طالِبٌ student, scholar

124 *Education*

عَبقَرِيٌّ a genius
غَباءٌ stupidity

Notes

1 The Arabic language uses synonyms and near synonyms stylistically to convey a single meaning.
2 Note that although the singular is feminine, grammatically it is used for both masculine and feminine.
3 In Levantine dialects this is also used to mean 'fat'.

4 Politics علِمُ السِّياسَةِ

Government and Politics الحُكومَةُ والسِّياسَةُ

No root

إرهاصٌ (إرهاصاتٌ) precursors, indicators; catalysts

أ م ر

أمَرَ – يَأمُرُ to order or command; to instruct
أمَّرَ – يُؤَمِّرُ to invest with authority; to make someone an emir
تَأمَّرَ – يَتَأمَّرُ to be imperious; to come to power
تآمَرَ – يَتآمَرُ to plot or conspire; to take counsel
أمرٌ (أوامِرُ) an order or decree; power
إمرةٌ power, influence
إمارةٌ (إماراتٌ) emirate
أميرٌ (أمَراءُ) prince, commander
أميرةٌ (أميراتٌ) princess
مُؤامَرَةٌ (مُؤامَراتٌ) plot, conspiracy
إستِمارةٌ (إستِماراتٌ) a form
مُؤتَمِرونَ / مُتآمِرونَ conspirators; members of a congress or convention
مُؤتَمَرٌ (مُؤتَمَراتٌ) conference, convention

أ م م

أمَّ – يَؤُمُّ to lead in prayer; to lead the way
أمَّمَ – يُؤَمِّمُ to nationalise
أمٌّ (أمَّهاتٌ) mother; origin, source
أمَّةٌ (أمَمٌ) a nation or people

DOI: 10.4324/9781003250890-5

126 Politics

الْأُمَمُ الْمُتَّحِدةُ United Nations (UN)
أُمِّيٌّ (أُمِّيّونَ) illiterate, uneducated
أُمومَةٌ motherhood
أَمامَ in front of, in the presence of (prep)
أَمامِيٌّ front, fore-, anterior
إمامٌ (أَئِمَّةٌ) leader; Imam, prayer leader
تَأْميمٌ nationalisation

ب د ر

بَدَرَ – يَبْدُرُ to come unexpectedly
بادَرَ – يُبادِرُ to embark; to enter
بَدْرٌ (بُدورٌ) full moon
مُبادَرَةٌ (مُبادَراتٌ) initiative, enterprise
بادِرَةٌ (بَوادِرُ) precursor, sign

No root

بَرْلَمانٌ parliament
دَوْرَةٌ بَرْلَمانِيَّةٌ parliamentary term or session

ب ط ش

بَطَشَ – يَبْطُشُ / يَبْطِشُ to attack violently or hit
بَطْشٌ power, force; tyranny

ب ع ث

بَعَثَ – يَبْعَثُ to send, dispatch, or delegate; to awaken (from death)
اِنْبَعَثَ – يَنْبَعِثُ to be sent out, dispatched, or delegated; to arise
بِعْثَةٌ (بِعْثاتٌ) mission, expedition; scholarship
مَبْعوثٌ (مَبْعوثونَ) delegate, envoy; dispatched

ب ل د

بَلَدَ – يَبْلُدُ to be stupid
تَبَلَّدَ – يَتَبَلَّدُ to become stupid; to show oneself as stupid
بَلَدٌ (بِلادٌ / بُلْدانٌ) country, town, city
بَلْدَةٌ / بَلْداتٌ town, city, rural township

Politics 127

بَلَدِيَّةٌ (بَلَدِيَّاتٌ) municipality, council
دارُ البَلَدِيَّةِ town hall, council, municipality
بَلادَةٌ stupidity, silliness

ج ب ر

جَبَرَ – يَجْبُرُ to restore; to force or compel
أجبَرَ – يُجبِرُ to force or compel
تَجَبَّرَ – يَتَجَبَّرُ to demonstrate one's strength; to oppress
جَبرٌ force, compulsion, power
عِلمُ الجَبرِ algebra
جَبّارٌ (جَبّارونَ) giant; tyrant, oppressor; omnipotent (God)
إجبارٌ compulsion, coercion
إجباريٌّ compulsory

ج ب ه

جَبَهَ – يَجبَهُ to face or confront
جابَهَ – يُجابِهُ to face or confront; to oppose or defy
جَبهَةٌ (جَبهاتٌ) front (political, military), movement; forehead
مُجابَهَةٌ confrontation, opposition
جَبهَةُ القِتالِ battlefield

ج ل س

جَلَسَ – يَجلِسُ to sit down
جَلسَةٌ (جَلساتٌ) session (parliament), seat; gathering
مَجلِسٌ (مَجالِسُ) session, meeting; commission, council
مَجلِسُ الوُزَراءِ Cabinet
مَجلِسُ الشُّيوخِ Senate
مَجلِسُ النُّوّابِ parliament, council of MPs
مَجلِسُ الأَمنِ the Security Council (UN)

ح د ا / ح د و

حَدا – يَحدو to urge, egg on, or prompt
تَحَدَّى – يَتَحَدَّى to challenge or compete; to defy or resist; to provoke or incite
تَحَدٍّ (تَحَدِّياتٌ) challenge, provocation

ح ر ر

حَرَّ – يَحِرُّ to be hot
حَرَّرَ – يُحَرِّرُ to liberate; to write or edit
تَحرَّرَ – يَتَحرَّرُ to be liberated
حَرٌّ heat, warmth
حُرٌّ (أَحْرارٌ) noble, unadulterated; a freeman; free, independent; liberal
حُرِّيَّةٌ (حُرِّيّاتٌ) freedom, liberty, independence
حُرِّيَّةُ الصَّحافةِ freedom of the press
حُرِّيَّةُ الفِكرِ freedom of thought
حُرِّيَّةُ الكلامِ freedom of speech
حُرِّيَّةُ التَّعبيرِ freedom of expression
الحُرِّيّاتُ المَدَنِيَّةُ civil liberties
حريرٌ (حرائرُ) silk
حَرارَةٌ heat, temperature; warmth; a fever
مقياسُ الحَرارَةِ thermometer
وَحْدَةٌ حَرارِيَّةٌ (حُرارِيّاتٌ)/السُّعراتُ الحَرارِيَّةِ calorie
تَحْريرٌ (تَحاريرُ) writing; freedom, liberation
حارٌّ hot
مُحرِّرٌ (مُحرِّرونَ) liberator; editor

ح ر ك

حَرَّكَ – يُحَرِّكُ to vowelise or put a vowel on a consonant; to move; to awaken
تَحرَّكَ – يَتَحرَّكُ to move or set in motion
حَرَكَةٌ (حَرَكاتٌ) vowel (grammar); movement, motion
مُحَرِّكٌ (مُحرِّكاتٌ) agent; instigator; motive, incentive; engine
مُتَحرِّكٌ vowelised (grammar); moving, mobile

ح ص ن

حَصُنَ – يَحْصُنُ to be well fortified or inaccessible; to be chaste
حَصَّنَ – يُحصِّنُ to fortify; to immunise; to make inaccessible
تَحَصَّنَ – يَتَحَصَّنُ to be fortified or secure
حِصْنٌ (حُصونٌ) stronghold, fortress; protection
حِصانٌ (حُصُنٌ) horse, stallion
حَصينٌ inaccessible, fortified; strong, secured; immune
أبو الحُصَيْنِ fox

Politics 129

حَصانةٌ (حَصاناتٌ) immunity, strength
حَصانةٌ دُبْلوماسِيَّةٌ diplomatic immunity
تَحْصينٌ (تَحْصيناتٌ) fortification, entrenchment
تَحَصُّنٌ protection, safeguarding
مُحَصَّنٌ fortified, immune

ح ك م

(Full treatment in Law chapter)

حَكَمَ – يحكُمُ to rule or govern; to judge; to sentence
حُكْمٌ (أحكامٌ) verdict; rule, order, law
حُكْمُ القانونِ rule of law
حُكْمٌ عُرفيٌّ martial law
حُكومَةٌ (حُكوماتٌ) government
مُوَظَّفٌ حُكوميٌّ civil servant
دائِرَةٌ حُكومِيَّةٌ governmental department
غيرُ حكوميٍّ non-governmental
مُنَظَّمةٌ غيرُ الحُكومِيَّةِ non-governmental organisation (NGO)
تَحَكُّمٌ rule, dominion, control
حاكِمٌ (حُكّامٌ) a ruler or judge; ruling
الأسْرةُ الحاكِمَةُ ruling family

خ ط ط

خَطَّ – يَخُطُّ to outline, sketch, or write
خَطَّطَ – يُخَطِّطُ to plan; to survey
خَطٌّ (خُطوطٌ) line, stroke; script, calligraphy
خُطَّةٌ (خُطَطٌ) plan, project
خُطَّةُ الطَّوارِئ emergency plan
خَطّاطٌ calligrapher
تَخطيطٌ planning, designing
تَخطيطٌ تَنْفيذيٌّ operational planning
مُخَطَّطٌ (مُخَطَّطاتٌ) planned; controlled (pl: plans, sketches; maps)

No root

دُسْتورٌ (دَساتيرُ) constitution
دُسْتوريٌّ constitutional

130 Politics

غَيْرُ دُسْتُورِيٍّ unconstitutional
النِّظامُ الدُّسْتُورِيُّ constitutional government
القانونُ الدُّسْتُورِيُّ constitutional law
حكومةٌ دُسْتُورِيَّةٌ constitutional government

د و ل

دالَ – يَدولُ to take turns or alternate
داوَلَ – يُداوِلُ to alternate; to discuss
دَوْلَةٌ (دُوَلٌ) state, country
دَوْلَةُ الرَّفاهِ utopia; welfare state
دُوَلُ الْخَليجِ the Gulf States
جامِعةُ الدُّوَلِ الْعَرَبِيَّةِ the Arab League
الدُّوَلُ الْعُظْمَى / الدُّوَلُ الْكُبْرى the Superpowers
الدُّوَلُ النَّامِيَةُ developing countries
الدَّوْلَةُ الإِسْلامِيَّةُ / داعِش Islamic State (ISIS), Daesh
مُداوَلَةٌ (مُداوَلاتٌ) negotiation, deliberation
تَداوُلٌ alternation, rotation; circulation (blood, money)
مُتَداوَلٌ current, in circulation, valid

No root

ذو (ذوو) possessor or owner of; endowed (m)
ذو مَكانةٍ influential
ذاتُ (ذواتُ) possessor or owner of; endowed (f)
الذَّاتِيَّةُ subjectivity; personality
الْحُكْمُ الذَّاتِيُّ self-determination, autonomy
الذَّاتُ الإِلهِيَّةُ God

ر أ س

رَأَسَ – يَرْأَسُ to be in charge; to head or lead
اِرْتَأَسَ – يَرْتَأَسُ to become or be the head
رَأْسٌ (رُؤوسٌ) head; leader; top, peak
قَطْعُ الرَّأْسِ beheading
رَأْسمالٌ (رَساميلُ) capital
رَأْسمالِيٌّ capitalist
الرَّأْسمالِيَّةُ capitalism

Politics

رَئِيسٌ (رُؤَساءُ) head, director, president
مَرؤوسٌ (مَرؤوسونَ) subordinates
رِئاسَةٌ leadership, presidency
الرَّئِيسُ the boss
رَئِيسٌ principal
المَقَرُّ الرَّئِيسُ head office
رَئِيسُ الوُزَراءِ prime minister

ر د د

رَدَّ – يَرُدُّ to bring back; to repel or resist
اِرتَدَّ – يَرتَدُّ to withdraw or retreat; to abandon (religion, principles)
رَدٌّ (رُدودٌ) answer, reply; rejection
مَرَدٌّ underlying factor
رِدَّةٌ apostasy
تَرديدٌ repetition, reiteration
تَرَدُّدٌ hesitation, indecision
مُرتَدٌّ renegade; apostate
مَردودٌ yield, returns

ر س خ

رَسَخَ – يرسَخُ to be deeply rooted; to be conversant
رَسَّخَ – يُرَسِّخُ to entrench or secure; to establish
راسِخٌ deep-rooted, stable; conversant

ر ك ز

رَكَزَ – يَركِزُ to set up; to embed firmly
رَكَّزَ – يُرَكِّزُ to concentrate (mind); to position or embed firmly
تَرَكَّزَ – يَتَرَكَّزُ to concentrate
تَركيزٌ setting up, installation; concentration, focus
مَركَزٌ (مَراكِزُ) centre; station, post, office
مَركَزُ حَجزٍ remand centre
مَركَزُ الشُّرطَةِ police station
مَركَزِيٌّ central
لامَركَزِيٌّ decentralised

س ف ر

سَفَرَ – يُسْفِرُ to unveil, to remove the veil
سَفَّرَ – يُسَفِّرُ to unveil or uncover; to dispatch or send away
سافَرَ – يُسافِرُ to travel; to depart
سَفَرٌ (أَسْفارٌ) travel, trip; departure
سَفْرَةٌ (سَفَراتٌ) trip, journey
سُفْرَةٌ (سُفَرٌ) dining table
سَفيرٌ (سُفَراءُ) ambassador
سَفارَةٌ (سَفاراتٌ) embassy
مُسافِرٌ (مُسافِرونَ) traveller; passenger

س ق ط

سَقَطَ – يَسْقُطُ to fall, drop, or stumble; to be abolished
أَسْقَطَ – يُسْقِطُ to drop (sth); to shoot down; to suffer a miscarriage; to eliminate
تَساقَطَ – يَتَساقَطُ to collapse or fall down; to come gradually
أَسْقَطَ النِظامَ to overthrow or topple the regime
سَقَطٌ (أَسْقاطٌ) rubbish, junk
سُقوطٌ collapse, ruin, decline, downfall
إِسْقاطٌ overthrow; miscarriage; abortion
ساقِطٌ (سُقّاطٌ) fallen, vile, disreputable

س ل ط

سَلَّطَ – يُسَلِّطُ to give power or establish as ruler; to impose, inflict, or load
تَسَلَّطَ – يَتَسَلَّطُ to exercise power or to command; to overcome
سُلْطَةٌ (سُلْطاتٌ) power, might, authority; sovereign power
سُلْطَةٌ قَضائِيَّةٌ judicial power
سُلْطَةٌ تَشْريعِيَّةٌ legislative power
سُلْطَةٌ مُطْلَقَةٌ absolute power
تَسَلُّطٌ dominion, control, authority

س و د

سادَ – يَسودُ to prevail; to be or become master or lord; to rule or govern
سَيَّدَ – يُسَيِّدُ to make someone master or chief
سَيِّدٌ (أَسْيادٌ) master, sir, gentleman
سَيِّدَةٌ (سَيِّداتٌ) lady, mistress

Politics   133

سِيادةٌ command, mastery; sovereignty, rule, dominion
سائِدٌ prevailing
دَولةٌ ذاتُ سِيادةٍ sovereign state

س و س

ساسَ – يَسوسُ to dominate, govern, or rule; to guide; to administer
سَوَّسَ – يُسَوِّسُ to be or become worm-eaten, to rot or decay (of teeth, bones)
سوسٌ (سِيسانٌ) woodworm
سوسٌ licorice
سِياسَةٌ (سِياساتٌ) politics; policy; administration
سِياسِيٌّ (سِياسِيّونَ) politician, political; diplomatic
حِزبٌ سِياسِيٌّ political party
السِّياسَةُ الخارجِيَّةُ foreign policy
جيوسياسِيَّةٌ geopolitical
شِقاقٌ سِياسِيٌّ / خِلافٌ سِياسِيٌّ / نِزاعٌ سِياسِيٌّ political dissension
واضِعو السِّياساتِ policymakers
ناشِطٌ سِياسِيٌّ political activist
دَوائِرُ سِياسِيَّةٌ political circles
اللُّجوءُ السِّياسِيُّ political asylum

س ي ط ر

سَيطَرَ – يُسَيطِرُ (على) to control or dominate
تَسَيطَرَ – يَتَسَيطَرُ to control or dominate
سَيطَرَةٌ rule, domination, supremacy, control
مُسَيطِرٌ ruler, sovereign

ش ر ط

شَرَطَ – يَشرُطُ to stipulate; to tear or make an incision
تَشَرَّطَ – يَتَشَرَّطُ to impose terms or conditions
اِشتَرَطَ – يَشتَرِطُ to stipulate
شَرطٌ (شُروطٌ) condition; stipulation; cut, incision
بِشرطِ أنْ .. on the condition that
جُملَةٌ شَرطِيَّةٌ conditional clause
مِشرَطٌ (مَشارِطُ) scalpel
شَرطِيٌّ conditional

134 *Politics*

شُرْطَةٌ police
شُرْطَةُ العاصِمَةِ metropolitan police
شُرْطَةٌ عَسْكَرِيَّةٌ military police
رَئِيسُ الشُّرْطَةِ police chief
شُرطِيٌّ / ضابِطُ شُرْطَةٍ police officer
مُحَقِّقُ شُرْطَةٍ police investigation
شَرِيطٌ (شَرائِطُ / أَشْرِطَةٌ) ribbon, tape; braid
اِشْتِراطٌ (اِشْتِراطاتٌ) condition, stipulation

ش ك ل

شَكَّلَ – يُشَكِّلُ to vowel (a text); to be dubious or ambiguous
شَكَّلَ – يُشَكِّلُ to form or shape; to create; to organise; to diversify
تَشَكَّلَ – يَتَشَكَّلُ to be formed or shaped
شَكْلٌ (أَشْكالٌ) form, shape, figure; appearance; resemblance
تَشْكِيلٌ / شَكْلٌ voweling, vowelisation
تَشْكِيلٌ (تَشْكِيلاتٌ) forming; creation, formation
تَشْكِيلَةٌ selection, variety
إِشْكالٌ ambiguity; obscurity
مُشْكِلٌ / مُشْكِلَةٌ (مَشاكِلُ / مُشْكِلاتٌ) problem, difficulty

ص ع د

صَعِدَ – يَصْعَدُ to rise or ascend; to escalate
صَعَّدَ – يُصَعِّدُ to ascend; to go upstream; to escalate
تَصْعِيدٌ escalation (political)
صُعودٌ rising, lifting, ascending; boom
مِصْعَدٌ (مَصاعِدُ) elevator

ض ه د

ضَهَدَ – يَضْهَدُ to suppress, oppress, or persecute
اِضْطَهَدَ – يَضْطَهِدُ to suppress, oppress, or persecute
اِضْطِهادٌ (اِضْطِهاداتٌ) persecution, oppression
مُضْطَهِدٌ oppressor, persecutor
مُضْطَهَدٌ oppressed, persecuted

Politics   135

طغو / طغى

طَغَى – يَطغَى to be tyrannical or to terrorise; to dominate; to flood or inundate
طُغْيانٌ flood; tyranny, oppression; terrorisation
طاغٍ (طُغاةٌ) tyrant, oppressor
طاغِيَةٌ tyrant, oppressor, bully

طول

طالَ – يَطولُ to be long, to extend or lengthen; to excel
طَوَّلَ – يُطَوِّلُ to lengthen, extend, or prolong; to be detailed
إستَطالَ – يَستَطيلُ to be long; to be overbearing or presumptuous
طَوْلٌ might, power
طولٌ (أَطوالٌ) length, size, height
طَويلٌ (طِوالٌ) tall, long
طائِلَةٌ might, power; retaliation
مُستَطيلٌ rectangle, oblong; elongated

عرض

عَرَضَ – يَعرِضُ to exhibit or demonstrate; to offer or suggest (sth); to be wide
عارَضَ – يُعارِضُ to resist, oppose, or contradict; to avoid
تَعَرَّضَ – يَتَعَرَّضُ to resist, oppose, or object; to expose; to risk
إعتَرَضَ – يَعتَرِضُ to object, protest, or resist; to hinder
إستَعرَضَ – يَستَعرِضُ to review or inspect; to consider
عَرضٌ (عُروضٌ) an offer or tender; exhibition or show; breadth or width
العَرضُ والطَّلَبُ supply and demand
عَرضُ أزياءٍ fashion show
عَرضُ حالٍ / عَرضحالٌ petition
عِرضٌ (أعراضٌ) honour, dignity
عَرَضٌ (أعراضٌ) accident; symptom (of disease)
عَريضٌ (عِراضٌ) broad, extensive
عَريضَةٌ (عَرائِضُ) petition
مَعرِضٌ (معارِضُ) exhibition, show; a stage or showroom
مُعارَضَةٌ opposition, resistance; contradiction
تَعارُضٌ conflict, clash; contradiction
إعتِراضٌ (إعتِراضاتٌ) objection, protest; resistance; exception

اِستِعراضٌ parade; examination; survey, review
عارِضٌ (عوارِضُ) obstacle, impediment; an attack or fit
مُعارَضَةٌ opposition, resistance; contradiction
مُعتَرِضٌ lying across something; opponent, antagonist

No root

عُضوٌ (أعضاءٌ) member, limb, organ
أعضاءُ الجِسمِ organs
غيرُ عُضوٍ non-member
أعضاءُ البَرلَمانِ members of parliament
عُضوِيٌّ organic
غيرُ عُضوِيٍّ inorganic
عُضوِيَّةٌ (عُضوِيّاتٌ) membership; organism

ع م ل

(Full treatment in Work chapter)

عَمِلَ – يَعمَلُ to do or act; to work or operate; to produce; to endeavour
عامَلَ – يُعامِلُ to treat or act towards; to trade or deal with; to proceed
تَعامَلَ – يَتَعامَلُ to trade or do business with
اِستَعمَلَ – يَستَعمِلُ to use or operate
عَمَلٌ work, practice, activity; production, operation; an act
تَعَطَّلَ عَنِ العَمَلِ to be unemployed
عَمَلِيٌّ practical; relating to work
عَمَلِيَّةٌ (عَمَلِيّاتٌ) activity, work; operation, process, technique; surgery
عَمَلِيَّةٌ سِرِّيَّةٌ covert operation
عَمَلِيَّةُ سَلامٍ peace process
عَمَلِيّاتٌ اِستِشهادِيَّةٌ martyr bombings
عَمَلِيّاتٌ اِنتِحارِيَّةٌ suicide bombings
عُملَةٌ (عُملاتٌ) money, currency
حِزبُ العُمّالِ Labour Party
عَميلٌ (عُملاءُ) agent, representative; ally; customer; patient
مُعامَلَةٌ (مُعامَلاتٌ) treatment
تَعامُلٌ (تَعامُلاتٌ) transactions, dealings; trade, business
اِستِعمالٌ use, application

Politics 137

عامِلٌ (عَوامِلُ) factor
مُستَعمَلٌ used

No root

عاهِلٌ (عَواهِلُ) monarch, ruler

No root

فِئَةٌ (فِئاتٌ) group, class; band; faction
فِئَوِيٌّ factional
فِئَوِيَّةٌ factionalism

ف ر ق

فَرَقَ – يَفْرُقُ to separate or divide; to differentiate or discriminate
فَرَّقَ – يُفَرِّقُ to separate or divide; to differentiate or discriminate
تَفَرَّقَ – يَتَفَرَّقُ to be or become separated; divided, separated
فَرِّقْ تَسُدْ divide and rule
فَرْقٌ (فُروقٌ) difference; division
فِرْقَةٌ (فِرَقٌ) part, portion, section; division
فُرْقَةٌ division, separation
فَريقٌ (فُروقٌ/فُرَقاءُ) team, party, faction, unit
فَريقُ تَفْكيرٍ think tank
فَريقُ عملٍ task force
فُرْقانٌ proof, evidence
الفُرْقانُ the Quran
مَفرَقٌ (مَفارِقُ) crossing, intersection
تَفرِقَةٌ separation, partition, division
تَفرِقَةٌ عُنصُرِيَّةٌ racism, racial discrimination
فِراقٌ separation, difference, parting
مُتَفَرِّقٌ scattered, dispersed; sporadic

ف ع ل

فَعَلَ – يَفعلُ to act or do; to affect or have an influence
تَفاعَلَ – يَتَفاعَلُ to interact; to combine
اِنفَعَلَ – يَنفعِلُ to be done; to be or become affected; to be agitated or excited

فِعْلٌ (أَفْعالٌ) verb (grammar); activity, work, action; impact
فِعْلِيٌّ actual, real, factual
فَعْلَةٌ (فَعَلاتٌ) deed, act
فَعّالٌ effective; actual
فَعّالِيَةٌ efficiency
تَفاعُلٌ (تَفاعُلاتٌ) interaction, interplay; chemical reaction
تَفاعُلٌ مُتسلسِلٌ / تَفاعُلٌ تَسلسُلِيٌّ chain reaction
اِنْفِعالٌ (اِنْفِعالاتٌ) agitation, irritation, excitement
فاعِلٌ (فاعِلونَ) effective, efficient; actor, perpetrator
فاعِلٌ (فَعَلَةٌ) workers, labourers; subject of a verbal clause
اِسمُ الْفاعِلِ active participle
فاعِلِيَةٌ effectiveness; activity
مَفعولٌ (مَفاعيلُ) object (grammar); effect, impact, or impression; validity
مَفعولٌ بِهِ object (grammar)
اِسمُ الْمَفعولِ passive participle
بالْفِعلِ / فِعلًا indeed, really
مُنْفَعِلٌ excited, agitated
مُفتَعَلٌ artificial, fabricated, forged

ف و ض

فَوَّضَ – يُفَوِّضُ to entrust; to authorise; to commit; to consign
فاوَضَ – يُفاوِضُ to negotiate; to confer
تَفاوَضَ – يَتَفاوَضُ to negotiate with each other; to confer
فَوْضى chaos, confusion
فَوْضى سِياسِيَّةٌ political anarchy
فَوْضَوِيٌّ anarchist; chaotic
تَفويضٌ (تَفويضاتٌ) power of attorney; entrusting; delegation; authority
مُفاوَضَةٌ (مُفاوَضاتٌ) negotiations, talk
مُفَوَّضٌ (مُفَوَّضونَ) commissioner; agent, proxy

ق ل ل

قَلَّ – يَقِلُّ to be small, insignificant, or scarce
قَلَّلَ – يُقَلِّلُ to diminish, decrease, or reduce
اِستَقَلَّ – يَستَقِلُّ to be independent; to despise or undervalue; to transport
قِلَّةٌ a few; insignificance; lack, want
قَليلٌ (أَقِلّاءُ / قَلائِلُ / قِلالٌ) little, few; insignificant

Politics   139

أَقَلِّيَّةٌ (أَقَلِّيَّاتٌ) small number, minority
حُكْمُ الأَقَلِّيَّةِ minority rule
أَقَلِّيَّةٌ عُنْصُرِيَّةٌ ethnic minority
اِسْتِقْلالٌ independence
مُسْتَقِلٌّ independent, autonomous; separate

ق م ع

قَمَعَ – يَقْمَعُ to suppress, repress, or prevent; to tame
قَمْعٌ oppression, repression; crackdown
نِظَامٌ قَمْعِيٌّ oppressive regime

No root

القُنْصُلُ the consul
قُنْصُلِيٌّ consular
قُنْصُلِيَّةٌ (قُنْصُلِيَّاتٌ) consulate
قُنْصُلِيَّةٌ عَامَّةٌ consulate general

ق و د

قَادَ – يَقُودُ to lead; to guide, steer, or pilot; to pimp
اِنْقَادَ – يَنْقَادُ to be led or guided; to follow or obey
قَوْدٌ leadership; pimping
قَوَّادٌ pimp
قِيَادَةٌ guidance, leadership
بِقِيَادَةِ under the leadership of (plus idafa)
قَائِدٌ (قُوَّادٌ) guide, leader; commander

No root

الكَابِنِتْ the Cabinet

No root

الكِنِيسِتْ the Knesset

No root

الكُونْغِرِس Congress

ل ح ق

لَحِقَ – يَلْحَقُ to follow or keep close; to overtake; to cling or join
لاحَقَ – يُلاحِقُ to follow, pursue, or chase
أَلْحَقَ – يُلْحِقُ to attach; to be annexed
إِلْحاقٌ attachment, annexation; enrolment
اِلْتِحاقٌ (بِـ) enrolment (in); affiliation (with)
لاحِقٌ subsequent, following; attached
مُلْحَقٌ (مُلْحَقونَ) attaché; assistant

No root

اللّوبي a lobby
اللّوبيّونَ / أَعْضاءُ اللّوبي lobbyists

م ث ل

مَثَلَ – يَمْثُلُ to resemble; to copy; to compare or liken
مَثَّلَ – يُمَثِّلُ to make similar; to liken; to represent; to act
تَمَثَّلَ – يَتَمَثَّلُ to become similar or imitate; to assimilate or absorb
مِثْلٌ (أَمْثالٌ) resemblance, similarity
مِثْلَما as (conj)
المِثْلِيَّةُ homosexuality
مَثَلٌ (أَمْثالٌ) metaphor, simile, proverb; example
مَثَلًا / على سبيلِ المِثالِ for example
مِثالٌ (أَمْثِلَةٌ) simile, parable, allegory; example; pattern
مِثالِيٌّ exemplary; allegorical, model
مَثيلٌ (مُثُلٌ) like, similar
تِمْثالٌ (تَماثيلُ) statue, sculpture
تَمْثيلٌ (تَماثيلُ) representation; portrayal
تَمْثيلٌ نِسْبِيٌّ proportional representation
تَمْثيلٌ acting
تَمْثيلِيَّةٌ series; play
مُمَثِّلٌ (مُمَثِّلونَ) representative, deputy; actor

م ك ن

مَكُنَ – يَمْكُنُ to be or become strong; to have power
مَكَّنَ – يُمَكِّنُ to strengthen or consolidate; to make possible
تَمَكَّنَ – يَتَمَكَّنُ to be able to; to have influence; to have or gain power

Politics

تَمْكينٌ strengthening, consolidation
إمْكانٌ power, ability; faculty
إمْكانيَّةٌ (إمْكانيّاتٌ) possibilities
تَمَكُّنٌ power, authority, self-control
مُمْكِنٌ possible, conceivable
مِنَ المُمْكِنِ it is possible
غَيْرُ مُمْكِنٍ / مِن غَيرِ المُمكِنِ not possible

م ل ك

مَلَكَ – يَمْلِكُ to rule or dominate; to acquire, possess, or seize
تَمَلَّكَ – يَتَمَلَّكُ to appropriate or seize
امْتَلَكَ – يَمْتَلِكُ to possess or own; to gain or acquire; to dominate or master
مُلْكٌ reign, dominion, power
مِلْكٌ (أَملاكٌ) property, possessions, goods, wealth
مَلِكٌ (مُلوكٌ) king, monarch
مَلَكِيَّةٌ monarchy, royalty
مَلِكَةٌ (مَلِكاتٌ) queen
مَلَكٌ / ملاكٌ (مَلائِكَةٌ) angel
مِلْكِيَّةٌ (مِلْكِيّاتٌ) property, ownership
مَمْلَكَةٌ (مَمالِكُ) kingdom, empire, country
تَمَلُّكٌ taking possession; ownership, domination, control
امْتِلاكٌ occupancy; possession; domination, control
مَمْلوكٌ (مَماليكُ) owned, belonging to; Mameluke
مُمْتَلَكٌ (مُمْتَلَكاتٌ) owned; property, estates

ن د ب

نَدَبَ – يَنْدُبُ to mourn or lament; to detail; to delegate or commission
انْتَدَبَ – يَنْتَدِبُ to appoint, commission, authorise, or empower; to detail
نَدْبٌ lamentation; deputation, delegation; authorisation
انْتِدابٌ (انْتِداباتٌ) mandate; assignment, mission; detailing; appointment
مَنْدوبٌ (مَنْدوبونَ) agent, delegate, representative; lamented
مَنْدوبيَّةٌ delegation; High Commission

ن ز ل

نَزَلَ – يَنْزِلُ to go down, descend, or fall; to camp or lodge
نَزَّلَ – يُنَزِّلُ to make come down; to dismount; to reveal; to lower

142 Politics

تَنازَلَ – يَتَنازَلُ to renounce, waive, or relinquish; to resign
نُزُلٌ (نُزُولٌ) quarters, lodging; hotel
نَزلَةٌ (نَزَلاتٌ) cold, catarrh
نُزُولٌ descending, dismounting; surrender
مَنزِلٌ (منازِلٌ) house; stopping place
مَنزِلَةٌ status, rank; dignity
تَنازُلٌ (تَنازُلاتٌ) concessions; transfer; surrender; abdication

ن ظ م

نَظَمَ – يَنْظِمُ to organise or arrange; to classify or group; to write poetry
تَنَظَّمَ – يَتَنَظَّمُ to be well arranged or well organised
نِظامٌ (نُظُمٌ / أَنظِمَةٌ) system, method; rule, order, law; organisation; regime
نِظامُ الأَكثَرِيَّةِ majority system
تَغييرُ النِّظامِ regime change
نِظامٌ سِياسِيٌّ political regime
تَنظيمٌ (تَنظيماتٌ) arrangement, organisation; reform; regulation
اِنتِظامٌ order, regularity; systematic
مُنظَّمَةٌ (مُنظَّماتٌ) organisation
مُنظَّمَةُ حِلفِ شَمالِ الأَطلَسِيِّ North Atlantic Treaty Organization (NATO)
مُنتَظِمٌ regular, even, uniform

ن ه ز

نَهَزَ – يَنهَزُ to push, shove, or thrust; to drive or urge on
اِنتَهَزَ – يَنتَهِزُ (فُرْصَةً) to seize or take (opportunity)
اِنتِهازِيٌّ opportunist

ن و ب

نابَ – يَنوبُ to act as representative; to substitute or replace; to frequent
نَوَّبَ – يُنَوِّبُ to deputise; to delegate or commission
ناوبَ – يُناوِبُ to alternate; to take shifts
نَوْبَةٌ (نَوَبٌ) change, rotation, shift; a calamity or misfortune
نَوْبَةٌ (نَوْباتٌ) a fit or attack; a crisis
نِيابَةٌ representation; replacement, substitution; proxy
بِالنِّيابَةِ عَن on behalf of
نِيابِيٌّ parliamentary; representative

Politics 143

مُناوَبةٌ alternation, rotation; successively, in shifts
بِالتَّناوُبِ successively, alternately
نائِبٌ (نُوَّابٌ) MP; deputy, representative, delegate
نائِبُ الرَّئيسِ deputy head
مجلِسُ النُّوَّابِ parliament
وَكيلُ النِّيابةِ public prosecutor, district attorney
مُناوِبٌ on duty

ه م ش

هَمَشَ – يَهمِشُ to bite
هامِشٌ (هَوامِشُ) margin
تَهميشٌ marginalising
على الهامِشِ on the sidelines
يضعُ على الهامِشِ to be marginalised

ه ي م ن

هَيمَنَ – يُهَيمِنُ to dominate or control; to guard or watch; to say amen
هَيمَنةٌ hegemony, control; supervision, surveillance
مُهَيمِنٌ supervising; controlling; guardian, master

و ح د

وَحَدَ – يوحِدُ to be alone; to be without equal
وَحَّدَ – يُوَحِّدُ to unify, unite, or standardise
اِتَّحَدَ – يَتَّحِدُ to be united or combined; to unite
وَحَّدَ اللهَ to declare God to be one, to be a monotheist
وَحْدةٌ (وَحْداتٌ) unit (military); oneness, unity; privacy, solitude
وَحيدٌ alone, solitary, lonely, single, individual
تَوحيدٌ union, combination, consolidation
التَّوحيد monotheism
اِتِّحادٌ (اِتِّحاداتٌ) union; concord, agreement; combination
الإتِّحادُ الأوروبِّيُ the European Union
اِتِّحادِيٌّ federal
واحِدٌ one (number); someone, somebody; separate, individual
مُتَّحِدٌ united; uniform

و ز ر

تَوَزَّرَ – يَتَوَزَّرُ to become a minister
وَزِيرٌ (وُزَرَاءُ) minister, vizier; queen (in chess)
وَزِيرُ الْخَارِجِيَّةِ foreign minister
وَزِيرُ الدَّاخِلِيَّةِ home secretary
وَزِيرُ الدِّفَاعِ defence minister
هَيْئَةُ الْوُزَرَاءِ Cabinet
وِزَارَةٌ (وِزَارَاتٌ) ministry
وِزَارَةُ الْخَارِجِيَّةِ foreign ministry
خَارِجِيٌّ external, exterior; outside
وِزَارَةُ الدَّاخِلِيَّةِ ministry of interior
دَاخِلِيٌّ internal, interior, inside
وِزَارَةُ الدِّفَاعِ ministry of defence
وِزَارَةُ الْعَدْلِ ministry of justice

و ط ن

وَطَنَ – يوطِنُ to live, reside, or stay
اِسْتَوْطَنَ – يَسْتَوْطِنُ to live, settle, or become naturalised
وَطَنٌ (أَوْطَانٌ) nation, homeland, country
وَطَنِيٌّ (وَطَنِيُّونَ) indigenous, national; patriotic, nationalist; patriot
وَطَنِيَّةٌ nationalism; patriotism
مَوْطِنٌ (مَوَاطِنُ) native land, residence, domicile
اِسْتِيطَانٌ immigration, colonisation; settling
مُوَاطِنٌ compatriot, citizen
مُسْتَوْطِنٌ (مُسْتَوْطِنُونَ) settler; domestic; resident
مُسْتَوْطَنَةٌ (مُسْتَوْطَنَاتٌ) settlement

و ف ق

وَفِقَ – يَوْفِقُ to be right, suitable, or appropriate
وَفَّقَ – يُوَفِّقُ to adapt or make suitable; to accommodate; to reconcile; to be lucky
وَافَقَ – يُوَافِقُ to befit; to agree; to be agreeable or convenient
اِتَّفَقَ – يَتَّفِقُ to agree, be consistent, or reach an agreement; to happen accidentally
وِفْقاً لِ according to
مُوَافَقَةٌ (مُوَافَقَاتٌ) agreement; analogy; suitability; consent, approval

Politics   145

تَوافُقٌ coincidence; agreement, conformity
اِتّفاقٌ (اِتّفاقاتٌ) agreement, treaty, pact; coincidence, accident
اِتّفاقِيَّةٌ (اِتّفاقِيَّاتٌ) agreement, treaty, convention

و ق ع

وَقَعَ – يَقَعُ to fall or drop; to occur or happen; to arrive; to meet
وَقَّعَ – يُوَقِّعُ to let fall; to sign (sth); to carry out; to register; to seize or confiscate
تَوَقَّعَ – يَتَوَقَّعُ to expect, anticipate, or dread
وَقْعَةٌ (وَقَعاتٌ) a fall, drop, tumble; an incident
وُقوعٌ occurrence, happening
مَوقِعٌ (مَواقِعُ) place, spot, location; event; website
تَحْديدُ المَوقِعِ الجُغرافِيِّ geolocation
مَوقِعَةٌ (مَواقِعُ) battlefield; a battle or combat
تَوقيعٌ (تَوقيعاتٌ) performance; registration; recording (pl: signature)
واقِعُ الحالِ state of affairs
واقِعِيٌّ realistic, real
واقِعِيَّةٌ reality
مُوَقَّعٌ signed, recorded, registered
مُتَوَقَّعٌ expected

Political Parties and Ideologies الأحزابُ السِّياسِيَّةُ والايديولوجيات

No root

اِمبراطوريٌّ imperialist
اِمبراطورِيَّةٌ empire; imperialism
اِمبراطورٌ (أَباطِرَةٌ) emperor

ب د د

بَدَّ – يَبِدُّ to distribute, spread, or disperse
اِستَبَدَّ – يَستَبِدُّ to rule tyrannically; to be independent; to be obstinate
بُدٌّ way out, escape
لا بُدَّ inevitably, definitely
اِستِبدادٌ tyranny, oppression, autocracy
اِستِبداديٌّ arbitrary; autocratic, despotic
الاِستِبداديَّةُ authoritarianism

146 *Politics*

No root

بوليس police
دَوْلَةٌ بوليسيَّةٌ police state

No root

الْبيروقراطيَّةُ bureaucracy

ج د د

جَدَّ – يَجِدُّ to be new; to be serious; to take seriously or strive earnestly
جَدَّدَ – يُجَدِّدُ to renew or fix; to limit; to establish; to be an innovator
تَجَدَّدَ – يَتَجَدَّدُ to be renewed; to revive
جَدٌّ (جُدُودٌ) good fortune
جداً very, much
جِدِّيٌّ serious
جَديدٌ (جُدُدٌ) new, recent, modern; unprecedented
تَجْديدٌ renewal, modernisation; innovation
مُجَدِّدٌ (مُجَدِّدونَ) modernists, reformists; innovator

ج م ه ر

جَمْهَرَ – يُجَمْهِرُ to gather, collect, or assemble
تَجَمْهَرَ – يَتَجَمْهَرُ to gather or flock together
جَمْهَرَةٌ crowd, multitude; the populace
جُمْهورٌ (جَماهيرُ) crowd, multitude; the public
الْجَماهيرُ the people, the masses
جُمهوريٌّ (جُمهوريّونَ) republican
جُمهوريَّةٌ (جُمهوريّاتٌ) republic
الْحِزْبُ الْجُمْهوريُّ the Republicans

ح ز ب

حَزَبَ – يَحزبُ to befall, happen, or occur
تَحَزَّبَ – يَتَحَزَّبُ to take sides; to form a party or join forces
حِزْبٌ (أحزابٌ) party, faction, group; one-sixtieth of the Quran
حِزْبٌ حاكِمٌ ruling party
حزبُ الْعُمَّالِ Labour party
حزبُ الْمُحافظينَ Conservative party

Politics 147

ح ف ظ

حَفِظَ – يَحْفَظُ to preserve, guard, or defend; to learn or observe; to comply
حافَظَ – يُحافِظُ to preserve or maintain; to supervise or control; to observe
تَحَفَّظَ – يَتَحَفَّظُ to be mindful or wary; to be on one's guard; to observe
حِفْظٌ preservation, maintenance, guarding, custody; memorisation
قَوّاتُ حِفْظِ السَّلامِ peacekeeping forces
حِفاظٌ (حِفاظاتٌ) dressing, bandage; a nappy
حَفيظٌ attentive; heedful, mindful
حَفيظَةٌ (حَفائِظُ) grudge, resentment
مَحفظَةٌ (مَحفظاتٌ / مَحافِظُ) folder, bag
حِفاظٌ defence, protection, guarding
مُحافَظَةٌ (مُحافَظاتٌ) district; guarding, preservation; defence
حافِظٌ (حُفّاظٌ) Hafiz;[1] guardian, custodian, caretaker
مُحافِظٌ conservative; governor
مُحافِظٌ جَديدٌ neoconservative
مُتَحَفِّظٌ cautious or vigilant; sedate

No root

دِكتاتوريَّةٌ hegemony, dictatorship, monopoly
دِكتاتورٌ dictator

No root

ديموقراطِيٌّ democratic
غَيْرُ ديموقراطِيٍّ undemocratic
ديموقراطِيَّةٌ democracy
الحِزْبُ الديموقراطِيُّ / الدّيموقراطِيّونَ the Democrats

ش م ل

شَمَلَ – يَشمَلُ to comprise or include
اِشتَمَلَ – يَشتَمِلُ to comprise or include
شامِلٌ total, comprehensive, universal
شُموليَّةٌ totalitarianism
شُموليٌّ totalitarian

No root

صَهْيون Zion

148 Politics

صَهْيونِيٌّ Zionist
الصَّهْيونِيَّةُ Zionism

No root

الفاشِيَّةُ fascism

No root

اللِّيبرالِيّونَ the Liberals
اللِّيبرالِيَّةُ liberalism

No root

مَارْكسِيٌّ Marxist
المَاركسِيَّةُ Marxism

No root

النَّازِيَّةُ Nazism
النازِيَّةُ الْجَديدةُ neo-Nazism
نازِيٌّ جديدٌ neo-Nazi

ي س ر

يَسِرَ – يَيْسِرُ to be or become easy; to be small or little
يَسَّرَ – يُيَسِّرُ to level, smooth, or pave; to ease or facilitate
تَيَسَّرَ – يَتَيَسَّرُ to become easy; to be possible; to thrive or prosper
يَسارٌ left side; ease, comfort; prosperity, affluence
يَسارِيٌّ left-wing, leftist
يَسيرٌ easy; small, little, slight
مُتَيَسِّرٌ facilitated, made easy; well off
اليَسارُ the Left

ي م ن

يَمَنَ – يَيْمِنُ to be lucky or fortunate
يَمَّنَ – يُيَمِّنُ to go to the right
يُمْنٌ good fortune
اليَمنُ السَّعيدُ the Yemen

Politics 149

يَمينٌ (أَيْمانٌ) the right-hand side; an oath
يَمينيٌّ right-wing
اليَمينُ the Right

الإجراءاتُ الأمنيَّةُ Security Measures

No root

الأيديولوجيَّةُ (الأيديولوجيّاتُ) ideology

No root

البِنتاغون Pentagon

No root

الدُّبلوماسِيَّةُ diplomacy

No root

الڤيتو veto

No root

اِستراتيجيٌّ strategic
اِستراتيجِيَّةٌ strategy

أ م ن

أَمِنَ – يَأْمَنُ to be faithful, reliable, or trustworthy
أَمَّنَ – يُؤَمِّنُ to reassure; to safeguard
آمَنَ – يُؤْمِنُ to believe
أَمْنٌ/أَمانٌ safety, protection, security, shelter, peace
أَمينٌ (أُمناءُ) reliable, loyal, trustworthy
بيتٌ آمِنٌ safe house
أَمْنٌ قوميٌّ national security
تهديدٌ للأَمنِ القوميِّ national security threat
مَجْلِسُ الأَمنِ Security Council
قُوّاتُ الأَمنِ security forces
أَمنُ الدَّوْلَةِ national security

أَمِينٌ عامٌّ secretary general
آمِين amen
أَمانةٌ (أَماناتٌ) reliability, trustworthiness; deposit
إيمانٌ faith, belief (also a girl's name)
تَأْمِينٌ insurance, guarantee, warranty
مُؤْمِنٌ (مُؤْمِنونَ) faithful; a believer; Muslim

أ ه ب

أَهَّبَ – يُؤَهِّبُ to prepare or make ready
تَأَهَّبَ – يَتَأَهَّبُ to get ready
أُهْبَةٌ (أُهَبٌ) preparation, readiness; equipment, gear
تَأَهُّبٌ (تَأَهُّباتٌ) preparedness, readiness (pl: preparation)
مُتَأَهِّبٌ ready, prepared
وَضَعَ في حالةِ تَأَهُّبٍ قُصوى to put on red alert

ب غ ت

بَغَتَ – يَبْغَتُ to come unexpectedly
اِنْبَغَتَ – يَنْبَغِتُ to be taken by surprise, to be taken aback
بَغْتَةٌ surprise, a surprising event
مُباغَتةٌ (مُباغَتاتٌ) surprise attack or raid; sudden arrival

No root

تَكْتيكاتٌ tactics

ج ذ ر

جَذَرَ – يَجْذُرُ to uproot
جَذَّرَ – يُجَذِّرُ to uproot; to extract the root (of number); to take root
جِذْرٌ (جُذورٌ) root, base, stem
جَذْرِيٌّ radical; root

ج ر ى

جَرى – يَجري to occur or come to pass; to flow or stream
جَرّى – يُجَرّي to cause to run
أَجْرى – يُجْري to cause to flow or run; to carry out, execute, or launch; to bestow

Politics 151

مَجرىً (مَجارٍ) sewage system; drain; stream, current; course (of events)
إِجراءٌ (إِجراءاتٌ) performance; measures
إِجراءاتٌ أَمنِيَّةٌ security measures
إِجرائِيٌّ operational
جارٍ flowing, circulating, current

ج س س

جَسَّ – يَجِسُّ to touch, handle, or probe
تَجَسَّسَ – يَتَجَسَّسُ to scout, explore, or spy
جاسوسٌ (جَواسيسُ) spy
تَجَسُّسٌ espionage

ح د د

حَدَّ – يَحُدُّ to sharpen; to delimit or restrict
حَدَّدَ – يُحَدِّدُ to sharpen; to establish; to determine; to restrict, define, or delimit
تَحَدَّدَ – يَتَحَدَّدُ to be scheduled; to be delimited; to be established
اِحتَدَّ – يَحتَدُّ to be or become angry or agitated
حَدٌّ (حُدودٌ) border, edge, limit, extremity, end
إِلى حَدٍّ ما to some extent
عَلى حَدٍّ سَواءٍ equally
شُرطَةُ الحُدودِ border police
حِدَّةٌ sharpness; violence, fury, anger; pitch
حِدادٌ mourning
حَديدٌ (حَدائِدُ) iron, hardware; forgings
حَدَّادٌ (حَدَّادونَ) blacksmith, ironmonger
تَحديدٌ (تَحديداتٌ) limitation, restriction; delimitation, delineation
حادٌّ sharp, keen; high pitched
مَحْدودٌ limited, restricted, circumscribed
مُحَدَّدٌ sharpened; clearly defined

ح ر س

حَرَسَ – يَحرُسُ to guard, watch, or protect; to control
اِحتَرَسَ – يَحتَرِسُ to be wary or on one's guard
حَرَسٌ guard, bodyguards, security, escort
الحَرَسُ الوَطَنِيُّ the national guard

Politics

جِراسةٌ guarding, supervision, protection, custody
حارسٌ (حُرّاسٌ) guard, bodyguard, porter (in a building)
حارسُ الْمَرْمى goalkeeper
مَحروسٌ guarded, secured, protected

ح ر ض

حَرَّضَ – يُحرِّضُ to incite, provoke, or instigate
تَحْريضٌ incitement, provocation, instigation
التَّحْريضُ على الإرهابِ incitement to terror
مُحرِّضٌ (مُحرِّضونَ) instigator, agitator

خ ر ق

خَرَقَ – يَخرُقُ to tear, pierce, or penetrate; to cross; to violate; to impair
أخرقَ – يُخرقُ to lie in wait
اِخْتَرَقَ – يَخْتَرِقُ to pierce; to cross, exceed, or go beyond
اِخْتِراقٌ أمنيٌّ security breach
خِرقةٌ (خِرَقٌ) cloth; rag
اِخْتِراقٌ (اِخْتِراقاتٌ) infiltration, penetration, hacking; disruption; crossing

خ ط ف

خَطَفَ – يَخْطُفُ to snatch or seize; to kidnap or abduct
اِنْخَطَفَ – يَنْخَطِفُ to be snatched away or carried away
اِخْتَطَفَ – يَخْتَطِفُ to hijack, take hostage, abduct, or kidnap; to seize or grab
خَطْفٌ grabbing, seizing; abduction, kidnapping
خَطَّافٌ kidnapper; robber
خاطِفُ طائراتٍ hijacker
اِخْتِطافٌ a hijacking; abduction

خ ل و

خلا – يَخْلو to be empty or vacant; to lack; to isolate
خلَّى – يُخلِّي to vacate or evacuate; to leave alone; to desist
تَخلَّى – يَتَخلَّى to relinquish or abandon; to withdraw or surrender
خلاءٌ emptiness, vacancy, void; open country, open space
خَليَّةٌ (خَلايا) cell; beehive

Politics 153

الْخَلايا النَّائِمَةُ sleeper cells
خَلِيَّةٌ إِرْهابِيَّةٌ terrorist cell

خ و ن

خانَ – يَخونُ to be disloyal or false; to cheat or deceive
خَوَّنَ – يُخَوِّنُ to regard as false or treacherous; to distrust
خِيانَةٌ treason, treachery, betrayal
الْخِيانَةُ الْعُظْمى high treason
خائِنٌ (خَوَنَةٌ) treacherous; traitor

د ه م

دَهَمَ – يَدْهَمُ to come or descend upon suddenly; to raid or invade; to surprise
دَهَّمَ – يُدَهِّمُ to blacken
داهَمَ – يُداهِمُ to seize; to attack suddenly; to catch in the act
دُهْمَةٌ blackness
أَدْهَمُ (دُهْمٌ) black
الدَّهْماءُ the masses, the populace
مُداهَمَةٌ (مُداهَماتٌ) raids, attacks; home search

ر ه ب

رَهِبَ – يَرْهَبُ to be frightened or afraid; to fear or dread
رَهَّبَ – يُرَهِّبُ to frighten, alarm, or intimidate
أَرْهَبَ – يُرْهِبُ to terrorise
تَرَهَّبَ – يَتَرَهَّبُ to threaten; to become a monk
رَهْبَةٌ fear, terror, fright
تَرْهيبٌ intimidation
إِرْهابٌ terror, terrorism, intimidation
مُكافَحَةُ الْإِرْهابِ counterterrorism
إِرْهابِيٌّ (إِرْهابِيّونَ) terroristic, terrorist
هُجومٌ إِرْهابِيٌّ terrorist attack
تَهْديدٌ إِرْهابِيٌّ terrorist threat
تَنْظيمٌ إِرْهابِيٌّ / مُنَظَّمَةٌ إِرْهابِيَّةٌ terrorist organisation
أَنْشِطَةٌ إِرْهابِيَّةٌ terrorist activities
إِرْهابٌ صادِرٌ عَنِ الدَّوْلَةِ state-sponsored terrorism
تَرَهُّبٌ monasticism

Politics

راهِبٌ (رُهْبانٌ) monk
راهِبَةٌ (راهِباتٌ) nun

ر ه ن

رَهَنَ – يَرهَنُ to pawn or mortgage
راهَنَ – يُراهِنُ to bet or make a wager
رَهنٌ (رُهونٌ) hostage; pawning; security
رَهنٌ عَقاريٌّ mortgage
رَهينَةٌ (رَهائِنُ) pawn, pledge, security, mortgage
اِحتَجَزَ رَهينَةً to hold to ransom
مُحتَجِزُ الرَّهائِنِ hostage taker
فَكُّ الرَّهائِنِ hostage release
رِهانٌ a bet or wager
مُراهَنَةٌ (مُراهَناتٌ) bet, wager

س ر ر

سَرَّ – يَسُرُّ to make (someone) happy or delight
سَرَّرَ – يُسَرِّرُ to make (someone) happy, delight, or cheer
سارَّ – يسارِرُ to confide a secret
سِرٌّ (أَسرارٌ) secret, mystery; heart
كاشِفُ الأَسرارِ whistle-blower
سِرِّيٌّ secret, private, confidential
سِرِّيٌّ لِلغايَةِ top secret
سُرَّةٌ (سُرَرٌ) navel, belly button
الحَبلُ السُّرِّيُّ umbilical cord
سُرورٌ joy, happiness
سَريرٌ (أَسِرَّةٌ) bed; throne
مَسرورٌ (بِ) glad, happy, delighted (at), pleased (with)

س ط و

سَطا – يَسطو to raid or attack; to burglarise; to rush; to pounce
سَطوٌ attack, assault, raid; burglary
السَّطوُ المُسَلَّحُ armed raid
سَطوَةٌ (سَطَواتٌ) attack, assault; influence, authority, power

س ل ل

سَلَّ – يَسِلُّ to withdraw or pull out; to remove gently
تَسَلَّلَ – يَتَسَلَّلُ to infiltrate, penetrate, or invade; to steal away
اِنسَلَّ – يَنسَلُّ to escape; to infiltrate; to have tuberculosis
سِلٌّ tuberculosis
سَلَّةٌ (سَلَّاتٌ / سِلالٌ) basket
سُلالَةٌ (سُلالاتٌ) descendants, offspring
تَسَلُّلٌ infiltration
مُتَسَلِّلٌ (مُتَسَلِّلونَ) infiltrator

ض د د

ضادَّ – يُضادِدُ to oppose, antagonise, or contravene; to be contrary; to violate
ضِدٌّ (أضدادٌ) adversary, opponent; anti-, opposite
ضِدَّ (prep) against, opposite
مُضادَّةٌ contrast, contradiction
تَدابيرُ أَمنٍ مُضادَّةٌ security countermeasures
مُراقَبَةٌ مُضادَّةٌ counter surveillance
مُضادٌّ opposed, opposite, anti-, counter-

ط ر ف

طَرَفَ – يَطرُفُ to blink, wink, or squint; to twinkle
تَطَرَّفَ – يَتَطَرَّفُ to be radical or extreme
طَرْفٌ eye, glance, look
طَرَفٌ (أطرافٌ) extremity, tip, edge; side, party
مِن طَرَفِ by
الطَّرَفُ الأغَرُّ Trafalgar, the glorious edge
طَريفٌ strange, odd; novel, rare; exquisite
تَطَرُّفٌ extremism, excess, immoderation, radicalism
مُتَطَرِّفٌ extremist, extreme, radical

ع د و

عَدا – يَعْدو to run, speed, or dash; to abandon or leave
عَدَّى – يُعَدِّي to cross or exceed
عادَى – يُعادي to feud or be at war; to contravene

Politics 155

أَعْدى – يُعدي to infect (with disease)
اِنْعَدى (مِن) – يَنْعَدي (مِن) to be infected (by)
اِعْتَدى على – يَعْتَدي على to overstep or infringe; to violate, attack, or raid
ما عَدا except
عَدْوى infection
عَدْوٌ running
العَدْوُ البَطيءُ jogging
عَدُوٌّ (أَعْداءٌ) enemy
عِداءٌ animosity
عَداوَةٌ (عَداواتٌ) enmity, hostility, aggression
عُدْوانٌ hostility, aggression; assault
اِعْتِداءٌ (اِعْتِداءاتٌ) assault, aggression, raid
مُعادٍ hostile, antagonistic
مُعْدٍ contagious, infectious
مُعاداةٌ anti-, against; fighting

No root

فَخٌّ (فُخوخٌ / فِخاخٌ) trap, snare
عَمَلِيَّةُ تَفْخيخٍ sting operation

ف د ى

فَدى – يَفْدي to sacrifice
تَفادى – يَتَفادى to beware or to guard; to prevent or avoid
اِفْتَدى – يَفْتَدي to free oneself; to obtain by sacrificing something else; to redeem oneself
فِدىً / فِداءٌ redemption; ransom; sacrifice
كَبْشُ الفِدى scapegoat
فِدْيَةٌ (فِدْياتٌ) redemption; ransom; sacrifice
فِدائِيٌّ (فِدائِيّونَ) Fedayeen; one who sacrifices himself
مَجْموعَةٌ فِدائِيَّةٌ guerrilla group

ق ح م

أَقْحَمَ – يُقْحِمُ to push, drag, or introduce forcibly
اِقْتَحَمَ – يَقْتَحِمُ to raid, storm, or invade; to defy

Politics   157

قُحْمَةٌ (قُحَمٌ) hazardous undertaking
اِقْتِحامٌ (اِقْتِحاماتٌ) intrusion; raids, invasion, capture by storm

ق و ي

قَوِيَ – يَقْوى to be strong, forceful, or powerful
قَوَّى – يُقَوِّي to strengthen, fortify, or intensify
قُوَّةٌ (قُوّاتٌ) power, strength, force; troops; intensity; courage
ميزانُ الْقُوى the balance of power
اِسْتِخدامُ الْقُوَّةِ use of force
قُوَّةٌ مُعادِيَةٌ hostile force
قُوَّةٌ دِفاعِيَّةٌ defence force
قُوَّةُ رَدْع deterrent force
قُوّاتُ الدَّرَكِ police force
قُوّاتٌ خاصَّةٌ special forces
الْقُوّاتُ الْجَوِّيَّةُ air force
قَوِيٌّ (أَقْوِياءُ) strong, powerful

ك م ن

كَمَنَ – يَكْمُنُ to hide, to be hidden or concealed
تَكَمَّنَ – يَتَكَمَّنُ to lie in wait or ambush
كَمينٌ (كَمائِنُ/كُمَناءُ) secret attack, ambush

ن ح ر

نَحَرَ – يَنْحَرُ to slaughter, butcher, or kill
اِنْتَحَرَ – يَنْتَحِرُ to commit suicide
نَحْرٌ (نُحورٌ) throat; killing, slaughter
نَحيرٌ/مَنْحورٌ slaughtered, butchered
مَنْحَرٌ throat, neck
اِنْتِحارٌ suicide

ن ص ت

نَصَتَ – يَنْصُتُ to listen
تَنَصَّتَ – يَتَنَصَّتُ to eavesdrop; bugging, tapping
كاشِفُ التَّنَصُّتِ bug detector
جِهازُ تَنَصُّتٍ a bug

ن ف ر

نَفَرَ – يَنْفِرُ to shy or run away; to avoid
نَفَّرَ – يُنَفِّرُ to startle, frighten, or chase away; to alienate
اِسْتَنْفَرَ – يَسْتَنْفِرُ to be frightened away; to fight or go to war
نَفَرٌ (أَنْفَارٌ) man, person, individual
نَفُورٌ shy; scared, fearful
نافورَةٌ (نَوافيرُ) fountain
تَنْفيرٌ alienation, deterrence, repulsion
تَنافُرٌ mutual aversion
اِسْتِنْفارٌ operational status; mobilisation

و ش ى

وَشى – يَشي to defame or slander; to inform on or denounce; to embroider
وِشايَةٌ defamation, slander
واشٍ (وُشاةٌ) informant, traitor; slanderer

و غ ل

وَغَلَ – يَغْلُ to penetrate deeply or intrude
تَوَغَّلَ – يَتَوَغَّلُ to advance further or penetrate
واغِلٌ intruder; parasite; deep-rooted
تَوَغُّلٌ incursions, penetration

و ف د

وَفَدَ – يَفِدُ to reach, arrive, or come; to travel or visit
وَفَّدَ – يُوَفِّدُ to send, dispatch, or delegate
أَوْفَدَ – يوفِدُ to send, delegate, or dispatch; to send a delegation
وَفْدٌ (وُفودٌ / أوفادٌ) deputation, delegation
وَفْدٌ أَمنيٌّ security delegation
وُفودٌ / تَوافُدٌ arrival
وافِدونَ migrants

No root

وَكْرٌ (أَوْكارٌ) nest, abode; retreat
وَكْرُ الإِرْهابِ terrorist den

Politics 159

War and Peace الحَربُ والسّلامُ

أ س ر

أَسَرَ – يَأسِرُ to capture or take prisoner; to shackle
اِسْتَأْسَرَ – يَسْتَأْسِرُ to surrender
أُسْرَةٌ (أُسَرٌ) family, dynasty, relatives
أَسيرٌ (أَسْرَى) captive, prisoner
آسِرٌ captor; winning, captivating

No root

أُسطولٌ (أَساطيلُ) fleet, flotilla

No root

بارجةٌ (بَوارجُ) warship, battleship; barge

No root

بُندُقيَّةٌ (بَنادِقُ) gun, rifle
بُنْدُقيَّةٌ آلِيَّةٌ automatic rifle
البندُقيَّةُ Venice

ب ي د

بادَ – يَبيدُ to perish, die, or become extinct
أَبادَ – يُبيدُ to annihilate or destroy
بَيْداءُ (بيدٌ) desert, steppe
إبادَةٌ annihilation, extermination
إبادَةٌ جَماعيَّةٌ genocide
بائِدٌ transitory, temporal; past

No root

تَرسانَةٌ / تَرسَخانَةٌ arsenal; shipyard, dockyard

ث ب ر

ثَبَرَ – يَثْبُرُ to destroy, ruin, or perish
ثابَرَ – يُثابِرُ to persist or persevere

160 *Politics*

ثُبُورٌ ruin, destruction

مُثابَرَةٌ persistence, perseverance, endurance

No root

ثُكَنَةٌ (ثُكَنٌ / ثَكَناتٌ) barracks

ثُكَنَةٌ عَسكَرِيَّةٌ military barracks

ج م ع

(Full treatment in Education chapter)

جَمَعَ – يَجمَعُ to gather or unite; to summarise; to convene

جَمعِيَّةٌ (جَمعِيّاتٌ) assembly; society, club, or organisation; association

مُجتَمَعٌ (مُجتَمَعاتٌ) society, community

المُجتَمَعُ الدُوَلِيُّ the international community

ج ن د

جَنَّدَ – يُجَنِّدُ to draft (into army) or conscript; to mobilise

تَجَنَّدَ – يَتَجَنَّدُ to be drafted or conscripted (military service)

جُندِيٌّ (جُنودٌ) a soldier

جُندِيُّ مُشاةِ البَحرِيَّةِ a marine

تَجنيدٌ draft, enlistment; recruitment

ج ه د

جَهَدَ – يَجهَدُ to endeavour or strive; to fatigue or exhaust

جاهَدَ – يُجاهِدُ to endeavour or strive; to fight; to wage holy war

جَهدٌ (جُهودٌ) strain, exertion, effort

جُهدٌ / إجهادٌ strain, exertion, stress

جِهادٌ struggle, battle, fight, striving; jihad

مَجهودٌ (مَجهوداتٌ) endeavour, effort, exertion

مُجاهِدٌ (مُجاهِدونَ) freedom fighter, warrior, mujahid

مُجتَهِدٌ (مُجتَهِدونَ) diligent, industrious

ج و ل

جالَ – يَجولُ to roam or wander

تَجَوَّلَ – يَتَجَوَّلُ to roam, patrol, wander, or tour; to surf (web)

جَولَةٌ (جَولاتٌ) circuit, round, patrol; tour, trip

جَوّالٌ wandering, travelling; a traveller

Politics

هاتِفٌ جَوّالٌ mobile phone
مَجالٌ (مَجالاتٌ) field, domain, sphere; theories
تَجَوُّلٌ roaming, wandering, migration
مَنعُ التَّجَوُّلِ curfew

ج ي ش

جاشَ – يَجيشُ to be excited or agitated; to rage, storm, or simmer
جَيَّشَ – يُجَيِّشُ to mobilise an army
جَيشٌ (جُيوشٌ) army

ح ر ب

حَرِبَ – يَحرُبُ to be furious or angry
حارَبَ – يُحارِبُ to fight or combat; to wage war
تَحارَبَ – يَتحارَبُ to fight one another or be engaged in war
حَربٌ (حُروبٌ) war,[2] fight, combat
الْحَربُ الْعالَمِيَّةُ world war
الْحَربُ على الإرهابِ war on terror
مُجرِمُ حَربٍ (مُجرِمو حَربٍ) war criminal
أسيرُ حَربٍ prisoner of war
جَرائِمُ حَربٍ war crime
حَربٌ أَهْلِيَّةٌ civil war
حَربٌ نَفسِيَّةٌ psychological warfare
حَربِيٌّ pertaining to law; military
مُحارَبَةٌ struggle, combat, battle, warfare
مُحارِبٌ (مُحارِبونَ) fighter, combatant
مُحارِبونَ قُدَماءُ veterans

ح ش د

حَشَدَ – يَحشُدُ to mobilise or gather troops
تَحَشَّدَ – يَتَحَشَّدُ to rally, assemble, or gather; to fall into line (troops)
حَشدٌ (حُشودٌ) crowd, assembly, gathering
حاشِدٌ numerous, crowded

ح ص ر

حَصَرَ – يَحصُرُ to surround, encircle, or enclose; to restrict; to besiege or blockade
حاصَرَ – يُحاصِرُ to besiege, surround, or blockade

Politics

حَصْرٌ restriction, detention; siege, enclosure
حِصَارٌ / مُحاصَرَةٌ blockade, siege; barrier
حَصيرَةٌ (حَصائِرُ) mat
مَحصورٌ besieged

ح ظ ر

حَظَرَ – يَحظُرُ to forbid or prohibit; to fence in
حَظْرٌ ban, embargo; prohibition
مَحظورٌ (مَحظوراتٌ) prohibited, forbidden; embargoes
حَظْرُ التَّجَوُّلِ curfew
موادٌ محظورَةٌ prohibited items
مَنطِقَةٌ مَحْظورَةٌ / مَمْنوعَةٌ prohibited or restricted zone
مَنطِقَةُ الْحَظرِ الْجَوِّيِّ no-fly zone

ح و ر

حارَ – يحورُ to return; to recede or diminish
حاوَرَ – يُحاوِرُ to talk, discuss, debate, or argue
تَحاوَرَ – يتَحاوَرُ to continue a discussion
حارَةٌ (حاراتٌ) district, quarter; section, part; side street
حِوارٌ (حِواراتٌ) dialogue, talk, conversation
مِحوَرٌ (مَحاوِرُ) axis, pivot; core
مَحارٌ oyster, shellfish, mussel
مُحاوَرَةٌ talk, dialogue, argument
تَحاوُرٌ discussion
حِوارٌ dialogue

خ ن د ق

خَنْدَقَ – يُخَندِقُ to dig a trench; to prepare for battle
خَنْدَقٌ (خَنادِقُ) trench, ditch

د ب ب

دَبَّ – يَدُبُّ to creep or crawl; to advance or enter; to invade
دَبَّبَ – يُدَبِّبُ to sharpen, point
دُبٌّ (دِبَبَةٌ) bear
دَبيبٌ creeping, crawling; infiltration, influx

Politics 163

دَبَّابَةٌ (دَبَّاباتٌ) tank, armoured car
دابَّةٌ (دَوابُّ) animal, beast; riding animal

د ث ر

دَثَرَ – يَدثُرُ to be obliterated, extinct, or wiped out
دَثَّرَ – يُدَثِّرُ to cover or envelop; to annihilate or destroy
تَدَثَّرَ – يَتَدَثَّرُ to wrap or cover oneself
دِثارٌ (دُثُرٌ) blanket, cover
اِندِثارٌ obliteration

د ر ع

دَرَّعَ – يُدَرِّعُ to arm or equip with armour
تَدَرَّعَ – يَتَدَرَّعُ to arm oneself or take up arms; to put on armour
دِرعٌ (دُروعٌ) armour, shield
دِرْعٌ بَشَرِيٌّ human shield
مُدَرَّعٌ reinforced, armoured
المُدَرَّعُ armadillo
مُدرَّعاتٌ armoured vehicles, tanks

د م ر

دَمَرَ – يَدمُرُ to perish, to be ruined or destroyed
دَمَّرَ – يُدَمِّرُ to destroy, ruin, or demolish
تَدَمَّرَ – يَتَدَمَّرُ to be destroyed, demolished, or ruined
دَمارٌ ruin, destruction
أَسلِحَةُ الدَّمارِ الشَّامِلِ weapons of mass destruction (WMD)
اِندِمارٌ utter defeat, destruction

ذ ب ح

ذَبَحَ – يَذبَحُ to kill, slaughter, or butcher
ذَبحٌ slaughtering, slaughter
ذَبيحَةٌ (ذَبائِحٌ) slaughter animal, sacrificial victim, blood sacrifice
مَذبَحَةٌ (مَذابِحٌ) massacre

ر د ع

رَدَعَ – يَردَعُ to keep from or prevent (someone) from

164 Politics

رادِعٌ (رَوادِعُ) deterrent; restriction, impediment
قُوّاتُ الرَّدعِ deterrent forces

No root

زِنادٌ (أَزِندةٌ) the trigger of a gun, the cock or hammer of a rifle
حَجرُ الزِّنادِ flint

ز و ل / ز ي ل

زالَ – يَزولُ to withdraw, abandon, or vanish; to cease (with negation)
أَزالَ – يُزيلُ to remove or eliminate; to cause to stop
ما زالَ / لَمْ يَزَلْ / لا يَزالُ to continue or carry on; it is still ...
إِزالةٌ removal, elimination
إِزالةُ القَنابِلِ bomb disposal
زائِلٌ transitory, fleeting

س ب ى

سَبى – يَسْبي to capture or take prisoner; to captivate
سَبْيٌ capture, captivity
سَبِيٌّ (سَبايا) captive, prisoner of war

س د س

سَدَّسَ – يُسَدِّسُ to multiply by six or make hexagonal
سُدْسٌ (أَسْداسٌ) one-sixth
سُداسِيٌّ hexagon
مُسَدَّسٌ (مُسَدَّساتٌ) revolver, pistol, gun; hexagon, hexagonal
مُسَدَّسةٌ pistol, gun, revolver

س ل ح

سَلَحَ – يَسْلَحُ to drop excrement (bird); to empty the bowels
سَلَّحَ – يُسَلِّحُ to arm
سِلاحٌ (أَسْلِحةٌ) weapon
سِلاحٌ ناريٌّ firearm
سِلاحٌ قَذائِفِيٌّ ballistic weapon
سِلاحُ الطَّيَرانِ air force

Politics 165

تَجْريدٌ مِن السِّلاحِ / نزعُ السِّلاحِ disarmament, demilitarisation
أَسْلِحَةٌ ذَكِيَّةٌ precision weapons (intelligent weapons)
تَهْريبُ الأَسْلِحَةِ weapons smuggling
تَسْليحٌ (تَسْليحاتٌ) arming
مُسَلَّحٌ (مُسَلَّحونَ) armed (man); gunman
غَيْرُ مُسَلَّحٍ unarmed
القُوّاتُ المُسَلَّحَةُ the armed forces

س ل م

سَلِمَ – يَسْلَمُ to be safe and sound, to be unharmed; to be certain or established
سَلَّمَ – يُسَلِّمُ to hand over; to deliver; to preserve or keep from harm; to greet
سالَمَ – يُسالِمُ to keep the peace; to make peace with someone
تَسَلَّمَ – يتسَلَّمُ to obtain or receive
اِسْتَلَمَ – يَسْتَلِمُ to receive or obtain; to touch
اِسْتَسْلَمَ – يَسْتَسْلِمُ to surrender or capitulate
سِلْمٌ / سَلامٌ / سِلْمٌ peace
سُلَّمٌ (سَلالِمُ) ladder, stairs
سَلامٌ (سلاماتٌ) peace, safety, well-being; a greeting
سَلامَةٌ safety, integrity, welfare
سَليمٌ (سُلَماءُ) safe, unhurt, healthy, secure; free (also a boy's name in the singular)
مُسالَمَةٌ conciliation, pacification
تَسْليمٌ handing over, submission, surrender; admission; extradition
إِسْلامٌ submission
الإِسْلامُ Islam
اِسْتِلامٌ receipt; taking over; acceptance
وَصْلُ اسْتِلامٍ receipt
اِسْتِسْلامٌ surrender, capitulation, submission; resignation
سالِمٌ safe, secure, free, intact
مُسالِمٌ peaceful, mild-tempered, gentle
مُسْلِمٌ (مُسلمونَ) Muslim

س و ح

ساحَ – يَسيحُ to travel or roam
ساحَةٌ (ساحاتٌ) courtyard, open square, arena, field
ساحَةُ الْحَرْبِ theatre of war

Politics

سائِحٌ (سُوّاحٌ / سُيَّاحٌ) traveller, tourist
الْمُنْتَجَعاتُ السِّياحِيَّةُ tourist resorts

No root

سيناريو (سيناريوهاتٌ) scenarios
سيناريو أَسْوَأُ الأَحْوالِ worst-case scenario

ش ب ك

شَبَكَ – يَشْبِكُ to entangle, fasten, or tighten
اِشْتَبَكَ – يَشْتَبِكُ to fight with; to be entangled or embroiled with; to be complicated
تَشَبَّكَ – يَتَشَبَّكُ to be entangled; to be or become complicated or involved
شَبَكَةٌ (شَبَكاتٌ / شَبَكٌ) network
شُبّاكٌ (شَبابِيكُ) window, grid
اِشْتِباكٌ (اِشْتِباكاتٌ) clash, scuffle

ش ظ ى

شَظِيَ – يَشْظى to be splintered or shattered
تَشَظَّى – يَتَشَظَّى to be splintered or shattered
شَظايا shrapnel (plural in Arabic)

ش ن ن

شَنَّ – يَشُنُّ to launch (war, attack, campaign)
أَشَنَّ – يَشِنُّ to launch (war, attack, campaign)
يَشُنُّ حَمْلَةً to campaign
شَنَّ حَرْباً to wage war

ص ر خ

صَرَخَ – يَصْرُخُ to cry, scream, or shout
صَرْخَةٌ (صَرَخاتٌ) a cry, scream, or yell
صُراخٌ crying, yelling, screams
صاروخٌ (صَواريخُ) missile, rocket; siren
قاذِفَةُ الصَّواريخ rocket or missile launcher

ص ر ع

صَرَعَ – يَصْرَعُ to throw down or bring to the ground; to be epileptic
صارَعَ – يُصارِعُ to wrestle; to fight

Politics   167

اِنصَرَعَ – يَنصَرِعُ to be or go mad
صَرَعٌ epilepsy
صِراعٌ struggle, fight; wrestling match
صِراعٌ مُسَلَّحٌ armed conflict
مُصارَعةٌ wrestling; wrestling match; a fight or struggle
مُصارِعٌ wrestler, fighter

ص ع ق

صَعَقَ – يَصعَقُ to strike (with lightning); to destroy or hit; to stun or stupefy
أَصعَقَ – يُصعِقُ to strike down, slay, or destroy; to stun or stupefy
صَعقٌ thunder
صاعِقٌ detonator
صاعِقةٌ (صَواعِقُ) thunderbolt, lightning bolt
مَصْعوقٌ struck by lightning, thunderstruck; destroyed; dumbfounded

ص ل ح

صَلَحَ – يَصلُحُ to be good, valid, or proper; to thrive
صَلَّحَ – يُصَلِّحُ to put in order; to repair; to make amends
صالَحَ – يُصالِحُ to make peace or reconcile
أَصلَحَ – يُصلِحُ to reform or repair; to make amends; to make peace
صُلحٌ peace, compromise, settlement
مَحكَمةُ الصُّلحِ reconciliation court
صَلاحٌ goodness, properness, piety (also a boy's name)
صَلاحِيّةٌ suitability
مَصلَحةٌ (مَصالِحُ) benefit, advantage, interest; (government) department
تَصليحٌ (تَصليحاتٌ) restoration, restitution; mending
مُصالَحةٌ reconciliation
إِصلاحٌ (إِصلاحاتٌ) reforms
إِصلاحاتٌ سياسِيّةٌ political reform
اِصطِلاحٌ (اِصطِلاحاتٌ) agreement; convention, usage; technical term
صالِحٌ good, right, virtuous
مُصالِحٌ peacemaker
مُصطَلَحٌ (مُصطَلَحاتٌ) idiom; terminology; technical term

ط ي ر

طارَ – يَطيرُ to fly or fly away; to hurry
طَيَّرَ – يُطَيِّرُ to make or let fly; to dispatch or forward without delay

168 Politics

تَطَيَّرَ – يَتَطَيَّرُ to see an evil omen
طَيْرٌ / طائِرٌ (طُيورٌ) birds; omen
طَيَّار (طَيَّارونَ) flying; pilot
طائِرَةٌ / طِيَّارَةٌ (طائِراتٌ / طِيَّاراتٌ) airplane; kite
طَيَرانٌ flight, flying, aviation
مَطارٌ (مَطاراتٌ) airport
طائِرَةٌ مِرْوَحَيَّةٌ helicopter
طائِرَةٌ بدون طَيَّارٍ drone, unmanned aerial vehicle

ع ب أ / ع ب و

عَبَّأ – يُعَبِّئُ to fill, pack, load, or charge; to load (a gun)
عِبءٌ (أَعْباءٌ) burden, load, encumbrance
تَعْبِئَةٌ mobilisation; drafting, conscription
عُبْوَةٌ (عُبْواتٌ) package, container
عُبوةٌ حارِقَةٌ incendiary device
عُبواتٌ ناسِفَةٌ booby traps, explosives
عُبْوَةٌ ناسِفَةٌ improvised explosive device (IED)
عَباءَةٌ (عَباءاتٌ) abaya, cloak-like wrap

ع ت د

عَتَدَ – يَعْتُدُ to be ready or prepared
أَعْتَدَ – يَعتِدُ to prepare (sth)
عَتادٌ (أَعْتادٌ) equipment; ammunition, material (for war)
مُسْتَوْدَعُ عَتادٍ / مُسْتَوْدَعُ ذَخيرةٍ ammunition depot

ع ر ك

عَرَكَ – يَعْرُكُ to play havoc with or damage severely
عارَكَ – يُعارِكُ to fight or struggle
عَرْكَةٌ fight, struggle, battle
مَعركةٌ (مَعارِكُ) battle
عِراكٌ battle, combat, struggle

ع ز ز

عَزَّ – يَعِزُّ to be strong or powerful; to be respected or cherished
عَزَّرَ – يُعَزِّرُ to strengthen or fortify; to confirm or corroborate
إعْتَزَّ – يَعتَزُّ to feel strong or powerful; to be proud or boastful

Politics 169

عِزٌّ power, might; high rank, honour; fight
عِزَّةٌ power, might; standing, honour
عَزيزٌ (أَعِزّاءُ) powerful, strong; noble; dear (also a boy's name in the singular)
مَعَزَّةٌ esteem, regard; affection, love
تَعزيزٌ (تَعزيزاتٌ) strengthening, consolidation, support
مُعتَزٌّ proud, mighty, powerful (also a boy's name)

No root

عَسْكَرٌ (عَساكِرُ) soldier; military, army, troops
عَسْكَريٌّ (عَسكريّونَ) military, of or relating to the army
عَسْكَرِيَّةٌ military service; militarism
مُعَسكَرٌ (مُعَسكراتٌ) army camp, camp
مُعَسكَرُ إعتِقالٍ concentration camp, detention centre
مُعَسكَرُ تَدريبٍ training camp
تَدَخُّلٌ عَسكَريٌّ military intervention
قاعِدةٌ عَسكَرِيَّةٌ military base
الخِدمةُ العَسْكَرِيَّةُ military service

ع م ر

عَمَرَ – يَعمُرُ to live long or flourish; to populate; to erect or build
عَمَّرَ – يُعَمِّرُ to grant long life (of God); to populate; to let someone live
إعتَمَرَ – يَعتَمِرُ to visit; to perform umra (in Mecca)
إستَعمَرَ – يَستَعمِرُ to settle or colonise
عُمرٌ (أعمارٌ) life, life span, age
عُمْرَةٌ umra, pilgrimage out of the Hajj season
عِمارَةٌ (عِماراتٌ) structure, building
مِعمارٌ builder, architect, mason
إستِعمارٌ colonialism, colonisation, imperialism
مُحارَبَةُ الإستِعمارِ anti-colonialism
المَعمورَةُ earth
مُستَعمِرٌ settler, colonist, imperialist
مُستَعمَرَةٌ (مُستَعمَراتٌ) colony, settlement

غ ر ب

غَرَبَ – يَغرُبُ to depart, leave, or withdraw; to be strange or odd
تَغَرَّبَ – يَتَغَرَّبَ to emigrate; to assimilate oneself into a Western culture
إغتَرَبَ – يَغتَرِبُ to emigrate or go to a foreign country

170 Politics

اِسْتَغْرَبَ – يَسْتَغْرِبُ to find strange or unusual; to deem absurd
غَرْبٌ west, occident
الضَّفَّةُ الْغربيَّةُ الْمُحتَلَّةُ the Occupied West Bank
غُربَةٌ exile; life outside of one's native country
غُرابٌ (غِربانٌ) crow, raven
غَريبٌ (غُرباءُ) a stranger; strange, bizarre
غُروبٌ setting (of the sun)
مَغربٌ (مَغاربٌ) place or time of sunset; west, occident
الْمَغربُ Maghrib; North Africa; prayer at sunset
تَغَرُّبٌ / اِغترابٌ emigration
اِستِغرابٌ wonder, astonishment
مُغتربٌ (مُغتربونَ) immigrants

غ ز و

غَزا – يَغْزو to attack, raid, or invade; to strive or aspire; to intend
غَزْوٌ raid, invasion, attack, conquest
غَزوَةٌ (غَزواتٌ) incursion, raid, attack, aggression
مَغزىً (مَغازٍ) intention, purpose
غازٍ (غُزاةٌ) invader, aggressor

غ ل ب

غَلَبَ – يَغْلِبُ to conquer, subdue, or defeat; to surmount; to seize
تَغَلَّبَ على – يَتَغَلَّبُ على to triumph or overcome; to master
غُلبَةٌ victory, conquest
أغْلَبُ (followed by genitive) the greater portion, majority
في الأغْلَب mostly, generally, in general
أغلبيَّةٌ / غالبيَّةٌ majority
مَغلوبٌ defeated (struggle, spirit), overcome

No root

غوانتانامو Guantanamo

غ و ر

غارَ – يَغورُ to penetrate deeply or sink in; to become hollow
أغارَ على – يُغيرُ على to raid, invade, or attack
غَوْرٌ (أغوارٌ) bottom; depression, declivity

Politics 171

غارٌ (أغوارٌ) cave, cavern
غارَةٌ (غاراتٌ) raid, invasion, attack
غاراتٌ جَوِّيَّةٌ air strikes
مَغارَةٌ (مَغاراتٌ) cave, grotto

ف ج ر

فَجَرَ – يَفجُرُ to break up; to dig up; to sin; to commit adultery
فَجَّرَ – يُفَجِّرُ to explode (sth) or split; to create an outlet
اِنفَجَرَ – يَنفَجِرُ to explode, detonate, or discharge; to overflow
فَجرٌ dawn, daybreak; the beginning; the morning prayer
تَفَجُّرٌ outbreak, eruption
اِنفِجارٌ (اِنفِجاراتٌ) explosion, outbreak, detonation
أَداةُ تَفجيرٍ explosive device
مُتَفَجِّرٌ (مُتَفَجِّراتٌ) explosives

ف ز ز

فَزَّ – يَفِزُّ to jump up; to startle or frighten
اِستَفَزَّ – يَستَفِزُّ to agitate, incite, or provoke; to startle
فَزَّةٌ a start or a jump (in surprise)
اِستِفزازٌ (اِستِفزازاتٌ) provocation; instigation
اِستِفزازيٌّ provocative

No root

فَشَكٌّ cartridges

ف و ز

فازَ – يَفوزُ to be triumphant or win; to defeat; to obtain
فَوَّزَ – يُفَوِّزُ to cross or travel through the desert
فَوزٌ success, victory
فائِزٌ successful, victorious; victor, winner

ق د م

قَدِمَ – يَقدُمُ to precede; to arrive, come, or reach; to be old
قَدَّمَ – يُقَدِّمُ to offer; to precede; to dispatch; to prefer
تَقَدَّمَ – يَتَقَدَّمُ to go forward, progress, or proceed; to be at the head

172 Politics

قِدَمٌ antiquity, time immemorial
قَدَمٌ (أَقدامٌ) foot, step
قَديمٌ (قُدماءُ) old, ancient, antique
تَقَدُّمٌ progress
مُقَدِّمَةٌ (مُقَدِّماتٌ) introduction, forefront, prelude, head
مُتَقَدِّمٌ advancing, moving forward

ق ذ ف

قَذَفَ – يَقْذِفُ to bomb, throw, drop, or toss
قَذْفٌ slander, false accusation
قَذيفَةٌ (قَذائِفُ) shell, projector, bomb; missile
قَذيفَةُ نَسْفِ السُّفُنِ / مُفرقَعَةٌ torpedo

ق ص ف

قَصَفَ – يَقصِفُ to bomb; to break; to oppress or harass
اِنقَصَفَ – يَنقَصِفُ to be broken; to break or snap
قَصْفٌ bombardment, shelling, thunder (of cannon)
قَصْفٌ صاروخِيٌّ rocket fire
قَصْفٌ دَقيقٌ precision bombing

ق ع د

قَعَدَ – يَقعُدُ to sit down; to stay or remain; to desist
أَقعَدَ – يُقعِدُ to make someone sit down, to seat; to hold back
تَقاعَدَ – يَتَقاعَدُ to retire; to withdraw; to abstain
مَقعَدٌ (مَقاعِدُ) seat, chair
تَقاعُدٌ retirement
مُتَقاعِدٌ retired; pensioner
قاعِدٌ (قُعودٌ) sitting, seated, inactive, idle
قاعِدَةٌ (قَواعِدُ) base; basis, foundation, rule, principle (pl: Arabic grammar)
النَّحوُ والقَواعِدُ grammar
قاعِدَةٌ جَوِّيَّةٌ air base
القاعِدَةُ Al-Qaeda
مُقعَدٌ infirm, lame, disabled

ق ن ب ل

قَنبَلَ – يُقَنبِلُ to bomb
قُنبُلَةٌ (قَنابِلُ) bomb, grenade, shell

Politics 173

مَوادُّ صُنْعِ القَنابِلِ bomb-making materials
قُنْبُلَةٌ يَدَوِيَّةٌ hand grenade
قُنْبُلة ذَرِّيّة atomic bomb

ق ن ص

قَنَصَ – يَقْنِصُ to hunt or shoot; to take advantage
قَنْصٌ hunting, shooting; a hunt
قَنَّاصٌ (قَنَّاصَةٌ) sniper; hunter
قانِصَةٌ (قانِصاتٌ) tank destroyer

ق ه ر

قَهَرَ – يَقْهَرُ to defeat or conquer; to subjugate
قَهْرٌ subjugation; coercion
لا يُقْهَرُ invincible
القاهِرَةُ Cairo
قَهَّارٌ conquering, vanquishing

ق ه ق ر

قَهْقَرَ – يُقَهْقِرُ to regress or deteriorate; to retreat or withdraw
تَقَهْقَرَ – يَتَقَهْقَرُ to regress or deteriorate; to retreat or withdraw
تَقَهْقُرٌ recession; a retreat
قَهْقَرَةٌ / قَهْقَرى backward movement; degeneration; retreat

ق و م

قامَ – يَقومُ to rise or stand; to rebel or revolt; to leave; to undertake
قاوَمَ – يُقاوِمُ to resist, withstand, or oppose; to fight or argue
أقامَ – يُقيمُ to live in; to set up, establish, or erect
قَوْمٌ (أقوامٌ) nation, people, tribe, race; kin
قَوْمِيٌّ national
قَوْمِيَّةٌ nationalism
المَصالِحُ القَوْمِيَّةُ national interests
قامَةٌ figure, stature
قيمَةٌ (قِيَمٌ) value, price
قِيامَةٌ resurrection; upheaval
يَوْمُ القِيامَةِ Judgement Day
مَقامٌ (مَقاماتٌ) place, location; shrine, tomb; rank

174   Politics

تَقْوِيمٌ (تَقَاوِيمُ) calendar; setting up; correction, amendment
التَّقْوِيمُ المِيلادِيُّ the Gregorian calendar
التَّقْوِيمُ الهِجْرِيُّ the Islamic (Hijri) calendar
تَقْوِيمُ الأسْنانِ braces (teeth)
مُقاوَمَةٌ resistance, opposition; fight
إقامَةٌ residency; establishment, setting up
قائِمَةٌ (قَوائِمُ / قائِماتٌ) list, register, schedule; leg, foot, pillar, stand
مُقَوِّمٌ (مُقَوِّماتٌ) factor; elements, components
مُقِيمٌ resident; permanent
مُسْتَقِيمٌ straight, upright, correct

ك ف ح

كَفَحَ – يَكْفَحُ to face, encounter, or confront
كافَحَ – يُكافِحُ to struggle, combat, or battle; to defend
كِفاحٌ / مُكافَحَةٌ opposition; fight, battle; struggle (also a girl's name[3] in the singular)

ل غ م

لَغَمَ – يَلْغُمُ to plant mines
لَغْمٌ (أَلْغامٌ) a mine
مَلْغومٌ ambushed; covered with mines

No root

مُناوَرَةٌ (مُناوَراتٌ) manoeuvre, military manoeuvres

م ي د

مادَ – يَمِيدُ to be moved; to be shocked or upset; to swing or sway; to be dizzy
مَيْدانٌ (مَيادِينُ) square, field, domain, arena, battleground
مَيْدانُ العَمَلِيَّاتِ field of operations
مَيْدانُ القِتالِ battlefield
مائِدَةٌ (مائِداتٌ / مَوائِدُ) table (with food on it)

No root

مِيلِيشِيا (مِيلِيشْياتٌ) militia

ن ز ع

نَزَعَ – يَنْزَعُ to remove; to spoil; to leave one's land; to dismiss or deprive

Politics 175

نازَعَ – يُنازِعُ to dispute with, fight, or challenge; to be on the verge of death
نَزْعُ السِّلاحِ disarmament
نِزاعٌ (نِزاعاتٌ) conflict, struggle, fight; dispute, controversy
بِلا نِزاعٍ indisputably
مُنازَعَةٌ (مُنازَعاتٌ) a fight or struggle; controversy, quarrel
تَنازُعٌ fight, struggle
اِنتِزاعٌ withdrawal, elimination

ن ض ل

نَضَلَ – يَنضُلُ to surpass, beat, or defeat
ناضَلَ – يُناضِلُ to compete, dispute, or struggle; to stand up for someone
نِضالٌ / مُناضَلَةٌ fight, dispute, defensive battle
حَرَكَةٌ نِضالِيَّةٌ resistance movement
مُناضِلٌ fighter, combatant, defender

ن ف ض

نَفَضَ – يَنفُضُ to shake or dust off; to shiver
اِنتَفَضَ – يَنتَفِضُ to be shaken off; to shiver or tremble
اِنتِفاضٌ shaking; a shiver, shudder, or tremor
اِنتِفاضَةٌ intifada, uprising
الاِنتِفاضَةُ the Palestinian Intifada

ن ه ب

نَهَبَ – يَنهَبُ to plunder, pillage, or loot
نَهْبٌ robbery, pillaging; booty
نَهّابٌ robber, looter

ن و ر

نَوَّرَ – يُنَوِّرُ to blossom or bloom; to fill with light; to enlighten
تَنَوَّرَ – يَتَنَوَّرُ to be lit or illuminated; to receive enlightenment
نارٌ (نيرانٌ) fire; gunfire
النّارُ hell
وقفُ إطْلاقِ النّارِ ceasefire
تَبادُلُ إطْلاقِ النّارِ to exchange fire
أَطلَقَ النّيرانَ to discharge or fire (a gun)
نورٌ (أنوارٌ) light, brightness, illumination; a ray

176 Politics

نُوّارٌ (نَواويرُ) blossom, flowers
مَنارَةٌ (مَناراتٌ / مَناورُ) lighthouse
تَنويرٌ enlightenment, illumination; flowering, blossoming

ن و ش

ناوَشَ – يُناوِشُ to engage in a skirmish; to brush against; to play
مُناوَشَةٌ (مُناوَشاتٌ) skirmishes, hostilities

ه ج م

هَجَمَ (على) – يَهجُمُ (على) to attack, assault, or raid
هاجَمَ – يُهاجِمُ to attack, raid, or assault
تَهجَّمَ (على) – يَتَهجَّمُ (على) to fall upon, attack, or assault
هُجومٌ / مُهاجَمَةٌ an attack, assault, or raid
هُجومٌ بَرِّيٌّ ground offensive, attack
هُجومٌ جَوِّيٌّ air raid
هُجومٌ مُعاكِسٌ / هُجومٌ مُضادٌّ counter-attack

ه د ف

هَدَفَ – يَهدِفُ to approach or draw near; to aim or target
إستَهدَفَ – يَستَهدِفُ to target or aim; to have in mind
هَدَفٌ (أَهدافٌ) target, aim, objective, purpose; goal (sport)
مُستَهدَفٌ exposed, open
القَتلُ المُستَهدَفُ targeted killings

ه د ن

هَدَنَ – يَهدِنُ to be quiet; to calm down
هادَنَ – يُهادِنُ to conclude a truce
هُدنَةٌ (هُدَنٌ / هُدناتٌ) truce, peace, calm (also a girl's name in the singular)
مُهادَنَةٌ truce negotiations

ه ز م

هَزَمَ – يَهزِمُ to defeat or vanquish; to neutralise (opponent)
إنهَزَمَ – ينهَزِمُ to be defeated
هَزيمَةٌ (هَزائِمُ) defeat
مُنهَزِمٌ defeated

Politics

اِنْهِزامٌ defeat, flight
اِنْهِزامِيّةٌ defeatism

Civil Disobedience العِصيانُ المَدَنِيُّ

ث و ر

ثارَ – يَثورُ to revolt, stir, excite, or arouse
ثَوْرٌ (ثيرانٌ) bull, ox; Taurus
ثَوْرَةٌ (ثَوْراتٌ) revolution, uprising, revolt; agitation, excitement
ثَوْرِيٌّ revolutionary
إثارَةٌ excitation, agitation; incitement
ثائِرٌ (ثُوّارٌ) insurgent, revolutionary; excited, agitated
مُثيرٌ exciting, provocative; stimulant

ح ج ج

حَجَّ – يَحُجُّ to overcome or defeat; to convince; to perform Hajj
اِحتَجَّ – يَحتَجُّ to justify; to plea or protest; to vindicate
حَجٌّ Hajj (pilgrimage to Mecca)
حُجّةٌ (حُجَجٌ) pretence; excuse; proof, evidence
تَحَجُّجٌ argumentation, pleading; pretence
اِحتِجاجٌ (اِحتِجاجاتٌ) plea, protest, argumentation; excuse; pretence
حاجٌّ (حُجّاجٌ) title given to people who have been on pilgrimage to Mecca
مُحتَجٌّ (مُحتَجّونَ) protestor

ش غ ب

شَغَبَ – يَشغَبُ to make trouble; to stir riots or provoke dissension
شاغَبَ – يُشاغِبُ to make trouble, disturb the peace, or riot
شَغَبٌ riot, unrest
شُرْطةُ مَنع الشَغَب anti-riot police
مُشاغَبةٌ (مُشاغَباتٌ) disorder, disturbance, riot, dissension, controversy
مُشاغِبٌ (مُشاغِبونَ) troublemaker, agitator, rioter

ظ ه ر

ظَهَرَ – يَظهَرُ to emerge or appear; to be visible; to publish
أظهَرَ – يُظهِرُ to make visible or apparent; to demonstrate; to initiate

تَظاهَرَ – يَتَظاهَرُ to demonstrate or show; to pretend or feign
ظَهْرٌ (ظُهورٌ) back, reverse, rear side; deck, surface
ظُهْرٌ (أَظْهارٌ) noon, midday; midday prayer
بَعدَ الظُّهر the afternoon
ظاهِرَةٌ (ظَواهِرُ) phenomenon
مَظْهَرٌ (مظاهِرُ) appearance, view, sight
مُظاهَرَةٌ (مُظاهَراتٌ) demonstration, rally, protest
مُتظاهِرٌ (مُتظاهِرونَ) demonstrator
تَظاهُرٌ (تَظاهُراتٌ) pretending, hypocrisy (pl: demonstration, rally)

No root

غَوْغاءُ mob, riff-raff; noise, clamour
الغَوْغائِيَّةُ mob chaos

غ و ل

غالَ – يَغولُ to snatch, grab, or seize; to destroy; to take unawares
اِغتالَ – يَغْتالُ to assassinate or murder
غولٌ (غِيلانٌ / أَغْوالٌ) ogre, desert demon, ghoul[4]
اِغتِيالٌ (اِغتيالاتٌ) assassination, murder
غائِلَةٌ (غَوائِلُ) calamity, disaster; danger

م ر د

مَرَدَ – يَمرُدُ to be rebellious; to revolt or rebel
تَمَرَّدَ – يَتَمَرَّدُ to revolt or rebel; to be insolent or arrogant
تَمَرُّدٌ revolt, insurrection, mutiny
مارِدٌ (مارِدونَ / مَرَدَةٌ) defiant; demon, evil spirit, devil; giant
مُتَمَرِّدٌ (مُتَمَرِّدونَ) rebel, insurgent
مُكافَحَةُ التَّمَرُّدِ counter-insurgency

الانتِخاباتُ والتَّصويتُ Elections and Voting

أ ي د

أَيَّدَ – يُؤَيِّدُ to support; to confirm or back
تَأَيَّدَ – يَتَأَيَّدُ to be supported
تَأْييدٌ support, confirmation, endorsement
مُؤَيِّدٌ (مُؤَيِّدونَ) supporter

Politics 179

ر ش ح

رَشَّحَ – يُرَشِّحُ to nominate
تَرَشَّحَ – يَتَرَشَّحُ to be qualified; to be nominated as a candidate; to catch a cold
رَشْحٌ a cold; perspiration, sweating
تَرشيحٌ nomination
مُرشَّحٌ (مُرشَّحونَ) candidate; nominated, voted in; having a cold
مُتَرَشِّحٌ (مُتَرَشِّحونَ) candidate, nominee

ص و ت

صاتَ – يَصوتُ to ring, sound, or shout
صَوَّتَ – يُصَوِّتُ to vote or cast ballots
صَوْتٌ (أَصْواتٌ) a vote; a voice; a sound (pl: interjections) (grammar)
كاتِمُ الصَّوتِ silencer (gun)
فَرْزُ الأَصواتِ vote count
صَوْتِيٌّ vocal; acoustic, phonetic
عِلمُ الأَصْواتِ / صَوْتِيَّاتٌ phonetics
تَصْويتٌ voting, a vote
مُصوِّت (مُصوِّتونَ) voters

ق ر ع

قَرَعَ – يَقرَعُ to hit, bump, knock, beat, or strike
اِقتَرَعَ – يَقتَرِعُ to cast lots or vote
قارِعَةٌ (قَوارِعُ) misfortune, calamity, adversity
مُقارَعَةٌ fight, struggle
اِقتِراعٌ (اِقتِراعاتٌ) ballot, vote; draft (military)
صُندوقُ الاِقتِراعِ ballot box
مَركَزُ الاِقتِراعِ polling station

ن خ ب

نَخَبَ – يَنخُبُ to select or choose; to vote or elect
اِنتَخَبَ – يَنتَخِبُ to select or choose; to vote or elect
نَخْبٌ selection, choice; a drink to one's health
نُخْبَةٌ (نُخَبٌ) elite, selected
اِنتِخابٌ (اِنتِخاباتٌ) election; choice, selection
اِنتِخاباتٌ رِئاسِيَّةٌ presidential elections
اِنتِخاباتٌ مَحَلِّيَّةٌ local elections

180 *Politics*

لائِحةٌ اِنتخابِيّةٌ electoral roll
حَملةٌ اِنتخابِيّةٌ election campaign
ناخِبٌ (ناخبونَ) voter; electorate
مُنتَخَبٌ (مُنتَخبونَ / مُنتَخَباتٌ) nominated, voted in; elected candidate; team (sports)

النُزوعُ والمُساعداتُ Displacement and Aid

ج و ر

جارَ – يَجورُ to deviate or stray; to persecute or oppress
جاوَرَ – يُجاوِرُ to live next to, to be the neighbour of; to adjoin or border
أجارَ – يُجيرُ to grant asylum; to protect or aid
جَوْرٌ injustice, oppression, tyranny
جارٌ (جيرانٌ) neighbours
مُجاوَرَةٌ neighbourhood; proximity
جائِرٌ (جَوَرَةٌ) aggressive, tyrannical, unjust
مُجاوِرٌ neighbouring, adjacent, near

خ ي م

خَيَّمَ – يُخَيِّمُ to pitch a tent or camp; to settle
خَيْمةٌ (خَيْماتٌ / خِيامٌ) tent, pavilion
مُخَيَّمٌ (مُخَيَّماتٌ) (refugee) camp, encampment

ر ح ل

رَحَلَ – يَرحَلُ to set out or depart; to leave, emigrate, or move away
رَحَّلَ – يُرَحِّلُ to make someone leave; to urge; to evacuate or emigrate
رِحْلةٌ (رحلاتٌ) journey, trip, tour
رَحيلٌ departure, emigration, exodus; demise
رَحّالةٌ (رَحّالونَ) explorer, globetrotter
مَرْحَلةٌ (مَراحِلُ) stage, phase; a leg of a journey
تَرحيلٌ emigration, exodus; deportation
راحِلٌ (رُحَّلٌ) departing, leaving, travelling; deceased

ش ر د

شَرَدَ – يَشْرُدُ to flee, run away, or desert
شَرَّدَ – يُشَرِّدُ to scare, frighten, or chase away
تَشَرَّدَ – يَتَشَرَّدُ to roam or be homeless

شَرِيدٌ fugitive, expelled; a vagrant
تَشْرِيدٌ expulsion, banishment, eviction
شارِدٌ (شَوارِدٌ/شُرُدٌ) deserter, fugitive; intimidated, frightened
مُشَرَّدٌ fugitive, refugee, displaced person

ص م د

صَمَدَ – يَصْمُدُ to withstand, defy, resist, or oppose; to apply oneself
صامَدَ – يُصامِدُ to fight or come to blows
صَمَدٌ lord; eternal, everlasting
صُمودٌ resistance, defiance, staying power

ط و ر

طَوَّرَ – يُطَوِّرُ to develop or advance; to promote
تَطَوَّرَ – يَتَطَوَّرُ to develop, evolve, or change
طَوْرٌ (أَطْوارٌ) one time; stage, degree; condition, state
طورٌ (أَطْوارٌ) mountain
طورُ سَيْناءَ Mount Sinai
تَطَوُّرٌ (تَطَوُّراتٌ) development, evolution
نَظَرِيَّةُ التَّطَوُّرِ the Theory of Evolution
تَطَوُّرِيٌّ evolutionary
تَطْوِيرٌ (تَطْوِيراتٌ) development
مُتَطَوِّرٌ (مُتَطَوِّرونَ) developed
البُلدانُ المُتَطَوِّرَةُ developed countries

ع و ن

عاوَنَ – يُعاوِنُ to help, assist, or support
أَعانَ – يُعِينُ to help, assist, or support; to free, liberate, or relieve
تَعاوَنَ – يَتَعاوَنُ to cooperate, help, or assist each other
عَوْنٌ (أَعْوانٌ) help, aid, assistance (pl: helper, assistant, servant)
وَكالَةُ الْعَوْنِ aid agency
مَعونَةٌ/مُعاوَنَةٌ help, aid, relief, assistance
تَعاوُنٌ cooperation
مُتَعاوِنٌ collaborator
تَعاوُنِيَّةٌ cooperation; cooperative spirit
مُعِينٌ (مُعِينونَ) helper, supporter

غ و ث

أغاثَ – يُغيثُ to help or succour
اِستَغاثَ – يَستَغيثُ to appeal for help, to seek the aid of
غَوْثٌ / إغاثَةٌ aid, succour, help
عامِلُ الإغاثَةِ aid worker

ق ر ر

قَرَّ – يَقَرُّ to settle down, reside, or dwell; to establish oneself
قَرَّرَ – يُقَرِّرُ to decide, determine, or establish
اِستَقَرَّ – يَستَقِرُّ to settle down, establish oneself, or dwell
قَرارٌ (قَراراتٌ) resolutions, decisions; abode, dwelling
قَرارُ الأُمَمِ المُتَّحِدَةِ UN resolution
مَقَرٌّ (مَقَرّاتٌ / مَقارٌّ) dwelling, residence
تَقريرٌ (تَقاريرُ) settlement, decision; report
تَقريرُ المَصيرِ self-determination
إقرارٌ acknowledgement; confirmation
اِستِقرارٌ constancy, stability; establishment
عَدَمُ الإستِقرارِ instability
قارَّةٌ (قارّاتٌ) continent; mainland
مُقَرَّرٌ (مُقَرَّراتٌ) decisions; established, settled

ق ط ن

قَطَنَ – يَقطُنُ to live, dwell, or reside
قُطنٌ (أَقطانٌ) cotton
قاطِنٌ (قُطّانٌ) resident, inhabitant

ل ب ث

لَبِثَ – يَلبَثُ to hesitate or linger; to remain or stay
تَلَبَّثَ – يَتَلَبَّثُ to hesitate or linger; to remain or stay

ل ج أ

لَجَأَ – يَلجَأُ to take refuge; to resort to; to seek information
اِلتَجَأَ – يَلتَجِئُ to flee or take refuge; to resort to
مَلجَأٌ (مَلاجِئُ) refuge, retreat, shelter, sanctuary
لاجِئٌ (لاجِئونَ) refugee; emigrant; inmate of asylum
لاجِئٌ سِياسِيٌّ political refugee

Politics   183

مُلْتَجِئٌ (مُلْتَجِئُونَ) refuge; one seeking refuge
لُجُوءٌ seeking refuge, asylum
مُلْتَمِسُ اللُّجوءِ / طالِبُ اللُّجوءِ asylum seeker

ل ز م

لَزِمَ – يَلْزَمُ to be necessary; to adhere; to belong; to accompany; to persist
أَلْزَمَ – يُلْزِمُ to force or compel; to press or obligate
اِلْتَزَمَ – يَلْتَزِمُ to adhere or stick; to persist or persevere; to be obligated or forced
لُزومٌ necessity, exigency; need, want
اِلْتِزامٌ (اِلْتِزاماتٌ) necessity, obligation, commitment, liability
لازِمٌ necessary, imperative; inevitable; intrinsic
لَوازِمُ (pl) necessities, requirements

م د د

مَدَّ – يَمُدُّ to extend or spread out; to help or aid; to provide; to reinforce (army)
أَمَدَّ – يُمِدُّ to help or aid; to reinforce (army); to supply; to postpone; to fester
تَمَدَّدَ – يَتَمَدَّدُ to be spread; to extend, lengthen, or stretch out
مَدٌّ (مُدودٌ) stretching, lengthening; extension
مَدَّةٌ long sign over *alif* (آ)
مُدَّةٌ (مُدَدٌ) period; interval; duration
مَدَدٌ (أَمْدادٌ) help, aid, assistance, support (pl: resources, supplies)
إمْدادٌ (إمْداداتٌ) supplies, provisions; sustenance
تَمَدُّدٌ expansion, spreading, stretching
اِمْتِدادٌ stretching, widening, extension
مادَّةٌ (مَوادٌّ) subject, topic, theme; chemical element; component, material
مادِّيٌّ materialistic
مُمْتَدٌّ stretched, extended; comprehensive

م ك ث

مَكَثَ – يَمْكُثُ to remain or stay; to dwell or reside
مَكْثٌ (مُكوثٌ) remaining, lingering, stay

ن ج د

نَجَدَ – يُنْجِدُ to help or assist; to sweat
نَجَّدَ – يُنَجِّدُ to upholster; to furnish
اِسْتَنْجَدَ – يَسْتَنْجِدُ to ask for help; to seek aid; to take liberties

184 Politics

نَجْدَةٌ (نَجَداتٌ) help, aid, succor, assistance, support
النَّجدة! help!
تَنجيدٌ upholstering

ن ز ح

نَزَحَ – يَنزَحُ to migrate; to be distant
اِنتَزَحَ – يَنتزِحُ to emigrate
نُزوحٌ emigration, forced migration
نازِحٌ emigrant, emigrating; distant, remote

ن ق ذ

نَقَذَ – يَنقِذُ to save or rescue; to escape
أَنقَذَ – يُنقِذُ to save, rescue, or recover
إنقاذٌ bailout (economic); rescue, relief, recovery; salvation
رِجالُ الإنقاذِ rescue men
اِستِنقاذٌ recovery, relief; salvation
مُنقِذٌ rescuer, saviour

ن ك ب

نَكَبَ – يَنكُبُ to afflict or distress
تَنَكَّبَ – يَتَنَكَّبُ to deviate, avoid, or shun
نَكْبٌ (نُكوبٌ) misfortune, calamity, catastrophe
نَكْبَةٌ (نَكَباتٌ) misfortune, calamity, catastrophe
النَّكْبَةُ the Palestinian Nakba
مَنكوبٌ afflicted by disaster, unfortunate, miserable; victim (of catastrophe)

ه ج ر

هَجَرَ – يَهجُرُ to emigrate; to separate; to abandon or surrender
هاجَرَ – يُهاجِرُ to emigrate
هَجرٌ abandonment, forsaking
هِجرَةٌ flight, migration, departure, exit, exodus
الهِجرَةُ النَّبَوِيَّةُ emigration of Prophet Muhammad from Mecca to Medina in AD 622
هِجرةٌ غيرُ شَرعِيَّةٍ illegal immigration
هِجريٌّ pertaining to Islamic calendar
مُهاجِرٌ (مُهاجِرونَ) immigrants
مُهاجِرٌ غيرُ شَرعِيٍّ illegal immigrant

Exercises

1) Give two derived nouns for each of the following roots:

أ م م
ح ر ر
د ب ب
ر أ س
ع ر ض
غ ر ب

2) Find the roots of these words:

إِجْبارِيٌّ
اِخْتِراقٌ
اِسْتِمارَةٌ
تَطَرُّفٌ
حُروبٌ
حَصانَةٌ
حُكومَةٌ
دَوْلَةٌ
سَلامٌ
سِياسَةٌ

3) Give the singular of these words (some may have more than one singular form):

إماراتٌ
جَواسيسُ
حَرَكاتٌ
سَفاراتٌ
شُروطٌ
عَمَلِيّاتٌ
قُوّاتٌ
مَراكِزُ
مُفاوَضاتٌ
مَمالِكُ
نُوّابٌ

4) Give the present tense of these verbs:

اِسْتَسْلَمَ to surrender or capitulate

اِسْتَغْرَبَ to find strange or unusual; to deem absurd

186 *Politics*

أَعانَ to help, assist, or support

تَطَوَّرَ to develop, evolve, or change

ثارَ to revolt, stir, excite, or arouse

حارَبَ to fight or combat; to wage war

شَرَدَ to flee, run away, or desert

صَوَّتَ to vote or cast ballots

قَرَّرَ to decide, determine, or establish

قَعَدَ to sit down; to stay or remain; to desist

نازَعَ to dispute with, fight, or challenge

5) Translate the following into English:

- الرَّئيسُ الرّوسيُّ يُقابِلُ الرَّئيسَ الفرنسيَّ لِبحثِ قَضيَّةِ الحرب في أوكرانيا.
- ما هَدَف التطبيعِ بين الإمارات وإسرائيل؟
- هل يُعتَبَرُ موقفُ الإمارات خيانةً لإخوَتِهم الفلسطينيّين؟
- قَدَّمَ وزيرُ الصَّحَّة البريطانيّ اِستقالَتَهُ بعدَ خرقِ قواعِدِ مكافحةِ فيروسِ كورونا.

6) Translate the following into Arabic:

- Israel kills two journalists in one month.
- The UN has declared the situation in Yemen a disaster.
- The UK has become a police state.

7) Give the Arabic words which best match these English definitions:

- To raid or attack
- To organise or arrange
- To resist, oppose, or contradict
- To take sides; to form a party
- To wage holy war

Notes

1 Someone who has memorised the Quran by heart.
2 This is a feminine word in Arabic.
3 This is particulary prevalent in Palestinian societies, reflecting the Palestinian struggle for independence.
4 This is usually feminine. In the dialects, however, غولٌ is used for the masculine and the feminine is made by adding the ة which gives غولة.

5 Work, Business, and Economics
العَمَلُ والتِّجارةُ والاقتِصادُ

Work and Employment العَمَلُ والتَّوظيفُ

أ ج ر

أجَرَ – يَأجُرُ to reward or remunerate
أجَّرَ – يُؤَجِّرُ to let out, rent, or lease
اِستأجَرَ – يَستأجِرُ to let out, rent, or lease; to engage the services of
أجرٌ (أجورٌ) wages, pay; fee, rate
زيادةُ الأجورِ wage increase
الحَدُّ الأدنى للأجورِ minimum wage
أجرةٌ hire, rent; fixed rate, price
أجيرٌ (أجَراءٌ) a workman or labourer
تأجيرٌ renting out, leasing, hiring out
إيجارٌ (إيجاراتٌ) rent, letting, leasing
مُستأجِرٌ tenant or leaseholder

أ ش ر

أشَرَ – يأشِرُ to saw or file; to sharpen
أشَّرَ – يُؤَشِّرُ to mark; to indicate; to state, record; to grant a visa
تأشيرةٌ / فيزا (تأشيراتٌ / فيزٌ) visa
تأشيرةُ عَمَلٍ work visa
مُؤَشِّرٌ (مُؤَشِّراتٌ) index; indicator, sign; needle

ب ش ر

بَشَرَ – يَبشُرُ to peel or scratch off; to grate or shred
باشَرَ – يُباشِرُ to pursue or practise (task, job); to touch; to have sex with
بَشَرٌ man, human being; mankind

DOI: 10.4324/9781003250890-6

بَشَرِيٌّ human, human being; of or relating to skin
طبيبٌ بَشَرِيٌّ dermatologist
بَشَرَةٌ skin, complexion; cuticle
الْبَشَرِيَّةُ humanity
الموارِدُ الْبَشَرِيَّةُ human resources
دائرةُ الْمَوارِدِ الْبَشَرِيَّةِ human resources department
مُباشَرَةٌ a pursuit or practice
مُباشَرَةً immediately, directly
مُباشِرٌ (مُباشِرونَ) direct, immediate; live (TV); director, operator, practitioner

ب ط ل

بَطَلَ – يَبْطُلُ to be or become invalid; to be false; to be untenable
بَطَّلَ – يُبَطِّلُ to thwart, frustrate; to counteract, invalidate, neutralise
بُطْلانٌ futility, vanity; falseness
بَطالةٌ unemployment; idleness; holidays
بَطالةٌ جَماعِيَّةٌ mass unemployment
مُعَدَّلُ الْبَطالةِ unemployment rate
باطِلٌ vain, futile; invalid or worthless

ح ر ف

حَرَّفَ – يُحَرِّفُ to distort, twist, or corrupt; to incline or deflect
اِنْحَرَفَ – يَنْحَرِفُ to deviate, digress, or depart from; to slant or to be twisted
اِحْتَرَفَ – يَحْتَرِفُ to practise (sth) as a profession; to strive for success
حَرْفٌ (حِرَفٌ) edge (knife); border, verge
حَرْفٌ (أَحْرُفٌ/حُروفٌ) letter, consonant; particle (grammar)
الْحُروفُ الأَبجَدِيَّةُ letters of the alphabet
حَرْفِيٌّ literal
حَرْفِيّاً literally
حِرفةٌ (حِرَفٌ) vocation, trade, craft, occupation, profession; skill
حِرفِيٌّ professional; craftsmen
تَحريفٌ (تَحريفاتٌ) alteration; distortion, corruption
اِنْحِرافٌ (اِنْحِرافاتٌ) deviation, digression; inclination, slant
مُحَرَّفٌ corrupted (word)
مُنْحَرِفٌ slanted, twisted; distorted, corrupted
مُحْتَرِفٌ professional, skilful

خ د م

خَدَمَ – يَخدِمُ to serve or wait on; to work or have a job
خَدَّمَ – يُخَدِّمُ to employ, hire, or engage services
اِستَخدَمَ – يَستَخدِمُ to use or employ; to hire or engage the services of
اِستِخدامٌ utilisation, use; employment, service, occupation
خِدمَةٌ (خِدَماتٌ) service, attendance; occupation, job, employment; office
خِدمَةُ الزَّبائِنِ customer services
الخِدمَةُ المَدنِيَّةُ civil service
الخِدماتُ اللَّوجِستِيَّةُ / لوجِستِيّاتٌ logistics
خادِمٌ / خَدّامٌ (خُدّامٌ / خَدَمٌ) servant / attendant
خادِمةٌ / خَدّامةٌ (خادِماتٌ / خَدّاماتٌ) maid, female servant

د ر ب

دَرِبَ – يَدرَبُ to be accustomed or used to; to be practised, trained, or skilled
دَرَّبَ – يُدَرِّبُ to habituate or accustom; to practise or train; to coach or tutor
دَرْبٌ (دُروبٌ) alley, lane; narrow mountain pass
دَربُ التَّبانةِ the Milky Way
تَدريبٌ habituation; practice, training, tutoring
مُدَرِّبٌ (مُدَرِّبونَ) instructor, trainer, coach
مُتَدَرِّبٌ (مُتَدَرِّبونَ) trainee

د و م

دامَ – يَدومُ to last or continue; to persevere or persist
داوَمَ – يُداوِمُ to persevere, persist, or pursue diligently
دَوْمٌ permanence, duration, continuance
دَوامٌ duration, perpetuity; working hours
ساعاتُ الدَّوامِ working hours
الدَّوامُ الكامِلُ full time (work)
الدَّوامُ الجُزئِيُّ part time (work)
دَوّامَةٌ vortex, whirlpool
مُداوَمَةٌ duration; perseverance, persistence
دائِمٌ lasting, eternal; continuous, constant
دائِماً always
ما دامَ so long as, as long as

Work, Business, and Economics

مُستَديمٌ constant, continuous, uninterrupted
عاهةٌ مُستَديمةٌ chronic disability

ر ت ب

رتَّبَ – يُرتِّبُ to arrange or organise; to appoint or fix; to decorate or dress
تَرَتَّبَ – يَتَرَتَّبُ to be arranged or organised; to result or follow; to fall in line
رُتبَةٌ (رُتَبٌ) grade, level, rank, class, degree, position
مَرتَبَةٌ (مَراتِبُ) elevation; step, grade, degree, status
تَرتيبٌ (تَرتيباتٌ) arrangement, order, sequence; set-up; succession
تَرتيبِيٌّ ordinal
رَقمٌ تَرتيبِيٌّ ordinal number
راتِبٌ (رَواتِبُ) salary, pay
راتِبٌ تَقاعُدِيٌّ pension
مُرَتَّبٌ (مُرتَّباتٌ) arranged, organised, regulated (pl: salary, wages)

ر ق ي

رَقِيَ – يَرقى to be promoted; to rise, climb, or mount
رَقَّى – يُرَقِّي to promote; to raise or advance
اِرتَقى – يَرتَقي to be promoted; to rise; to ascend (as a martyr); to increase
رُقِيٌّ rise; progress
تَرقِيَةٌ (تَرقِياتٌ) a promotion, upgrade, or advancement

ز م ل

زامَلَ – يُزامِلُ to accompany or to be a companion; to be a colleague or associate
تَزامَلَ – يَتَزامَلُ to be comrades or close companions
زَميلٌ (زُملاءُ) colleague, associate
زَمالَةٌ comradeship, fellowship

No root

سِكرِتيرٌ secretary

ش غ ل

شَغَلَ – يَشغَلُ to work; to occupy, distract, or divert
شَغَّلَ – يُشَغِّلُ to busy, occupy; to employ; to work; to fabricate; to invest
أَشغَلَ – يُشغِلُ to employ; to occupy or busy

Work, Business, and Economics   191

اِنْشَغَلَ – يَنْشَغِلُ to occupy or busy oneself; to be concerned
شُغْلٌ (أَشْغالٌ) work, job, occupation; activity; distraction
شَغّالٌ (شَغّالون) worker, labourer; very busy
شَغّيلٌ (شَغّيلة) worker, employee, labourer; hard working
مَشْغَلٌ (مَشاغِلُ) workshop
اِنْشِغالٌ being busy or occupied; work or occupation
مَشْغولٌ busy, occupied, distracted

ط ر د

طَرَدَ – يَطْرُدُ to fire or expel; to banish, exile, or drive away
طارَدَ – يُطارِدُ to assault or attack; to pursue, follow, or stalk (an animal)
طَرْدٌ eviction; firing; a parcel
طَريدٌ evicted, expelled; banished, exiled; a fugitive

ط و ع

طاعَ – يُطيعُ to be obedient or to obey
طَوَّعَ – يُطَوِّعُ to subdue or subjugate; to subject
طاوَعَ – يطاوِعُ to obey, consent, or comply with
تَطَوَّعَ – يَتَطَوَّعُ to volunteer
اِسْتَطاعَ – يَسْتَطيعُ to carry out; to be able or capable of
طَوْعٌ subjugation; voluntariness; spontaneity
طَوْعِيٌّ / تَطَوُّعِيٌّ voluntary
مُنَظَّمَةٌ طَوْعِيَّةٌ / مُنَظَّمَةٌ تَطَوُّعِيَّةٌ voluntary organisation
طَوْعاً / طَوْعِيّاً voluntarily
تَطَوُّعٌ volunteering, voluntary service; obedience, compliance
تَطْويعٌ subjugation
عَمَلٌ تَطَوُّعِيٌّ voluntary work
طاعَةٌ (طاعاتٌ) obedience, compliance, submissiveness (pl: pious deeds)
مُطيعٌ / طائِعٌ obedient, compliant
مُتَطَوِّعٌ (مُتَطَوِّعون) volunteer
مُسْتَطاعٌ possible, feasible

ع ط ل

عَطَلَ – يَعْطِلُ to lack or be destitute; to be idle or unemployed
تَعَطَّلَ – يَتَعَطَّلُ to be or become unemployed; to be delayed; to be out of order

Work, Business, and Economics

عُطلَةٌ (عُطَلٌ / عُطَلاتٌ) holiday, leisure; unemployment
عُطلَةٌ رَسميَّةٌ public holiday
عُطلَةٌ مَصرَفيَّةٌ bank holiday
تَعطيلٌ obstruction, closure, suspension
تَعَطُّلٌ unemployment; inactivity, idleness
عاطِلٌ (عاطِلونَ) unemployed; inactive, idle; destitute
مُعَطَّلٌ unemployed; inactive, idle; out of work; out of order

ع م ل

عَمِلَ – يَعمَلُ to do or act; to work or operate; to produce
عامَلَ – يُعامِلُ to treat; to trade or deal with
تَعامَلَ – يَتَعامَلُ to trade or do business with
عَمَلٌ (أَعمالٌ) work, labour, job, business, trade; production, operation
التَّدريبُ على العَمَلِ apprenticeship; work experience
صاحِبُ العَمَلِ employer
رَجُلُ أَعمالٍ businessman
سَيِّدَةُ أَعمالٍ businesswoman
إدارةُ الأَعمالِ business administration
عَمَلِيٌّ practical
جَدوَلُ الأَعمالِ agenda
عَمَلِيَّةٌ (عَمَلِيّاتٌ) activity, work; operation, process, method; surgery
عُملَةٌ (عُملاتٌ) money, currency
عُملَةٌ أَجنَبيَّةٌ foreign exchange
تَبادُلُ العُملاتِ currency exchange
عَميلٌ (عُمَلاءُ) agent or representative; customer; ally
خِدمَةُ العُمَلاءِ customer services
عُمولَةٌ (عُمولاتٌ) commission
مَعمَلٌ (مَعامِلُ) laboratory, factory, workshop; establishment
مُعامَلَةٌ (مُعامَلاتٌ) treatment; business relations
تَعامُلٌ (تَعامُلاتٌ) transactions, trade relations, business
إستِعمالٌ use, utilisation, handling
عامِلٌ (عَوامِلُ) factor
عامِلٌ (عُمَّالٌ) worker; agent
حِزبُ العُمَّالِ Labour party
العامِلونَ staff
العَمالَةُ / القُوى العامِلَةُ / اليَدُ العامِلَةُ the workforce; manpower

Work, Business, and Economics   193

عَمَلٌ فَرِيقِيٌّ teamwork
طَلَبُ عَمَلٍ application form
فُرَصُ العملِ job opportunities
خِبْرَةُ العملِ work experience
تَعَطَّلَ عن العملِ to become unemployed
العملُ للحِسابِ الخاصِّ self-employment
رَبُّ العملِ/صاحِبُ العَمَلِ employer
ظُروفُ العملِ working conditions
عَمالةُ الأَطْفالِ child labour

ف ر ص

فَرَّصَ – يُفرِّصُ to go on holiday
فُرْصَةٌ (فُرَصٌ) opportunity, chance; holiday, vacation

ف ل ح

فَلَحَ – يَفلَحُ to split or cleave; to cultivate or plough
أَفلَحَ – يُفلِحُ to thrive or prosper; to become happy; to be lucky
اِستَفلَحَ – يَستَفلِحُ to thrive or prosper; to become happy; to be lucky
فَلاحٌ prosperity, success; welfare, salvation
فِلاحَةٌ cultivation, agriculture
فَلّاحٌ (فلّاحونَ) farmer, peasant
فالِحٌ/مُفلِحٌ lucky, successful

ق ي ل

قالَ – يَقيلُ to take a midday nap
أَقالَ – يُقيلُ to abolish, cancel, dismiss, or discharge
اِستَقالَ – يَستَقيلُ to resign; to demand the cancellation (of); to apologise
إِقالةٌ cancellation, annulment; dismissal (work)
اِستِقالةٌ retirement, resignation; withdrawal
مُستَقيلٌ retired, discharged, resigned

ك د ح

كَدَحَ – يَكْدَحُ to work hard, toil, or slave

194 · *Work, Business, and Economics*

اِكْتَدَحَ – يَكْتَدِحُ to earn a living
كَدْحٌ exertion; toil
كادِحٌ (كادِحونَ) labourer

ك د د

كَدَّ – يَكِدُّ to work hard, exhaust, wear out, slave away
كَدٌّ hard work, labour, pains
كَدُودٌ industrious, hard working
مَكدودٌ worn out, exhausted, overworked

ك س ب

كَسَبَ – يَكْسِبُ to earn, gain, or win; to acquire (knowledge)
كَسَّبَ – يُكَسِّبُ to make or let someone gain
اِكْتَسَبَ – يَكْتَسِبُ to possess; to earn
كَسْبٌ acquisition; gains, earnings
مَكْسَبٌ (مَكاسِبُ) gain, profit
اِكْتِسابٌ acquisition, gaining
كاسِبٌ winner

ك س ل

كَسِلَ – يَكْسَلُ to be lazy or negligent
تَكاسَلَ – يَتَكاسَلُ to be lazy or negligent
كَسَلٌ laziness, inactivity, negligence
كَسولٌ / مُتَكاسِلٌ lazy, idle
كَسْلانٌ (كَسالى) lazy, idle

م ه ن

مَهَنَ – يَمْهَنُ to serve; to degrade; to treat; to wear out by use
ماهَنَ – يُماهِنُ to practise (a profession)
مِهْنَةٌ (مِهَنٌ / مِهْناتٌ) job, vocation, profession
مِهْنِيٌّ professional, vocational; employed
الإرْشادُ المِهْنِيُّ career advice
تدريبٌ مِهْنِيٌّ apprenticeship
سيرةٌ مِهْنِيَّةٌ career
مَهينٌ despised, despicable, contemptible

Work, Business, and Economics 195

ن ط ر

نَطَرَ – يَنْطُرُ to watch or guard
نَطْرٌ / نِطارَةٌ watch, protection; a guard
ناطِرٌ / ناطورٌ (نُطّارٌ / نَواطيرُ) a guard, warden, or lookout

ن ق ب

نَقَبَ – يَنْقُبُ to pierce or perforate; to dig or excavate; to inquire
تَنَقَّبَ – يَتَنَقَّبُ to examine, study, or investigate; to be perforated; to veil the face (of women)
نَقْبٌ (أَنْقابٌ) digging, drilling, excavation; a perforation, hole, or opening
نِقابٌ (نُقُبٌ) a veil
نِقابَةٌ (نِقاباتٌ) syndicate, corporation, union, association
نِقابَةُ العُمّالِ trade union
نَقيبٌ (نُقَباءُ) chief or head; lieutenant

No root

هَنْدَسَةٌ engineering; architecture; geometry
الهَنْدَسَةُ الكَهْرَبائيَّةُ electrical engineering
الهَنْدَسَةُ المَدَنيَّةُ civil engineering
الهَنْدَسَةُ الميكانيكيَّةُ mechanical engineering
الهَنْدَسَةُ المِعْماريَّةُ architecture
هَنْدَسيٌّ technical; industrial; geometrical
مُهَنْدِسٌ (مُهَنْدِسونَ) engineer, technician; architect
مُهَنْدِسٌ مِعْماريٌّ architect
مُهَنْدِسٌ كَهْرَبائيٌّ electrical engineer

و ب خ

وَبَّخَ – يُوَبِّخُ to reprimand or scold
تَوْبيخٌ a reproach or reproof

No root

وَرْشَةٌ (وَرْشاتٌ) workshop

و ظ ف

وَظَّفَ – يُوَظِّفُ to employ, appoint, or give office to; to invest; to burden or impose

تَوَظَّفَ – يَتَوَظَّفُ to get a job or obtain a position; to be appointed to an office
وَظيفةٌ (وَظائِفُ) work, job, post, duty, task, assignment
وَظائِفُ شاغِرةٌ job vacancies
تَوْظيفٌ employment, hiring
مكتبُ التَّوظيفِ employment office
مُوَظَّفٌ (مُوَظَّفونَ) employed; a worker or employee; an official
مُوَظَّفُ اِسْتِقبالٍ receptionist
مُوَظَّفٌ حُكوميٌّ civil servant
شُؤونُ الْمُوَظَّفينَ personnel department

و ق ت

وَقَّتَ – يُوَقِّتُ to fix, appoint, or determine a time
وَقْتٌ (أَوْقاتٌ) time; a period of time, a moment, or an instant
في نَفسِ الْوَقتِ simultaneously
تَوْقيتٌ timing
مَوْقوتٌ appointed; fixed; temporary or limited in time
مُوَقَّتٌ / مُؤَقَّتٌ temporary, transient, provisional; a fixed or set time
مُؤَقَّتاً temporarily, provisionally

و ه ب

وَهَبَ – يَهَبُ to give, donate, grant, present, or endow
هِبةٌ (هِباتٌ) a gift, present, donation, or grant
وَهَبةٌ tip, gratuity
الوَهابيّةُ Wahabism
مَوْهِبةٌ (مَواهِبُ) skill, talent, gift
إيهابٌ donation; granting (also a boy's name)
واهِبٌ giver, donor
مَوْهوبٌ gifted, talented

Business, Trade, and Commerce العَمَلُ والتِّجارةُ

أ س س

أَسَّسَ – يُؤَسِّسُ to establish, set up, or lay the foundation
تَأَسَّسَ – يَتَأَسَّسُ to be founded, established, or set up
أَساسٌ (أُسُسٌ / أَساساتٌ) foundation, basis, groundwork

Work, Business, and Economics 197

أَساسِيٌّ / أَساسٌ fundamental; basic, elementary
أَساسِيّاتٌ fundamentals, principles
تَأسيسٌ (تَأسيساتٌ) setting up or establishing (pl: facilities, utilities)
مُؤَسِّسٌ (مُؤَسِّسونَ) founder
مُؤَسَّسَةٌ (مُؤَسَّساتٌ) institution, establishment, organisation

ب د ل

بَدَلَ – يَبْدُلُ to replace or exchange
بَدَّلَ – يُبَدِّلُ to change, alter, substitute, or exchange
تَبَدَّلَ – يَتَبَدَّلُ to change or be exchanged
تَبادَلَ – يَتَبادَلُ to exchange
بَدَلٌ (أَبْدالٌ) substitute, replacement; compensation, reimbursement; price, rate
بَدَلَ (prep) instead of, in place of
بَدَلًا مِن (prep) in place of, instead of
بَدْلَةٌ (بَدَلاتٌ) suit, costume
بَديلٌ substitute
تَبَدُّلٌ change, shift, transformation
تَبادُلٌ exchange
مُتَبادَلٌ mutual, reciprocal

ب ض ع

بَضَعَ – يَبْضَعُ to cut or slash; to dissect
تَبَضَّعَ – يَتَبَضَّعُ to trade or make purchases
اِسْتَبْضَعَ – يَسْتَبْضِعُ to trade
بَضْعٌ amputation
بِضاعَةٌ (بَضائِعُ) products, commodities, merchandise
بَضائِعُ وخَدَماتٌ goods and services

ب ك ر

بَكَرَ – يَبْكُرُ to set out early in the morning; to come early
باكَرَ – يُباكِرُ to be ahead of someone; to anticipate
اِبْتَكَرَ – يَبْتَكِرُ to be the first to do something; to deflower; to invent or create
بَكْرٌ (أَبْكُرٌ) young camel
بِكْرٌ (أَبْكارٌ) firstborn, eldest; new; virgin, virginal
بُكْرَةٌ early morning

198 Work, Business, and Economics

بَكِّيرٌ / باكِرٌ coming early, premature, precocious
اِبتِكارٌ (اِبتِكاراتٌ) invention, innovation; foresight
باكِراً / مُبَكِّراً early; in the morning
مُبتَكِرٌ creator, inventor

ب ي ع

باعَ - يَبيعُ to sell
تَبايَعَ - يَتَبايَعُ to agree the terms of a sale, to conclude a bargain
اِبتاعَ - يَبتاعُ to buy or purchase
بَيْعٌ selling
البَيْعُ بِالجُملَةِ wholesale
بَيْعٌ بِالتَّجزِئَةِ retail
بَيْعَةٌ agreement, arrangement; business deal, bargain, sale, purchase
بَيّاعٌ / بائِعٌ salesman, merchant, dealer
مَبيعٌ (مَبيعاتٌ) sales
مُديرُ مَبيعاتٍ sales manager
بائِعٌ (باعَةٌ / بائِعونَ) salesman

ت ج ر

تَجَرَ - يَتجُرُ to trade, deal, or do business
تاجَرَ - يُتاجِرُ to trade, deal, or do business
تِجارَةٌ commerce, trade; merchandise
التِّجارَةُ العادِلَةُ fair trade
تِجاريٌّ commercial, business, or trade related
مَعرِضٌ تِجاريٌّ trade fair
التَّبادُلُ التِّجاريُّ trade exchange
حَظرٌ تِجاريٌّ trade embargo
الغُرفَةُ التِّجارِيَّةُ chamber of commerce
مَتجَرٌ (مَتاجِرُ) business; store; dealing; merchandise
تاجِرٌ (تُجّارٌ) merchant, trader; businessman
اِتِّجارٌ trade, business

No root

جُمرُكٌ (جَمارِكُ) customs, duty
رَسمُ الجَمارِكِ customs duty, tariff

Work, Business, and Economics   199

جُمْرُكِيٌّ customs, tariff
رَقابةٌ جُمرِكيَّةٌ customs control
مُجَمْرَكٌ duty paid

ح ك ر

اِحتَكَرَ – يَحتَكِرُ to buy up; to hoard; to monopolise
حُكْرةٌ hoarding of goods; monopoly
اِحتِكارٌ (اِحْتِكاراتٌ) monopoly, cartel; supremacy, hegemony

د م ج

دَمَجَ – يَدْمِجُ to merge; to enter; to be inserted or incorporated
اِندَمَجَ – يَندَمِجُ to be inserted or incorporated; to merge
إدماجٌ insertion, incorporation
اِندِماجٌ (اِندِماجاتٌ) merger, annexation, incorporation
مُدَمَّجٌ compact

د و ر

دارَ – يَدورُ to turn, revolve, or circle; to circulate or spread; to roam; to lead or guide
دَوَّرَ – يُدَوِّرُ to turn into a circle; to spin, revolve, or circulate; to set in motion
أدارَ – يُديرُ to turn; to direct, set in motion, or initiate; to administer, lead, or guide
تَدَوَّرَ – يَتَدَوَّرُ to be circular
اِستَدارَ – يَستَديرُ to rotate or spin; to look back
دارٌ (دورٌ) home, house, residence
دَوْرٌ (أدوارٌ) a role or part; a round; a degree or step; age, period; rotation
دَوْرةٌ (دَوْراتٌ) cycle; procession; circulation; parliamentary session
دَوْرِيَّةٌ (دَوْرِيّاتٌ) patrol, round, squad
دَيْرٌ (أَديْرَةٌ) monastery, convent
ديرةٌ region, area, land
إدارةٌ (إداراتٌ) management, administration; committee, department; turning
إدارةُ الأعمالِ business administration
إداريٌّ administrative
دائِرٌ turning, spinning, revolving
دائِرةٌ (دَوائِرُ) circle; circumference, perimeter; field, domain, department, office
مُدَوَّرٌ / مُستَديرٌ round, circular

مُديرٌ (مُدَراءُ/مُديرونَ) director, head, chief, manager, administrator
المُديرُ العامُّ managing director, director general

ر ز ق

رَزَقَ – يَرْزُقُ to provide with means of subsistence; to bestow or endow
ارْتَزَقَ – يَرْتَزِقُ to make a living or gain one's livelihood; to live
رِزْقٌ (أَرْزاقٌ) livelihood, subsistence, income; nourishment
مَرْزوقٌ blessed, prosperous, successful
مُرْتَزَقٌ (مُرْتَزِقَةٌ) hired; mercenary
مُرْتَزَقٌ livelihood, living

ر س م

رَسَمَ – يَرْسُمُ to draw, trace, or sketch; to describe or depict
رَسَّمَ – يُرَسِّمُ to enter, mark, or indicate; to appoint to public office
رَسْمٌ (رُسومٌ/رُسوماتٌ) drawing, sketch; impression, mark; fees
رَسْمُ الدُّخولِ admission fee
رُسومٌ مُتحرِّكةٌ animation, cartoons
رَسْمِيٌّ official, formal, conventional
رَسّامٌ (رَسّامونَ) painter, artist
مَراسِمُ ceremonies; ceremonial, ritual; protocol
مَرْسومٌ (مَراسيمُ) drawn; decreed, ordered; a decree; ceremonies; an act

ر و ج

راجَ – يَروجُ to circulate; to be current or in demand
رَوَّجَ – يُرَوِّجُ to promote or put into circulation; to make propaganda
رَواجٌ circulation; sales; marketability
تَرْويجٌ promotion, spreading, circulation, distribution; sale
رائِجٌ circulating, widespread, common; selling well
نَشاطٌ تَرْويجِيٌّ promotional activity

No root

زَبونٌ (زَبائِنُ) customer, client
زَبانةٌ clientele; custom

س ل ع

سَلِعَ – يَسْلَعُ to crack or become cracked

Work, Business, and Economics

سِلْعةٌ (سِلَعٌ) commodity, goods
سِلعةٌ رائجةٌ popular goods

س و ق

ساقَ – يَسوقُ to drive or herd; to draft or conscript; to send; to convey
سَوَّقَ – يُسوِّقُ to market or sell
تَسَوَّقَ – يَتَسَوَّقُ to trade in the market, to buy and sell
اِنْساقَ – يَنْساقُ to drift; to be driven or carried away
سَوْقٌ / سِواقةٌ driving (car); conscription; mobilisation (of troops/forces)
ساقٌ (سيقانٌ / سوقٌ) thigh, leg, side; stem, stalk
سوقٌ (أَسْواقٌ) market, bazaar, fair
الأَسْواقُ الحُرَّةُ duty free shop
السّوقُ المُشْتَرَكةُ the Common Market
السوقُ السَّوْداءُ black market
سوقُ الأوراقِ الماليَّةِ / البورصةُ the Stock Exchange
الأَسْواقُ النّاشِئةُ emerging or developing markets
قُوّاتُ السّوقِ market forces
سَوّاقٌ / سائِقٌ (سَوّاقونَ / سائِقونَ) driver
تَسْويقٌ marketing, sale

س و م

سامَ – يَسومُ to offer for sale; to impose, force, or demand
ساوَمَ – يُساوِمُ to bargain, haggle, or negotiate
مُساوَمةٌ (مُساوَماتٌ) bargaining, haggling

ش ر ك

شَرِكَ – يَشْرَكُ to share or participate; to be or become a partner or associate
شارَكَ – يُشارِكُ to share or participate; to be or become a partner or associate
اِشْتَرَكَ – يَشْتَرِكُ to enter into partnership or collaborate; to participate or share
شِرْكٌ polytheism; share, lot
شَرِكةٌ (شَرِكاتٌ) company, corporation, partnership, firm
شَرِكةٌ عِملاقةٌ / شَرِكةٌ عبرَ القارّاتِ multinational corporation
مَجْموعةُ شَرِكاتٍ conglomerate
شَريكٌ (شُرَكاءُ) partner, associate; companion; ally
شَريكٌ تِجاريٌّ trade partner
مُشارَكةٌ في participation (in); cooperation, collaboration

Work, Business, and Economics

اِشْتِراكٌ (اِشْتِراكاتٌ) cooperation, partnership; sharing; subscription
اِشْتِراكِيٌّ socialist
اِشْتِراكِيَّةٌ socialism
مُشْرِكٌ (مُشْرِكونَ) polytheist
مُشْتَرِكٌ (مُشْتَرِكونَ) participant; subscriber
مُشْتَرَكٌ common, joint, combined

ش ر ى

شَرى – يَشري to sell or vend; to buy or purchase
اِشْتَرى – يَشْتَري to buy, purchase, or acquire; to sell
شِراءٌ purchase, buying
قُوَّةُ الشِّراءِ purchasing power
شَرْوَةٌ purchase
شِرْيانٌ (شَرايينُ) artery
شارٍ (شُراةٌ) seller, salesman
مُشْتَرٍ purchaser, customer; seller, vendor
المُشْتَري Jupiter
مُشْتَرىً (مُشْتَرَياتٌ) purchases, buying; goods

ص د ر

صَدَرَ – يَصْدُرُ to leave; to proceed; to arise or stem from; to appear; to be published
صَدَّرَ – يُصَدِّرُ to export; to send off, dispatch, or forward; to publish
صادَرَ – يُصادِرُ to seize, impound, or confiscate; to urge or press
صَدْرٌ (صُدورٌ) chest, heart; a part or portion
صُدورٌ coming out, appearance; publication (book, article)
مَصْدَرٌ (مَصادِرُ) starting point, source; the infinitive (grammar); a verbal noun
مُصادَرَةٌ seizure, confiscation
إِصْدارٌ export; issue, bringing out; publication
صادِرٌ (صادِراتٌ) exports; yield; originating, emanating; published
مُصَدِّرٌ exporter

ص ف ق

صَفَقَ – يَصْفِقُ to slap, smack, or bang; to set in motion; to be thick or heavy
صَفْقَةٌ (صَفْقاتٌ) a deal or bargain; the conclusion of a contract
تَصْفيقٌ applause, hand clapping

Work, Business, and Economics

ص ن ع

صَنَعَ – يَصْنَعُ to make, manufacture, produce, build; to stage or arrange
صَنَّعَ – يُصَنِّعُ to industrialise
تَصَنَّعَ – يَتَصَنَّعُ to pretend, simulate, or affect
صُنْعٌ production, manufacture, fabrication
صُنْعٌ يَدَوِيٌّ handmade
صَنْعَةٌ work, manufacture; trade, skill; workmanship; fabrication, art
صاحِبُ الصَّنْعَةِ artisan
صِناعَةٌ (صِناعاتٌ) industry, manufacturing; skill, occupation, profession
صِناعِيٌّ artificial, synthetic; trade, industrial
مَصْنَعٌ (مَصانِعُ) factory, plant, works; establishment, firm
مَصْنَعِيَّةٌ wages, pay; workmanship
تَصْنِيعٌ industrialisation
تَصَنُّعٌ hypocrisy, affectation
اِصْطِناعٌ production, making
اِصْطِناعِيٌّ artificial, synthetic
صانِعٌ (صُنَّاعٌ) manufacturer, producer
مَصْنوعٌ (مَصْنوعاتٌ) products, articles, produce, manufactured goods
مُتَصَنِّعٌ fake, affected, stilted

ع د د

عَدَّ – يَعُدُّ to count or calculate
أَعَدَّ – يُعِدُّ to prepare, make ready, or arrange
تَعَدَّدَ – يَتَعَدَّدُ to be or become numerous; to be manifold or multiple
اِسْتَعَدَّ – يَسْتَعِدُّ to get or be ready; to prepare oneself; to be willing
عَدٌّ counting, enumeration, calculation
عُدَّةٌ (عُدَدٌ) readiness; equipment, tools; outfit
عِدَّةٌ a number (of); several, many, numerous
عَدَدٌ (أَعْدادٌ) number, figure, digit
عَديدٌ numerous, many
إِعْدادٌ preparation, readying, arranging
تَعَدُّدٌ variety, diversity
اِسْتِعْدادٌ (اِسْتِعْداداتٌ) readiness, willingness; inclination, tendency
مُعَدَّاتٌ equipment, material
مُتَعَدِّدٌ multiple, plural, diverse
مُسْتَعِدٌّ (لِ) prepared, ready (for)

204 Work, Business, and Economics

ع ر ب ن

عَرْبَنَ – يُعرْبِنُ to make a down payment
عَرَبونٌ (عَرابينُ) deposit, token, down payment

غ ل ل

غَلَّ – يَغِلُّ to enter, penetrate, or insert; to handcuff; to produce or yield
اِستَغَلَّ – يَستَغِلُّ to utilise; to profit, capitalise, or gain
غُلٌّ (أَغلالٌ) burning thirst; shackles, handcuffs
غَلَّةٌ (غِلالٌ) daily income; yield
اِستِغلالٌ utilisation; exploitation; working
مُستَغِلٌّ exploiter; beneficiary

ف ض ل

فَضَلَ – يَفضُلُ to be surplus or in excess; to be excellent or superior
فَضَّلَ – يُفَضِّلُ to prefer or give preference
فَضلٌ (فُضولٌ) surplus, excess, remainder; importance
فَضلَةٌ (فَضَلاتٌ) remainder, surplus, residue; waste, scraps (pl: excrements)
فُضولٌ / فُضولِيَّةٌ curiosity, inquisitiveness
فَضيلةٌ (فَضائِلُ) virtue, merit, advantage, excellence
تَفضيلٌ preference, favouring, esteem
مُفَضَّلٌ preferable, preferred

ق ط ع

قَطَعَ – يَقطَعُ to cut, sever, or amputate; to divide or interrupt
قاطَعَ – يُقاطِعُ to dissociate or snub; to boycott; to cut or interrupt
اِنقَطَعَ – يَنقَطِعُ to be cut off, severed, or chopped; to be torn apart; to be disrupted
اِستَقطَعَ – يَستَقطِعُ to deduct
قَطعٌ cutting off, amputation; disruption
قَطعِيٌّ positive, decided, final, decisive
قِطعَةٌ (قِطَعٌ) piece, fragment, part, portion, section, division
قِطاعٌ (قِطاعاتٌ) sector, section
مَقطَعٌ (مَقاطِعُ) crossing, passage; section, division
مَقطَعُ فيديو / مَقطَعٌ مَرئِيٌّ video clip
مُقاطَعَةٌ boycott; interruption; indifference

Work, Business, and Economics

مُقاطَعَةٌ (مُقاطَعاتٌ) area, region, district; section
اِنْقِطاعٌ separation, break, severance
قِطاعُ الخَدَماتِ service sector
قِطاعٌ عامٌّ public sector
قِطاعٌ خاصٌّ private sector

ك ف ى

كَفى – يَكْفي to be sufficient or enough; to suffice; to save or spare
كافى – يُكافي to suffice; to recompense or reward
اِكْتَفى – يَكْتَفي to be content
كِفايَةٌ enough, sufficient; degree, extent; sufficiency
مُكافَأَةٌ reward, gratification
اِكْتِفاءٌ contentment
الإِكْتِفاءُ الذَّاتِيّ self-sufficiency
كافٍ (كُفاةٌ) enough, sufficient; skilled, qualified; appropriate

ك ل ف

كَلِفَ – يَكْلَفُ to like; to be in love; to be intent or set on (sth)
كَلَّفَ – يُكَلِّفُ to give a task, commission, or assign; to go to the trouble
كُلْفَةٌ (كُلَفٌ) expenditure, cost; inconvenience; formality; ceremonial
تَكْليفٌ (تَكاليفُ) expenses, costs; burdening, nuisance, bother
مُكَلَّفٌ commissioned, authorised, charged; liable

No root

ماركَةٌ (ماركاتٌ) mark, sign, token
ماركَةٌ تِجارِيَّةٌ / ماركَةٌ مُسَجَّلَةٌ trademark

ن ف ذ

نَفَذَ – يَنْفُذُ to pierce, penetrate, or break through; to arrive; to communicate
نَفَّذَ – يُنَفِّذُ to implement or execute; to pierce or penetrate; to send; to be effective
نَفَذٌ (أَنْفاذٌ) opening, outlet, hole, vent
نُفوذٌ penetration, influence; person of interest
ذو نُفوذٍ influential; person of influence
مَنْفَذٌ (مَنافِذُ) outlet, exit, way out; window

Work, Business, and Economics

تَنْفيذٌ execution, fulfilment, implementation
تَنْفيذِيٌّ executive
مُوَظَّفٌ تَنْفيذِيٌّ an executive
المُديرُ التَّنْفيذِيُّ executive manager
الرَّئيسُ التَّنْفيذِيُّ chief executive
نافِذَةٌ (نَوافِذُ) window

ن ف ع

نَفَعَ – يَنْفَعُ to be useful, profitable, or advantageous
اِنْتَفَعَ – يَنْتَفِعُ to utilise, use, or take advantage of; to profit, benefit, or enjoy
مَنْفَعَةٌ (مَنافِعُ) use, benefit, advantage, profit
نافِعٌ useful, profitable, advantageous (also a boy's name)

ن ف ق

نَفَقَ – يَنْفُقُ to be active; to sell well; to die or perish
نَفَّقَ – يُنَفِّقُ to sell
نافَقَ – يُنافِقُ to be a hypocrite
أَنْفَقَ – يُنْفِقُ to spend: to squander; to disburse; to support or bear the costs of
نَفَقٌ (أَنْفاقٌ) tunnel
نَفَقَةٌ (نَفَقاتٌ) expense, cost; maintenance, support
مُنافَقَةٌ / نِفاقٌ hypocrisy
إِنْفاقٌ spending, expenses
مُنافِقٌ (مُنافِقونَ) hypocrite

ن ق ص

نَقَصَ – يَنْقُصُ to decrease or diminish; to be reduced
ناقَصَ – يُناقِصُ to invite bids
أَنْقَصَ – يُنْقِصُ to decrease, diminish, reduce, or cut
نَقْصٌ decrease, deficit, loss
عُقْدَةُ النَّقْصِ inferiority complex
مُناقَصَةٌ (مُناقَصاتٌ) competition; tender (commerce); public auction
ناقِصٌ defective, diminished; incomplete

No root

نَموذَجٌ (نَماذِجُ) sample, model, type
نَموذَجِيٌّ exemplary, model

Work, Business, and Economics 207

ه ل ك

هَلَكَ – يَهْلَكُ to perish, die, or be destroyed
أَهْلَكَ – يُهْلِكُ to ruin or destroy
اِسْتَهْلَكَ – يَسْتَهْلِكُ to exert oneself; to squander, spend, or consume
هَلاكٌ / هُلْكٌ ruin, destruction
اِسْتِهْلاكٌ consumption; attrition; wear and tear
ثَقافَةٌ اِسْتِهْلاكِيَّةٌ consumer culture
سِلَعٌ اِسْتِهْلاكِيَّةٌ consumer goods
مُهْلِكٌ destructive, devastating, annihilating
مُسْتَهْلِكٌ (مُسْتَهْلِكونَ) consumer

ه ي ئ

هَيُوَ – يَهْيُوْ to be shapely, well formed, or beautiful to look at
هَيَّأَ – يُهَيِّئُ to prepare, get ready, fix up, or arrange
هَيْئَةٌ (هَيْئاتٌ) form, shape, appearance; group, council, corporation, organisation
تَهْيِئَةٌ preparation, training; adjustment
مُهَيَّأٌ prepared, ready
هَيْئَةُ الأُمَمِ المُتَّحِدَةِ United Nations
هَيْئَةُ الإِذاعَةِ البِريطانِيَّةِ British Broadcasting Corporation (BBC)

و ر د

وَرَدَ – يَرِدُ to arrive, reach, appear, or show up; to be said or mentioned
وَرَّدَ – يُوَرِّدُ to bring, import, supply, or deposit
اِسْتَوْرَدَ – يَسْتَوْرِدُ to import, supply, buy, or get
وَرِيدٌ (أَوْرِدَةٌ) vein
مَوْرِدٌ (مَوارِدُ) source, well; destination
المَوارِدُ البَشَرِيَّةُ human resources
وُرودٌ coming, arrival
اِسْتيرادٌ importing
وارِدٌ (وارِداتٌ) imports
مُسْتَوْرَداتٌ imported goods, imports

و ز ع

وَزَّعَ – يُوَزِّعُ to distribute, apportion, share, or deal out
تَوَزَّعَ – يَتَوَزَّعُ to be distributed or divided
تَوْزيعٌ distribution, division, delivery, sale

208 *Work, Business, and Economics*

مُوَزِّعٌ distributor; distributing
مُوَزَّعٌ distributed, scattered
التَّوْزِيعُ وَالتَّسْوِيقُ distribution and marketing

الاِقْتِصادُ وَالمالُ Economics and Finance

No root

بَنْكٌ (بُنوكٌ) bank
البَنْكُ الدُّوَلِيُّ the World Bank
البُنوكُ banking

ث ر ى / ث ر و

ثَرِيَ – يَثْرى to become wealthy
ثَرىً moist earth, ground, or soil
ثَرِيٌّ (أَثْرِياءُ) wealthy, rich; wealthy people
ثَرْوَةٌ / ثَراءٌ wealth, riches, fortune
ثُرَيَّا (ثُرَيَّاتٌ) chandelier (also a girl's name in the singular)

ث م ر

ثَمَرَ – يُثْمِرُ to bear fruit
اِسْتَثْمَرَ – يَسْتَثْمِرُ to invest or exploit; to profit or benefit
ثَمَرٌ / ثَمَرَةٌ (ثِمارٌ / ثَمَراتٌ) fruit, fruits; result; yield, profit, gain
اِسْتِثْمارٌ (اِسْتِثْماراتٌ) investment; utilisation, exploitation
الاِسْتِثْمارُ الأَجْنَبِيُّ المُباشِرُ foreign direct investment
الاِسْتِثْماراتُ الأَجْنَبِيَّةُ foreign investments
مُثْمِرٌ fruitful, productive, profitable
مُسْتَثْمِرٌ (مُسْتَثْمِرونَ) investor; exploiter; beneficiary

ح س ب

حَسَبَ – يَحْسِبُ to compute, count, or reckon; to charge; to debit or credit
حاسَبَ – يُحاسِبُ to settle an account; to hold accountable
اِحْتَسَبَ – يَحْتَسِبُ to take into account or consideration; to debit or credit
حَسْبَما (conj) according to
حِسابٌ (حِساباتٌ) account, invoice, reckoning; arithmetic, calculation
الحِسابُ the bill; arithmetic

قِسْمُ الْحِساباتِ accounts department
مُدَقِّقُ الْحِساباتِ auditor
مُقَدَّمٌ تحتَ الْحِسابِ deposit
رَقَمُ حِسابٍ account number
مُحاسَبَةٌ (مُحاسَباتٌ) accounting, bookkeeping
حاسِبٌ calculator
مُحاسِبٌ (مُحاسِبونَ) accountant
الْمُحاسَبةُ accountancy
الحاسوبُ / الكومبيوتَرُ computer; ICT

ح ص ل

حَصَلَ – يَحصُلُ to originate; to happen, arise, result, or attain
حَصَّلَ – يُحَصِّلُ to attain, obtain, or acquire; to deduce; to sum up
تَحَصَّلَ – يَتَحَصَّلُ to result from; to be obtained; to be collected or demanded
حُصولٌ obtainment, attainment; achievement; acquisition
حَصيلةٌ (حَصائِلُ) income, proceeds, revenue, receipts
حَصَّالَةٌ money box, piggy bank
تَحصيلٌ (تَحصيلاتٌ) gain, acquisition; learning; income, revenue, returns
حاصِلٌ (حَواصِلُ) occurring; revenues, receipts, proceeds, income
مَحْصولٌ (مَحاصيلُ / محصولاتٌ) result, outcome; yield, gain, crop, harvest

ح ص ى

أحصى – يُحصي to count, enumerate, or calculate
إحصاءٌ (إحصاءاتٌ) statistics; calculation, count
إحصاءُ السُّكَّانِ census
إحصائِيَّةٌ (إحصائِيَّاتٌ) statistics
إحصائِيٌّ statistician

خ ز ن

خَزَنَ – يَخْزُنُ to amass or accumulate; to store; to keep secret
خَزَّنَ – يُخَزِّنُ to store or accumulate; to put into safekeeping; to dam
خَزْنٌ / تَخزينٌ storing, hoarding, amassing; accumulation, storage
خَزْنَةٌ vault, safe
خَزانَةٌ (خَزاناتٌ / خَزائِنُ) treasury, safe, vault; wardrobe, closet
خَزّانٌ (خَزّاناتٌ) tank, reservoir, dam

مَخْزَنٌ (مَخازِنُ) storage room, stockroom, warehouse
خازِنٌ (خُزّانٌ) treasurer
مَخْزونٌ stored, deposited, warehoused; reserve

خ س ر

خَسِرَ – يَخْسَرُ to forfeit, lose, or incur a loss; to suffer damage
خَسَّرَ – يُخَسِّرُ to cause loss or do harm; to damage, destroy, or corrupt
خُسْرٌ / خُسْرانٌ loss, damage; decline, deterioration, depravity
خَسارَةٌ (خَسائِرُ) loss, damage; casualties
المَكسبُ والْخَسارةُ profit and loss
خاسِرٌ / خَسْرانٌ lost, hopeless; a loser; incurring losses; depraved, corrupted
مُخَسِّرٌ detrimental; causing damage or harm

خ ص ص

خَصَّ – يَخُصُّ to distinguish, favour, or single out; to demand; to bestow
تَخَصَّصَ – يَتَخَصَّصُ to specialise; to apply oneself or devote all of one's attention
اِخْتَصَّ – يَخْتَصُّ to distinguish or favour; to devote; to claim or demand
خَصيصَةٌ (خَصائِصُ) special characteristic or quality
خُصوصاً / خِصّيصاً especially, particularly
خُصوصِيٌّ private; personal
تَخْصيصٌ (تَخْصيصاتٌ) specialisation; specification, designation; allocation
تَخَصُّصٌ (تَخَصُّصاتٌ) specialisation
اِخْتِصاصٌ (اِخْتِصاصاتٌ) competence; privileges; jurisdiction
اِخْتِصاصِيٌّ (اِخْتِصاصِيّونَ) specialist
خاصٌّ special, particular, specific; private, exclusive, not public
خاصِّيَةٌ (خَصائِصُ) feature, characteristic, trait; speciality; peculiarity
خَصْخَصَةٌ privatisation

خ ط ر

خَطَرَ – يَخْطُرُ to shake or tremble; to vibrate or swing
خاطَرَ – يُخاطِرُ to risk, hazard, bet, or wager
أَخْطَرَ – يُخْطِرُ to notify or inform; to warn or caution
خَطَرٌ (أَخْطارٌ) dangers, perils; consequence; significance
خَطَرٌ مُحْدِقٌ imminent danger
تَحْليلُ الْخَطَر risk analysis

Work, Business, and Economics   211

خَطِيرٌ / خَطِرٌ dangerous, risky; important, significant; serious
مَخاطِرُ dangers, perils, risk, hazard
إدارةُ المَخاطِر risk management
مُخاطَرَةٌ (مُخاطَراتٌ) venture; risk, hazard
خاطِرٌ (خَواطِرُ) idea, thought, notion; mind; desire, inclination
مُخاطِرٌ daring, bold, venturesome
مُخطِرٌ dangerous, risky, hazardous; in a critical state

خ ف ض

خَفَضَ – يَخفِضُ to lower, decrease, reduce, or drop
خَفَّضَ – يُخَفِّضُ to lower, decrease, or reduce
انخَفَضَ – يَنخَفِضُ to be reduced (price); to decrease or be diminished
خَفضٌ decrease, lowering, reduction; subduing
خَفضُ الإنفاق spending cuts
خَفيضٌ / مُنخَفِضٌ low, soft, subdued
تَخفيضٌ (تَخفيضاتٌ) cutbacks, reductions; limitations
تَخفيضُ القيمَة devaluation
انخِفاضٌ decrease, diminution, lowering, sinking, dropping
مُخَفَّضٌ lowered, reduced; moderate

د خ ل

دَخَلَ – يَدخُلُ to enter; to join
أَدخَلَ – يُدخِلُ to admit, introduce, or bring in; to let enter; to incorporate
تَدَخَّلَ – يَتَدَخَّلُ to meddle or interfere
دَخلٌ income, revenue, takings, receipts
دَخلٌ مُنخَفِضٌ low income
دَخيلٌ (دُخَلاءُ) inner, internal, core; foreign, alien; a stranger; false
كَلِمَةٌ دَخيلَةٌ loanword
دُخولٌ entry, entrance, admission
مَدخَلٌ (مَداخِلُ) entrance, hallway, foyer
داخِلٌ inside
داخِلِيٌّ interior
وِزارةُ الدَّاخلِيَّة ministry of the interior
تَدَخُّلٌ interference, meddling; invasion
مدخولٌ (مَداخيلُ) revenue, returns, takings

د ع م

دَعَمَ – يَدعَمُ to support or prop; to consolidate or strengthen
إدَّعَمَ – يَدَّعِمُ to be supported; to rest; to be based (on)
دَعْمٌ a subsidy, support, or prop
مَدْعومٌ subsidised, supported
تَدعيمٌ support; subsidising; strengthening, consolidation

د ف ع

دَفَعَ – يَدفَعُ to push, repel, or drive back; to dislodge
دافَعَ – يُدافِعُ to resist, oppose, or withstand; to defend
دَفعَةٌ (دَفَعاتٌ) a shove, push, or thrust; a payment or deposit; installments
دَفعَةٌ مُقَدَّمةٌ down payment
مِدفَعٌ (مَدافِعُ) gun; cannon
دِفاعٌ defence, protection
الدِّفاعُ المَدَنِيُّ civil defence
دِفاعٌ عَنْ النَّفسِ self-defence
دافِعٌ (دَوافِعُ) incentive, motive, impetus, impulse
مُدافِعٌ defender
مَدْفوعاتٌ payments

د ه و ر

دَهْوَرَ – يُدَهْوِرُ to topple, overthrow, or tear down
تَدَهْوَرَ – يَتَدَهْوَرُ to deteriorate or worsen; to be torn down
تَدَهْوُرٌ decline or slump (economic/health)

د ي ن

دانَ – يَدينُ to borrow or take up a loan; to owe or be indebted; to have as a religion
دايَنَ – يُدايِنُ to have a debt or be indebted; to be the creditor
تَدَيَّنَ – يتدَيَّنُ to be indebted or have debts
دَيْنٌ (دُيُونٌ) debt, claim, obligation
الدَّيْنُ العامُّ public debt
دَيْنٌ مُسْتَحَقٌّ outstanding debt
دَيْنونَةٌ judgement; Last Judgement
أزمةُ الدُّيونِ debt crisis

Work, Business, and Economics   213

سَدَّ الدَّيْنَ to repay a debt
إدانَةٌ (إداناتٌ) conviction; guilty conviction
دائِنٌ / مُدينٌ creditor, moneylender
مَديونٌ / مَدينٌ indebted, in debt
مُدانٌ convicted, condemned; guilty
مَدينَةٌ / مدائِنٌ / مُدُنٌ town, city
المَدينَةُ المُنَوَّرَةُ Medina (in Saudi Arabia)

ذ ب ذ ب

ذَبْذَبَ – يُذَبْذِبُ to swing; to dangle
تَذَبْذَبَ – يَتَذَبْذَبُ to swing, vibrate, or fluctuate; to hesitate
ذَبْذَبَةٌ (ذَبْذَباتٌ) oscillation; vibration
تَذَبْذُبٌ fluctuation, oscillation, swinging
مُذَبْذَبٌ variable, wavering, hesitant, unsteady

ذ خ ر

ذَخَرَ – يَذْخُرُ to keep, preserve, or save
إِدَّخَرَ – يَدَّخِرُ to save, amass, preserve, or hoard
ذُخْرٌ (أَذْخارٌ) stores, supplies; treasure
ذَخيرَةٌ (ذَخائِرُ) treasure; stores, supplies, provisions; food; ammunition
إِدِّخارٌ storage, hoarding, accumulation

ر ب ح

رَبِحَ – يَرْبَحُ to gain or profit
رَبَّحَ – يُرَبِّحُ to make (someone) gain; to allow (someone) a profit
رِبْحٌ (أَرْباحٌ) profit, gain, yield, revenues, dividends
مُرْبِحٌ profitable, lucrative

ر خ ص

رَخُصَ – يَرْخُصُ to be cheap or inexpensive
رَخَّصَ – يُرَخِّصُ to permit, authorise, license, or empower; to reduce the price
اِسْتَرْخَصَ – يَسْتَرْخِصُ to find cheap; to request someone's permission
رُخْصٌ inexpensiveness, cheapness
رُخْصَةٌ (رُخَصٌ) permit, licence, authorisation

رَخيصٌ cheap; low, base, mean
تَرخيصٌ (تَرخيصاتٌ) permission, authorisation; concession; a price reduction

ر ص د

رَصَدَ – يَرصُدُ to observe or watch; to control; to lie in wait; to observe (stars); to conjure (a demon)
رَصَّدَ – يُرَصِّدُ to provide; to set aside or earmark (funds); to balance (accounts)
رَصَدٌ (أَرصادٌ) observation; a spy; a watchdog; post; talisman
رَصدُ الأفلاكِ stargazing, astronomy
الأرصادُ الجَوِّيَّةُ meteorological observation
مَرصِدٌ جَوِّيٌّ meteorological station; weather station
رَصيدٌ (أَرصِدةٌ) balance, available funds
رَصيدٌ دائِنٌ / إئتمانٌ / تَسليفٌ credit
مَرصَدٌ (مَراصِدُ) observatory
مِرصادٌ telescope

ر ك د

رَكَدَ – يَركُدُ to be motionless, stagnant, or still
رُكودٌ recession; stagnation, stillness, suspension
راكِدٌ stagnant; sluggish

ز ي د

زادَ – يَزيدُ to increase, multiply, or exceed; to be compounded
زايَدَ – يُزايِدُ to outbid
إزدادَ – يَزدادُ to grow, increase, or multiply
زِيادةٌ growth, increase, intensification; elevation; surplus, extra pay
مَزادٌ / مُزايَدةٌ (مَزاداتٌ / مُزايَداتٌ) auction
مَزادٌ عَلَنِيٌّ auction
تَزايُدٌ gradual increase, growth
زائِدٌ increasing, growing; immoderate
مُزايِدٌ (مُزايِدونَ) bidder

ز ي ف

زافَ – يَزيفُ to be false
زَيَّفَ – يُزَيِّفُ to counterfeit (money); to declare something to be false

Work, Business, and Economics 215

تَزْيِيفٌ forgery, counterfeiting
زائِفٌ false, counterfeit, forged
مُزَيِّفٌ forger, counterfeiter

س ع ر

سَعَرَ – يَسعَرُ to kindle or start (fire, war)
سَعَّرَ – يُسَعِّرُ to kindle or start (fire, war); to set a price
ساعَرَ – يُساعِرُ to bargain or haggle over the price
سِعرٌ (أَسعارٌ) rate, price; exchange rate
سِعرُ التَّشغيلِ running cost
سِعرُ البَيعِ retail price
سِعرُ الفائِدَةِ interest rate
ضَبطُ الأَسعارِ price control
تَسعيرٌ / تَسعيرَةٌ pricing; price fixing

س م س ر

سَمسَرَ – يُسَمسِرُ to act as broker or middleman
سَمسَرَةٌ brokerage
سِمسارٌ (سَماسِرَةٌ) broker, middleman, agent

س ه م

سَهَمَ – يَسهَمُ to look grave or have a grave expression
ساهَمَ – يُساهِمُ to cast or draw lots; to participate or partake; to show
أَسهَمَ – يُسهِمُ to give a share
سَهمٌ (أَسهُمٌ) share, portion, lot; arrow, dart
سُهومٌ sadness, mourning
مُساهَمَةٌ participation, sharing, contribution
مُساهِمٌ (مُساهِمونَ) shareholder
حَمَلَةُ الأَسهُمِ shareholders
الأَسهُمُ والسَّنَداتُ shares and bonds
مُؤَشِّرُ الأَسهُمِ share or stock index

ص ر ف

صَرَفَ – يَصرِفُ to turn or turn away; to spend or change (money); to inflect (a word)

صَرَّفَ – يُصَرِّفُ to dispatch; to circulate; to liquidate (business); to inflect (word)
تَصَرَّفَ – يَتَصَرَّفُ to behave or act; to move freely; to be inflected (word)
اِنصرفَ – يَنصَرِفُ to depart or turn away; to spend
صَرْفٌ expenditure; money changing; averting or turning away
سِعرُ الصَّرفِ exchange rate
عِلْمُ الصَّرفِ morphology
مَمْنُوعٌ مِنَ الصَّرفِ indeclinable (grammar)
مَكْتَبُ الصِّرافةِ exchange bureau
صِرْفٌ pure, unadulterated, absolute
صَرَّافٌ money changer, teller, banker
صَرَّافٌ آلِيٌّ ATM
مَصرِفٌ (مَصارِفُ) bank; drain
تَحويلٌ مَصرَفِيٌّ bank transfer
تَصَرُّفٌ (تَصَرُّفاتٌ) behaviour, conduct; measures, regulations
اِنصِرِفْ! Go! Get lost! (imperative)
مَصْرُوفٌ (مَصْرُوفاتٌ / مَصاريفُ) expenses, costs; devoted, dedicated
مَصْرُوفُ الجيبِ pocket money

ض ب ط

ضَبَطَ – يَضبِطُ to grab, grasp, seize, or catch; to control
ضَبْطٌ capture, detention, restraint, suppression
الضَّوابِطُ controls

ض خ م

ضَخُمَ – يَضخُمُ to be or become big; large, voluminous
ضَخَّمَ – يُضَخِّمُ to inflate
تَضَخَّمَ – يَتَضَخَّمُ to swell or expand
ضَخْمٌ (ضِخامٌ) big, large, great, heavy; magnificent, splendid
ضَخامَةٌ greatness, heaviness, volume; obesity; pomp, splendor
تَضَخُّمٌ inflation, expansion, swelling
مُعَدَّلُ التَّضَخُّمِ rate of inflation

ض ر ب

ضَرَبَ – يَضرِبُ to beat, strike, or shoot; to play (an instrument); to impose (tax)
ضارَبَ – يُضارِبُ to contend, vie, or fight; to speculate

Work, Business, and Economics 217

أَضْرَبَ – يُضْرِبُ to go on strike; to leave or abandon
ضَرْبٌ (ضُروبٌ) beating, striking, hitting; species
ضَرْبَةٌ (ضَرَباتٌ) a blow, knock, punch, or strike
ضَرْبَةٌ اسْتِباقِيَّةٌ pre-emptive strike
ضَريبَةٌ (ضَرائِبُ) tax, duty, levy
ضَريبَةُ الدَّخْلِ income tax
ضَريبَةُ التَّرِكاتِ/ضَريبَةُ الإِرْثِ inheritance tax
ضَريبَةُ القيمةِ المُضافةِ value added tax (VAT)
ضَريبَةُ الأَرْباحِ الرَّأْسْماليَّةِ capital gains tax (CGT)
تَخْفيضاتٌ ضَريبيَّةٌ tax cuts
مَصْلَحَةُ الضَّرائِبِ inland revenue
مِضْرَبٌ (مَضارِبُ) racket, bat; mallet
مُضارَبَةٌ (مُضارَباتٌ) speculation; partnership
إِضْرابٌ (إِضْراباتٌ) strike
اِضْطِرابٌ (اِضْطِراباتٌ) riots, unrest; confusion, muddle
اِضْطِراباتُ الطَّعامِ eating disorder
مُتَضارِبٌ contradictory

ض م ن

ضَمِنَ – يَضْمَنُ to be or become responsible; to vouch or guarantee; to insure (sth)
ضَمَّنَ – يُضَمِّنُ to have something insured; to insert or enclose
تَضامَنَ – يَتَضامَنُ to be in accord; to have joint liability
ضِمْنَ inside, within
ضَمانٌ responsibility, guarantee, security, insurance
ضَمانٌ إِجْتِماعِيٌّ social security
ضَمينٌ (ضُمَناءُ/ضامِنونَ) liable; guarantor
ضَمانَةٌ guarantee, warranty, security; bail
تَضامُنٌ mutuality; solidarity; joint liability
مَضْمونٌ guaranteed; insured

ع ج ز

عَجَزَ – يَعْجِزُ to be weak; to be unable or incapable
عَجْزٌ weakness, incapacity, impotence; failure; shortage
عَجْزٌ في ميزانِيَّةِ الدَّوْلَةِ budget deficit
عَجْزٌ تِجارِيٌّ trade deficit

Work, Business, and Economics

عَجوزٌ (عَجائِزُ) old woman; old man; old

إعْجازٌ inimitability of the Quran

عاجِزٌ (عواجِزُ / عَجَزَةٌ) physically weak, feeble, impotent

مُعْجِزَةٌ (مُعْجِزاتٌ) miracle

ع م م

عَمَّ – يَعُمُّ to be or become common or universal; to include, encompass, or extend

عَمَّمَ – يُعَمِّمُ to generalise; to popularise

تَعَمَّمَ – يَتَعَمَّمُ to put on a turban

عِمامَةٌ (عَمائِمُ) turban

عَمٌّ (أعمامٌ) paternal uncles

عَمَّةٌ (عَمَّاتٌ) paternal aunts

عُمومِيٌّ public, universal, general

تَعميمٌ making something public; generalisation; popularisation

عامٌّ public, general, universal

النَّقْلُ العامُّ public transport

الرَّأيُ العامُّ public opinion

المُدَّعي العامُّ the attorney general; public prosecutor

المَرافِقُ العامَّةُ public utilities

عامَّةُ النَّاسِ the masses

عامَّةً / عُموماً / بِشَكلٍ عامٍّ generally, in general

عامِّيٌّ common, popular, vulgar, ordinary

العامِّيَّةُ colloquial language

ع و ر

عَوِرَ – يَعْوَرُ to lose an eye; to be or become one-eyed

أعارَ – يُعيرُ to lend or loan

إسْتَعارَ – يَسْتَعيرُ to borrow

عَوْرَةٌ (عَوْراتٌ) defectiveness, faultiness, imperfection, weakness (pl: genitals)

عيرَةٌ false (body parts)

أعْوَرُ (عُورٌ) one-eyed

إعارَةٌ lending

إسْتِعارَةٌ borrowing; metaphor

إسْتِعارِيٌّ metaphorical, figurative

مُعيرٌ lender

مُسْتَعيرٌ (مُسْتَعيرونَ) borrower
مُسْتَعارٌ borrowed; false or artificial; figurative
اسمٌ مُسْتَعارٌ pseudonym

ع و ض

عاضَ – يَعوضُ to compensate; to substitute or replace; to pay as a price
عَوَّضَ – يُعَوِّضُ to compensate; to substitute or replace; to pay as a price
تَعَوَّضَ – يَتَعَوَّضُ to seek or receive compensation
لا يُعَوَّضُ irreplaceable; irreparable
عِوَضٌ substitute, exchange; compensation, indemnity
عِوَضاً عن instead of
تَعويضٌ (تَعويضاتٌ) compensation, reparations; replacement, substitution
تَعويضاتُ الإقالَة redundancy pay
التَّعويضاتُ المالِيَّةُ financial reparations

غ ر م

غَرِمَ – يَغرَمُ to pay (a fine/tax); to suffer a loss
غَرَّمَ – يُغَرِّمُ to fine or impose a fine
تَغَرَّمَ – يَتَغَرَّمُ to be fined
غُرمٌ damage or loss
غَريمٌ (غُرَماءُ) opponent, adversary; creditor
غَرامَةٌ (غَراماتٌ) fine; compensation, damages
مَغرَمٌ (مَغارِمُ) damages, loss; debt, fine

غ ل و

غَلا – يَغلو to be excessive or to go too far; to become expensive
غَلَّى – يُغَلِّي to raise the price of something
إسْتَغلى – يَسْتَغلي to find (something) costly or expensive
غَلاءٌ rise in prices; high cost, high price
غالٍ expensive; dear, beloved

غ ن ي

غَنِيَ – يَغنى to be free from want; to be rich or wealthy
غَنَّى – يُغَنِّي to sing or chant; to sing the praises or extol

اِسْتَغْنَى – يَسْتَغْنِي to become rich; to have no need
غَنَاءٌ / غِنىً wealth, riches, affluence
غَنِيٌّ (أَغْنِيَاءُ) rich, wealthy, prosperous
غِنَاءٌ singing; song
أُغْنِيَةٌ (أَغَانٍ / أُغْنِيَاتٌ) song, melody
مُغَنٍّ singer

ف ل س

فَلَّسَ – يُفَلِّسُ to declare someone bankrupt
أَفْلَسَ – يُفْلِسُ to be or become bankrupt; to fail; to be ruined
فِلْسٌ (فُلُوسٌ) fils (small coin) (pl: money)
تَفْلِيسٌ / إِفْلاسٌ bankruptcy
مُفْلِسٌ (مُفْلِسُونَ / مَفَالِيسُ) bankrupt

ف ي د

أَفَادَ – يُفِيدُ to benefit, help, or be useful; to notify, advise, or inform
اِسْتَفَادَ – يَسْتَفِيدُ to acquire, gain, or learn; to benefit or profit from
إِفَادَةٌ (إِفَادَاتٌ) utility, benefit, advantage; notice, notification
اِسْتِفَادَةٌ utilisation, use
فَائِدَةٌ (فَوَائِدُ) interest (money); benefit, advantage, profit
مُفِيدٌ useful, beneficial, profitable
مُفَادٌ contents; substance, meaning

ق ر ض

قَرَضَ – يَقْرِضُ to cut, sever, bite, or eat; to write poetry
أَقْرَضَ – يُقْرِضُ to loan or lend money
اِنْقَرَضَ – يَنْقَرِضُ to die out, perish, or become extinct
اِقْتَرَضَ – يَقْتَرِضُ to raise a loan, to borrow
قَرْضٌ (قُرُوضٌ) loan
قَرْضٌ حَسَنٌ interest-free loan
قَرْضٌ دِرَاسِيٌّ student loan
اِنْقِرَاضٌ extinction, disappearance
مُقْرِضٌ (مُقْرِضُونَ) lender, moneylender
مُنْقَرِضٌ extinct, perished

ق س ط

قَسَّطَ – يُقَسِّطُ to distribute, to pay in instalments
أَقْسَطَ – يُقْسِطُ to act justly
قِسْطٌ (أَقْساطٌ) justice, rightness, equity; part, share, instalments
تَقْسيطٌ payment in instalments
مُقْسِطٌ just, fair

ق ش ف

قَشِفَ – يَقْشِفُ to live in squalor and misery
تَقَشَّفَ – يَتَقَشَّفُ to become rough and chapped (of skin); to live in squalor and misery
تَقَشُّفٌ austerity; a simple or primitive way of life
سِياسَةُ التَّقَشُّفِ austerity policy
مُكافَحَةُ التَّقَشُّفِ anti-austerity
إجراءاتٌ تَقَشُّفِيَّةٌ austerity measures

ق ص د

قَصَدَ – يَقْصِدُ to aim or strive for; to pursue; to be economical or to save
أَقْصَدَ – يُقْصِدُ to induce to go; to compose poetry (qasidas)
اِقْتَصَدَ – يَقْتَصِدُ to be frugal or save; to compose poetry (qasidas)
قَصْدٌ purpose, intent, object, goal, aim; endeavour
قَصيدَةٌ (قَصائِدُ) poetry; qasida[1]
مَقْصَدٌ (مَقاصِدُ) purpose, object, goal, intention; destination; significance
اِقْتِصادٌ economy; saving; thrift, providence
الاِقْتِصادُ العالَمِيُّ the global economy
اِقْتِصادُ الحَجْمِ economies of scale
اِقْتِصادِيٌّ economic
الاسْتِقْرارُ الاِقْتِصادِيُّ economic stability
حَفَّزَ الاِقْتِصادَ / نَشَّطَ الاِقْتِصادَ to stimulate the economy
عُقوباتٌ اِقْتِصادِيَّةٌ economic sanctions
اِقْتِصادِيٌّ (اِقْتِصادِيّونَ) economist
مَقْصودٌ intended, deliberate

ق ل ص

قَلَصَ – يَقْلِصُ to contract, decrease, diminish, or decline

222 Work, Business, and Economics

قَلَّصَ – يُقَلِّصُ to contract, draw together, or roll up
تَقَلُّصٌ contraction, shrinking

ك ث ر

كَثُرَ – يَكْثُرُ to outnumber; to increase or multiply; to happen frequently
كَثَّرَ – يُكَثِّرُ to increase, augment, or multiply
كَثْرَةٌ large quantity, abundance, copiousness
كَثيرٌ (كِثارٌ / كَثيرونَ) much, many, numerous

ك س د

كَسَدَ – يَكْسَدُ to be stagnant; to find no market (to sell sth)
أَكْسَدَ – يُكْسِدُ to be dull or listless
كَسادٌ recession, economic depression, slump, stagnation (market)

م ك س

مَكَسَ – يَمْكُسُ to collect taxes
ماكَسَ – يُماكِسُ to haggle or bargain
مَكْسٌ (مُكوسٌ) tax, custom, duty
مَكَّاسٌ tax collector

م و ل

مَوَّلَ – يُمَوِّلُ to make rich; to finance
تَمَوَّلَ – يَتَمَوَّلُ to be financed; to become rich or wealthy
مالٌ (أَموالٌ) wealth, property, money, capital; revenue
ماليٌّ monetary, financial, fiscal
اِنْهِيارٌ ماليٌّ financial meltdown
ماليَّةٌ monetary affairs, finance; public revenue
مُساعدةٌ ماليَّةٌ financial aid
أَزمةٌ ماليَّةٌ financial crisis
التَّخْفيضاتُ الماليَّةُ financial cuts
العامُ الماليُّ / السَّنةُ الماليَّةُ the financial year
وَزيرُ الماليَّةِ finance minister
غَسيلُ الأَموالِ money laundering
تَمويلٌ funding; finance
مُمَوِّلٌ (مُمَوِّلونَ) financier; taxpayer

ن ت ج

نَتَجَ – يَنْتُجُ to produce, manufacture; to bring forth; to follow, result, or ensue
أَنْتَجَ – يُنتِجُ to bring forth, generate, or yield; to originate
اِسْتَنْتَجَ – يَسْتَنْتِجُ to conclude or deduce
نِتَاجٌ brood, litter, offspring
نَتِيجَةٌ (نَتَائِجُ) result, conclusion, consequence; proceeds, gain, profit
إِنْتَاجٌ production, producing, generation, manufacture, cultivation
نَاتِجٌ resulting, following, proceeding, deriving
النَّاتِجُ المَحَلِّيُ الإِجْمَالِيُّ / إِجْمَالِيُ النَّاتِجِ الدَّاخِلِيِّ Gross Domestic Product (GDP)
اِسْتِنْتَاجٌ (اِسْتِنْتَاجَاتٌ) inference, deduction, conclusion
مَنتوجٌ (مَنتوجاتٌ) product, creation; work, production
مُنْتَجَاتٌ products; proceeds, returns, yields

ن ق د

نَقَدَ – يَنْقُدُ to pay in cash; to criticise or examine critically; to peck
أَنْقَدَ – يَنْقُدُ to pay
نَقْدٌ (نُقودٌ) cash; coins, change; criticism
صُنْدوقُ النَّقْدِ fund
صُنْدوقُ النَّقْدِ الدُّوَلِيِّ the International Monetary Fund (IMF)
نَاقِدٌ (نُقَّادٌ) critic, reviewer
اِنْتِقَادٌ (اِنْتِقَادَاتٌ) objection, exception, criticism, critique, disapproval

ن م ى

نَمَى – يَنْمِي to grow, increase, or multiply; to progress; to thrive or prosper
نَمَّى – يُنَمِّي to make grow or increase; to promote or advance
اِنْتَمَى – يَنْتَمِي to be descended from; to depend or be dependent; to belong
نَمَاءٌ / نَمِيٌّ / نُمُوٌّ growth, expansion, increase, augmentation
تَنْمِيَةٌ growth, expansion, increase; promotion, advancement
الدُّوَلُ النَّامِيَةُ developing countries
اِنْتِمَاءٌ membership; belonging
نَامِيَةٌ (نَوَامٍ) growth; tumour
النَّوَامِي السَّرَطَانِيَّةُ cancerous growths
مُنْتَمٍ belonging, pertaining to

ه ب ط

هَبَطَ – يَهْبِطُ to descend, fall down, sink, or settle

224 *Work, Business, and Economics*

أَهْبَطَ – يُهْبِطُ to cause to sink; to descend; to lower
هَبْطٌ / هُبُوطٌ reduction, lowering, decline
مَهْبِطٌ (هابِطٌ) place of descent, landing place

و د ع

وَدَعَ – يَدَعُ to put down or deposit; to leave; to give up or omit
وَدَّعَ – يُوَدِّعُ to see off, take leave, or bid farewell
اِسْتَوْدَعَ – يَسْتَوْدِعُ to put down, place, deposit, or store
وَدْعٌ / إيداعٌ depositing; lodging
وَداعٌ farewell, leave-taking
وَديعةٌ (وَدائِعُ) deposit; trust, charge
تَوْديعٌ farewell; leave-taking
مُسْتَوْدِعٌ depositor
مُسْتَوْدَعٌ (مُسْتَوْدَعاتٌ) storehouse, depot; lodged

و ز ن

وَزَنَ – يَزِنُ to weigh; to balance or compensate; to make a comparison
تَوازَنَ – يَتَوازَنُ to be balanced or in equilibrium
وَزْنٌ (أَوْزانٌ) noun or verb pattern; metre (poetry); weight, measure
ميزانٌ (مَوازينُ) scales
ميزانيةٌ budget; balance, equilibrium
تَوازُنٌ / اِتِّزانٌ balance, equilibrium, harmony
مُتَوازِنٌ balanced; in equilibrium

و ف ر

وَفَرَ – يَفِرُ to be abundant; to increase, augment, grow
وَفَّرَ – يُوَفِّرُ to economise or save; to increase
تَوَفَّرَ – يَتَوَفَّرُ to be ample or plentiful; to prosper or thrive
وَفْرٌ economy, saving; abundance, wealth, excess, surplus
وَفْرَةٌ plenty, abundance
وافِرٌ / وَفيرٌ abundant, plentiful, numerous
مُتَوَفِّرٌ ample, abundant; thrifty, economical; savings
تَوْفيرٌ savings
حِسابُ تَوْفيرٍ savings account

Exercises

1) Give two derived nouns for each of the following roots:

أ ج ر
ب د ل
د و م
ش غ ل
ن ف ذ

2) Find the roots of these words:

اِستِهلاكٌ
تَعويضٌ
خَسارةٌ
دَعْمٌ
رَخيصٌ
ضَريبَةٌ
مُحاسِبٌ
نافِعٌ

3) Give the plural of the following words (some may have more than one plural form):

أَساسٌ
اِستِثمارٌ
أُغنِيَّةٌ
حَرْفٌ
راتِبٌ
شُغْلٌ
غَرامَةٌ
فِلسٌ
مالٌ
مَصْروفٌ

4) Give the past tense of these verbs:

يَبيعُ to sell
يَدورُ to turn, revolve, or circle
يُساوِمُ to bargain, haggle, or negotiate
يَشتَري to buy, purchase, or acquire
يُصنِعُ to industrialise

يَطْرُدُ to fire or expel

يَعمَلُ to do or act; to work or operate

يَكسِبُ to earn, gain, or win

5) Translate the following sentences into Arabic:

   a) The lawyer was very professional but his rates were very high.
   b) The rate of unemployment has decreased in Dubai.
   c) She complained to her manager about the long working hours.
   d) Everyone needs a work visa.
   e) These days work experience is essential.

6) Translate the following into English:

   - أصبَحَتْ لَندنُ أكبَرَ سوقٍ لِلاقتِصادِ الإسلاميِّ.
   - يَرفَعُ بنكُ إنجلترا سِعرَ الْفائِدَةِ لِرابعِ مرَّةٍ هذِهِ السَّنَةِ.
   - يَعتَمِدُ الأردنُ اعتِماداً كُلِّيّاً على الطَّاقةِ المُستَوردَةِ.
   - حُكومةُ لُبنانَ تُعلِنُ إفلاسَ الدَّوْلَةِ والْبنكِ الْمَرْكَزيِّ.

7) Give antonyms for each of the following words:

   بَطالةٌ unemployment

   خَفْضٌ decrease, lowering, reduction

   وارداتٌ imports

Note

1 Arabic poems which have a rigid tripartite structure.

6 Media وَسائلُ الإعلامِ

Journalism and News الصَّحافةُ والأَخبارُ

ب ث ث

بَثَّ – يَبُثُّ to spread or scatter; to broadcast
اِنْبَثَّ – يَنْبَثُّ to be spread or scattered
بَثٌّ spreading, dissemination
بَثٌّ إذاعِيٌّ broadcasting

ت ل ف ز

تَلْفَزَ – يُتَلْفِزُ to televise, to transmit by television
تِلْفازٌ (تِلِفِزْيونٌ) television
تِلِفِزْيونٌ فَضائِيٌّ / الفَضائِيّاتُ satellite television
إذاعةٌ تَلَفَزِيَّةٌ / إذاعةٌ تِلِفِزيونِيَّةٌ television broadcast

ج ل ل

جَلَّ – يَجِلُّ to be great; to be lofty or sublime
جَلَّلَ – يُجَلِّلُ to honour or dignify; to clothe or drape
جَلَلٌ important, significant
جَلِيلٌ (أَجِلّاءُ) great, important; revered, honourable
جَلالٌ splendour, loftiness, glory
جَلالةٌ majesty
مَجَلَّةٌ (مَجَلّاتٌ) periodical, magazine
مَجَلّاتٌ دَوْرِيَّةٌ periodicals
مَجَلَّةٌ إلِكترونِيَّةٌ online journal

DOI: 10.4324/9781003250890-7

خ ب ر

خَبَرَ – يَخبَرُ to try or test; to experience or know well
خَبَّرَ – يُخَبِّرُ to inform, tell, or advise
أَخبَرَ – يُخبِرُ to inform, advise, tell, or communicate
اِختَبَرَ – يَختَبِرُ to explore or search; to test or examine; to know well
اِستَخبَرَ – يَستَخبِرُ to inquire or ask about
خَبَرٌ (أَخبارٌ) news, information, intelligence; report; predicate of a nominal clause
الأَخبارُ the news
نَشْرَةُ الأَخبارِ news bulletin
أَخبارٌ عاجِلَةٌ breaking news
خَبيرٌ (خُبَراءُ) an expert or specialist; familiar, conversant
مُختَبَرٌ (مُختَبَراتٌ) laboratory
المُخابَراتُ intelligence service
إِخبارٌ notification, communication; information; message; report
اِختِبارٌ (اِختِباراتٌ) test, examination; study, investigation
تَحتَ الاِختِبارِ on probation
فَترةُ الاِختِبارِ probationary period
اِستِخبارٌ (اِستِخباراتٌ) inquiry; intelligence (information)
الاِستِخباراتُ intelligence bureau
مَصدَرٌ اِستِخباريٌّ intelligence source
مَعلوماتٌ اِستِخباريَّةٌ investigative information
مُخبِرٌ (مُخبِرونَ) informant; reporter; detective
خِبرَةٌ (خِبراتٌ) experience
خِبرَةُ العَمَلِ work experience
ذو خِبرَةٍ experienced
لَجنَةُ خُبَراءَ expert committee

د م غ

دَمَغَ – يدمَغُ to refute or invalidate; to triumph
دِماغٌ (أَدمِغَةٌ) brain
حُجَّةٌ دامِغَةٌ irrefutable argument
غَسيلِ الدِماغِ brainwashing

ذ ي ع

ذاعَ – يَذيعُ to circulate, or spread; to become public

Media

أَذاعَ – يُذيعُ to broadcast, spread, publish, or announce
ذُيوعٌ spreading, dispersion, circulation (news)
مِذياعٌ (مَذاييعُ) radio or broadcasting station
إِذاعةٌ (إِذاعاتٌ) broadcasting, spreading; radio; broadcast, transmission
مُذيعٌ broadcaster

ر س ل

رَسِلَ – يَرسَلُ to be long and flowing (of hair)
راسَلَ – يُراسِلُ to correspond with
أَرسَلَ – يُرسِلُ to send out or dispatch
رَسِلٌ easy, gentle, leisurely (adj)
رَسولٌ (رُسُلٌ) messenger, delegate, envoy
رَسولُ اللهِ Messenger of God (i.e. Prophet Muhammad)
رِسالةٌ (رِسالاتٌ/رَسائِلُ) letter, message, report, communication; consignment
رِسالةُ الدُّكتوراةِ PhD thesis
مُراسَلَةٌ correspondence
جِهازُ إِرسالٍ transmitter
مُراسِلٌ (مُراسِلونَ) correspondent, reporter
مُراسِلٌ أَجنَبِيٌّ foreign correspondent

ر و ي

رَوى – يَروي to tell a story or report
تَرَوَّى – يَتَرَوَّى to ponder or reflect
اِرتَوى – يَرتَوي to quench one's thirst; to be watered or irrigated
رِيٌّ irrigation, moistening
رِوايةٌ (رِواياتٌ) tale, story, novel
رَيّانٌ (رِواءٌ) well-watered; verdant, lush (also a boy's name in the singular)
راوٍ (رُواةٌ) narrator, storyteller

ص ح ف

صَحَّفَ – يُصَحِّفُ to misread, misspell, or distort; to misplace diacritical marks
صَحفةٌ (صِحافٌ) bowl, dish, platter
صَحيفةٌ (صُحُفٌ/صَحائِفُ) a newspaper, journal; a page (of a book); surface
صُحُفِيٌّ (صُحُفِيّونَ) journalist; journalistic
مُؤتَمَرٌ صُحُفِيٌّ press conference

Media

صِحافَةٌ journalism, the press
صِحافِيٌّ journalist
تَصريحٌ صُحُفِيٌّ press release
حَملَةٌ صِحافِيَّةٌ press campaign
مُصحَفٌ (مَصاحِفُ) volume, book; a copy of the Quran

ص و ر

صَوَّرَ – يُصَوِّرُ to represent form or shape; to mould; to illustrate; to photograph
تَصَوَّرَ – يَتَصَوَّرُ to have been represented; to be shaped or illustrated
صورَةٌ (صُوَرٌ) picture, image, form, representation
صورَةٌ نَمَطِيَّةٌ stereotype
تَصويرٌ photography, drawing, sketching; portrayal
تَصَوُّرٌ (تَصَوُّراتٌ) imagination, fancy; idea
مُصَوِّرٌ (مُصَوِّرونَ) photographer, cameraman; creator

ع ل م

(Full treatment in Education chapter)

عَلِمَ – يَعلَمُ to know; to be aware, familiar, or acquainted; to learn
عَلَّمَ – يُعَلِّمُ to teach, instruct, or train; to designate; to mark
تَعَلَّمَ – يَتَعَلَّمُ to learn or study; to know
إستَعلَمَ – يَستَعلِمُ to inquire or ask; to gather information
عِلمٌ (عُلومٌ) knowledge, learning; information (pl: sciences)
عَلَمٌ (أعلامٌ) sign, token; flag
عالَمٌ (عَوالِمُ) world; universe, cosmos
عالَمِيٌّ international
تَعليمٌ (تَعليماتٌ/تَعاليمُ) teaching, education; information, instructions; doctrines
إعلامٌ notification; information; advice
وَسائِلُ الإعلامِ mass media, media
إعلامِيٌّ journalist
إستِعلامٌ (إستِعلاماتٌ) inquiry; information; news or press agency
مَعلومَةٌ (مَعلوماتٌ) information

ع ل ن

عَلَنَ – يَعلِنُ to be known, manifest, or evident; to announce

Media

أَعْلَنَ – يُعْلِنُ to publicise, advertise, or publish; to manifest or reveal
الْعَلَنُ the public
عَلَناً publicly, openly
عَلانِيَةٌ openness, overtness; publicity
إِعْلانٌ (إِعْلاناتٌ) advertising; statement; revelation
إِعْلانٌ مُمَوَّلٌ sponsored ads
الإِعْلاناتُ advertising

غ ط و

غَطا – يَغْطو to cover or cover up
غَطَّى – يُغَطِّي to cover, conceal, or envelop
تَغَطَّى – يَتَغَطَّى to be covered, enveloped, or concealed
غِطاءٌ (أَغْطِيَةٌ) cover, wrap, wrapper, envelope
تَغْطِيَةٌ coverage
تَغْطِيَةٌ حَيَّةٌ live coverage
مُحاوَلَةُ تَغْطِيَةٍ attempted cover-up

ق ب ل

قَبِلَ – يَقْبَلُ to accept or receive; to approve
قَبَّلَ – يُقَبِّلُ to kiss
قابَلَ – يُقابِلُ to interview; to be opposite someone; to confront or face
تَقابَلَ – يَتَقابَلُ to face each other; to meet or get together
اِسْتَقْبَلَ – يَسْتَقْبِلُ to meet, face, or confront; to receive (guest)
قَبْلُ / مِن قَبْلِ / مِن قَبْلُ (adv) before, previously
قَبْلَ أَنْ (conj) before
مِن قِبَلِ by
قُبْلَةٌ (قُبْلاتٌ / قُبَلٌ) a kiss
قِبْلَةٌ qibla, direction to which Muslims turn to pray Mecca
قُبولٌ approval, acceptance, admission; reception, welcome
قَبيلَةٌ (قَبائِلُ) tribe
مُقابِلٌ (مُقابِلونَ) interviewer
مُقابَلَةٌ (مُقابَلاتٌ) encounter, meeting; talk, discussion; interview
اِسْتِقْبالٌ (اِسْتِقْبالاتٌ) reception; opposition
مَقْبولٌ reasonable, acceptable
غَيرُ مَقْبولٍ unacceptable

232   *Media*

مُقابِلَ in exchange for; in relation to; in comparison to
مُقبِلٌ coming, next
مُقَبِّلاتٌ appetisers
مُستَقبِلٌ radio receiver
المُستَقبَلُ the future

ق ر أ

قَرَأَ – يَقرَأُ to recite, read, or study
اِستَقرَأَ – يَستَقرِئُ to recite or read; to investigate or explore
قِراءَةٌ (قِراءاتٌ) recitation, a reading
القُرآنُ الكَريمُ the Holy Quran
اِستِقراءٌ (اِستِقراءاتٌ) investigation, examination, exploration
قارِئٌ (قُرّاءٌ / قارِئونَ) editor; reader, reciter (of Quran)
بَريدُ القُرّاءِ letters to the editor
مَقروءٌ read; legible

ق ص ص

قَصَّ – يَقُصُّ to cut or shear; to relate or tell
قاصَصَ – يقاصِصُ to retaliate or take vengeance; to avenge
قَصٌّ clippings, cuttings
قِصَّةٌ (قِصَصٌ) narrative, story; cut
أُقصوصَةٌ (أَقاصيصُ) short story
مِقَصٌّ (مِقَصّاتٌ / مَقاصُّ) scissors
قِصاصٌ punishment; retaliation

ق و ل

قالَ – يَقولُ to speak, tell, or state; to voice
قاوَلَ – يُقاوِلُ to confer; to negotiate or dispute
تَقَوَّلَ – يَتَقَوَّلُ to spread rumours; to pretend; to allege
قَولٌ (أَقوالٌ / أَقاويلُ) word, speech, statement, utterance; doctrine, proverbs
مَقالٌ speech; proposition; teaching, doctrine; article
مَقالٌ اِفتِتاحِيٌّ editorial
مَقالَةٌ (مَقالاتٌ) article, essay, piece of writing
مَقولَةٌ statement
مَقولٌ (مَقولاتٌ) saying, utterance, speech

ك ت ب

كَتَبَ – يَكْتُبُ to write; to note, record, or register
كَتَّبَ – يُكَتِّبُ to make (someone) write; to deploy troops
كاتَبَ – يُكاتِبُ to correspond
أَكْتَبَ – يُكْتِبُ to dictate
تَكاتَبَ – يَتَكاتَبُ to correspond or write to each other
اِكْتَتَبَ – يَكْتَتِبُ to write or copy; to subscribe; to contribute
كِتابٌ (كُتُبٌ) book; paper, letter; contract; piece of writing
الْكِتابُ the Bible; the Quran; the Torah
أَهْلُ الْكِتابِ people of the Book (Christians and Jews)
كِتابٌ إِلِكْترونِيٌّ e-book
كَتْبُ الْكِتابِ to write the marriage contract
كُتَيِّبٌ (كُتَيِّباتٌ) booklet
مَكْتَبٌ (مكاتِبُ) office, school, study (room)
مَكْتَبُ الأَخْبارِ / مَكْتَبُ الأَنْباءِ news agency
مَكْتَبُ الاِسْتِعْلاماتِ information office
مَكْتَبُ التَّسْجيلِ registration office
مَكْتَبُ الْقُبولِ admissions office
مَكْتَبةٌ (مَكْتَباتٌ) library
مَكْتَبةٌ (مَكاتِبُ / مَكْتَباتٌ) bookshop
مَكْتَبةٌ عامَّةٌ public library
كِتابةٌ (كِتاباتٌ) writing; essay
اِسْمُ الْكِتابةِ pen name
اِكْتِتابٌ subscription, registration
كاتِبٌ (كُتّابٌ) writer, scribe
كاتِبُ عَمودٍ columnist
مَكْتوبٌ (مَكاتيبُ) written, destined, pre-ordained (pl: letters)
كَتيبةٌ (كَتائِبُ) battalion, regiment

ن ب أ

نَبَّأَ – يُنَبِّئُ to inform, tell, or advise
أَنْبَأَ – يُنْبِئُ to inform, tell, or advise
تَنَبَّأَ – يَتَنَبَّأُ to predict or foretell; to claim to be a prophet
اِسْتَنْبَأَ – يَسْتَنْبِئُ to ask for news, to inquire
نَبَأٌ (أَنْباءٌ) news, information, report, newsflash

وَكالةُ أنباءٍ press agency
نُبوءةٌ (نُبوءاتٌ) prophecy
نَبِيٌّ (أَنبِياءُ) prophet
تَنَبُّؤٌ (تَنَبُّؤاتٌ) prediction, prophecy

ن ظ ر

نَظَرَ – يَنظُرُ to watch, observe, or look; to perceive or see
ناظَرَ – يُناظِرُ to equal; to liken or compare; to argue; to supervise
تَناظَرَ – يَتَناظَرُ to face each other; to argue or fight
اِنتَظَرَ – يَنتَظِرُ to wait, expect, or anticipate
نَظَرٌ (أنظارٌ) vision, eyesight; look, glance; theory, trial
نَظرَةٌ (نَظَراتٌ) a look or glance (pl: reflections)
نَظَرِيٌّ visual; theoretical
نَظَرِيَّةٌ theory; contemplation
نَظّارَةٌ (نَظّاراتٌ) telescope (pl: binoculars, glasses)
مَنظَرٌ (مَناظِرُ) view, panorama; appearance; outlook
مِنظارٌ (مَناظيرُ) telescope; magnifying glass; mirror
مُناظَرَةٌ dispute; rivalry, competition
اِنتِظارٌ waiting, expectation; a wait or delay
فَترةُ اِنتِظارٍ waiting period
ناظِرٌ (نُظّارٌ) inspector, manager, supervisor

و ج ز

وَجَزَ – يَجِزُ to be brief or concise
أَوجَزَ – يوجِزُ to be brief or concise; to abridge or summarise
وَجيزٌ short, brief
إيجازٌ brevity, conciseness
مُوجَزٌ a summary, abstract, or outline; concise
مُوجَزُ الأخبارِ / مُوجَزُ الأنباءِ news summary

و ج ه

وَجُهَ – يَوجُهُ to be a man of distinction
وَجَّهَ – يُوَجِّهُ to distinguish or honour; to face; to head
واجَهَ – يُواجِهُ to face or encounter; to defy or oppose
تَوَجَّهَ – يَتَوَجَّهُ to face or turn

Media

اِتَّجَهَ – يَتَّجِهُ to aim or point; to face; to head
جِهَةٌ (جِهاتٌ) side, section, part; direction (compass)
وَجْهٌ (وُجوهٌ) face; intent, aim, objective
وِجْهَةٌ direction (compass); intention, aim
وِجْهَةُ نَظَرٍ point of view
وَجيهٌ (وُجَهاءُ) notable, distinguished
تُجاهَ (prep) in front of, facing; towards
مُواجَهَةٌ (مُواجَهاتٌ) confrontation, encounter
اِتِّجاهٌ (اِتِّجاهاتٌ) direction; inclination; trend
الاِتِّجاهاتُ الحالِيَّةُ current trends
واجِهَةٌ (واجِهاتٌ) face, front, façade

و س ل

تَوَسَّلَ – يَتَوَسَّلُ to ingratiate oneself; to entreat
وَسيلَةٌ (وَسائِلُ) the means
وَسائِلُ الإعلامِ المَرئِيَّةُ visual media
وَسائِلُ الإعلامِ المَكتوبَةُ printed media

Publishing النَّشرُ

ج ر د

جَرَدَ – يَجرُدُ to peel or strip; to take inventory
تَجَرَّدَ – يَتَجَرَّدُ to be free; to renounce; to be stripped or divested of
جَرْدٌ bare; worn; stocktaking
جَرِدٌ / أَجرَدُ (جُردٌ) bald, hairless; bleak; shabby, worn; without vegetation
جَرادٌ locusts
جَريدَةٌ (جَرائِدُ) newspaper; register, index
كِشكُ الجَرائِدِ news kiosk
مُجَرَّدٌ bare, naked; free; pure, mere (with idafa); first stem of the verb; root (grammar)
مُجَرَّدٌ ثُلاثِيٌّ triliteral root
مُجَرَّدٌ رُباعِيٌّ quadrilateral root

ح ر ر

(Full treatment in Politics chapter)

حَرَّ – يَحِرُّ to be hot

236 *Media*

حَرَّرَ – يُحَرِّرُ to write or edit; to liberate or set free
حُرِّيَّةٌ (حُرِّيَّاتٌ) freedom, liberty, independence
تَحْرِيرٌ (تَحَارِيرُ) writing, editing; freedom, liberty
رَئِيسُ التَّحْرِيرِ editor-in-chief
إدارةُ التَّحْرِيرِ editorial staff
مُحَرِّرٌ (مُحَرِّرُونَ) editor; liberator
مُحَرِّرُ النُّصُوصِ text editor (computer)
تَحْرِيرِيٌّ in writing; liberal

س ب ع

سَبَّعَ – يُسَبِّعُ to make sevenfold; to divide into seven
سَبُعٌ (أَسْبُعٌ / سُبُوعٌ) lion; beast of prey
سَبُعٌ (سِبَاعٌ) lion; predatory animal
سَبْعَةٌ seven
سَبْعُونَ seventy
أُسْبُوعٌ (أَسَابِيعُ) week
عُطْلَةُ نِهَايَةِ الأُسْبُوعِ weekend
أُسْبُوعِيٌّ weekly
أُسْبُوعِيّاً weekly

No root

سَنَةٌ (سَنَوَاتٌ / سِنُونٌ) year
سَنَةٌ كَبِيسَةٌ leap year
عَلَى مَدَارِ السَّنَةِ all year round
سَنَوِيٌّ annual
اِكْتِتَابٌ سَنَوِيٌّ annual subscription
سَنَوِيّاً annually

ش ه ر

شَهَرَ – يَشْهَرُ to be famous or well-known; to spread; to divulge
أَشْهَرَ – يُشْهِرُ to announce or make known; to spread
اِشْتَهَرَ – يَشْتَهِرُ to be or become well-known
شَهْرٌ (أَشْهُرٌ / شُهُورٌ) month
شَهْرُ العَسَلِ honeymoon
شَهْرِيٌّ / شَهْرِيّاً monthly
اِشْتِرَاكٌ شَهْرِيٌّ monthly subscription

Media 237

نِصفُ شَهْرِي fortnightly
شَهْرِيَّةٌ monthly; monthly salary
شُهْرَةٌ / اِشْتِهارٌ fame
شَهيرٌ / مَشْهورٌ famous
إِشْهارٌ announcement, declaration; publicity

ص د ر

(Full treatment in Work chapter)

صَدَرَ – يَصْدُرُ to be published; to go out; to happen; to originate
صَدَّرَ – يُصَدِّرُ to send off, dispatch, or forward; to publish; to preface or introduce
صُدورٌ publication (book, article); issuing, coming out, appearance
تاريخُ الصُّدور date of issue
مَصْدَرٌ (مَصادِرُ) source or point of origin; infinitive (grammar)
مَصادِرُ مُطَّلِعَةٌ informed sources
مَصادِرُ مَوْثوقَةٌ reliable sources
مَجْهولُ المَصدر unknown sources
إِستِصدارٌ issue, issuance
صادِرٌ (صادِراتٌ) exports; yield; originating; published

ط ب ع

(Full treatment in Earth chapter)

طَبَعَ – يَطْبَعُ to impress, print, stamp, or seal
اِنطَبَعَ – يَنطَبِعُ to be impressed on or printed
طَبْعٌ (طِباعٌ) characteristic; nature, disposition; print, stamp
طَبْعَةٌ (طَبَعاتٌ) edition, issue; printing
طَبَّاعٌ / طابِعٌ printer
مَطْبَعةٌ (مَطابِعُ) printing press; publishing house
طابَعٌ (طَوابِعُ) character; stamp, seal
مَطْبوعٌ (مَطْبوعاتٌ) printed materials, newspapers and magazines; printed (adj)
اِنطِباعٌ (اِنطِباعاتٌ) impression

ع ن و ن

عَنْوَنَ – يُعَنْوِنُ to furnish with an address; to title; to give someone a title
عُنوانٌ (عَناوينُ) headline, title; address; sign, token
العَناوينُ الرَّئيسِيَّةُ the headlines

ع و م

عامَ – يَعومُ to swim or float
عَوَّمَ – يُعَوِّمُ to launch or float; to flood
عَوْمٌ swimming
عامٌ (أَعْوامٌ) year
الْعامُ الْحالِيُّ / الْعامُ الْجاري present year, current year
الْعامُ الْمُنصَرِمُ / الْعامُ الْماضي last year
الْعامُ الْقادِمُ / الْعامُ الْمُقْبِلُ the coming year, next year

ن ش ر

نَشَرَ – يَنْشُرُ to publish, publicise, spread, or diffuse
اِنْتَشَرَ – يَنْتَشِرُ to be spread out, unfolded, extended, or expanded
نَشْرٌ publishing; diffusion, propagation; spreading, unfolding
نَشْرٌ إِلِكْتْرونيٌّ electronic publishing
نَشْرَةٌ (نَشَراتٌ) announcement, bulletin; publication, leaflet, report
مِنْشارٌ (مَناشيرُ) a saw
اِنْتِشارٌ dissemination; spreading; circulation
ناشِرٌ publisher
مَنْشورٌ (مَنْشوراتٌ) made public, published (pl: leaflets, pamphlets)
مُنْتَشِرٌ widespread; current

ي و م

يَوَّمَ – يُيَوِّمُ to hire by the day
يَوْمٌ (أَيّامٌ) day
الْيَوْمُ today
ذاتَ يَوْمٍ one day; once
يَوْمَ أَمْسِ yesterday
يَوْماً / يَوْماً ما some day; one of these days
كُلَّ يَوْمٍ every day, daily
يَوْمِيّاً daily
يَوْمَئِذٍ then, at that time, on that day
يَوْمَذاكَ on that day, then
يَوْمِيٌّ (adj) daily
جَريدةٌ يَوْمِيَّةٌ daily newspaper
يَوْمِيَّةٌ daily wages; daily ration; journal

Commentary التَّعليقُ

أ د ى

أَدَّى – يُؤَدِّي to lead to; to contribute; to convey
أَداءٌ (أَداءاتٌ) pursuit; execution, performance
تَأدِيَةٌ pursuit; performance, execution

أ ك د

أَكَّدَ – يُؤَكِّدُ to confirm; to assure
تَأَكَّدَ – يَتَأَكَّدُ to be or become convinced; to make sure
تَأكيدٌ (تَأكيداتٌ) assurances; confirmation; emphasis
أَكيدٌ certain, sure
مُؤَكَّدٌ certain, definite, confirmed
مُتَأَكِّدٌ (مِن) convinced (of), certain

ب ع د

بَعُدَ – يَبعُدُ to be distant or remote; to exceed
أَبعَدَ – يُبعِدُ to remove or eliminate; to banish or exile
اِبتَعَدَ – يَبتَعِدُ to move away, quit, or leave; to avoid
اِستَبعَدَ – يَستَبعِدُ to rule out or regard as unlikely; to disqualify
بُعدٌ (أَبعادٌ) distance, remoteness
بَعدَ (prep) after
بَعيدٌ (بُعَداءُ) far, distant, remote
مُستَبعَدٌ improbable, unlikely

ب ي ن

بانَ – يَبينُ to be plain, clear, or evident; to come to light
بَيَّنَ – يُبَيِّنُ to make clear, plain, or evident; to announce; to show or demonstrate
تَبَيَّنَ – يَتَبَيَّنُ to be or become clear; to appear; to turn out
اِستَبانَ – يَستَبينُ to be or become clear
بَينَ (prep) between, among
بَينَما (conj) while, whereas
بَيِّنٌ clear, evident, obvious
بَيانٌ (بَياناتٌ) statement, announcement, declaration
بَيانٌ اِنتِخابِيٌّ election manifesto

240 Media

بَيانٌ مُقْتَضَبٌ brief statement
بَيِّنَةٌ (بَيِّناتٌ) clear proof, indisputable evidence
مُبينٌ clear, plain, evident, obvious[1]

ح و ز

حازَ – يَحوزُ to possess, own, or have
تَحَيَّزَ – يَتَحَيَّزُ to stay away; to seclude or isolate oneself
حَوْزٌ possession, holding
تَحَيُّزٌ prejudice, bias
عَدَمُ الانحيازِ non-alignment
مُتَحَيِّزٌ partial, prejudiced, biased
غَيرُ مُنحازٍ non-aligned

ح ي د

حادَ – يَحيدُ to depart or abandon; to deviate; to swerve
حَيَّدَ – يُحَيِّدُ to keep or put aside
حَيْدٌ / حَيْدَةٌ deviation, digression; departure; swerving
حِيادٌ / مُحايَدَةٌ neutrality
مُحايِدٌ / حِياديٌّ / على الْحِيادِ neutral

خ ت م

خَتَمَ – يَخْتِمُ to finish or conclude; to seal or stamp
تَخَتَّمَ – يَتَخَتَّمُ to wear a ring
اِخْتَتَمَ – يَخْتَتِمُ to conclude or finish
خَتْمٌ (أَختامٌ) a seal, stamp, or imprint
خاتِمٌ (خَواتِمُ) a ring or stamp
خاتِمَةٌ (خاتِماتٌ / خَواتِمُ) end, termination, conclusion

خ ط ب

خَطَبَ – يَخْطُبُ to preach, make a speech, or deliver a sermon; to propose
خاطَبَ – يُخاطِبُ to address; to speak or talk
خَطْبٌ (خُطوبٌ) situation, conditions; business; mishap
خِطْبَةٌ courtship, engagement
خِطابٌ (خِطاباتٌ) letter, speech, message, note
خَطيبٌ (خُطباءُ) speaker, lecturer, preacher; fiancé

خِطابَةٌ preaching, oratory
خُطوبَةٌ engagement
مُخاطَبَةٌ (مُخاطَباتٌ) public address or speech

خ ل ص

خَلَصَ – يَخلُصُ to be pure or unadulterated; to arrive or come; to be free
خَلَّصَ – يُخَلِّصُ to clear, purify, or purge; to clarify
خالَصَ – يُخالِصُ to act with integrity or sincerity; to get even
أخلَصَ – يُخلِصُ to be loyal, devoted, or faithful
تَخَلَّصَ – يَتَخَلَّصُ to get rid or rid oneself of; to be saved or rescued
اِستَخلَصَ – يَستَخلِصُ to deduce or infer; to choose or select
خُلاصَةٌ (خُلاصاتٌ) essence; extract; abstract, résumé
تَخليصٌ clearing, purification; rectification
إخلاصٌ sincere devotion, loyal attachment, sincerity
تَخَلُّصٌ (مِن) freedom, liberation, release, escape (from)
اِستِخلاصٌ extraction; selection; collecting (money)
خالِصٌ (خُلَّصٌ) clear, pure, unadulterated, sincere
مُخلِصٌ sincere, faithful

ر أ ى

رَأى – يَرى to see, notice, observe, or discern; to express one's opinion
أرى – يُري to show or demonstrate
اِرتَأى – يَرتَئي to contemplate; to be of the opinion
رَأيٌ (آراءٌ) opinion, view, idea, notion, suggestion
الرَّأيُ العامُّ public opinion
اِستِطلاعُ الرَّأي opinion poll
تَبادُلُ الآراءِ exchanging opinions and views
رايَةٌ (راياتٌ) banner, flag
رُؤيَةٌ seeing, looking; insight, vision (real)
رُؤيا vision (dream)
مِرآةٌ (مَرايا) mirror, looking glass; reflection
مِرايَة (مِراياتٌ) mirror

ز ع م

زَعَمَ – يَزعُمُ to claim or allege; to pretend
تَزَعَّمَ – يَتَزَعَّمُ to be or pretend to be the leader

زَعْمٌ allegation
زَعيمٌ (زُعَماءُ) leader; colonel (also a boy's name in the singular)
زَعامَةٌ leadership
مَزاعِمُ claims, allegations; assumptions
مَزْعومٌ claimed, alleged

س أ ل

سَأَلَ – يَسْأَلُ to ask, inquire, or request; to demand or claim
تَسَوَّلَ – يَتَسَوَّلُ to beg
سُؤالٌ (أَسْئِلَةٌ) question; request; demand
مَسْأَلَةٌ (مَسائِلُ) problem, question, matter
سائِلٌ (سائِلونٌ) questioner; beggar
مُتَسَوِّلٌ (مُتَسَوِّلونَ) beggar
مَسْؤولٌ (مَسْؤولونَ) an official; responsible or accountable for
كِبارُ الْمَسْؤولينَ high-ranking officials
مَسْؤوليَّةٌ (مَسْؤوليّاتٌ) responsibility
عَديمُ الْمَسْؤوليَّةِ irresponsible

س ب ل

سَبَّلَ – يُسَبِّلُ to dedicate to charitable purposes
أَسْبَلَ – يُسْبِلُ to let fall or drop; to close (eyes); to shed (tears); to form (ears of corn)
سَبَلٌ ears of corn
سَبيلٌ (سُبْلٌ) way, road, path; access; possibility
عَلى سَبيلِ الْمِثالِ for example
في سَبيلِ اللهِ for God's sake, for the love of God (not expecting anything in return)
اِبْنُ السَّبيلِ tramp; traveller

ش د د

شَدَّ – يَشُدُّ to be firm or solid; to be intense or harsh; to tighten or pull
شَدَّدَ – يُشَدِّدُ to emphasise or stress; to strengthen; to exert pressure
تَشَدَّدَ – يَتَشَدَّدُ to be strict, severe, or intense; to be violent
اِشْتَدَّ – يَشْتَدُّ to be or become harsher or more violent; to intensify
شَدَّةٌ intensification; stress (grammar)
شِدَّةٌ (شَدائِدُ) strength, forcefulness; adversity, misery
شَديدٌ (أَشِدَّاءُ / شِدادٌ) powerful, intense, severe; difficult

Media 243

شَديدَةٌ (شَدائِدُ) misfortune, calamity, misery
تَشَدُّدٌ intolerance, strictness
مَشدودٌ tense, tight, taut
مُشَدَّدٌ doubled (letter grammatically); emphatic; intense, severe
مُتَشَدِّدٌ (مُتَشَدِّدونَ) radical, bigot, fanatic; stern

ش ر ح

شَرَحَ – يَشرَحُ to explain or illustrate; to expose or cut open
شَرَّحَ – يُشَرِّحُ to cut in slices; to dissect
اِنشَرَحَ – يَنشَرِحُ to be relaxed, glad, or happy
شَرحٌ (شُروحٌ) explanation, commentary
شَريحَةٌ (شَرائِحُ) thin or long slice
تَشريحٌ dissection; anatomy
شارِحٌ (شُرَّاحٌ) explainer, interpreter, commentator

ش م ل

شَمِلَ – يَشمَلُ to incorporate, take in, include, or comprehend
اِشتَمَلَ – يَشتَمِلُ to contain, comprise, comprehend, or include
شَملٌ uniting, gathering; union
شامِلٌ comprehensive; general, universal
مُشتَمِلٌ comprising, including
مُشتَمَلاتٌ contents

ش ه د

(Full treatment in Law chapter)

شَهِدَ – يَشهَدُ to witness, testify, or attest; to attend or be present
شاهَدَ – يُشاهِدُ to see or witness; to view or inspect
شاهِدٌ (شُهودٌ/شواهِدُ) witness; notary public
شاهِدُ عِيانٍ (شُهودُ عِيانٍ) eyewitness
مَشهَدٌ (مَشاهِدُ) view, scene

ص ر ح

صَرُحَ – يَصرُحُ to be pure, unadulterated, or clear; to clarify or explain
صَرَّحَ – يُصَرِّحُ to state or declare; to explain or clarify

صَريحٌ (صُرحاءُ) clear; frank, outspoken, sincere
صَراحَةٌ clarity; sincerity, openness
تَصريحٌ (تَصريحاتٌ) statement, declaration; permission
تَصريحٌ صَحَفيٌّ press release
تَصريحٌ أَمنيٌّ security clearance

ص ر ر

صَرَّ – يَصِرُّ to chirp, creak, or screech; to chatter; to bind
أَصَرَّ – يُصِرُّ to resolve, determine, or decide; to persist
صَريرٌ chirping, screeching
صَرّارٌ / صَرّارُ اللَّيلِ a cricket
إِصرارٌ persistence, perseverance
مُصِرٌّ persistent

ظ ن ن

ظَنَّ – يَظُنُّ to believe, think, or consider; to assume
تَظَنَّنَ – يَتَظَنَّنُ to surmise or form conjectures
ظَنٌّ (ظُنونٌ) opinion, idea, assumption, belief
حُسْنُ الظَّنِّ benefit of the doubt
سوءُ الظَّنِّ mistrust, distrust
ظِنَّةٌ (ظِنَنٌ) suspicion
ظَنينٌ suspicious, untrustworthy, unreliable

ع ب ر

عَبَرَ – يَعبُرُ to cross or pass; to swim; to ferry
عَبَّرَ – يُعَبِّرُ to state, declare, or express clearly; to interpret (a dream)
اِعتَبَرَ – يُعتَبِرُ to consider, deem, or regard; to take into account; to learn a lesson; to hold in esteem
عَبْرَ over (prep), beyond (prep), across (prep); crossing, passage
عُبورٌ crossing, transit
عَبيرٌ fragrance, scent, perfume (also a girl's name)
عِبْريٌّ Hebrew
عِبْرَةٌ (عِبَرٌ) warning, advice, lesson; example
عِبارَةٌ (عِباراتٌ) explanation, interpretation; word, clause, phrase, expression
عِبْرانيٌّ Hebrew

مَعْبَرٌ (مَعابِرُ) a passage or crossing
تَعْبِيرٌ (تَعْبِيراتٌ) declaration, expression, utterance
اِعْتِبارٌ (اِعْتِباراتٌ) consideration, regard, deference, esteem, respect
مُعَبِّرٌ expressive; significant

ع ر ب

عَرَّبَ – يُعَرِّبُ to Arabise; to express or state clearly; to translate into Arabic
أَعْرَبَ – يُعْرِبُ to express or state clearly; to Arabise; to declare; to decline (a verb)
تَعَرَّبَ – يَتَعَرَّبُ to assimilate oneself to the Arabs; to become an Arab
اِسْتَعْرَبَ – يَسْتَعْرِبُ to pretend to be an Arab; to become an Arab
إِعْرابٌ declension; inflection (grammar); declaration, utterance
عَرَبٌ (أَعْرابٌ) Arabs, Bedouins
عَرَبِيٌّ an Arab; Arabian
عَرَبَةٌ (عَرَباتٌ) carriage, vehicle, cart; a swift river
عَرَبِيَّةٌ (عَرَبِيّاتٌ) carriage, vehicle, coach
عَرّابٌ godfather; sponsor
عَرّابَةٌ godmother; sponsor
عُروبَةٌ Arabism
تَعْرِيبٌ translating into Arabic; incorporation (of loanwords) into Arabic
مُسْتَعْرِبٌ Arabist

ع ل ق

عَلِقَ – يَعْلَقُ to hang or be suspended; to stick, cling, or adhere
عَلَّقَ – يُعَلِّقُ to comment, remark, or state; to hang; to fasten; to leave undecided
عَلاقَةٌ (عَلاقاتٌ) relation; affiliation, connection; affection
العَلاقاتُ العامَّةُ public relations
العَلاقاتُ الدُّوَلِيَّةُ international relations
العَلاقاتُ الدُّبْلوماسِيَّةُ diplomatic relations
عَلاقاتٌ وَثيقَةٌ close relations
تَعْليقٌ (تَعْليقاتٌ) commentary; comment, remark; hanging, suspended
بِدون تَعْليقٍ no comment
مُعَلِّقٌ (مُعَلِّقونَ) news, radio, or press commentator
مُعَلَّقٌ suspended, hanging; in suspense, undecided
بَرْلَمانٌ مُعَلَّقٌ hung parliament

غ ر ض

أَغْرَضَ – يُغْرِضُ to attain (goal); to take sides
تَغَرَّضَ – يَتَغَرَّضُ to take sides or have a bias
غَرَضٌ (أَغْراضٌ) target, objective; interest (personal); bias, prejudice; things
تَغَرُّضٌ prejudice, bias
مُغْرِضٌ (مُغْرِضونَ) partial, biased

ف ت ح

فَتَحَ – يَفْتَحُ to open; to turn on; to build or dig
فاتَحَ – يُفاتِحُ to address first; to confront
انْفَتَحَ – يَنْفَتِحُ to open up or unfold
افْتَتَحَ – يَفْتَتِحُ to inaugurate; to introduce or preface; to conquer or capture
فَتْحٌ (فُتوحٌ / فتوحاتٌ) opening, introduction; conquest, victory
فَتْحَةٌ the (a) ó vowel in Arabic
فُتْحَةٌ (فُتحاتٌ / فُتَحٌ) opening, aperture
مِفتاحٌ (مَفاتيحُ) key
افْتِتاحٌ opening, introduction, inauguration
افْتِتاحِيَّةٌ editorial; introductory, preliminary
فاتِحٌ light (colour); beginner; victor, conqueror
فاتِحَةٌ (فَواتِحُ) start, opening, beginning
الفاتِحَةُ first sura of Quran
مَفتوحٌ opened; open

ق ر ح

قَرَحَ – يَقْرَحُ to wound; to ulcerate or fester
اقْتَرَحَ – يَقْتَرِحُ to suggest or propose; to invent or improvise
قَرْحٌ (قُروحٌ) wound, sore, ulcer
قُرْحَةٌ (قُرحاتٌ) ulcer, sore, abscess
اقْتِراحٌ (اقْتِراحاتٌ) suggestion, proposal; invention
مُقْتَرَحٌ (مُقْتَرَحاتٌ) proposal, suggestion, proposition

ك ش ف

كَشَفَ – يَكْشِفُ to expose, reveal, or disclose; to remove
انْكَشَفَ – يَنْكَشِفُ to be uncovered, disclosed, or revealed
اكْتَشَفَ – يَكْتَشِفُ to discover or detect; to uncover

اِستَكشَفَ – يَستَكشِفُ to explore, investigate, or inquire
كَشفٌ (كُشوفٌ) discovery; investigation, examination (medical); statement (bank)
عَدَمُ كَشفِ الهُوِيَّةِ anonymity
كَشّافٌ (كَشّافَةٌ) boy scout; explorer; inventor
اِكتِشافٌ (اِكتِشافاتٌ) discovery, disclosure, uncovering
اِستِكشافٌ uncovering; exploration
مَكشوفٌ revealed, uncovered, exposed, naked
مُكتَشِفٌ discoverer, explorer

ك ل م

كَلَّمَ – يُكَلِّمُ to speak, talk, or address
تَكَلَّمَ – يَتَكَلَّمُ to speak, express, or voice
كَلِمَةٌ (كَلِماتٌ) word, speech, utterance; address; maxim
كَلامٌ sentence or clause (grammar); talking, speech; language
كَلامٌ فارِغٌ nonsense
كَليمٌ (كُلَماءُ) spokesperson, speaker; person addressed
مُكالَمَةٌ (مُكالَماتٌ) talk, conversation, discussion
مُتَكَلِّمٌ first person (grammar); speaker, spokesman; outspoken

ل خ ص

لَخَّصَ – يُلَخِّصُ to extract; to summarise or outline
تَلَخَّصَ – يَتَلَخَّصُ to be summarised, summed up, or condensed
تَلخيصٌ summary, résumé, abstract, synopsis
مُلَخَّصٌ (مُلَخَّصاتٌ) summarised, abridged, extract

ل ق ي

لَقِيَ – يَلقى to encounter or meet; to experience; to endure
لاقى – يُلاقي to meet or encounter; to experience
أَلقى – يُلقي to throw, drop, or discard
تَلَقّى – يَتَلَقّى to receive, take, or accept; to learn or be informed
اِلتَقى – يَلتَقي to meet, come together, or encounter
أَلقى خِطاباً to give a speech
أَلقى الضَّوءَ عَلى to throw light on
تِلقاءَ (prep) opposite, in front of
تِلقائيٌّ automatic, spontaneous

مَلْقىً (ملاقٍ) meeting place; junction, crossing
لِقاءٌ (لِقاءاتٌ) encounter, meeting
إلْقاءٌ throwing, casting, flinging; delivering a speech
إلْتِقاءٌ (مع) meeting (with); reunion
مُلْتَقىً (مُلْتَقَياتٌ) meeting place; rendezvous; junction

ل م ح

لَمَحَ – يَلْمَحُ to glance, see, or notice; to flash or sparkle
لَمَّحَ – يُلَمِّحُ to insinuate, hint, or allude
ألْمَحَ – يُلْمِحُ to glance casually
لَمْحٌ quick look, glance; moment
لَمْحَةٌ (لَمْحاتٌ) glance; moment, instant
مَلامِحُ features, traits
تَلْميحٌ (تَلْميحاتٌ / تَلاميحُ) allusion, insinuation, hint; refutation

ن ق ش

نَقَشَ – يَنْقُشُ to engrave or paint; to sculpt or chisel
ناقَشَ – يُناقِشُ to discuss, argue, or debate; to criticise; to examine
تَناقَشَ – يَتَناقَشُ to debate, to carry on a dispute
نَقْشٌ (نُقوشٌ) painting, drawing, engraving; inscription
نَقّاشٌ sculptor, engraver
مُناقَشَةٌ (مُناقَشاتٌ) discussion, negotiation, argument
نِقاشٌ (نِقاشاتٌ) discussion, debate
مُناقِشٌ (مُناقِشونَ) disputant, person in dispute

ن ق ض

نَقَضَ – يَنْقُضُ to destroy, demolish, or violate; to invalidate
ناقَضَ – يُناقِضُ to contradict; to be opposite
إنْتَقَضَ – يَنْتَقِضُ to be destroyed or demolished; to revolt; to attack
نَقْضٌ destruction, demolition; breach, violation
نَقيضٌ opposite, contrary; antithesis
على النَّقيضِ (مِن ذلِكَ) on the contrary
تَناقُضٌ contradiction, inconsistency
مُتَناقِضٌ (مُتَناقِضاتٌ) contradictions, contrasts

ن ق ل

نَقَلَ – يَنْقُلُ to communicate; to remove; to transport
نَقَّلَ – يُنَقِّلُ to move or displace; to advance
تَنَقَّلَ – يَتَنَقَّلُ to move about, migrate, or wander
اِنتَقَلَ – يَنتَقِلُ to be carried or transported
اِنتَقَلَ إِلى رحمةِ اللهِ he died
نَقْلٌ transmission, transfer; carrying, removal, transport
نَقْلُ المَعْلوماتِ information transfer
نَقْلُ التِّكنولوجيا technology transfer
النَّقْلُ العامُّ / وَسائلُ النَّقْلِ العامِ public transport
نَقْلًا عن according to
اِنتِقالٌ transportation, moving, removal
مُتَنَقِّلٌ mobile, itinerant, roaming
تَنَقُّلٌ / اِنتِقالٌ change of residence; roaming, wandering; transmission
مُتَنَقِّلٌ / نَقّالٌ portable, mobile

ه م م

هَمَّ – يَهُمُّ to disquiet or worry; to grieve; to be important
أَهَمَّ – يُهِمُّ to grieve, worry, or trouble; to be of interest or importance
اِهتَمَّ – يَهتَمُّ to be concerned, distressed, or worried; to pay attention
هَمٌّ (هُمومٌ) worry, anxiety, concern, solitude
هِمَّةٌ (هِمَمٌ) ambition, resolution, intention
أَهَمِّيَّةٌ importance, significance; interest
مَهَمَّةٌ (مَهامُّ) mission, task, duty
اِهتِمامٌ (اِهتِماماتٌ) interest, concern, attention; an endeavour
هامٌّ important, serious, interesting
مَهْمومٌ concerned, worried, stressed
مُهِمٌّ important, significant; interesting
مُهِمَّةٌ (مُهِمّاتٌ) important things; requirements, provisions
مُهْتَمٌّ (بِـ) interested (in), concerned, anxious

No root

هَوَجٌ folly; light-headedness, rashness
أَهوَجُ (هُوجٌ) reckless, impatient; violent, frantic

250   Media

هائِجٌ raging (of discussion)
هَوجاءُ (هوجٌ) hurricane, tornado, cyclone

و ز ع

وَزَعَ – يَزَعُ to curb or restrain
وَزَّعَ – يُوَزِّعُ to distribute, divide, or deliver
تَوَزَّعَ – يَتَوَزَّعُ to be distributed or divided
تَوزيعٌ distribution, division, allotment
وازِعٌ obstacle, impediment; conscience; restraint
مُوَزِّعٌ distributor; distributing
مُوَزِّعُ البَريدِ postman
مُوَزَّعٌ distributed, scattered, dispersed

و ض ح

وَضَحَ – يَضِحُ to be clear or evident; to appear or come to light
أَوْضَحَ – يوضِحُ to clarify, explain, or illustrate
تَوَضَّحَ – يَتَوَضَّحُ to be clear or evident; to appear or come to light
اِستَوضَحَ – يَستَوضِحُ to ask for explanation or clarification
وُضوحٌ clarity, distinctness
تَوضيحٌ clarification, explanation, elucidation
إيضاحٌ (إيضاحاتٌ) explanation, clarification
واضِحٌ clear, plain, distinct

Censorship رِقابةُ المَطبوعاتِ

ح ذ ف

حَذَفَ – يَحذِفُ to delete, omit, or suppress; to shorten; to deduct or subtract
حَذَّفَ – يُحَذِّفُ to give something shape; to trim or clip
حَذْفٌ omission, suppression; ellipsis (grammar); shortening; cancelling

ر ق ب

رَقَبَ – يَرقُبُ to observe, supervise, or control
راقَبَ – يُراقِبُ to observe, supervise, or control; to detect
تَرَقَّبَ – يَتَرَقَّبُ to expect, anticipate, or await; to look for
اِرتَقَبَ – يَرتَقِبُ to expect or anticipate

Media 251

مُراقِبٌ (مُراقِبونَ) observer; censor
رَقَبةٌ (رِقابٌ/رَقَباتٌ) neck
رَقيبٌ (رُقباءُ) vigilant; guardian
رَقابةٌ censorship (of press); supervision, control
مُراقَبةٌ surveillance, supervision, control
بُرجُ المُراقَبةِ control tower
نِظامُ المُراقَبةِ surveillance system
مُراقِبٌ (مُراقِبونَ) supervisor, inspector, controller

س ت ر

سَتَرَ – يَستُرُ to cover, veil, hide, or conceal
تَسَتَّرَ – يَتَسَتَّرُ to cover up (for someone); to be covered or veiled
اِستَتَرَ – يَستَتِرُ to be veiled, hidden, or concealed
سِترٌ (سُتورٌ/أَستارٌ) veil, screen, curtain, covering
سِتارٌ (أَستارٌ) screen, veil, curtain, covering
قِصّةٌ لِلتَّسَتُّرِ على cover story
سِتارٌ دُخانيٌّ smokescreen
مَستورٌ hidden, invisible, masked

ع ت م

عَتَمَ – يَعتِمُ to darken; to hesitate (with negative)
أَعتَمَ – يُعتِمُ to hesitate or waver
عَتمةٌ dark, gloom, darkness
تَعتيمٌ darkening, clouding, obscurity
مُعتِمٌ dark
التَّعتيمُ الكامِلُ complete darkness (no news coverage)

ك ظ م

كَظَمَ – يَكظِمُ to suppress; to keep silent
كَظيمٌ one who suppresses his anger; to be filled with anger

ك م م

كَمَّ – يَكُمُّ to cover up, conceal, or hide; to muzzle
كَمَّمَ – يُكَمِّمُ to muzzle; to provide with sleeves

252 *Media*

كِمامَةٌ (كِمامَاتٌ/كَمائِمُ) muzzle; mask
تَكْمِيمُ الإعْلامِ muzzling the media

ل غ ز

لَغَزَ – يَلْغُزُ to speak in riddles, to equivocate
أَلْغَزَ – يُلْغِزُ to speak in riddles, to equivocate
لُغْزٌ (أَلْغازٌ) riddle, enigma, puzzle
لُغْزُ الْكَلِماتِ الْمُتَقاطِعَةِ crossword puzzle

و ض ع

وَضَعَ – يَضَعُ to lay, put, or impose
تَواضَعَ – يَتَواضَعُ to behave humbly or modestly
اِتَّضَعَ – يَتَّضِعُ to humble oneself
وَضْعٌ (أَوْضاعٌ) circumstances; principles; recording, fixing
مَوْضِعٌ (مَواضِعُ) place, spot, site, position, situation
تَواضُعٌ humility, modesty; lowliness
مَوْضوعٌ (مَواضيعُ) subject, theme; matter; article
مَوْضوعُ جَدَلٍ controversial matter
الْمَوْضوعِيَّةُ objectivity
غَيْرُ مَوْضوعِيّ subjective

Exercises

1) Give two derived words for each of the following roots:

    خ ب ر
    ر س ل
    ع ل م

2) Find the roots of the following words:

    أُسْبوعٌ
    تَوْزيعٌ
    جَريدَةٌ
    شَهيرٌ
    طِباعٌ
    عامٌّ
    قِصَّةٌ

مَصادِرٌ
مَقالاتٌ

3) Give the plural of these words (some may have more than one plural):

إعلانٌ
تَعليمٌ
خاتِمةٌ
قُبلةٌ
كِتابٌ
وَسيلةٌ

4) Give the present tense of these verbs:

أعلنَ
حَرَّرَ
صَدَرَ
قابَلَ
كَتَبَ
واجَهَ

5) Translate the following sentences into Arabic
   a) The journalist published his first book.
   b) The PM gave a brief statement.
   c) The president spoke about the allegations in a television broadcast.
   d) The correspondent confirmed his neutrality.
   e) My friend owns the largest news agency in England.

6) Translate the following sentences into English:

   ـ آخِرُ الأخْبارِ العالميَّةِ.
   ـ الصَّحَفيّون أساسيّون لِلْحِفاظِ على الديمقراطيَّةِ.
   ـ ما هُوَ دَوْرُ الصّحفي اليَومَ؟
   ـ تَلعبُ وسائلُ الإعلامِ دَوْراً هاماً في عَصرِنا هذا.
   ـ ذَكَرتْ وَكالةُ الأنباءِ البِريطانيَّة أنَّ رئيسَ الوزراءِ قدَّمَ استِقالَتَهُ.

Note

1 This is frequently used as an epithet of the Quran القُرآنُ المُبينُ

7 Law and Order القانونُ والأَمنُ

الإجراءاتُ القانونِيَّةُ The Legal Process

ب و ح

باحَ – يَبوحُ to be revealed; to disclose or divulge
أَباحَ – يُبيحُ to disclose, reveal, release; to permit, allow
اِسْتباحَ – يَسْتبيحُ to reveal; to deem permissible or lawful
بَوْحٌ confession, disclosure
باحَةٌ (باحاتٌ) a wide open space or courtyard
إِباحَةٌ permission; disclosure; licentiousness
إِباحِيَّةٌ libertinism; anarchism; freethinking
اِسْتِباحَةٌ capture or seizure; confiscation
مُباحٌ permitted, legal; legitimate

ج د ل

جَدَلَ – يَجدِلُ to twist or plait; to tighten
جَدَّلَ – يُجدِّلُ to plait
جادَلَ – يُجادِلُ to quarrel, argue, or debate
جَدَلٌ a quarrel, argument, or debate
أَثارَ جَدَلًا to cause controversy
مُثيرٌ لِلْجَدَلِ / جَدَلِيٌّ controversial
جَديلَةٌ (جَدائِلُ) a plait
جِدالٌ / مُجادَلَةٌ (جِدالاتٌ / مُجادَلاتٌ) a quarrel, argument, or debate
لا جِدالَ / بِلا جِدالٍ indisputably
مُجادِلٌ a disputant or opponent

ج ن ى

جَنى – يَجني to commit a crime; to pocket or secure; to gather or harvest

DOI: 10.4324/9781003250890-8

Law and Order 255

تَجَنَّى – يَتَجَنَّى to incriminate; to accuse
جِنايَةٌ (جِناياتٌ) a crime or felony
مَحْكَمَةُ الجِناياتِ / مَحْكَمَةٌ جِنائِيَّةٌ criminal court
جِنائِيٌّ criminal (adj)
تَحقيقٌ جِنائِيٌّ criminal investigation
المَحْكَمَةُ الجِنائِيَّةُ الدَّوَلِيَّةُ the International Criminal Court

ج و ب

جابَ – يجوبُ to travel or traverse; to wander or roam
جاوَبَ – يُجاوِبُ to answer or respond
إستَجوَبَ – يَستَجوِبُ to interrogate or examine
جَوابٌ (أَجْوِبَةٌ) a reply; an octave (music)
إجابةٌ (إجاباتٌ) an answer or reply
إستِجوابٌ (إستِجواباتٌ) an interrogation or hearing; a debriefing

ج و ز

جازَ – يَجوزُ to pass, come, travel; to be allowed; to be possible
جَوَّزَ – يُجَوِّزُ to permit, authorise, warrant
إستجازَ – يَستجيزُ to deem permissible; to ask permission
جَوازٌ permissibility or legality; license or permission
جَوازُ سَفَرٍ passport
إجازةٌ (إجازاتٌ) a holiday; permission, license, or approval
جائِزٌ permitted or lawful; conceivable; passing
جائِزَةٌ (جوائِزُ) a prize or reward; a premium

ح ت م

حَتَّمَ – يُحَتِّمُ to decree or make necessary; to decide or determine
حَتْمٌ (حُتومٌ) imposition; resolution; final decision
حَتمِيٌّ final, conclusive
مَحْتومٌ imposed, determined, definite

ح ر م

حَرَمَ – يَحرِمُ to be prohibited or unlawful; to deprive or dispossess
حَرَّمَ – يُحَرِّمُ to forbid; to declare unlawful
تَحَرَّمَ – يَتَحَرَّمُ to be forbidden or prohibited

اِحْتَرَمَ – يَحْتَرِمُ to honour, respect, or esteem
اِسْتَحْرَمَ – يَسْتَحْرِمُ to deem sacred or inviolable
الْحَرَمانِ الشَّريفانِ the two Holy Places, i.e. Mecca and Medina
حُرْمَةٌ (حُرَماتٌ) holiness, sacredness; deference, veneration; woman or wife
حَرامٌ (حُرُمٌ) unlawful, prohibited or inviolable
حَرامٌ Poor thing!
حِرامٌ (أَحْرِمةٌ) blanket
حَريمٌ (حُرَمٌ) sacred or inviolable; women; harem
حَرامِيٌّ thief
حِرمانٌ deprivation
تَحْريمٌ interdiction, prohibition
اِحْتِرامٌ (اِحْتِراماتٌ) deference, respect, tributes
مَحرومٌ deprived; bereaved
مُحَرَّمٌ forbidden; the name of the first Islamic month
الْمُحَرَّماتُ taboos
مُحْتَرَمٌ honoured, esteemed
مَحْرَمَةٌ (مَحارِمُ) handkerchief

ح ظ ر

حَظَرَ – يَحْظُرُ to fence or hem in; to forbid or prohibit
حَظْرٌ a ban, embargo, or prohibition
حَظْرُ التَّجَوُّلِ curfew
مَحْظورٌ (مَحْظوراتٌ) prohibited; forbidden things or restrictions

ح ق ق

حَقَّ – يَحِقُّ to be true or suitable; to be necessary
حَقَّقَ – يُحَقِّقُ to investigate or interrogate; to achieve; to determine or verify
تَحَقَّقَ – يَتَحَقَّقُ to check; to ascertain or prove true; to convince
اِسْتَحَقَّ – يَسْتَحِقُّ to be entitled or to claim; to merit; to necessitate
حَقٌّ (حُقوقٌ) truth; rights; law; duty
حَقّاً in reality/truly
الْحُقوقُ law, jurisprudence
حَقيقةٌ (حَقائِقُ) truth, reality, fact
حَقيقةً / في الْحَقيقةِ truly, really
حَقيقيٌّ real or true

Law and Order 257

تَحْقيقٌ (تَحْقيقاتٌ) investigation, inquiry, interrogation; realisation (of); conviction
مُحَقِّقٌ (مُحَقِّقونَ) investigator, examiner, detective; magistrate
مُستحِقٌّ deserving, worthy, entitled
حَقُّ العَمَلِ right of employment
حَقُّ الْمُحاكَمةِ العادِلةِ right to fair trial
حُقوقُ الإنسانِ human rights
قانونَ حُقوقِ الإنسانِ Human Rights Act
جمعيّاتُ حُقوقِ الإنسانِ human rights organisations
الْحُقوقُ المدنِيَّةُ civil rights
حُقوقُ الْمَرْأةِ women's rights
حُقوقُ الحَيْوانِ animal rights

ح ك م

حَكَمَ – يَحكُمُ to rule or govern; to judge; to sentence
حَكَّمَ – يُحَكِّمُ to appoint as a ruler or judge
حاكَمَ – يُحاكِمُ to try, prosecute, or interrogate; to hear (a defence or prosecution)
تَحَكَّمَ – يَتَحَكَّمُ to be in control; to proceed at random
تَحاكَمَ – يَتَحاكَمُ to appeal
حُكْمٌ (أحْكامٌ) rule, order, law; judgement; verdict
حَكيمٌ (حُكماءُ) a sage or wise person; a doctor
حِكْمةٌ (حِكَمٌ) wisdom; an aphorism or witticism
حُكومةٌ (حُكوماتٌ) government
مَحْكَمةٌ (محاكِمُ) court; tribunal
جَلسةُ مَحْكَمةٍ court hearing
مُحاكَمةٌ (مُحاكَماتٌ) a trial or hearing
مَحْكومٌ عليهِ بِـ sentenced to
تَحَكُّمٌ rule, domination, power, control
حاكِمٌ (حُكّامٌ) a ruler or judge; ruling, governing
أخَذَ لِلْمَحْكَمةِ to take to court
بانْتِظارِ الْمَحاكَمةِ on remand
حُكْمُ براءةٍ acquittal
حُكْمُ الإعدامِ death penalty
محكمةُ الاسْتِئنافِ Court of Appeal
اسْتِئنافٌ appeal
أمرُ الْمَحْكَمةِ a warrant
مَحْكَمةُ التّاجِ / مَحْكَمةُ الجِنايات Crown court

258 Law and Order

مَحْكَمَةُ الصُّلْح Magistrates' court
مَحْكَمَةٌ عُلْيا the high or supreme court

ح ل ف

حَلَفَ – يَحْلِفُ to swear or take an oath
حَلَّفَ – يُحَلِّفُ to make (someone) swear or take an oath; to swear in
حِلْف اليَمين taking the oath
حِلْفٌ (أَحْلافٌ) alliance, pact
حَليفٌ (حُلَفاءُ) ally, confederate
حَلّوفٌ (حَلاليفُ) pig, swine¹
تَحالُفٌ alliance
مُحَلَّفٌ (مُحَلَّفونَ) juror
هَيْئَةُ المُحَلَّفينَ jury

ح ل ل

حَلَّ – يَحُلُّ to untie or solve; to resolve or settle (a dispute); to release
حَلَّلَ – يُحَلِّلُ to dissolve or break up; to declare lawful, to allow
اِحْتَلَّ – يَحْتَلُّ to occupy; to hold or have
اِسْتَحَلَّ – يَسْتَحِلُّ to regard (sth) as lawful; to regard as fair game
حَلٌّ (حُلولٌ) solution, explanation; untying, undoing, breaking up
حَلٌّ وَسَطٌ compromise
حَلُّ النِّزاعاتِ conflict resolution
حَلالٌ lawful, legal, legitimate
مَحَلٌّ (مَحَلّاتٌ) place, location; a shop or store
مَحَلِّيٌّ local
تَحْليلٌ (تَحاليلُ/تَحْليلاتٌ) analysis, resolution; dissolution, breaking up
اِنْحِلالٌ dissolution, breakup
اِحْتِلالٌ occupation
الأَراضي المُحْتَلَّةُ the Occupied Territories
مُحَلِّلٌ (مُحَلِّلونَ) analyst

ح م ى

حَمى – يَحْمي to defend, guard, or protect
حامى عَن – يُحامي عَن to defend (someone in court); to stand up for
حِمايةٌ (حِماياتٌ) protection; patronage; sponsorship

Law and Order 259

مُحاماةٌ defence; the legal profession; the practice of law
المُحاماةُ law (the discipline)
مُحامٍ (مُحامونَ) lawyer
مَحْمِيٌّ protected
حِمايةُ البياناتِ data protection

خ ص م

خَصَمَ – يَخصِمُ to defeat in an argument; to deduct or subtract
خاصَمَ – يُخاصِمُ to argue or dispute; to sue
تَخاصَمَ – يَتَخاصَمُ to have a fight; to litigate
خَصمٌ (خُصومٌ) adversary, opponent, enemy
خَصْمٌ reduction, discount, rebate
خَصيمٌ (خُصماءُ) adversary, enemy
خِصامٌ/خُصومَةٌ argument, dispute, quarrel

د ع و / د ع ى

دَعا – يَدْعو to call or summon; to appeal to someone
داعى – يُداعي to challenge; to prosecute
إدَّعى – يَدَّعي to claim, allege, charge, or testify (in court)
إستَدْعى – يَستَدعي to call or summon; to appeal (a judgement)
دَعْوةٌ (دَعَواتٌ) an appeal; a demand; an invitation, call or prayer
دَعوى (دَعاوى/دَعاوٍ) allegation, claim; a case or legal proceedings
دُعاءٌ (أدعِيَةٌ) prayer; request; good wish
دِعايةٌ propaganda
إدِّعاءٌ (إدِّعاءاتٌ) claim, allegation, accusation
الإدِّعاءُ prosecution
إستِدعاءٌ summons; citation
داعٍ (دُعاةٌ) cause or reason; host
مُدَّعٍ (مُدَّعونَ) a plaintiff or claimant
رفَعَ دَعْوى عَلى to sue
المُدَّعى عَليهِ/مُدَّعٍ عليهِ defendant

ز ع م

زَعَمَ – يَزعُمُ to allege, claim, declare, or assert; to pretend
تَزَعَّمَ – يَتَزَعَّمُ to lead; to pretend to be a leader

Law and Order

زَعْمٌ allegation, claim
زَعِيمٌ (زُعَماءُ) leader, general, ringleader
مَزاعِمُ allegations, claims; assumptions
مَزعومٌ alleged

ش ج ر

شَجَرَ – يَشْجُرُ to happen, take place or occur; to break out
شاجَرَ – يُشاجِرُ to quarrel, fight, or dispute
شَجَرٌ (أَشْجارٌ) trees, shrubs, bushes
شِجارٌ / مشاجَرةٌ fight, quarrel, dispute

ش ح ن

شَحَنَ – يَشْحَنُ to load; to ship, freight, or consign
شاحَنَ – يُشاحِنُ to quarrel or argue
شَحْنةٌ (شَحَناتٌ) cargo, load, freight
مُشاحَنةٌ (مُشاحَناتٌ) a grudge, feud, dispute or quarrel; hatred
شاحِنٌ a charger
شاحِنةٌ (شاحِناتٌ) truck, lorry

ش ر ع

شَرَعَ – يَشْرَعُ to enter, begin or go; to make laws
شَرَّعَ – يُشَرِّعُ to legislate or make laws
اِشتَرَعَ – يَشتَرِعُ to enact (laws); to make laws
شَرعيٌّ legitimate, lawful
غَيْرُ شَرعِيٍّ illegitimate, illegal
الطِّبُّ الشَّرعِيُّ forensic medicine
شَرعِيَّةٌ lawfulness, legality, legitimacy
المحاكمُ الشَّرعِيَّةُ religious courts
شَريعَةٌ (شَرائِعُ) law, legitimacy; a watering hole
الشَّريعَةُ الإِسْلامِيَّةُ Islamic law, Sharia law
تَشْريعِيٌّ legislative
شارِعٌ (شَوارِعُ) street
مَشْروعٌ (مَشْروعاتٌ / مَشاريعُ) scheme, project, plan
مُشَرِّعٌ (مُشَرِّعونَ) legislators, lawmakers

Law and Order 261

ش ك ك

شَكَّ – يَشُكُّ to doubt or suspect; to pierce or stab
شَكٌّ (شُكُوكٌ) doubt, suspicion; uncertainty
تَشَكُّكٌ doubt, scepticism
مَشْكُوكٌ بِهِ suspicious, doubtful
بِدُونِ شَكٍّ / بِلا شَكٍّ doubtlessly, no doubt

ش ك و

شَكا – يَشْكُو to complain or make a complaint; to suffer from (an illness)
اِشْتَكَى – يَشْتَكِي to complain
شَكْوَى (شَكاوَى) a complaint
مُشْتَكٍ complainant, plaintiff
مُشْتَكًى عَلَيْهِ defendant, accused, charged

ش ه د

شَهِدَ – يَشْهَدُ to witness, testify, or attest; to attend or be present
شاهَدَ – يُشاهِدُ to witness, observe or see; to view or inspect
اِسْتَشْهَدَ – يَسْتَشْهِدُ to call (someone) as a witness; to be martyred; to die
شَهْدٌ honey; honeycomb
شَهِيدٌ (شُهَداءُ) martyr; witness
شاهِدٌ (شَواهِدُ / شُهُودٌ) witness; notary public
شاهِدُ عِيانٍ (شُهُودُ عِيانٍ) eyewitness
شَهادَةٌ (شَهاداتٌ) certificate, diploma; witness statement, affidavit
الشَّهادَةُ testimony
شَهادَةُ البَكالوريوس bachelor's degree
مَشْهَدٌ (مَشاهِدُ) assembly, meeting; scene
مُشاهِدٌ (مُشاهِدونَ) spectator, onlooker, observer
اِسْتِشْهادٌ martyrdom; quotation

ش و ر

شَوَّرَ – يُشَوِّرُ to make a sign or signal; to beckon; to wink or blink
شاوَرَ – يُشاوِرُ to seek advice or consult
أَشارَ – يُشيرُ to make a sign or signal; to beckon; to hint
اِسْتَشارَ – يَسْتَشيرُ to ask for advice or counsel

مُوَشِّراتٌ signs, indicators
مُشاوَرَةٌ (مُشاوَراتٌ) consultation
إِشارَةٌ (إِشاراتٌ) signs, precursors
اِسْتِشارَةٌ (اِسْتِشاراتٌ) consultation, guidance, advice
مُسْتَشارٌ (مُسْتَشارونَ) advisor, consultant
مُستشارونَ قانونيّونَ legal advisors

ع د ل

عَدَلَ – يَعْدِلُ to act justly or fairly
عَدَّلَ – يُعَدِّلُ to straighten, balance, or rectify
تَعَدَّلَ – يَتَعَدَّلُ to be changed, altered, or modified
عَدْلٌ justice, impartiality, fairness; straightness, honesty
عَدْلِيٌّ legal, judicial; forensic
عَديلٌ equal; corresponding; brother-in-law
عَدالَةٌ justice, fairness, impartiality; integrity
العَدالَةُ الإِجْتِماعِيَّةُ social justice
تَعديلٌ (تَعديلاتٌ) regulation; alteration, modification
تَعادُلٌ balance, equilibrium; equivalence
اِعْتِدالٌ straightness, evenness, symmetry; moderation (also a girl's name)
عادِلٌ just, upright (also a boy's name)
مُعَدَّلٌ (مُعَدَّلاتٌ) average; rates
مُعْتَدِلٌ straight; moderate, temperate

ع ر ق ل

عَرْقَلَ – يُعَرْقِلُ to impede, hinder, obstruct, or delay
تَعَرْقَلَ – يَتَعَرْقَلُ to be hindered, impeded, or obstructed; to be aggravated
عَرْقَلَةٌ (عَراقيلُ) obstacles, difficulty, handicap

ف ت ش

فَتَّشَ – يُفَتِّشُ to inspect, examine, or investigate; to search for
تَفْتيشٌ (تَفاتيشُ) examination, search, investigation
مُفَتِّشٌ (مُفَتِّشونَ) inspector; supervisor
نُقْطَةُ تَفْتيشٍ (نِقاطُ تَفْتيشٍ) checkpoint
أَمْرُ التَفْتيشِ search warrant

ف ت و / ف ت ى

فَتِىَ – يَفْتَأُ to be youthful; young or adolescent
أَفْتَى – يُفْتِي to give a formal legal opinion; to deliver an opinion
اِسْتَفْتَى – يَسْتَفْتِي to ask for a formal legal opinion; to request information
فَتَىً (فِتْيانٌ) a youth or adolescent; young people
فَتاةٌ (فَتَياتٌ) a young woman
فَتْوى (فَتاوٍ / فَتاوى) a fatwa or Islamic legal opinion
إِفْتاءٌ delivery of a formal legal opinion
اِسْتِفْتاءٌ request for a formal legal opinion; referendum, poll
مُفْتٍ (مُفْتونَ) a mufti or deliverer of formal legal opinion

ف س ر

فَسَّرَ – يُفَسِّرُ to interpret
اِسْتَفْسَرَ – يَسْتَفْسِرُ to seek an explanation
تَفْسيرٌ (تَفاسيرُ) explanation, elucidation, commentary (esp. of the Quran)
اِسْتِفْسارٌ (اِسْتِفْساراتٌ) inquiry, question
مُفَسِّرٌ commentator

ف ص ل

فَصَلَ – يَفْصِلُ to separate or divide; to divorce
اِنْفَصَلَ – يَنْفَصِلُ to be separated; to dissociate oneself
فَصْلٌ (فُصولٌ) separation, division; season; term; chapter; class
فاصِلَةٌ (فَواصِلُ) comma
فَصيلَةٌ (فَصائِلُ) genus, species, group
فَيْصَلٌ (فَياصِلُ) judge, arbiter (also a boy's name in the singular)
مَفْصِلٌ (مَفاصِلُ) joint; articulation
تَفْصيلٌ (تَفاصيلُ / تَفْصيلاتٌ) details, particulars; a detailed statement
اِنْفِصالٌ separation; withdrawal, secession
اِنْفِصالِيٌّ separatist
مُنْفَصِلٌ separate, detached

ف ق ه

فَقِهَ – يَفْقَهُ to understand or comprehend
فَقَّهَ – يُفَقِّهُ to teach or make (someone) understand

264 Law and Order

تَفَقَّهَ – يَتَفَقَّهُ to understand or comprehend; to gain information; to study Fiqh
فِقهٌ Fiqh; jurisprudence; understanding, comprehension
فَقيهٌ (فُقهاءُ) legislator; man of knowledge

ق س م

قَسَمَ – يَقسِمُ to divide; to distribute
قَسَّمَ – يُقَسِّمُ to divide; to distribute
أَقسَمَ – يُقسِمُ to take or swear an oath
اِنقَسَمَ – يَنقَسِمُ to be divided or separated
قِسمٌ (أَقسامٌ) part, section, department
قِسمَةٌ dividing, distribution; fate or destiny; kismet
قَسَمٌ (أَقسامٌ) an oath
القَسَمُ الكاذِبُ perjury
تَقسيمٌ (تَقسيماتٌ) exorcism; division, partition, distribution
مَقسومٌ / مُقَسَّمٌ divided

ق ض ى

قَضى – يَقضي to act as judge; to settle; to execute or finish; to spend time
قاضى – يُقاضي to prosecute or sue; to summon before a judge
تَقاضى – يَتَقاضى to claim; to litigate
اِنقَضى – يَنقَضي to pass away, cease, or end
قَضاءٌ decree, judgement, sentence; fate or destiny
قَضِيَّةٌ (قَضايا) affair, case, matter, issue or lawsuit
قاضٍ (قُضاةٌ) judge, magistrate; decisive; lethal
قاضي الصُّلحِ justice of the peace
النِّظامُ القَضائِيُّ the judicial system
مُتَقاضٍ (مُتَقاضونَ) litigants

ق ن ع

قَنَعَ – يَقنَعُ to be content or satisfied; to be convinced
قَنَّعَ – يُقَنِّعُ to mask (the face); to veil; to satisfy or persuade
أَقنَعَ – يُقنِعُ to convince or persuade
اِقتَنَعَ – يَقتَنِعُ to be content; to be convinced
قَناعَةٌ satisfaction, contentment; moderation
قِناعٌ (أَقنِعَةٌ) veil, mask

Law and Order 265

اِقْتِناعٌ contentment; conviction
مُقْنِعٌ convincing

ق ن ن

قَنَّنَ – يُقَنِّنُ to legalise; to legislate or make laws
قانونٌ (قَوانينُ) law, rule, canon
القانونُ law (the discipline)
قانونيٌّ legal
غَيْرُ قانونيٍّ illegal
خالَفَ القانونَ to break the law
تَطبيقُ القانونِ applying the law
قُوّاتُ إنفاذِ القانونِ law enforcement forces
القانونُ الدُّوَليُّ international law

ك ت م

كَتَمَ – يَكتُمُ to hide or conceal; to stifle, muffle, or repress
تَكَتَّمَ – يَتَكَتَّمُ to keep silent
كَتْمٌ / كِتمانٌ silence, concealment, secrecy
كَتيمٌ impenetrable, impermeable, impervious
كاتِمُ السِّرِ secretary
مَكتومٌ silenced; hidden
سِرّيٌّ ومكتومٌ private and confidential

ك ذ ب

كَذَبَ – يَكذِبُ to lie or deceive
كَذَّبَ – يُكَذِّبُ to accuse of lying; to refute or deny
مِكشافُ الكَذِبِ lie detector
كِذبةٌ (أَكاذيبُ) a lie
كاذِبٌ / كَذّابٌ a liar

م ن ع

مَنَعَ – يَمنَعُ to prevent or forbid; to restrain or hinder
مانَعَ – يُمانِعُ to prevent someone from doing; to put up resistance; to oppose
اِمتَنَعَ – يَمتَنِعُ to refrain or abstain; to stop or cease; to refuse
مَمْنوعاتٌ forbidden things

مَناعَةٌ immunity; hardiness; inaccessibility
مُمانَعَةٌ opposition, resistance
ممْنوعٌ forbidden, prohibited

ن ص ف

نَصَفَ – يَنصِفُ to reach noon
ناصَفَ – يُناصِفُ to share in halves; to share equally
أنصَفَ – يُنصِفُ to be fair or just; to halve; to act impartially
اِنتَصَفَ – يَنتَصِفُ to appeal for justice; to stand in the middle
نِصفٌ (أنصافٌ) half
إنصافٌ justice; impartiality (also a girl's name)
مُنتَصَفٌ middle

ن ط ق

نَطَقَ – يَنْطِقُ to speak, utter, or articulate
أنطَقَ – يُنطِقُ to make (someone) speak or talk
اِستَنطَقَ – يَسْتَنطِقُ to interrogate, question, or examine
نُطْقٌ articulated speech; word; utterance; pronouncement
نِطاقٌ (نُطُقٌ) limit, boundary; range, scope
مَنْطِقٌ logic; speech, diction, enunciation
مِنْطَقَةٌ (مَناطِقُ) area, zone, territory
اِستِنْطاقٌ interrogation, questioning; hearing
ناطِقٌ spokesperson, speaker; eloquent
ناطِقٌ بِاسمِ spokesperson
مُستَنطِقٌ examining judge; interrogator

ن ك ر

نَكِرَ – يُنكِرُ to deny or disavow; to be ignorant or not to know
نَكَّرَ – يُنَكِّرُ to disguise; to use in its indefinite form (grammar)
أنكَرَ – يُنكِرُ to deny; to renounce or refuse
نُكْرٌ / نُكْرانٌ denial, disavowal
نَكِرٌ unknown
إنكارٌ denial, disavowal, rejection, negation
تَنَكُّرٌ a disguise or masquerade
اِستِنكارٌ disapproval; aversion; horror
مُنْكَرٌ (مُنْكَراتٌ) objectionable; denied, unacknowledged (pl: forbidden actions)

Law and Order 267

ن و ه / ن ه ى

نَهَى – يَنْهَى to forbid, prohibit, or ban; to reach
أَنْهَى – يُنْهِي to finish or terminate; to communicate or transmit; to inform or decide
اِنْتَهَى – يَنْتَهِي to be concluded; terminated, concluded
نَهْيٌ prohibition, ban, interdiction
نُهَى intelligence, understanding, reason (also a girl's name)
نِهايَةٌ (نِهاياتٌ) ending, termination; limit, extremity
نِهائِيٌّ extreme; final, ultimate
لانِهائِيٌّ infinite
إِنهاءٌ finishing, termination, completion
اِنْتِهاءٌ end; termination

و س ط

وَسَّطَ – يُوَسِّطُ to place in the middle; to appoint as a mediator
تَوَسَّطَ – يَتَوَسَّطَ to be in the middle or centre; to mediate or act as mediator
وَسَطٌ (أَوْساطٌ) middle, centre, heart; medium, average
بِواسِطَةِ by means of, through
الشَّرْقُ الأَوْسَطُ the Middle East
مُتَوَسِّطٌ middle; medium
وَساطَةٌ mediation; intervention
وَسيطٌ (وُسَطاءُ) mediator, intermediary; middle

و ص ى

وَصَّى – يُوَصِّي to make a will; to recommend or advise; to order; to bequeath
وَصِيٌّ (أَوْصِياءُ) guardian, executor; commissioner
وَصِيَّةٌ (وَصايا) testament or will; a command or order
الوَصايا العَشْرُ the Ten Commandments
تَوْصِيَةٌ (تَوْصِياتٌ) recommendations, proposal; advice, counsel; instruction

و ك ل

وَكَلَ – يَكِلُ to entrust, assign, commission
وَكَّلَ – يُوَكِّلُ to authorise or empower; to engage as legal counsel
تَوَكَّلَ – يَتَوَكَّلُ to be appointed as representative; to put one's trust in God
تَوَكُّلٌ / اِتِّكالٌ trust, confidence; trust in God
وَكيلٌ (وُكلاءُ) representative; authority, agent
وَكالَةٌ (وَكالاتٌ) power of attorney; agency
مُوَكِّلٌ (مُوَكِّلونَ) lawyer; commissioned, charged

و ه م

وَهَمَ – يَهِمُ to imagine or fancy; to think or believe
أَوْهَمَ – يُوهِمُ to make someone believe; to instil a prejudice
تَوَهَّمَ – يَتَوَهَّمُ to suspect, think, believe, or imagine
اِتَّهَمَ – يَتَّهِمُ to accuse or charge; to question or suspect
تُهَمَةٌ (تُهَمٌ) accusation, charge
وَهْمٌ (أَوْهَامٌ) imagination, fancy; delusion; bias, prejudice
إِيهَامٌ (إِيهَامَاتٌ) deception, fraud; delusion
اِتِّهَامٌ (اِتِّهَامَاتٌ) indictment, accusation
مُتَّهَمٌ suspected, charged; defendant

Treaties and Contracts المُعَاهَدَاتُ وَالعُقُودُ

No root

بَنْدٌ (بُنُودٌ) article (of law), clause; banner; group of troops

س ن د

سَنَدَ – يَسْنِدُ to support oneself; to prop, lean, or recline
سَانَدَ – يُسَانِدُ to support, help, or aid
أَسْنَدَ – يُسْنِدُ to make someone rest; to rest or support; to establish a tradition
سَنَدٌ (سَنَدَاتٌ) document, bill, deed, bonds; support or prop
سَنَدُ تَوْكِيلٍ power of attorney
إِسْنَادٌ (أَسَانِيدُ) chain of authorities on which an Islamic tradition is based
مَسْنَدٌ (مَسَانِدُ) a prop or cushion; the Islamic tradition of tracing sources
مُسْتَنَدٌ (مُسْتَنَدَاتٌ) official papers, document, record; a reason or cause

No root

شَأْنٌ (شُؤُونٌ) matter, affairs, circumstance, case
بِشَأْنِ ... regarding, with regard to

ط ر ح

طَرَحَ – يَطْرَحُ to throw or throw away; to suggest
طَرَّحَ – يُطَرِّحُ to cause a miscarriage
اِنْطَرَحَ – يَنْطَرِحُ to be thrown; to be thrown out or rejected

Law and Order 269

طَرْحٌ (طُروحاتٌ) expulsion, rejection; miscarriage, abortion; propositions
أُطْروحَةٌ dissertation
مَطْرَحٌ (مَطارِحُ) place, location; place where something is thrown

ع ق د

عَقَدَ – يَعْقِدُ to convene (a meeting); to conclude; to delegate
تَعَقَّدَ – يَتَعَقَّدُ to be complicated; to clot or thicken
تَعاقَدَ – يَتَعاقَدُ to make a contract or reach a mutual agreement
اِنْعَقَدَ – يَنْعَقِدُ to hold, convene, or assemble; to contract; to be knotted
اِعْتَقَدَ – يَعْتَقِدُ to believe
عَقْدٌ (عُقودٌ) a contract; a decade; a necklace; knitting
إبرامُ عَقْدٍ signing a contract
فَسْخُ الْعَقْدِ annulment of a contract
عُقْدَةٌ (عُقَدٌ) a knot or joint (in the body); a dilemma
عَقيدَةٌ (عَقائِدُ) a belief or article of faith; dogma
تَعْقيدٌ (تَعْقيداتٌ) complications, problems
مُعْتَقَدٌ (مُعْتَقَداتٌ) believed or received (belief, idea); doctrine, tenet
مُتعاقِدٌ / مُعاقِدٌ contractor
عَقيدٌ (عُقَداءُ) general, colonel

ع ه د

عَهِدَ – يَعْهَدُ to fulfil a promise; to entrust or commission
عاهَدَ – يُعاهِدُ to contract, promise, or undertake (to do sth)
تَعَهَّدَ – يَتَعَهَّدُ to support or advocate; to maintain; to promise
عَهْدٌ (عُهودٌ) a contract, covenant, or obligation; an era or epoch
الْعَهْدُ الْقَديمُ the Old Testament
الْعَهْدُ الْجَديدُ the New Testament
مَعْهَدٌ (مَعاهِدُ) a place or locality; an institute
مُعاهَدَةٌ (مُعاهَداتٌ) a treaty, agreement, or arrangement; an institute
تَعَهُّدٌ (تَعَهُّداتٌ) a pledge, commitment, or promise; contracting (to do sth)
مُعاهَدَةُ سَلامٍ peace treaty

ف س خ

فَسَخَ – يَفْسَخُ to annul, invalidate, or cancel; to sever
فَسْخٌ cancellation, abolition, voiding

و ث ق

وَثِقَ (بِ) – يَثِقُ (بِ) to trust, have confidence in; to rely or depend on
وَثَّقَ – يُوَثِّقُ to document, authenticate, or notarise; to make firm or strengthen
واثَقَ – يُواثِقُ to enter into an agreement; to intend
اِستَوْثَقَ – يَسْتَوْثِقُ to make sure, verify or check; to have confidence
ثِقَةٌ (ثِقاتٌ) confidence, trust; authority
ثِقَةٌ بِالنَّفْسِ self-confidence
عَدَمُ الثِّقَةِ lack of confidence; mistrust
وَثيقٌ strong, reliable, secure
وَثيقَةٌ (وَثائِقُ) documents, deed, record; charter, bill
فيلْمٌ وَثائِقيٌّ documentary
ميثاقٌ (مَواثيقُ) convention, covenant, charter, contract
ميثاقُ جِنيف Geneva Convention
تَوْثيقٌ authentication, documentation, strengthening
مَوْثوقٌ بِهِ trustworthy, reliable; dependable

الجَرائِمُ Crimes

ب ز ز

اِبتَزَّ – يَبتَزُّ to rob, fleece, or steal; to blackmail
اِبتِزازٌ blackmail, extortion

ب غ ى

بَغى – يَبْغي to seek; to desire or covet; to wrong, oppress, or treat unjustly
يَنْبَغي it is desirable; it is necessary; it is proper
بَغيٌ injustice, wrong
بَغيٌّ (بَغايا) whore, prostitute
البِغاءُ prostitution
اِبتِغاءٌ desire
باغٍ (بُغاةٌ) oppressive, tyrannical, unjust; tyrant

ث أ ر

ثَأَرَ – يَثْأَرُ to avenge or take revenge
ثَأْرٌ (أَثْآرٌ) revenge, vengeance, blood feud
ثائِرٌ avenger

Law and Order 271

ج ر م

جَرَمَ – يَجرِمُ to commit an offence; to injure or harm
جَرَّمَ – يُجَرِّمُ to incriminate; to charge with a crime
أَجرَمَ – يُجرِمُ to commit a crime, sin, or do harm
جُرمٌ (أَجرامٌ/جُرومٌ) crime, offence, sin
لا جَرَمَ of course, certainly
جَريمةٌ (جرائمُ) crime, offence, sin
إجرامٌ crime
مُجرِمٌ (مُجرمونَ) criminal
اِرتِكابُ جُرمٍ to commit an offence
جرائمُ حَربٍ war crimes

ح ر ش

حَرَشَ – يَحرُشُ to scratch
حَرَّشَ – يُحَرِّشُ to incite or provoke; to sow discord
تَحَرَّشَ – يَتَحَرَّشُ to provoke or harass
تَحَرُّشٌ provocation or harassment
تَحَرُّشٌ جِنسيٌّ sexual harassment

ح و ل / ح ي ل

حالَ – يَحيلُ to change; to be transformed
حَوَّلَ – يُحَوِّلُ to change, transform, or convert; to transfer
تَحايَلَ – يَتَحايَلُ to trick, deceive, or cheat; to outsmart or outwit
اِحتالَ – يَحتالُ to defraud
اِستَحالَ – يَستَحيلُ to be impossible, absurd, or inconceivable
حالٌ (أَحوالٌ) condition, state, situation
حالَما (conj) as soon as
حالةٌ (حالاتٌ) condition, state, situation
حالةُ الطَّوارِئ state of emergency
الحالةُ الاِجتِماعيّةُ marital status
الحالةُ الرّاهِنةُ the status quo
حاليٌّ current, present, actual
حَوْلٌ (أَحوالٌ) year; might or power
حَوْلَ (prep) around
حيلةٌ (حِيَلٌ) a trick or ruse; artifice

حَوالَيْ (prep) around, about, approximately
تَحْويلٌ transformation, conversion, change; transfer
مُحاوَلةٌ (مُحاوَلاتٌ) an attempt, effort, or endeavour
تَحايُلٌ / اِحتيالٌ trickery, malice, treachery, fraud
مُكافحةُ الإحتيالِ anti-fraud
مُسْتَحيلٌ impossible; absurd

خ د ع

خَدَعَ – يَخدَعُ to cheat, mislead, dupe
اِنخَدَعَ – يَنخَدِعُ to be deceived, deluded, or misled
خُدْعةٌ (خُدَعٌ) deception, cheating
خِداعٌ / خَديعةٌ (خدائعُ / أَخاديعُ) deception, deceit, betrayal, treachery; swindles, tricks
مُخادِعٌ / خَدّاعٌ swindler, imposter, cheat

خ ر ب

خَرِبَ – يَخرِبُ to destroy, wreck, demolish, or shatter
خَرَّبَ – يُخَرِّبُ to devastate, lay waste (to), or destroy
خَرْبٌ / خَرابٌ destruction, devastation
تَخريبٌ (تَخريباتٌ) sabotage, destruction, devastation
تَخريبٌ مُتَعَمَّدٌ vandalism
مُخرِّبٌ (مُخرِّبونَ) saboteur, annihilator, terrorist

خ ل س

خَلَسَ – يخْلِسُ to steal, pilfer, or swipe
اِختَلَسَ – يَختَلِسُ to steal, pilfer, or embezzle
خُلْسةً / خِلْسةً stealthily, furtively
اِختِلاسٌ (اِختِلاساتٌ) embezzlement, misappropriation

خ ن ق

خَنَقَ – يَخنُقُ to strangle, choke, smother
خانَقَ – يُخانِقُ to have a fight or quarrel with
اِنخَنَقَ – يَنْخنِقُ to be strangled, choked, or smothered
خَنْقٌ strangulation
خِناقٌ a fight, quarrel, or row

Law and Order

اِختِناقٌ asphyxiation, suffocation
مَخنوقٌ strangled, suffocated, choked

د ع ر

دَعِرَ – يَدعَرُ to be immoral
دَعرٌ / دَعارَةٌ indecency, immorality, prostitution
بَيتُ دَعارةٍ brothel

ذ ب ح

ذَبَحَ – يَذبَحُ to slaughter, kill, murder, slay
ذَبحٌ slaughter, slaughtering
ذَبيحَةٌ (ذَبائِحُ) slaughter animal, sacrificial victim, blood sacrifice
مَذبَحَةٌ massacre, slaughter

ر ش و

رَشا – يَرشو to bribe
اِرتَشى – يَرتَشي to accept a bribe or be corrupt
رَشوٌ / اِرتِشاءٌ bribery, corruption
رِشوةٌ (رِشْواتٌ / رَشاوي) bribe, bribery

ز و ر

زارَ – يَزورُ to visit or call
زَوَّرَ – يُزَوِّرُ to forge, falsify, or fake
تَزاوَرَ – يَتَزاوَرُ to exchange visits
زَورٌ throat; upper part of chest
زُورٌ a lie or untruth
شَهادةُ الزّورِ false testimony, perjury
تَزويرٌ falsification, forgery
زِيارَةٌ (زِياراتٌ) a visit or call
زائِرٌ (زُوّارٌ) visitor

س ر ق

سَرَقَ – يَسرِقُ to steal, loot, rob
سَرِقةٌ (سَرِقاتٌ) burglary, theft, stealing

سارِقٌ thief (سارقونَ/سَرَاقُونَ) سَرّاقٌ/
مَسْروقٌ stolen; stolen goods (مَسْروقاتٌ)

س ف ح

سَفَحَ – يَسْفَحُ to spill or shed
تَسافَحَ – يَتَسافَحُ to whore or fornicate
سَفْحٌ foot (of mountain); a flat, rocky surface (سُفوحٌ)
سَفّاحٌ serial killer (سَفّاحونَ)
سِفاحٌ fornication

س و ء

ساءَ – يَسوءُ to be or become bad, evil, or wicked; to vex or torment
أَساءَ – يُسيءُ to do badly; to spoil, harm, or wrong
سوءٌ evil, ill, misfortune; injury, offence
لِسوءِ الحَظِّ unfortunately
سَيِّئٌ bad, evil, ill
سَيِّئَةٌ sin, offense, misdeed (سَيِّئاتٌ)
مَساءَةٌ an evil deed or vile action; disadvantages (مَساوِئُ)
إِساءَةٌ misdeed, sin; offense, insult
إِساءَةُ المُعامَلَةِ mistreatment

ش ت م

شَتَمَ – يَشْتِمُ to abuse or swear at someone; to vilify or scold
شَتْمٌ/مُشاتَمَةٌ abuse, vilification
شَتيمَةٌ abuse, vilification (شَتائِمُ)

ش ر ر

شَرَّ – يَشِرُّ to be evil, wicked, or vicious
شَرٌّ evil, ill (thing); mischief, calamity, disaster (شُرورٌ)
شِرّيرٌ bad, evil, wicked (person) (أَشِرّاءُ/أَشْرارٌ)

ض ا ق

ضاقَ – يَضيقُ to be narrow or confined; to be anguished
ضايَقَ – يُضايِقُ to vex, annoy, anger, harass, or oppress

Law and Order

تَضايَقَ – يَتَضايَقُ to become irritated; to be angry; to be or become narrow
ضيقٌ narrowness, confinement; anxiety
ضَيِّقٌ narrow, tight, cramped; limited, restricted
مُضايَقَةٌ (مُضايَقاتٌ) harassment, molestation; distress, annoyance; disturbance
مُتَضايِقٌ annoyed, angry, exasperated

ط ع ن

طَعَنَ – يَطْعَنُ to contest; to thrust; to pierce; to defame
طَعْنٌ (طُعونٌ) defamation, slander; piercing; attacks
طَعنَةٌ (طَعَناتٌ) a stab, thrust, or attack
طاعونٌ (طَواعينُ) a plague
مَطْعونٌ stabbed; plagued

ع ص ى

عَصى – يَعصي to disobey, defy, oppose, or resist
اِستَعصى – يَستَعصي to resist, oppose, defy, revolt; to be insidious; to escape
عَصِيٌّ (أَعصِياءُ) rebel
عِصْيانٌ disobedience; insubordination, rebellion, mutiny
عِصْيانٌ مَدَنِيٌّ civil disobedience, unrest
مَعْصِيَةٌ (مَعاصٍ) disobedience; insurrection, revolt, rebellion; sin
عاصٍ (عُصاةٌ) disobedient; insubordinate, rebellious; sinful

ع ن ف

عَنَّفَ – يُعَنِّفُ to treat severely; to reprimand or berate
أَعنَفَ – يُعنِفُ to treat severely or harshly
عُنفٌ violence; harshness
عُنفٌ مَنزِلِيٌّ domestic violence
أَعمالُ العُنفِ acts of violence
نَبْذُ العُنفِ renunciation of violence
عَنيفٌ severe, harsh, blunt

ع ه ر

عَهَرَ – يَعْهُرُ to commit adultery; to whore
عُهْرٌ / عَهارَةٌ adultery, fornication; prostitution

عاهِرَةٌ (عاهِراتٌ) prostitute
عاهِرٌ (عُهّارٌ) adulterer; prostitute

غ ب ن

غَبَنَ – يَغْبُنُ to cheat, dupe, or defraud
غُبْنٌ (غُبونٌ) fraud, deceit, cheating
غُبْنٌ فاحِشٌ criminal fraud (Islamic law)
غَبَنٌ stupidity

غ ش ش

غَشَّ – يَغُشُّ to act dishonestly; to deceive, mislead, or cheat
اِنْغَشَّ – يَنْغَشُّ to be deceived, cheated, or duped
اِسْتَغَشَّ – يَسْتَغِشُّ to regard (someone) as dishonest or as a fraud; to suspect of fraud
غَشٌّ adulteration, corruption, debasement; fraud, deceit
غَشّاشٌ a cheat, swindler, or impostor; deceptive, false
مَغْشوشٌ corrupted; deceived, cheated, duped

غ ص ب

غَصَبَ – يَغْصِبُ to take by violence; to rape; to usurp
اِغْتَصَبَ – يَغْتَصِبُ to take by force; to rape; to usurp
غَصْبٌ force, compulsion; illegal seizure
اِغْتِصابٌ force, compulsion; rape
غاصِبٌ (غاصِبونَ) usurper
مَغْصوبٌ forced, compelled, coerced
مُغْتَصِبٌ a rapist; violent, brutal

ف ز ع

فَزِعَ – يَفْزَعُ to fear or be afraid; to flee or take refuge
فَزَّعَ – يُفَزِّعُ to frighten, scare, or alarm
تَفَزَّعَ – يَتَفَزَّعُ to be terrified, startled, or frightened
فَزَعٌ (أَفْزاعٌ) fear, fright, terror, panic
فَزّاعَةٌ scarecrow; someone who inspires fear

ق ت ل

قَتَلَ – يَقْتُلُ to kill, slay, or murder

Law and Order 277

قاتَلَ – يُقاتِلُ to fight, combat, or battle
تَقاتَلَ – يَتَقاتَلُ to fight one another
قَتْلٌ murder, assassination, killing
قَتيلٌ (قَتْلى) deceased
قاتِلٌ (قَتَلَةٌ) murderer, killer, hitman, assassin
مَقتَلٌ (مَقاتِلُ) death, murder, killing
قِتالٌ fight, struggle, combat
قاتِلٌ deadly, lethal
جَريمةُ القَتْلِ homicide
قَتْلٌ بالرَّصاصِ shooting

ك ي د

كادَ – يَكيدُ to deceive, outwit, ensnare; to plot
كَيدٌ (كِيادٌ) a ruse or scheme; artifice; cunning
مَكيدةٌ (مَكايدُ / مُكائِدُ) a ruse, trick, or conspiracy; entrapment, schemes

ل ب س

لَبِسَ – يَلبَسُ to put on, wear, or dress
لَبَّسَ – يُلَبِّسُ to dress, clothe, or cover; to seize; to deceive
تَلَبَّسَ – يَتَلَبَّسُ to be involved or implicated; to dress or clothe
لَبْسٌ / أَلْبْسٌ confusion, tangle; obscurity
لِبْسٌ (أَلبوسٌ) clothes, dress, costume
لِباسٌ (لِباساتٌ) clothes, costume, garment
مَلابِسُ clothes
تَلَبُّسٌ / في حالةِ تَلَبُّسٍ caught in the act, caught red-handed
اِلتِباسٌ confusion, obscurity, ambiguity
مُتَلَبِّسٌ involved, implicated

ل ص ص

لَصَّ – يَلِصُّ to rob or steal; to do secretly
تَلَصَّصَ – يَتَلَصَّصُ to become a thief; to act stealthily
لِصٌّ (لُصوصٌ) robber

م س س

مَسَّ – يَمَسُّ to infringe or violate; to feel or touch; to harm or wrong

مَاسَّ – يُمَاسُّ to touch or be in contact (physically)

مَسٌّ touch, touching; misfortune, calamity; an attack; madness

مِسَاسٌ touching; violation, infringement; connection, relation

مَاسٌّ urgent, pressing; touching, tangency

حَاجَةٌ مَاسَّةٌ urgent matter

ن ص ب

نَصَبَ – يَنصُبُ to swindle or dupe; to raise or rear; to erect; to show or display

اِنتَصَبَ – يَنتَصِبُ to get up; to be appointed or hold an office; to be pronounced with a final *a* ◌َ (fatha)

نَصبٌ setting up, erection, raising

نَصبٌ تِذكاريٌّ monument

نِصَابٌ quorum; origin, beginning

نَصَّابٌ a cheat, swindler, or imposter; deceitful, fraudulent

نَصِيبٌ a share or dividend; participation; change; fate, lot

يَا نَصِيبٌ lottery

مَنصِبٌ (مَنَاصِبُ) position, post, rank, office

مَنصُوبٌ raised, erected, set-up; a word in the accusative (grammar)

ن ق م

نَقَمَ – يَنقُمُ to take vengeance; to be hostile

اِنتَقَمَ – يَنتَقِمُ to take vengeance

نَقمَةٌ (نِقَمٌ / نَقَمَاتٌ) revenge, vengeance; a grudge or resentment; spite

اِنتِقَامٌ vengeance, revenge

ه د د

هَدَّ – يَهُدُّ to break, demolish, ruin, undermine

هَدَّدَ – يُهَدِّدُ to threaten, menace, frighten, or intimidate

تَهَدَّدَ – يَتَهَدَّدُ to threaten or menace; to demolish or ruin

اِنهَدَّ – يَنهَدُّ to be demolished or wrecked; to collapse; to be a wreck

تَهدِيدٌ (تَهدِيدَاتٌ) threat, menace, intimidation

مَهدُودٌ destroyed, wrecked

مُهَدَّدٌ threatened, menaced

ه ر ب

هَرَبَ – يَهرُبُ to escape, flee, or desert

Law and Order

هَرَّبَ – يُهَرِّبُ to smuggle; to put to flight; to liberate or free
تَهَرَّبَ – يَتَهَرَّبُ to escape or evade
تَهْريبٌ smuggling, trafficking
مُهَرِّبٌ (مُهَرِّبونَ) smuggler, trafficker
هارِبٌ fugitive

Under Arrest الإعتِقالُ

أ ز ق

أَزَقَ – يَأْزِقُ to be narrow
مَأْزِقٌ (مَآزِقُ) predicament, dilemma; impasse or strait

ب ص م

بَصَمَ – يَبصُمُ to imprint, print, stamp
بَصْمَةٌ (بَصَماتٌ) imprint, impression
بَصْمَةُ الأصابِعِ fingerprinting

ح ج ز

حَجَزَ – يَحجِزُ to arrest, detain, restrain, or prevent; to seize
حَجْزٌ arrest, detention, prevention; isolation; a booking or reservation
حاجِزٌ (حَواجِزُ) obstacle, barrier, block, wall; boarders
حَواجِزُ على الطُّرُقِ road blocks

ر ب ك

رَبَكَ – يَربِكُ to muddle, entangle, complicate, confuse
اِرتَبَكَ – يَرتَبِكُ to be confused; to become involved
اِرتِباكٌ (اِرتِباكاتٌ) confusion, mess, tangle; involvement
مُرتَبِكٌ confused, bewildered

س ب ق

سَبَقَ – يَسبِقُ to be or come before; to precede; to anticipate
سابَقَ – يُسابِقُ to try to outdo, defeat, or beat; to compete or vie
تَسابَقَ – يَتَسابَقُ to try to outdo each another; to compete or vie
سَبْقٌ precedence, priority
سِباقٌ / تَسابُقٌ contest

مُسابَقةٌ (مُسابَقاتٌ) contest, competition, race
سابِقٌ (سابِقونَ) antecedent, preceding; previous, former, retired, ex-
سابِقَةٌ (سَوابِقُ) priority; previous (pl: previous convictions)
ذو السَّوابِقِ مِن has a criminal record
غَيْرُ مَسْبوقٍ / غَيْرُ مَسبوقةٍ unprecedented
مُسابِقٌ / مُتَسابِقٌ (مُسابِقونَ / مُتَسابِقونَ) competitor, contestant

ش ب ه

شَبَّهَ – يُشَبِّهُ to make equal, similar, comparable; to compare
شابَهَ – يُشابِهُ to resemble or be similar to
تَشابَهَ – يَتَشابَهُ to resemble one another; to be ambiguous or unclear
اِشتَبَهَ – يَشتَبِهُ to be in doubt; to suspect; to resemble one another
شِبهٌ (أَشْباهٌ) resemblance, similarity; image, picture
شُبْهَةٌ (شُبْهاتٌ) obscurity; vagueness, uncertainty, doubt
مَشْبوهٌ under suspicion, suspect, dubious
مُشابَهةٌ (مُشابَهاتٌ) resemblance, similarity
مُشتَبَهٌ بِهِ suspect, suspected

ص ف د

صَفَدَ – يَصفِدُ to bind, shackle, or handcuff
صِفادُ الْيَدَينِ handcuffs

ع ق ل

عَقَلَ – يَعقِلُ to confine; to detain, arrest; to comprehend; to be reasonable
اِعتَقَلَ – يَعتَقِلُ to arrest, apprehend, detain, or restrain
عَقلٌ (عُقولٌ) mind, intellect; understanding; comprehension
ضَعيفُ الْعَقلِ feeble-minded
العَقلُ الْمُوَجِّهُ mastermind
عَقليٌّ intellectual; mental
الْعُمرُ الْعَقليُّ mental age
عَقليَّةٌ (عَقليَّاتٌ) mentality
عُقلَةٌ (عُقَلٌ) a knot, joint, or knuckle
عَقيلَةٌ (عَقيلاتٌ / عَقائِلُ) a wife or spouse
اِعتِقالٌ (اِعتِقالاتٌ) arrest, detention
اِعتِقالٌ وِقائيٌّ protective custody

Law and Order

عاقِلٌ (عُقلاءُ) reasonable, sensible
مَعقولٌ reasonable, plausible, logical, sensible; possible

ق ب ض

قَبَضَ – يَقبِضُ to seize, grab, or take; to arrest
قَبْضٌ arrest, seizing, taking possession
أمرُ قَبْضٍ arrest warrant
ألقى القَبْضَ على to arrest
قَبْضَةٌ (قَبْضاتٌ) seizure, grip, hold, grasp
مَقبوضٌ عليهِ person who has been detained or arrested

ق ي د

قَيَّدَ – يُقَيِّدُ to bind or shackle; to restrict or limit; to stipulate
تَقَيَّدَ – يَتَقَيَّدُ to bind oneself; to be bound, limited, or restricted
قَيْدٌ (قُيودٌ) restrictions; shackles, handcuffs; specification, registering
تَقييدٌ (تَقييداتٌ) shackling, binding; booking; restriction, confinement

ك ف ل

كَفَلَ – يَكفُلُ to feed; to support; to vouch, sponsor, or bail; to be legal guardian
كَفَّلَ – يُكَفِّلُ to feed or support; to sponsor or bail
تَكَفَّلَ – يَتَكَفَّلُ to bail or vouch for
كَفيلٌ (كُفلاءُ) guarantor, sponsor; liable, responsible
كَفالَةٌ security, bail, sponsorship; guarantee, warranty
وَضَعَ تَحتَ الكَفالَةِ to remand on bail
أُطلِقَ سَراحُهُ بِكَفالَةٍ he was released on bail
تَكافُلٌ mutual responsibility; mutual agreement

No root

كَلبَشٌ handcuffs
كَلبَشَةٌ (كَلبَشاتٌ) handcuffs, manacles

ن ك ل

نَكَلَ – يَنكُلُ to abstain; to withdraw; to recoil or shrink from
نَكَّلَ – يُنَكِّلُ to punish severely; to torture or maltreat; to deter or repel

282　Law and Order

نِكلٌ (أَنْكالٌ) a shackle, fetter, or chain
نَكالٌ exemplary punishment; warning example

و ر ط

ورَّطَ – يُورِّطُ to entangle, embroil, involve, implicate
تَورَّطَ – يَتَورَّطُ to be involved or embroiled in; to get into trouble
ورْطَةٌ (ورْطاتٌ) dilemma, difficulty, trouble
مُتَورِّطٌ in a bind, in a fix; involved in

و ق ف

وَقَفَ – يَقِفُ to stop; to come to a standstill; to stand up
وَقَّفَ – يُوَقِّفُ to seize or arrest; to erect
تَوَقَّفَ – يَتَوَقَّفُ to stop or halt; to desist or refrain
وَقْفٌ (أَوقافٌ) Wakf; religious endowment; stagnation, stopping
وَقْفَةٌ (وَقَفاتٌ) position or standing; stance; halt
مَوْقِفٌ (مَواقِفُ) position, stance, stand, attitude; situation; place; car park
واقِفٌ standing; upright, erect
مَوْقوفٌ arrested, apprehended, detained

الأَدِلَّةُ والبَراهينُ Evidence and Proof

ب ر ر

بَرَّ – يَبَرُّ to be devoted or treat with reverence; to obey or be dutiful
بَرَّرَ – يُبَرِّرُ to justify; to vindicate or acquit; to warrant
بِرٌّ piety; kindness, righteousness
مَبَرَّةٌ (مَبَرّاتٌ) act of charity, good deed; charitable organisation
تَبريرٌ (تَبريراتٌ) justification, vindication, explanation
مُبَرِّرٌ (مُبَرِّراتٌ) justification, excuse
لا مُبَرَّرَ لَهُ unjustifiable

ب ر ه ن

بَرْهَنَ – يُبَرْهِنُ to prove or demonstrate
بُرْهانٌ (بَراهينُ) proof
بَرْهَنَةٌ demonstration

Law and Order

ث ب ت

ثَبَتَ – يَثْبُتُ to stand or remain firm; to hold one's ground
ثَبَّتَ – يُثَبِّتُ to convict; to stabilise, secure, or fasten
أَثْبَتَ – يُثْبِتُ to assert; to confirm or prove; to bear witness
ثُبوتٌ constancy, steadiness, permanence
إِثْباتٌ confirmation, proof, evidence; stabilisation, strengthening
شاهِدُ إِثْباتٍ witness for prosecution
عِبءُ الثَّباتِ burden of proof
ثابِتٌ firm, fixed, established, steady, stable
مُثَبَّتٌ established, confirmed, proven, certain

د ل ل

دَلَّ – يَدُلُّ to show, demonstrate, point out, indicate
دَلَّلَ – يُدَلِّلُ to confirm, to prove, corroborate, or furnish the proof
تَدَلَّلَ – يَتَدَلَّلُ to be coquettish or coy; to flirt; to dally
دَلالٌ coquetry (also a girl's name)
دَليلٌ (أَدِلَّةٌ/دلائلُ) evidence, sign, token; indication, guide
دَلالَةٌ (دلالاتٌ) pointing; guidance, leadership
تَدليلٌ reasoning; demonstration; confirmation; pampering
اِستِدلالٌ proof, evidence, demonstration; reasoning, argumentation

س ب ب

سَبَّ – يَسُبُّ to insult, abuse, revile, or curse
سَبَّبَ – يُسَبِّبُ to cause, arouse, provoke, or produce
سَبٌّ abuse, insults, cursing
السَّبَّابَةُ index finger
سَبَبٌ (أَسْبابٌ) reason, cause
سَبَبِيَّةٌ causality
مَسَبَّةٌ (مَسَبّاتٌ) curses, insults
مُسَبِّبٌ (مُسَبِّباتٌ) agent (of action); causative factor
السَّبَبُ والمُسَبَّبُ cause and effect

ف ض ح

فَضَحَ – يَفْضَحُ to expose, shame, or disgrace; to compromise

284 *Law and Order*

اِنْفَضَحَ – يَنْفَضِحُ to be exposed or disgraced; to be compromised

فَضِيحَةٌ (فَضَائِحُ) exposure; humiliation, mortification, shame, ignominy

فَاضِحٌ disgraceful, shameful, dishonourable

مَفْضُوحٌ exposed; compromised, humiliated, shamed, disgraced

ي ق ن

يَقِنَ – يَيْقَنُ to be sure or certain; to be convinced

تَيَقَّنَ – يَتَيَقَّنُ to convince oneself; to be convinced; to ascertain or make sure

يَقِينٌ certainty, conviction; belief

أنا على يَقينٍ أنَّ I am convinced that

يقيناً certainly

يَقِينِيَّاتٌ established truths, axioms

مُتَيَقِّنٌ convinced, positive

Verdicts and Convictions أحكامُ الإدانةِ

ب ر ئ

بَرِئَ – يَبْرَأُ to be or become free; to be cleared of guilt; to recover (from illness)

بَرَّأَ – يُبَرِّئُ to free or acquit

أَبْرَأَ – يُبْرِئُ to acquit, absolve, or discharge

تَبَرَّأَ – يَتَبَرَّأُ to disassociate; to clear oneself from suspicion

بَرِيءٌ (أَبْرِياءُ) innocent, guiltless; healthy

بَرَاءَةٌ acquittal, innocence; license, patent

بَرَاءةُ اخْتِراعٍ patent

تَبْرِئَةٌ acquittal; exoneration

ج ن ح

جَنَحَ – يَجْنَحُ to incline, tend, or lean; to diverge or depart

جَنَّحَ – يُجَنِّحُ to provide (sth) with wings

جُنْحَةٌ (جُنَحٌ) misdemeanour

جَناحٌ (أَجْنِحَةٌ) wing, side, flank

جُناحٌ misdemeanour; sin

جُنوحٌ delinquency; inclination

جانِحٌ side, wing; delinquent

جانِحَةٌ (جَوانِحُ) rib, bosom; heart, soul

Law and Order 285

ح ذ ر

حَذِرَ – يَحْذَرُ to be cautious or wary; to beware or be on one's guard
حَذَّرَ – يُحَذِّرُ to warn or tip off
تَحَذَّرَ – يَتَحَذَّرُ to beware, be wary
حَذِرٌ caution, alertness, precaution
تَحْذيرٌ (تَحْذيراتٌ) warning, cautioning
مَحْذورٌ (مَحْذوراتٌ) object of caution; danger, difficulty, misfortune

ذ ن ب

أَذْنَبَ – يُذْنِبُ to do wrong; to commit a sin or crime; to be guilty or culpable
اِسْتَذْنَبَ – يَسْتَذْنِبُ to find guilty of a crime or sin; to repent
ذَنْبٌ (ذُنوبٌ) offense, sin, crime
ذَنَبٌ (أَذْنابٌ) tail, end; a follower
مُذَنَّبٌ comet
مُذْنِبٌ (مُذْنِبونَ) guilty, culpable; a sinner, delinquent, or criminal

س م ح

سَمَحَ – يَسْمَحُ to permit or allow; to be generous or kind
سامَحَ – يُسامِحُ to pardon, excuse, forgive
تَسامَحَ – يَتَسامَحُ to be indulgent or tolerant; to show good will
سَماحٌ forgiveness; kindness/generosity; tolerance, grace (also a girl's name)
فَتْرَةُ سَماحٍ grace period
مُسامَحَةٌ pardon, forgiveness
تَسامُحٌ tolerance, lenience
عَدَمُ التَّسامُحِ zero tolerance; intolerance
مَسْموحٌ permissible

ش ف ع

شَفَعَ – يَشْفَعُ to mediate or intercede; to attach, add, or double
تَشَفَّعَ – يَتَشَفَّعُ to mediate, intercede, intervene, or plead
شَفْعٌ (أَشْفاعٌ) an even number; part of a pair
شَفيعٌ (شُفعاءُ) intercessor, advocate; mediator
شافِعٌ mediator; advocate

ط ل ق

طَلَقَ – يَطْلُقُ to be cheerful or happy; to get a divorce; to be in labour
طَلَّقَ – يُطَلِّقُ to release, set free; to divorce; to repudiate
أَطْلَقَ – يُطْلِقُ to free (someone); to set free; to divorce; to shoot or launch (missile etc.)
طَلْقٌ free; uninhibited, unrestrained; labour pains
طَلْقٌ (أَطْلاقٌ) shot (gun)
طَلاقٌ divorce
طَلِيقٌ (طُلَقاءُ) freed, released, set free
إِطْلاقٌ liberation, freeing, release
على الإِطْلاقِ / إِطْلاقاً absolutely
أَطْلَقَ سَراحَهُ to set him free
مُطْلَقٌ free; unlimited, unrestricted; absolute; general

ع د م

عَدِمَ – يَعْدَمُ to be deprived or devoid (of); to lack; to lose
أَعْدَمَ – يُعْدِمُ to execute; to destroy; to be or become poor; to deprive
عَدَمٌ non-; non-existence, absence; lack, want
عَدَمُ ... lack of ...
عَدَمُ التَّسامُحِ intolerance
إِعْدامٌ execution

ع ذ ب

عَذُبَ – يَعْذُبُ to be sweet, pleasant, or agreeable
عَذَّبَ – يُعَذِّبُ to pain, afflict, torment, torture, or to punish
تَعَذَّبَ – يَتَعَذَّبُ to be punished or suffer punishment; to feel pain
عَذْبٌ (عِذابٌ) sweet, pleasant, agreeable
عَذابٌ (عَذاباتٌ / أَعْذِبَةٌ) punishment, torture, torment; pain
تَعْذيبٌ torture, punishment, affliction

ع ر ف

عَرَفَ – يَعْرِفُ to know, be aware, or discover; to recognise or perceive
عَرَّفَ – يُعَرِّفُ to advise; to introduce or acquaint
تَعَرَّفَ – يَتَعَرَّفُ to become acquainted, meet, or familiarise; to reveal oneself

Law and Order

اِعْتَرَفَ – يَعْتَرِفُ to confess, admit, acknowledge, or concede
عُرْفٌ (أَعْرافٌ) custom, usage, tradition; kindness (pl: horse's mane, cock's comb)
عُرْفِيٌّ traditional, conventional, customary, habitual
عَرِيفٌ (عُرَفاءُ) an expert, authority, or specialist; a teaching assistant; aware
مَعْرِفَةٌ (مَعارِفُ) acquaintance, friend; knowledge, learning; skill, experience
المَعارِفُ cultural affairs; education
تَعْرِيفٌ (تَعْرِيفاتٌ) communication; notification, announcement, introduction
أَداةُ التَّعْرِيفِ definite article
اِعْتِرافٌ admission, confession, recognition
مَعْرُوفٌ known, famous; universally accepted, conventional

ع ف و

عَفا – يَعْفو to pardon or forgive; to free; to be eliminated; to be exempt
عافى – يُعافي to restore to health, heal, or cure; to guard or protect
تَعافى – يَتَعافى to recuperate or recover
اِسْتَعْفى – يَسْتَعْفي to ask someone's pardon; to ask for a reprieve; to resign
عَفْوٌ pardon, amnesty, forgiveness
عفوٌ عامٌّ general amnesty
عَفَوِيٌّ spontaneous
مُعافاةٌ / إعْفاءٌ exemption, dispensation, excuse
اِسْتِعْفاءٌ apology; excuse; resignation
عافِيَةٌ (عافِياتٌ / عَوافٍ) good health, well-being

ع ق ب

عَقَبَ – يَعْقُبُ to follow, succeed, ensue, continue, or come after
عاقَبَ – يُعاقِبُ to punish; to alternate
عَقِبٌ (أَعْقابٌ) heel; end, last part of; offspring
عَقَبَةٌ (عَقَباتٌ) difficulty, obstacle, impediment
عُقابٌ (عُقْبانٌ) eagle
عُقُوبَةٌ (عُقُوباتٌ) punishment, penalty (pl: sanctions)
قانونُ الْعُقوباتِ penal code
تَعْقِيبٌ (تَعْقِيباتٌ) follow-up procedures; pursuit, chase; investigation
مُعاقَبَةٌ (مُعاقَباتٌ) sanctions; punishment
عِقابٌ punishment
عاقِبَةٌ (عَواقِبُ) end, result, consequence, outcome

288   Law and Order

العُقوباتُ الجَماعِيَّةُ collateral damage
عُقوباتٌ sanctions

ف ر ج

فَرَّجَ – يُفَرِّجُ to open; to separate or part; to comfort; to show
أَفْرَجَ عَن – يُفْرِجُ عَن to release, free, liberate; to leave (a place)
تَفَرَّجَ – يَتَفَرَّجُ to watch or observe; to part or divide
فَرْجٌ (فُروجٌ) an aperture or opening; female privates (vulva)
إِفْراجٌ liberation, release
إِفْراجٌ عَنِ السَّجينِ release of a prisoner
مُتَفَرِّجٌ (مُتَفَرِّجونَ) viewer, observer, watcher

ف ر ض

فَرَضَ – يَفْرِضُ to impose, order, or decree; to decide or determine
اِفْتَرَضَ – يَفْتَرِضُ to suppose or assume; to impose
فَرْضٌ (فُروضٌ) duty; an order or decree; homework; religious duty
فَرْضِيٌّ hypothetical
فَريضَةٌ (فَرائِضُ) religious duty; homework
اِفْتِراضٌ (اِفْتِراضاتٌ) assumption, supposition, hypothesis
اِفْتِراضِيٌّ hypothetical

ل و م

لامَ – يَلومُ to blame, censure, reproach
لَوَّمَ – يُلَوِّمُ to reprimand sharply
لَوْمٌ / مَلامَةٌ blame, reproach, censure
لائِمٌ (لُوَّامٌ) accuser/critic
مَلومٌ / مُلامٌ blamed; blameworthy

ن د د

نَدَّ – يَنِدُّ to run or slip away; to flee
نَدَّدَ – يُنَدِّدُ to expose or show up; to compromise or criticise
نِدٌّ (أَنْدادٌ) antagonist, rival; equal, partner
تَنديدٌ defamation, criticism

Law and Order 289

ن ذ ر

نَذَرَ – يَنذِرُ to dedicate; to vow
أَنذَرَ – يُنذِرُ to warn or caution; to admonish; to announce
نَذْرٌ (نُذورٌ) a vow or solemn pledge
إِنذارٌ (إِنذاراتٌ) a warning, announcement, or alarm

السِّجنُ Prison

أ ب د

أَبَدَ – يَأبِدُ to stay or linger; to run wild; to shy away from
تَأَبَّدَ – يَتَأَبَّدُ to be perpetuated, to become lasting or permanent
أَبَدٌ (آبادٌ) eternity; endless, eternal; duration
الأَبَدِيَّةُ eternity, endless time
مُؤَبَّدٌ life sentence; endless, forever
سِجنٌ مُؤَبَّدٌ life imprisonment

ح ب س

حَبَسَ – يَحبِسُ to detain, imprison, or apprehend; to block or obstruct
اِحتَبَسَ – يَحتَبِسُ to confine or detain; to obstruct
حَبْسٌ (حُبوسٌ) confinement, imprisonment, prison, arrest
حُبْسَةٌ speech impediment
اِحتِباسٌ / اِنحِباسٌ retention; restraint, obstruction
مَحبوسٌ (مَحابيسُ) imprisoned; inmate, captive
حَبْسٌ اِنفِرادِيٌّ solitary confinement

No root

زِنزانَةٌ (زِنزاناتٌ / زَنازينُ) prison cell

س ج ن

سَجَنَ – يَسجُنُ to imprison
سِجنٌ (سُجونٌ) prison
سَجْنٌ imprisonment
سَجينٌ (سُجَناءُ) prisoner, captive
سَجّانٌ / مَأمورُ السِّجنِ prison warden

ش ن ق

شَنَقَ – يَشْنُقُ to hang someone
شَنْقٌ hanging
مَاتَ شَنْقاً death by hanging
مِشْنَقَةٌ (مَشَانِقُ) gallows

ع ز ل

عَزَلَ – يَعْزِلُ to remove; to set aside, isolate, or segregate
اِنْعَزَلَ – يَنْعَزِلُ to be isolated, separated, segregated
اِعْتَزَلَ – يَعْتَزِلُ to withdraw; to resign or retire; to segregate
عَزْلٌ removal; dissociation; isolation
الْعَزْلُ الإنفرادِيُّ solitary confinement
عُزْلَةٌ retirement; isolation, seclusion, separation
اِنْعِزالٌ seclusion, isolation
مُنْعَزِلٌ isolated, single, solitary

No root

عَنْبَرٌ (عَنَابِرُ) prison wing; ward or wing; warehouse

الإِسْتِئْنافُ والتَّسْوِيةُ Appeals and Settlements

ت و ب

تَابَ – يَتُوبُ to repent or be penitent; to renounce
تَوَّبَ – يُتَوِّبُ to make (someone) repent
تَوْبَةٌ repentance, contrition, penance
تَائِبٌ repentant, penitent

س و ي

سَوِيَ – يَسْوى to be equivalent or equal
سَاوى – يُساوي to be equivalent or equal; to equalise; to be worth
تَساوى – يَتَساوى to be equal or similar
اِسْتَوى – يَسْتَوي to be straight; to ripen
سَواءٌ equal, sameness; except
على حدٍ سواءٍ equally
سَوِيٌّ (أَسْوِياءٌ) straight, right, correct, intact

Law and Order

سَوِيَّة / سَوِيّاً together, jointly
مُساواةٌ equality, equivalence; equal rights
عَدَمُ المُساواةِ الاجْتِماعِيّةِ social inequality
اسْتِواءٌ straightness, evenness, equality
خطُّ الإسْتِواءِ the equator
مُسْتَوىً (مُسْتَوياتٌ) level; standard
تَسْوِيةٌ settlement (of a dispute or bill)
تَسْوِيَةُ الْخِلافِ to resolve a dispute
تَسْوِيَةُ الْمَطالِبِ settlement of demands

ع ك س

عَكَسَ – يَعكِسُ to reverse, invert, or reflect
عاكَسَ – يُعاكِسُ to counteract, oppose, or contradict; to disturb, harass, or tease
إنعكَسَ – يَنعكِسُ to be reversed, inverted, or reflected
عَكْسٌ opposite, reverse; inversion
بِالعكسِ on the contrary
على عكْسِ / على العَكسِ مِن ... contrary to
مُعاكِسٌ counter-, contra-, anti-
مُعاكَسةٌ (مُعاكَساتٌ) disturbance; pestering, harassment
إنعِكاسٌ (إنعِكاساتٌ) reflection; repercussion

ك ف أ

كفأ – يَكفأُ to reverse, turn over, or invert
كافأ – يُكافِئُ to reward, recompense, or repay
كفاءةٌ (كفاءاتٌ) equality; adequacy; qualifications, capabilities
مُكافأةٌ (مُكافآتٌ) reward, recompense; compensation
تَكافُؤٌ mutual correspondence; equivalence
مبدأ تكافُؤ الفُرَصِ principle of equal opportunities

ن د م

نَدِمَ – يَندَمُ to repent or regret
نَدَمٌ / نَدامَةٌ remorse, regret, repentance
نادِمٌ (نُدّامٌ) repentant/regretful
نَديمٌ (نُدماءُ) friend, confidant (also a boy's name in the singular)
نَدْمانٌ (نُدامى) remorseful, penitent
مُتندِّمٌ remorseful, penitent

292 *Law and Order*

Exercises

1) Give two derived nouns for each of the following roots:

ج د ل
ح ر م
ش ر ع
ع ق ل
و ث ق

2) Find the roots of these words:

اِعتِقالٌ
اِفتِراضٌ
تَبريرٌ
جُناحٌ
جَوابٌ
حَرامِيٌّ
سَجينٌ
شَريعَةٌ
كَفيلٌ
مُتَوَرِّطٌ
مَسموحٌ

3) Give the singular of the following plurals:

إجاباتٌ
إشاراتٌ
أَشْجارٌ
تَحْقيقاتٌ
جِناياتٌ
حُقوقٌ
دَعواتٌ
زُعَماءُ
فُقهاءُ
قُضاةٌ
مُجادَلاتٌ
مُحامونَ
وَصايا

Law and Order 293

4) Give the present tense of these verbs:

اِبْتَزَّ to blackmail

اِتَّهَمَ to accuse or charge; to question or suspect

اِسْتَغَشَّ to regard (someone) as dishonest or as a fraud; to suspect of fraud

اِنْتَقَمَ to take vengeance

جَرَّمَ to incriminate; to charge with a crime

خَدَعَ to cheat, mislead, dupe

رَشا to bribe

عَقَدَ to convene (a meeting); to conclude; to delegate

فَسَخَ to annul, invalidate, or cancel; to sever

وَكَّلَ to authorise or empower; to engage as legal counsel

5) Translate the following sentences into Arabic.
   a) The man regretted his behaviour.
   b) My friend sued the police for discrimination.
   c) It is forbidden to go out during curfew.
   d) He was charged with fraud.
   e) The prisoner fled.
   f) My neighbour has a criminal record.

6) Translate the following sentences into English:

   - اِرتِفاعُ مُعدّلاتِ جَرائِمُ القَتلِ في أمريكا بِشكلٍ غيرِ مَسبوقٍ.
   - جَرائِمُ الطَّعنِ في بريطانيا تَصِلُ أعلى مُعدّلاتِها.
   - أصبحتْ لندنُ عاصمةَ السَّرقاتِ في بريطانيا.

7) Give the antonyms of the following words:

اِدَّعى
بَريءٌ
زُورٌ
سَمَحَ
وَثِقَ (بِـ)

Note

1 In spoken Arabic, this is only used by North Africans.

8 Culture, Religion, and Society
الدّينُ والثَّقافةُ والمُجتَمَعُ

Religion الدّينُ

No root

آيَةٌ (آياتٌ) Quranic verse; sign, token (also a girl's name in the singular)

أ خ ر

أَخَّرَ – يُؤَخِّرُ to delay or postpone; to obstruct; to defer
تَأَخَّرَ – يَتَأَخَّرُ to be late or delayed; to be in arrears
آخِرٌ (آخِرونَ / أواخِرُ) last; ultimate, extreme
الآخِرةُ the hereafter
آخَرُ another (m)
أُخرى another (f)
أخيرٌ / آخِرٌ last, latest
أخيراً finally
تَأخيرٌ delay, postponement
تَأَخُّرٌ delay, lag; hesitation
مُؤَخَّرةٌ rear part, tail, end
مُؤَخَّراً recently, lately; finally
مُتَأَخِّرٌ delayed, belated, late

أ ذ ن

أَذِنَ – يَأذَنُ to listen or hear; to allow or permit
أَذَّنَ – يُؤَذِّنُ to call to prayer; to call
اِستَأذَنَ – يَستَأذِنُ to ask permission or take leave
إذنٌ permission, authorisation

أُذُنٌ (آذانٌ) ear
أذانٌ call to prayer
مُؤذِّنٌ (مُؤذِّنونَ) muezzin (person who does the call to prayer)
مِئذَنَةٌ / مَأذَنَةٌ (مَآذِنُ) minaret

No root

أَزَلٌ (آزالٌ) eternity
أَزَلِيٌّ eternal
الأَزَلُ / الأَزَلِيَّةُ eternity

No root

أُسْقُفٌ (أَساقِفَةٌ / أَساقِفُ) bishop
رَئيسُ الأَساقِفَةِ archbishop
أُسْقُفِيٌّ episcopal

No root

البابا the Pope

No root

البوذيّةُ Buddhism

No root

التَّوراةُ the Torah

No root

الزَّرادِشتِيّةُ Zoroastrianism

No root

السِّيخِيّةُ Sikhism

No root

الفاتيكانُ the Vatican

296 *Culture, Religion, and Society*

No root

الفِرْدَوْسُ (فَراديسُ) paradise
فِرْدَوْسِيٌّ heavenly

No root

القِبطُ (الأَقْباطُ) the Copts
قِبطيٌّ Coptic

أ ل ه

أَلَّهَ – يُؤَلِّهُ to deify
تَأَلَّهَ – يَتَأَلَّهُ to become a deity or to deify oneself
إِلَهٌ (آلِهَةٌ) a god or deity, divinity
اللهُ Allah, God in Christianity and Islam
إلاهةٌ (إلاهاتٌ) goddess
إلاهِيٌّ / إلَهِيٌّ celestial, divine
أُلوهِيَّةٌ divine power, divinity

No root

الهِنْدوسِيّةُ Hinduism

No root

اليَسوعُ / عيسى Jesus
يَسوعِيٌّ Jesuit

No root

إنجيلٌ (أناجيلُ) the Gospel, the Bible
إنجيليٌّ / إنجيليّةٌ evangelical; evangelist

No root

أُورثوذوكسِيٌّ (الأُورثوذوكسُ) Orthodox
الأَرثوذكسيّةُ اليونانيّةُ Greek Orthodox

No root

إيزيديٌّ / يَزيديٌّ (إيزيديّونَ / يَزيديّونَ) Yazidi

Culture, Religion, and Society

ب ر ق ع
بَرْقَعَ – يُبَرْقِعُ to veil or drape
تَبَرْقَعَ – يَتَبَرْقَعُ to veil oneself
بُرْقُعٌ (بَراقِعُ) burqa

ب ر ك
بَرَكَ – يَبْرُكُ to kneel down (of a camel)
بارَكَ – يُبارِكُ to bless
تَبارَكَ – يَتَبارَكُ to be blessed; to delight in
بَرَكَةٌ (بَرَكاتٌ) blessing
مُبارَكٌ blessed
مَبروكٌ congratulations

No root

بُروتُسْتانتِيٌّ (بُروتُسْتانِيّونَ) Protestant
البُروتُسْتانتِيَّةُ Protestantism

ب ش ر
بَشَرَ – يَبْشُرُ to rejoice, to be delighted or happy
بَشَّرَ – يُبَشِّرُ to announce or spread; to preach
أَبْشَرَ – يُبْشِرُ to rejoice at good news
بِشْرٌ joy
بِشارَةٌ (بِشاراتٌ / بَشائِرُ) good news, prophecy, good omen; messenger
تَبْشيرٌ preaching the Gospel, evangelism
مُبَشِّرٌ (مُبَشِّرونَ) missionary (Christian), preacher, messenger

ب ه ل
بَهَلَ – يَبْهَلُ to curse
اِبْتَهَلَ – يَبْتَهِلُ to supplicate or pray
اِبْتِهالٌ (اِبْتِهالاتٌ) supplication, prayer

ب ه و
بَها – يَبْهو to be beautiful
تَباهى – يَتَباهى to compete with another; to be proud or boast
بَهاءٌ beauty, splendour

البَهائِيَّةُ Bahai'ism
بَهائِيٌّ (بَهائِيُّونَ) adherent of the Bahai sect
مُباهاةٌ / تَباهٍ pride, boastfulness

No root

جَحيمٌ fire, hell
جَحيمِيٌّ hellish, infernal

ج س د

جَسَّدَ – يُجَسِّدُ to embody or represent in a corporeal form
تَجَسَّدَ – يَتَجَسَّدُ to materialise; to become incarnate (Christianity)
جَسَدٌ (أَجْسادٌ) body
عيدُ الجَسَدِ Corpus Christi
تَجْسيدٌ portrayal
تَجَسُّدٌ materialisation, incarnation
جَسَدِيٌّ carnal
مُجَسَّدٌ embodied

ج ل ب

جَلَبَ – يَجْلِبُ to attract; to gain or win; to bring; to heal (wound)
جَلَّبَ – يُجَلِّبُ to shout or be noisy
أَجْلَبَ – يُجْلِبُ to earn, gain, or acquire
جَلْبٌ bringing, procurement
جَلّابِيَّةٌ (جَلّابِيّاتٌ / جَلاليبُ) loose, shirt-like garment, jalabiya

ج ل ب ب

تَجَلْبَبَ – يَتَجَلْبَبُ to be clothed
جِلْبابٌ (جَلابيبُ) garment, dress, gown

No root

جَهَنَّمُ hell
جَهَنَّمِيٌّ hellish

No root

حاخامٌ rabbi

ح ج ب

حَجَّبَ – يُحَجِّبُ to veil, hide, conceal, or mask
تَحَجَّبَ – يَتَحَجَّبُ to conceal oneself or hide; to flee from sight
حَجْبٌ seclusion
حِجابٌ (أَحْجِبَةٌ) hijab, cover, wrap; a screen
حاجِبٌ (حَواجِبُ) eyebrows
مَحْجوبٌ concealed, veiled

ح س د

حَسَدَ – يَحسِدُ to envy or be envious; to bear a grudge
حَسَدٌ envy
حَسودٌ envious
حاسِدٌ (حُسّادٌ / حَسَدَةٌ) envious; an envious person
مَحسودٌ envied, afflicted by the evil eye

ح م د

حَمَدَ – يَحمُدُ to praise or commend
حَمَّدَ – يُحَمِّدُ to praise highly
حَمدٌ commendation, praise, laudation
الْحَمدُ لِلّهِ thank God
حَميدٌ praiseworthy, laudable, commendable
الحَميدُ the Benign (one of Allah's names)
أَحمَدُ more laudable, more praiseworthy; another one of the Prophet Muhammad's names (also a boy's name)
مَحمَدَةٌ (مَحامِدُ) praises
مَحمودٌ praised; praiseworthy
مُحَمَّدٌ praised, commended; Muhammad

خ ت ن

خَتَنَ – يَختِنُ to circumcise (a boy)
اِختَتَنَ – يَختَتِنُ to be circumcised
خِتانٌ / خِتانةٌ / خَتْنٌ circumcision
خِتانُ البَناتِ female circumcision

300 *Culture, Religion, and Society*

خ ش ع

خَشَعَ – يَخْشَعُ to be submissive or humble

تَخَشَّعَ – يَتَخَشَّعُ to act with humility; to be humble or moved (in spiritual worship)

خُشُوعٌ submission (to God); submissiveness, humility

خاشِعٌ (خاشِعونَ / خُشَّعٌ) submissive, humble

خ ل د

خَلَدَ – يَخْلُدُ to last forever or be immortal

خَلَّدَ – يُخَلِّدُ to immortalise

تَخَلَّدَ – يَتَخَلَّدُ to become eternal or immortal

خُلْدٌ eternity

خَلَدٌ (أَخلادٌ) mind, heart, spirit

خُلودٌ / تَخَلُّدٌ eternity; immortality

خالِدٌ eternal, immortal (also a boy's name)

خ ل ق

خَلَقَ – يَخْلُقُ to create, make, or shape

تَخَلَّقَ – يَتَخَلَّقُ to be created, made, or shaped

اِخْتَلَقَ – يَخْتَلِقُ to invent or fabricate

خَلْقٌ creation; mankind

خُلُقٌ (أَخلاقٌ) morals, character, nature

سوءُ الخُلُقِ bad manners

حُسْنُ الخُلُقِ good manners

خُلُقِيٌّ ethical, moral

أَخلاقِيٌّ moral

أَخلاقِيَّةٌ morality

خِلْقَةٌ (خِلَقٌ) creation; nature, constitution

خَليقٌ (خُلَقاءُ) fit, suitable, worthy

خَلّاقٌ / خالِقٌ creator, maker

مَخلوقٌ (مَخلوقاتٌ / مَخاليقُ) created; creature, created being

الخَليقَةُ the creation, nature; people

No root

خوريٌّ (خوارِنَةٌ) reverend, parson, priest

خ ي ر

خَارَ – يَخِيرُ to choose; to prefer
خَيَّرَ – يُخَيِّرُ to make choose; to prefer; to alternate
اِختَارَ – يَختَارُ to choose or select
اِستَخَارَ – يَستَخِيرُ to seek what is best; to consult; to ask God
خَيرٌ (خِيَارٌ / أَخيَارٌ) good, excellent, superior
خَيرٌ good thing, blessing; wealth; charity
خَيرِيٌّ charitable, beneficent
عَمَلٌ خَيرِيٌّ charity, voluntary work
جَمعِيَّةٌ خَيرِيَّةٌ / مُنَظَّمَةٌ خَيرِيَّةٌ charitable organisation
خِيَارٌ choice, option
اِختِيَارٌ (اِختِيَارَاتٌ) choice, selection, preference; free will
حُرِّيَّةُ الاِختِيَارِ free will
مُختَارٌ (مَخَاتِيرُ) chosen, preferred; voluntary; village chief or elder, a Mukhtar

د ج ل

دَجَلَ – يَدجُلُ to deceive or cheat; to be a cheat
دَجَّلَ – يُدَجِّلُ to smear; to deceive or cheat
دَجَلٌ deceit, trickery, swindle
دَجَّالٌ (دَجَّالُونَ) charlatan, pretender

No root

دُرزِيٌّ (دُرُوزٌ) Druze

د ع ر

دَعِرَ – يَدعَرُ to be immoral
دَعَرٌ / دَعَارَةٌ immorality, indecency, debauchery
بَيتُ دَعَارَةٍ brothel

د ن و / د ن ى

دَنَا – يَدنُو to be near or close; to approach or approximate
أَدنَى – يُدنِي to be near or close; to approach or approximate
تَدَنَّى – يَتَدَنَّى to approach gradually; to sink low or decline; to abase oneself
دَنِيٌّ (أَدنِيَاءُ) infamous, depraved, despicable, lowly, mean

Culture, Religion, and Society

أَدْنَى nearer, closer
الشَّرْقُ الأَدْنَى the near East
الدُّنيا the world, earth
دُنْيَوِيٌّ (دُنْيَوِيّونَ) secular, worldly
دانٍ low; near, close

د ي ن

(Same root letters as 'to borrow, take up a loan' but different root)

دانَ – يَدينُ to profess (a conviction, belonging to a religion)
تَدَيَّنَ – يَتَدَيَّنُ to profess (a religion)
دينٌ (أَدْيانٌ) religion, faith, belief
يَوْمُ الدّينِ day of judgement
دينيٌّ religious (objects)
دَيِّنٌ / مُتَدَيِّنٌ religious (person)
دِيانَةٌ (دِياناتٌ) religion
تَدَيُّنٌ devoutness, piety

ذ ه ب

ذَهَبَ – يَذْهَبُ to leave or depart; to decline or perish
ذَهَّبَ – يُذَهِّبُ to gild
ذَهَبٌ gold; gold coin
مُذَهَّبٌ gilded
ذَهابٌ going, passing; passage
مَذْهَبٌ (مَذاهِبُ) way; sect, ideology, doctrine; an escape
مَذْهَبِيٌّ sectarian
مَذْهَبِيَّةٌ sectarianism

ر ب ب

رَبَّ – يَرَبُّ to be master or lord; to control or have possession
رَبَّبَ – يُرَبِّبُ to raise or bring up; to idolise or deify
رَبٌّ (أَرْبابٌ) lord, master, owner; God (with definite article)
رَبَّةٌ (رَبَّاتٌ) mistress, lady
رَبَّةُ مَنزِلٍ housewife
رُبَّما perhaps, maybe

Culture, Religion, and Society

رَبابٌ / رَبابةٌ fiddle
رُبوبيَّةٌ divinity, deity
رَبّانيٌّ divine, pertaining to God

ر ج م

رَجَمَ – يَرجُمُ to stone; to curse, damn, or revile
رَجْمٌ (رُجومٌ) stoning (pl: a missile)
رَجيمٌ cursed, damned
الشَّيطانُ الرَّجيمُ the cursed devil

ر ح م

رَحِمَ – يَرحَمُ to show mercy or compassion; to be merciful
تَرَحَّمَ – يَتَرَحَّمُ to plead for God's mercy
اِستَرحَمَ – يَستَرحِمُ to plead for mercy
رَحْمٌ (أَرْحامٌ) a womb; relationship, kinship
رَحْمَةٌ mercy, pity, compassion
رَحيمٌ (رُحَماءُ) merciful, compassionate
الرَّحْمنُ the Merciful (one of Allah's names)
الرَّحيمُ the Merciful (one of Allah's names)
مَرْحومٌ late, deceased

ر ذ ل

رَذِلَ – يَرذِلُ to be low, vile, or despicable; to despise or scorn
أَرذَلَ – يُرذِلُ to reject, discard, or disown
رَذْلٌ (رُذولٌ / أَرذالٌ) rejection; low, base, despicable, mean
رَذيلٌ (رُذَلاءُ) base, mean, vile
رَذالةٌ depravity, baseness
رَذيلةٌ (رَذائِلُ) vice, depravity

ر ض ى

رَضِيَ – يَرضى to be satisfied or content; to approve or agree
راضى – يُراضي to try to please
أَرضى – يُرضي to satisfy, gratify, or please
تَرضيةٌ satisfaction, gratification; compensation
رَضِيَ اللهُ عنهُ may God be pleased with him

رِضًى/رِضَاءٌ contentment, satisfaction; approval, acceptance
رِضْوَانٌ consent, agreement, approval; good will (also a boy's name)

ر ك ع

رَكَعَ – يَرْكَعُ to kneel down; to bow down (in prayer)
أَرْكَعَ – يُرْكِعُ to make someone kneel down
رَكْعَةٌ (رَكَعَاتٌ) prostrations, bending (as in Muslim prayer)
رُكُوعٌ kneeling

No root

رَمَضَانُ Ramadan (the month of fasting), ninth month in Islamic calendar

ر و ح

رَاحَ – يَرُوحُ to go away or leave; to set out to do
رَوَّحَ – يُرَوِّحُ to fan (air); to refresh or revive
أَرْوَحَ – يُرُوحُ to stink or smell bad
أَرَاحَ – يُرِيحُ to give rest; to deliver, release, or relieve
اِرْتَاحَ – يَرْتَاحُ to find rest, to relax; to be satisfied
اِسْتَرَاحَ – يَسْتَرِيحُ to be calm; to take a rest or a break
رِيحٌ (رِيَاحٌ) wind; smell; fart
رُوحٌ (أَرْوَاحٌ) soul, spirit; breath
رُوحِيٌّ spiritual
رَاحَةٌ rest, leisure, vacation
رِيحَةٌ/رَائِحَةٌ smell, odour
رَيْحَانٌ (رَيَاحِينٌ) sweet basil (pl: aromatic plants)
مِرْوَحَةٌ (مَرَاوِحُ) fan, ventilator
صَلَاةُ التَّرَاوِيحِ prayer performed during the nights of Ramadan
اِسْتِرَاحَةٌ (اِسْتِرَاحَاتٌ) relaxation, recreation; break, intermission
مُرِيحٌ comfortable
مُرْتَاحٌ resting, relaxing; calm

ز ك و / ز ك ى

زَكَا – يَزْكُو to thrive or flourish; to be just or righteous
زَكَّى – يُزَكِّي to increase; to justify, commend, or praise
تَزَكَّى – يَتَزَكَّى to be purified

Culture, Religion, and Society   305

زَكاءٌ growth; purity, integrity
زَكاةٌ alms (one of Islam's pillars), charity; integrity, honesty
تَزْكِيَةٌ purification

ز م ت

تَزَمَّتَ – يَتَزَمَّتُ to be prim; to be sedate
تَزَمُّتٌ primness; gravity, sedateness
مُتَزَمِّتٌ (مُتَزَمِّتونَ) narrow-minded, intolerant; grave, stern

ز ن د ق

تَزَندقَ – يَتَزَندقُ to be a freethinker; to be an atheist
زَندقَةٌ disbelief, atheism
زِنديقٌ (زَنادِقَةٌ) freethinker; atheist; unbelievable

ز ن ى

زَنى – يَزني to fornicate, to commit adultery
زِنىً/زِناءٌ adultery, fornication

ز ه د

زَهَدَ – يَزْهَدُ to abstain from or renounce; to forsake; to lead a pious, ascetic life
زَهَّدَ – يُزَهِّدُ to induce to withdraw; to spoil someone's pleasure in (sth)
اِسْتَزْهَدَ – يَسْتَزْهِدُ to deem (sth) insignificant or trifling
زُهْدٌ indifference; renunciation, abstinence
زَهيدٌ little, low, insignificant
تَزَهُّدٌ asceticism
زاهِدٌ (زُهّادٌ) ascetic; abstinent (adj) (also a boy's name in the singular)

س ج د

سَجَدَ – يَسْجُدُ to bow down or prostrate oneself; to worship (God)
سَجْدةٌ (سَجَداتٌ) prostration in prayer
سُجودٌ prostration; adoration, worship
سَجّادةٌ (سَجاجيدُ) carpet; prayer rug
مَسْجِدٌ (مَساجِدُ) mosques
المَسْجِدُ الحَرامُ the Holy Mosque in Mecca
المَسْجِدُ الأَقْصى الشَّريفُ the Holy Al-Aqsa Mosque in Jerusalem

س ح ر

سَحَرَ – يَسْحَرُ to bewitch, enchant, or fascinate
تَسَحَّرَ – يَتَسَحَّرُ to have a light meal (before daybreak)
سِحرٌ (سُحورٌ / أَسحارٌ) magic, sorcery, witchcraft
سَحَرٌ (أَسحارٌ) early morning, dawn (also a girl's name in the singular)
سَحورٌ / سُحورٌ meal taken at night before the start of a fast
ساحِرٌ (سَحَرَةٌ) sorcerer, magician, wizard
ساحِرةٌ (ساحِراتٌ / سَواحِرُ) witch, sorceress

س ل م

(Full treatment in Politics chapter)

سَلِمَ – يَسْلَمُ to be safe and sound, to be unharmed; to be certain or established
اِسْتَسْلَمَ – يَسْتَسْلِمُ to surrender, capitulate, submit, or succumb
سَلامٌ (سلاماتٌ) peace, safety, security, well-being; a greeting
إِسْلامٌ submission
الإِسْلامُ Islam
الرّابِطةُ الإِسْلامِيّةُ the Muslim League
اِسْتِسْلامٌ surrender, capitulation, submission
مُسلِمٌ (مُسلمونَ) Muslim

س ن ن

سَنَّ – يَسُنُّ to sharpen or hone; to introduce or establish (laws, customs)
أَسَنَّ – يُسِنُّ to teethe or grow teeth; to age or grow old
اِسْتَنَّ – يَسْتَنُّ to take or follow (a way); to establish or enact (law, custom)
سَنٌّ introduction; enactment (law, custom)
سِنٌّ (أَسْنانٌ) a tooth or tusk; age
سِنُّ التَّقاعُدِ retirement age
سُنَّةٌ (سُنَنٌ) custom, tradition, practice
السُّنَّةُ Prophet's Sunna, teaching of the Prophet Muhammad
سُنِّيٌّ Sunni
مُسِنٌّ advanced in years

س و ر

سَوَّرَ – يُسَوِّرُ to enclose, fence in, or surround

Culture, Religion, and Society 307

ساوَرَ – يُساوِرُ to leap, attack, or assault
سورٌ (أَسْوارٌ) wall, enclosure, fence
سُورَةٌ (سُوَرٌ) sura, chapter of the Quran

No root

شَبَحٌ (أَشْباحٌ) ghost, apparition; an indistinct shape

ش ي أ

شاءَ – يَشيءُ to want or wish
شَيءٌ (أَشْياءُ) thing, something
شُوَيَّةٌ a little, a bit
مَشيئَةٌ wish, will, desire
بِمشيئَةِ اللهِ by God's will

ش ي ط ن

تَشَيْطَنَ – يَتَشَيْطَنُ to behave like a devil
شيطانٌ (شَياطينُ) Devil, Satan
شَيطانيٌّ devilish, demonic
شَيطَنَةٌ villainy

ش ي ع

شاعَ – يَشيعُ to be spread or become public; to dominate
أَشاعَ – يُشيعُ to spread, publish, or publicise
تَشَيَّعَ – يَتَشَيَّعُ to take sides; to join; to become a Shiite
شيعةٌ (شِيَعٌ) followers, disciples; sect; party
الشّيعَةُ the Shiites
شيعيٌّ (شيعيّونَ / شِيَعَةٌ) Shiite
شُيوعٌ spread or circulation (of news)
شُيوعيٌّ (شُيوعيّونَ) Communist
الشُّيوعِيَّةُ communism
إشاعةٌ rumour
شائِعٌ common, widespread
شائِعَةٌ (شائِعاتٌ) rumour
مُشاعٌ the public domain; widespread

ص ب ر

صَبَرَ – يَصْبِرُ to be patient; to bind or tie
صَبَّرَ – يُصَبِّرُ to ask someone to be patient; to console or comfort
تَصَبَّرَ – يَتَصَبَّرُ to be patient or persevere
صَبْرٌ patience, endurance; self-control; shackling
صَبْرَةٌ / صَبَارَةٌ severe cold
صَبُورٌ (صُبُرٌ) patient, enduring, steadfast
صَابِرٌ (صَابِرُونَ) patient, long suffering, steadfast

ص ل ب

صَلَبَ – يَصْلُبُ to crucify
صَلَّبَ – يُصَلِّبُ to crucify; to make the sign of the cross; to fold (arms)
صَلْبٌ crucifixion
صَلِيبٌ (صُلْبَانٌ) crucifix, cross
الْحُرُوبُ الصَّلِيبِيَّةُ the Crusades
الصَّلِيبِيُّونَ the Crusaders

ص ل و

صَلَّى – يُصَلِّي to pray or worship
صَلَاةٌ (صَلَوَاتٌ) Islamic prayer; blessing, benediction
الصَّلَاةُ الرَّبَّانِيَّةُ the Lord's Prayer
مُصَلًّى prayer place

No root

صُوفٌ (أَصْوَافٌ) wool
صُوفِيٌّ woollen; Sufi, Islamic mystic
الصُّوفِيَّةُ Sufism

ص و م

صَامَ – يَصُومُ to fast; to abstain from food, drink, and sexual intercourse
صَوْمٌ fasting; abstinence
الصَّوْمُ الْكَبِيرُ Lent
صِيَامٌ fasting (noun); fast
صَائِمٌ (صَائِمُونَ) fasting (adj); one who fasts

ض ح و / ض ح ى

ضَحِيَ – يَضحى to appear or become visible
ضَحَّى – يُضَحِّي to sacrifice
أَضحى – يُضحي to begin, start, or commence
ضُحىً forenoon
ضَحِيَّةٌ (ضَحايا) forenoon; sacrifice, victim
عيدُ الأَضحى Eid al-Adha
تَضحِيَةٌ (تَضحِيَاتٌ) sacrifice
ضاحِيَةٌ (ضَواحٍ) vicinity; suburb, outskirts

ط ه ر

طَهَرَ – يَطهُرُ to be clean or pure
طَهَّرَ – يُطَهِّرُ to clean, disinfect, or sterilise; to circumcise
تَطَهَّرَ – يَتَطَهَّرُ to clean oneself; to do one's ablutions
طُهرٌ cleanliness, purity
طَهارَةٌ cleanliness; sanctity; circumcision
تَطهيرٌ cleansing, cleaning, purification
تَطهيرٌ عِرقِيٌّ ethnic cleansing
طاهِرٌ clean, pure
مُطَهِّرٌ (مُطَهِّراتٌ) antiseptic

ط و ف

طافَ – يَطوفُ to circle, go about, or wander; to overflow
تَطَوَّفَ – يَتَطَوَّفُ to roam, wander, or walk (around Kaaba)
طَوافٌ round, circuit, circumambulation (of the Kaaba)
طوفانٌ flood, inundation, deluge
طائِفٌ itinerant, migrant
طائِفِيٌّ factional, sectarian; confessional
طائِفَةٌ (طَوائِفُ) faction, sect, party; number
طائِفَةٌ أَقَلِّيَّةٌ minority faction
طائِفِيَّةٌ sectarianism

ع ب د

عَبَدَ – يَعبُدُ to worship; to serve; to adore or idolise

عَبَّدَ – يُعَبِّدُ to enslave or subjugate
تَعَبَّدَ – يَتَعَبَّدُ to devote oneself to God
اِستَعبَدَ – يَستَعبِدُ to enslave or subjugate
عَبدٌ (عَبيدٌ) slave, servant
عِبادَةٌ (عِباداتٌ) worship, adoration (pl: acts of worship)
عِبادَةُ الشَّخصِ cult of personality
عُبوديَّةٌ slavery, servitude; worship
مَعبَدٌ (مَعابِدُ) place of worship
تَعَبُّدٌ worship, devotion
اِستِعبادٌ enslavement, subjugation
عابِدٌ (عابِدونَ) worshipper
مَعبودٌ worshipped, adored; an idol
مُتَعَبِّدٌ pious, devout

ع ذ ر

عَذَرَ – يَعذُرُ to excuse or forgive
اِعتَذَرَ – يَعتَذِرُ to excuse oneself or apologise
عُذرٌ (أعذارٌ) an excuse
عَذراءُ (عَذارى/عَذراواتٌ) virgin
مَريَمُ العَذراءُ the Holy Virgin Mary
مَعذِرةٌ (مَعاذِرُ) an excuse, a pardon
اِعتِذارٌ (اِعتِذاراتٌ) apology, excuse
مَعذورٌ excused, justified

ع ف ر ت

تَعَفرَتَ – يَتَعَفرَتُ to behave like a demon
عِفريتٌ (عَفاريتُ) demon, devil; sly, cunning
عَفرَتَةٌ villainy; a dirty trick

ع ف ف

عَفَّ – يَعِفُّ to refrain or abstain; to be chaste or virtuous
تَعَفَّفَ – يَتَعَفَّفُ to refrain or abstain; to be chaste or virtuous; to be shy
عِفَّةٌ abstinence; virtue, decency, chastity
عَفيفٌ (أعِفّاءُ) modest, virtuous, pure (also a boy's name in the singular)
تَعَفُّفٌ abstinence, restraint; chastity, modesty
مُتَعَفِّفٌ chaste, modest, decent

ع ل و

عَلا – يَعلو to be high or elevated; to rise or ascend
عَلَّى – يُعَلِّي to raise, lift, or elevate
اِستَعلى – يَستَعلي to rise; to master; to become haughty
عُلُوٌّ height, elevation; greatness
عَلَوِيٌّ (العَلَوِيّونَ) upper; heavenly, celestial; Alawi (pl: Alawites)
عَلى (prep) on, above, over
عَلِيٌّ high, tall, elevated (also a boy's name)
تَعلِيَةٌ elevation, raising; enhancement
اِستِعلاءٌ superiority

ع ن ق

عَنَّقَ – يُعَنِّقُ to grab by the neck or collar
عانَقَ – يُعانِقُ to embrace or hug; to associate closely
اِعتَنَقَ – يَعتَنِقُ to adopt or embrace (a religion/person); to be converted
عُنُقٌ (أَعناقٌ) neck, nape
عِناقٌ / مُعانَقَةٌ an embrace or hug
اِعتِناقٌ adoption (of a religion, doctrine)

ع ي د

عَيَّدَ – يُعَيِّدُ to celebrate, to observe a feast; to wish a merry feast
عيدٌ (أَعيادٌ) festival, feast, celebratory day
عيدِيَّةٌ gift presented on a feast day
عيدُ ميلادٍ birthday
عيدُ ميلادٍ سَعيدٍ happy birthday
كُلُّ عامٍ وأَنتَ بِخَيرٍ many happy returns of the day (birthdays, religious festivals)
الأَعيادُ الوَطَنِيَّة national holidays
عيدُ الأُمِّ Mother's Day
عيدُ الأَبِ Father's Day
عيدُ الحُبِّ Valentine's Day
عيدُ الفِطرِ Eid al-Fitr (at the end of Ramadan)
عيدٌ مُبارَكٌ Blessed Eid, Blessed festival[1]
الأَعيادُ الإسلامِيَّة Muslim festivals
الأَعيادُ المَسيحِيَّة Christian festivals
عيدُ ميلادِ المَسيح Jesus's birthday
عيدُ الميلادِ المَجيدِ Christmas

312 Culture, Religion, and Society

عيدُ ميلادٍ سَعيدٌ Merry Christmas
عيدُ الرُّقاقِ Passover
عيدُ العُرشِ / يُومُ كيپور Yom Kippur

غ ف ر

غَفَرَ – يَغفِرُ to forgive or pardon
اِستَغفَرَ – يَستَغفِرُ to ask someone's pardon or forgiveness
غَفورٌ / غَفّارٌ very forgiving
الغَفور / الغَفّار Very Forgiving (two of Allah's names)
غُفرانٌ forgiveness, pardon (also a girl's name)
عيدُ الغُفران Day of Atonement, Yom Kippur
أَستَغفِرُ اللهَ I ask for God's forgiveness, forgive me; Heaven forbid
اِستِغفارٌ asking for forgiveness (from God), repentance
مَغفِرَةٌ pardon, forgiveness
مَغفورٌ forgiven

ف ت ن

فَتَنَ – يَفتِنُ to seduce, tempt, or entice; to torture or torment; to denounce
فِتنَةٌ (فِتَنٌ) sedition; temptation

ف ح ش

فَحُشَ – يَفحُشُ to behave atrociously; to exceed accepted bounds; to be shameless
أَفحَشَ – يُفحِشُ to use obscene language; to commit atrocities
فُحشٌ / فاحِشَةٌ indecency, obscenity
فَحشاءُ abomination, atrocity; fornication
فاحِشٌ monstrous, excessive, obscene
فاحِشَةٌ (فَواحِشُ) sin, abomination, atrocity; fornication

ف س د

فَسَدَ – يَفسِدُ to be or become rotten; to be wicked or corrupt
فَسَّدَ – يُفَسِّدُ to spoil, corrupt, or degrade
أَفسَدَ – يُفسِدُ to spoil, destroy, or corrupt; to undermine
فَسادٌ decay, decomposition; corruption, depravity
مَفسَدَةٌ (مَفاسِدُ) cause of evil; scandalous deed
فاسِدٌ (فاسِدونَ) bad, rotten, spoiled, corrupt

ف ص ح

(Same root letters as 'to be eloquent' but different root)

أفصَحَ – يُفصِحُ to celebrate Easter; to celebrate Passover
فِصحٌ (فُصوحٌ) Passover, Easter
عيدُ الفِصحِ Easter
أحَدُ الفِصحِ المَجيدِ Easter Sunday

ف ط ر

فَطَرَ – يَفطِرُ to break the fast, to have breakfast; to split or cleave
أفطَرَ – يُفطِرُ to break the fast, to have breakfast
فَطرٌ (فُطورٌ) a crack or rupture
فِطرٌ fast breaking
فُطرٌ mushrooms, fungi
فِطرَةٌ (فِطَرٌ) nature, disposition, constitution
إفطارٌ breaking the fast during Ramadan
فَطورٌ breakfast outside of Ramadan
الفاطِرُ the Creator (one of Allah's names)

ق د ر

قَدَرَ – يَقدِرُ to decree or ordain (of God); to decide; to be able or to possess strength
قَدَّرَ – يُقَدِّرُ to determine or decree; to value or assess
أقدَرَ – يُقدِرُ to enable
إستَقدَرَ – يَستَقدِرُ to ask (God) for strength
قَدَرٌ (أقدارٌ) fate, divine decree; value; extent, scope
ليلَةُ القَدرِ Lailat al-Qadr[2]
القَضاءُ والقَدَرُ fate and pre-destiny
قُدرَةٌ power, might
مِقدارٌ (مَقاديرُ) amount, quantity, measure
مُقَدَّرٌ destined, written
مُقتَدِرٌ powerful, potent; capable

ق د س

قَدُسَ – يَقدُسُ to be holy or pure
قَدَّسَ – يُقَدِّسُ to sanctify, glorify, or worship

314 *Culture, Religion, and Society*

تَقَدَّسَ – يَتَقَدَّسُ to be sacred, or sanctified
قُدسٌ (أَقداسٌ) holiness, sanctity; sanctuary; shrine
الْقُدسُ / بيتُ المقدِس Al-Quds/Jerusalem
تَقديسٌ sanctification, hallowing; celebration
مُقَدَّسٌ (مُقَدَّساتٌ) holy, sacred, sanctified
الْكِتابُ المُقَدَّسُ the Bible
الرُّوحُ الْقُدُسُ the Holy Ghost

ق ر أ

(Full treatment in Education chapter)

القُرْآنُ الكَريمُ the Holy Quran

ق س س

قَسَّ – يَقُسُّ to seek, strive for, or aspire
قِسٌّ (قُسُسٌ) priest, pastor, minister
قِسّيسٌ (قِسّيسونَ) priest, pastor, minister

No root

كاتدرائِيَّةٌ cathedral

ك ث ل ك

تَكَثْلَكَ – يَتَكَثْلَكُ to become a Catholic
كاثوليكِيٌّ (كَثلَكَةٌ) Catholic
الكَثلَكَةُ / الكاثوليكِيَّةُ Catholicism

ك ف ر

كَفَرَ – يَكْفُرُ to be irreligious, to disbelieve in God; to cover or hide
كَفَّرَ – يُكَفِّرُ to make (someone) an infidel; to charge with unbelief; to atone
كَفرٌ (كُفورٌ) small village, hamlet
كُفرٌ atheism
كَفّارَةٌ penance, atonement; money paid when a fast is not kept
تَكفيرٌ (عَن) expiation (of), atonement, penance
كافِرٌ (كافِرونَ / كُفّارٌ) those who don't believe in one God, kafirs

ك ن س

كَنَسَ – يُكَنِّسُ to sweep
كَنْسٌ sweeping, cleaning
كَنَّاسٌ street sweeper or cleaner
كَنِيسٌ synagogue
كَنِيسَةٌ (كَنائِسُ) temple; church, synagogue
مِكْنَسَةٌ (مَكانِسُ) broom
مِكْنَسَةٌ كَهْرَبائِيَّةٌ vacuum cleaner

No root

كوشير / كوشَر kosher

No root

لاهوتٌ deity, divinity; divine nature
عِلمُ اللّاهوتِ theology
لاهوتِيٌّ theological
اللّاهوتِيَّةُ theology

ل ث م

لَثَمَ – يَلْثِمُ to kiss; to strike, hit, or wound
لَثَّمَ – يُلَثِّمُ to veil (face); to cover (sth)
تَلَثَّمَ – يَتَلَثَّمُ to veil one's face; to cover oneself up
لَثْمَةٌ kiss
لِثامٌ veil, cover, wrapping
مُلَثَّمٌ veiled

ل ح د

لَحَدَ – يَلْحَدُ to dig a grave, to bury; to deviate from the straight path
اِلْتَحَدَ – يَلْتَحِدُ to deviate or digress; to tend to or be inclined; to abandon one's faith
لَحْدٌ (ألحودٌ) grave, tomb
إلْحادٌ atheism, apostasy, heresy
مُلْحِدٌ (مُلْحِدونَ) apostate, heretic, atheist

ل ع ن

لَعَنَ – يَلعَنُ to curse or damn
لاعَنَ – يُلاعِنُ to utter oaths of condemnation
لَعنٌ cursing, malediction
لَعنةٌ (لَعناتٌ) curse, imprecation
لَعينٌ / مَلعونٌ (مَلاعينُ) cursed, damned; detested
اللَّعينُ the cursed one, the Devil

ل ه م

أَلْهَمَ – يُلهِمُ to inspire; to swallow
اِستَلْهَمَ – يَستَلْهِمُ to ask for inspiration or advice; to pray or turn to God
إِلهامٌ (إِلهاماتٌ) revelation; inspiration; instinct (also a girl's name in the singular)
مُلْهَمٌ inspired

م س ح

مَسَحَ – يَمسَحُ to stroke with the hand; to wipe, polish, or clean
مَسَّحَ – يُمَسِّحُ to wipe off; to rub or anoint; to persuade
مَسحٌ wiping, cleaning, anointing
مَسّاحٌ land surveyor
المَسيحُ the Messiah, Christ
مَسيحيٌّ (مَسيحيّونَ) Christian
مِمسَحةٌ (مَماسِحُ) dust cloth, dish rag; doormat
المَسيحيَّةُ Christianity
المَسيحُ المُخَلِّصُ Messiah

ن ب ر

نَبَرَ – يَنبِرُ to raise or elevate; to sing in a high pitched voice; to emphasise
اِنتَبَرَ – يَنتَبِرُ to swell or become swollen
نَبرٌ accent, stress
نَبرَةٌ (نَبَراتٌ) swelling; stress, accent (pl: inflection or intonation of voice)
مِنبَرٌ (مَنابِرُ) pulpit, platform

ن ج س

نَجُسَ – يَنجُسُ to be impure or dirty
نَجَّسَ – يُنَجِّسُ to defile, soil, or dirty

Culture, Religion, and Society

تَنَجَّسَ – يَتَنَجَّسُ to be or become impure, soiled, or defiled
نَجَسٌ / نَجَاسَةٌ impurity, dirt, filth, squalor
تَنْجِيسٌ soiling, defilement, contamination

No root

نَجْمةُ داوودَ Star of David

ن س ك

نَسَكَ – يَنسُكُ to lead a devout life; to live an ascetic life
تَنَسَّكَ – يَتَنَسَّكُ to be pious, to lead a devout life
نَسْكٌ piety, devoutness, asceticism
نُسْكٌ sacrifice; ceremonies (of pilgrimage)
مَنسِكٌ (مَناسِكُ) hermitage; place of sacrifice; ceremony, ritual (of pilgrimage)

ن ص ر

نَصَرَ – يَنصُرُ to help or aid; to protect or save
نَصَّرَ – يُنَصِّرُ to Christianise or convert to Christianity
تَنَصَّرَ – يَتَنَصَّرُ to try to help; to convert to Christianity
اِنْتَصَرَ – يَنْتَصِرُ to come to someone's aid; to conquer or vanquish
نَصْرٌ aid, victory, help, assistance
نُصْرَةٌ help, aid, assistance
نَصرانِيٌّ (نَصارى) Christian
النَّصْرانِيَّةُ Christianity
نَصيرٌ (نُصَراءُ) helper, supporter, protector; follower
اِنْتِصارٌ (اِنْتِصاراتٌ) victory, triumph; revenge
ناصِرٌ (أنصارٌ) helper, supporter, protector; follower (also a boy's name in the singular)
النَّاصِرَة Nazareth
مَنصورٌ / مُنْتَصِرٌ triumphant; victor, conqueror (also a boy's name)

ن ق و / ن ق ي

نَقِيَ – يَنقى to be pure
أنقى – يُنقي to purify, cleanse, or clean
اِنْتَقى – يَنْتَقي to pick out or select
نَقاءٌ / نَقْوَةٌ purity; fineness

318 *Culture, Religion, and Society*

نَقِيٌّ (أَنْقِيَاءُ) pure, clean, immaculate
تَنْقِيَةٌ cleaning, purification, sifting
اِنْتِقَاءٌ selection
مُنْتَقًى selected, select

ه د ى

هَدَى – يَهدي to guide, direct, or show; to supply
أَهدى – يُهدي to bring, lead, or conduct; to give as a present; to dedicate
تَهَدَّى – يَتَهَدَّى to be well led or rightly guided
اِهتَدى – يَهتَدي to be rightly guided; to find or discover
هُدًى guidance (religious), the right way
هَدِيَّةٌ (هَدايا) a gift, present, or donation
هِدايةٌ guidance
إِهْداءٌ presentation, award, donation

ه و د

هادَ – يَهودُ to be a Jew
هَوَّدَ – يُهَوِّدُ to make Jewish; to intoxicate; to proceed slowly
تَهَوَّدَ – يَتَهَوَّدُ to convert to Judaism
اليَهودُ the Jews
اليَهوديَّةُ Judaism
يَهوديٌّ (يَهودٌ) Jew; Jewish
اليَهوديَّةُ الأُرْثوذوكْسيَّةُ Orthodox Judaism

No root

وَثَنٌ (أَوْثانٌ) idol, image
وَثَنِيٌّ pagan, heathen, idolater
الوَثَنِيَّةُ paganism

و ح ى

وَحَى – يَحي to inspire or reveal
أَوْحى – يَوحي to inspire or reveal
وَحْيٌ (divine) inspiration, revelation
إيحاءٌ suggestion; inspiration
مُوحٍ inspiring; revealing

و س و س

وَسْوَسَ – يُوَسْوِسُ to whisper or instill evil (usually devil); to prompt or tempt
تَوَسْوَسَ – يَتَوَسْوَسُ to feel uneasy or anxious; to be suspicious or in doubt
وَسْوَسَةٌ (وَساوِسُ) devilish insinuation, temptation; suspicion
وَسْواسٌ (وَساوِسُ) whisperer, suggester (Satan); devilish insinuation
الوَسْواسُ Satan
مُوَسْوَسٌ obsessed with delusions; suffering from OCD

و ض و

وَضُوَ – يَوْضُوُ to be pure or clean
تَوَضَّأَ – يَتَوَضَّأُ to perform religious ablutions
وُضاءٌ brilliant, radiant
وَضاءَةٌ purity, cleanliness
وُضوءٌ ritual ablution before prayer; purity, cleanliness

و ع ظ

وَعَظَ – يَعِظُ to preach; to appeal to someone's conscience; to admonish
عِظَةٌ (عِظاتٌ) a moral, sermon, or warning
وَعْظٌ/وَعْظَةٌ admonition, warning, sermon
مَوْعِظَةٌ (مَواعِظُ) religious lecture, spiritual counsel
واعِظٌ (وُعَّاظٌ) a preacher

الثَّقافَةُ والمُجتَمَعُ Culture and Society

أ د ى

أَدَّى – يُؤَدِّي to lead to or bring about; to convey; to contribute
تَأَدَّى – يَتَأَدَّى to lead to; to be carried out; to contribute; to arrive
أَداءٌ (أَداءاتٌ) rendering (of a service); pursuit, performance, realisation (of a task)
تَأْدِيَةٌ pursuit; performance, discharge (of duty)
مُؤَدَّىً assignment, task; function

أ ذ ى

أَذِيَ – يَأذى to suffer damage or be harmed
أَذَّى – يُؤَذِّي to harm, hurt, or wrong

تَأَذَّى – يَتَأَذَّى to suffer damage; to feel offended, to be hurt
أَذًى / أَذِيَّةٌ evil, harm, injury, trouble
مُؤْذٍ hurtful, painful, harmful

أ س و / أ س ى

أَسِيَ – يَأْسَى to be sad, grieved, or distressed
أَسَا – يَأْسُو to nurse or treat; to make peace
أَسَّى – يُؤَسِّي to console, comfort, or nurse
أَسًى grief, sorrow, distress
مَأْسَاةٌ (مَآسٍ) tragedy, disaster
تَأْسِيَةٌ / مُوَاسَاةٌ consolation, comfort

أ ص ل

أَصُلَ – يَأْصُلُ to be or become firmly rooted; to be of noble origin
تَأَصَّلَ – يَتَأَصَّلُ to be ingrained or firmly rooted
اِسْتَأْصَلَ – يَسْتَأْصِلُ to uproot or annihilate; to remove surgically
أَصْلٌ (أُصُولٌ) root, trunk; origin, source; cause; principles
أَصْلِيٌّ original, primary, authentic
أَصِيلٌ (أَصِلَاءُ) original, authentic, proper; of noble birth
أُصُولِيٌّ in accordance with the rules, traditional
أُصُولِيٌّ fundamentalist
أُصُولِيَّةٌ fundamentalism
أَصَالَةٌ steadfastness; nobility of descent (also a girl's name)
مُتَأَصِّلٌ deep-rooted; chronic (illness)

أ م ل

أَمِلَ – يَأْمُلُ to hope or entertain hopes
أَمَّلَ – يُؤَمِّلُ to hope or expect; to raise one's hopes
تَأَمَّلَ – يَتَأَمَّلُ to look closely or regard; to contemplate or meditate
أَمَلٌ (آمَالٌ) hope, expectation
خَيْبَةُ أَمَلٍ disappointment
مَأْمَلٌ (مَآمِلُ) hope
تَأَمُّلٌ (تَأَمُّلَاتٌ) consideration, contemplation, meditation
آمِلٌ hopeful

ب د و

بَدا – يَبدو to appear, show, or become evident
أَبدى – يُبْدي to disclose, reveal, or show
تَبَدَّى – يَتَبَدَّى to live in the desert; to show or appear
بَدْوٌ desert nomads, Bedouins
بَدَوِيٌّ Bedouin, nomadic
بَداوَةٌ desert life, Bedouin life, nomadism
بَيْداءُ desert, wilderness
إبداءٌ expression, manifestation; declaration
بادٍ apparent, evident, obvious
بادِيَةٌ (بَوادٍ) desert nomads, Bedouins

ب ذ ل

بَذَلَ – يَبْذُلُ to grant or give freely and generously; to offer or sacrifice
اِبتَذَلَ – يَبتَذِلُ to make commonplace; to use vulgar language
بَذْلٌ giving, spending; sacrifice
بَذْلَةٌ suit (clothes)
اِبتِذالٌ vulgarity, degradation, commonness
مُبتَذَلٌ base, vulgar, common

No root

بُرجٌ (بُروجٌ / أَبراجٌ) tower, castle; horoscope
بُرجُ آيْفِل Eiffel Tower
بُرجُ الحَمامِ dovecot
بُرجُ الأَسَدِ Leo
بُرجُ الثَّورِ Taurus
بُرجُ الجَدْيِ Capricorn
بُرجُ الجَوْزاءِ Gemini
بُرجُ الحَمَلِ Aries
بُرجُ الحوتِ Pisces
بُرجُ الدَّلْوِ Aquarius
بُرجُ السَّرَطانِ Cancer
بُرجُ العَذراءِ Virgo
بُرجُ العَقرَبِ Scorpio

322 Culture, Religion, and Society

بُرجُ القَوسِ Sagittarius
بُرجُ الميزانِ Libra

ب ل و / ب ل ى

بَلا – يَبْلو to test or put (someone) to the test; to afflict
بالى – يُبالي to care, to be concerned, to take into consideration
ابتَلَى – يَبتَلي to afflict; to put (someone) to the test
بالٍ / بَالِيةٌ worn, old, shabby, threadbare
بَلِيَّة (بَلايا) trial, tribulations, misfortune, calamity
بَلاءٌ / ابتلاءٌ trial, tribulation, affliction, distress
بَلْوى calamity, trial, tribulation, misfortune
مُبالاةٌ consideration, regard, attention
لا مُبالاةٌ / اللّامُبالاةُ indifference, carelessness

ت ح ف

أتحفَ – يُتحِفُ to present
تُحْفةٌ (تُحَفٌ) precious article, masterpiece; gift
مَتحَفٌ / مُتحَفٌ (مَتاحِفُ) museum

ث ر ث ر

ثَرثَرَ – يُثَرثِرُ to chatter
ثَرثَرَةٌ gossip
ثَرثارٌ (ثَرثارونَ) chatterbox

ث ق ف

ثَقِفَ – يَثقَفُ to find or meet; to be skilful
ثَقَّفَ – يُثَقِّفُ to straighten or correct; to train
ثاقَفَ – يُثاقِفُ to fence (sport)
تَثاقَفَ – يَتَثاقَفُ to be trained or educated
ثَقافةٌ (ثَقافاتٌ) culture
مُتداخِلُ الثَّقافاتِ multicultural
ثَقافِيٌّ educational, intellectual, cultural
فَجوةٌ ثَقافِيَّةٌ cultural gap
تَثقيفٌ cultivation of the mind; education, training

Culture, Religion, and Society

مُثاقَفَةٌ fencing (sport), swordsmanship
مُثَقَّفٌ educated, trained, cultured

ج ن ز

جَنَّزَ – يُجَنِّزُ to conduct the funeral service, to say the burial prayers
جَنازَةٌ (جَنازاتٌ / جَنائِزُ) funeral, funeral procession

ح ظ ظ

حَظَّ – يَحِظُّ to be lucky or fortunate
حَظٌّ (حُظوظٌ) good fortune; fate, destiny
لِحُسنِ الحَظِّ fortunately
لِسوءِ الحَظِّ unfortunately
مَحْظوظٌ lucky, fortunate

ح ف ل

حَفَلَ – يَحفِلُ to gather or congregate; to be replete; to pay attention
حَفَّلَ – يُحَفِّلُ to adorn, decorate, or ornament
اِحتَفَلَ – يَحتَفِلُ to gather or rally; to celebrate or honour; to pay attention
حَفْلٌ gathering, congregation; performance
حَفْلَةٌ (حَفَلاتٌ) assembly, gathering, congregation; concert, performance
حَفْلَةُ التَّأبينِ commemoration
حَفْلَةٌ موسيقيَّةٌ concert
حَفيلٌ diligent, eager
اِحتِفالٌ (اِحتِفالاتٌ) celebration, ceremony, festival
حافِلَةٌ (حافِلاتٌ / حَوافِلُ) bus

No root

خُزَعْبَلٌ idle talk
خُزَعْبَلَةٌ (خُزَعْبَلاتٌ) superstitions; idle talk; joke

خ ط و

خَطا – يَخطو to step, pace, or walk; to proceed
تَخَطَّى – يَتَخَطَّى to overstep, transgress, or traverse; to overflow; to surpass
خَطْوَةٌ (خَطَواتٌ / خُطىً) a step, pace, or stride

ذ ل ل

ذَلَّ – يَذِلُّ to be low, humble, or contemptible
أَذَلَّ – يُذِلُّ to debase, degrade, humiliate, or humble
تَذَلَّلَ – يَتَذَلَّلُ to humble oneself; to be humble
اِستَذَلَّ – يَستَذِلُّ to think oneself low or despicable; to disparage
ذُلٌّ lowness, insignificance, humility; disgrace, shame, humiliation
ذِلَّةٌ lowness, baseness, depravity
ذَلِيلٌ (أَذِلَّةٌ / أَذِلاَّءُ) low, abject, despised, humble
مَذَلَّةٌ humiliation; submissiveness, meekness
تَذلِيلٌ / إِذلاَلٌ degradation, humiliation

ذ م م

ذَمَّ – يَذِمُّ to blame, criticise, or find fault
ذَمَّمَ – يُذَمِّمُ to criticise, rebuke, or censure
ذَمٌّ censure, disparagement
ذِمَّةٌ (ذِمَمٌ) conscience; protection, care; guarantee; debt
ذَمِيمَةٌ (ذَمَائِمُ) blame, censure
مَذمُومٌ objectionable, reprehensible

ر ح ب

رَحُبَ – يَرحُبُ to be wide, spacious, or roomy
رَحَّبَ – يُرَحِّبُ to welcome or receive graciously
رَحبٌ wide, spacious
مَرحباً hello
مَرحباً بِكم welcome
تَرحِيبٌ welcoming

ر د ى

رَدَى – يَردِي to perish or be destroyed
تَرَدَّى – يَتَرَدَّى to fall, tumble, or deteriorate; to clothe
اِرتَدَى – يَرتَدِي to wear or put on; to be clothed
الرَّدى death
رِداءٌ (أَردِيَةٌ) garment, cloak, robe

ر و ع

رَاعَ – يُرِيعُ to frighten, scare, or startle; to please or delight

Culture, Religion, and Society 325

رَوَّعَ – يُرَوِّعُ to frighten, scare, or alarm
تَرَوَّعَ – يَتَرَوَّعُ to be frightened or alarmed
رَوْعٌ fright, alarm; beauty
رَوْعَةٌ fright, alarm, fear; awe, splendour
رائِعٌ splendid, admirable, wonderful
مُرِيعٌ dreadful, horrible

ز ح م

زَحَمَ – يَزحَمُ to push, shove, or jostle
تَزاحَمَ – يَتَزاحَمُ to press or crowd together; to compete with one another
اِزدَحَمَ – يَزدَحِمُ to be crowded; to swarm
زَحمَةٌ/زِحامٌ crowd; traffic jam
مُزاحَمَةٌ (مُزاحَماتٌ) competition, rivalry
مُزاحِمٌ (مُزاحِمونَ) competitor, rival
مُزدَحِمٌ overcrowded, packed, crowded
اِزدِحامٌ crowding, overcrowding

س خ ر

سَخِرَ – يَسخَرُ to mock, ridicule, or make fun of
سَخَّرَ – يُسَخِّرُ to make subservient; to employ or utilise
سُخرَةٌ labour, forced labour; ridicule
مُسَخِّرٌ oppressor
تَسخيرٌ subjugation, exploitation
ساخِرٌ satirical
سُخرِيٌّ ridiculed (person); forced labour
سُخرِيَةٌ scorn, derision, mockery; irony; ridiculed (person)
مَسخَرَةٌ (مَساخِرُ) laughing stock, object of ridicule; ridiculous, ludicrous

س خ ط

سَخِطَ – يَسخَطُ to be annoyed, displeased, or angry
أَسخَطَ – يُسخِطُ to embitter, anger, or enrage
سَخَطٌ/تَسَخُّطٌ anger, resentment, indignation
مَسخوطٌ (مساخيطُ) loathsome, odious (pl: idols)

س ط ر

سَطَرَ – يَسطُرُ to rule or draw lines; to write or compose

سَطرٌ (سُطورٌ) line, row
ساطورٌ (سواطيرُ) cleaver
أُسطورَةٌ (أَساطيرُ) fable, legend, myth
أُسطوريٌّ legendary, mythical
مِسطَرَةٌ (مَساطِرُ) ruler
تَسطيرٌ recording, writing down
مُسَطَّرٌ ruled

ش أ م

تَشاءَمَ – يَتَشاءَمُ to perceive an evil omen; to regard as ominous; to be pessimistic
إستَشأَمَ – يَستَشئِمُ to perceive an evil omen; to regard as ominous
الشّامُ Syria, Damascus
شاميٌّ Syrian
شُؤمٌ bad omen; bad luck, calamity
تَشاؤُمٌ pessimism
مَشؤومٌ / مَشومٌ (مَشائيمُ) inauspicious, ominous
مُتَشائِمٌ pessimist

ش ر ف

شَرَفَ – يَشرُفُ to be high-born, noble, or illustrious
شَرَّفَ – يُشَرِّفُ to honour, elevate, exalt, or ennoble
أَشرَفَ – يُشرِفُ to be high or mighty; to supervise; to look down on, to overlook
تَشَرَّفَ – يَتَشَرَّفُ to be honoured, to have the honour of
شَرَفٌ honour, glory, nobility
شُرفَةٌ (شُرفاتٌ) balcony
شَريفٌ (شُرَفاءُ / أَشرافٌ) distinguished, illustrious, noble, exalted; Sherif (title)
إشرافٌ (على) supervision, control (over); patronage
مُشرِفٌ supervisor, overseer, superintendent

ش ع ب

شَعَبَ – يَشعَبُ to gather, assemble, or rally
تَشَعَّبَ – يَتَشَعَّبُ to branch, diverge, or separate
شَعبٌ (شُعوبٌ) people, tribe
شَعبيٌّ national, the people's; folksy
شَعبيَّةٌ popularity

Culture, Religion, and Society

شِعبٌ (شِعابٌ) mountain path, ravine, canyon
شَعْبانُ eighth Islamic month

ش م ت

شَمِتَ – يَشْمَت to gloat or rejoice in someone's misfortune
شَمَّتَ – يُشَمِّتُ to disappoint
أَشْمَتَ – يُشْمِتُ to take malicious pleasure in another's misfortunes
شَماتَةٌ malicious joy, schadenfreude
شامِتٌ (شُمَّاتٌ / شَوامِتُ) gloating

ش ق و / ش ق ى

شَقِيَ – يَشْقى to make someone wretched or miserable
أَشْقى – يُشْقي to make someone wretched or miserable
شَقاءٌ / شَقىً misfortune, distress, misery
شَقِيٌّ (أَشْقِياءُ) miserable, unhappy, wretched
شَقْوَةٌ misfortune, distress, misery
شَقاوَةٌ mischief, naughtiness; misery

ص د ف

صَدَفَ – يَصْدِفُ to turn away, avoid, or shun; to discourage or restrain
صادَفَ – يُصادِفُ to meet or encounter by chance; to come across; to coincide
تَصادَفَ – يَتَصادَفُ to happen by chance; to come to pass
صَدَفٌ (أَصدافٌ) seashell, oyster
صُدْفَةٌ (صُدَفٌ) chance occurrence, coincidence; accidentally
مُصادَفَةٌ (مُصادفاتٌ) encounter, meeting; chance, coincidence
بِالصُّدْفَةِ by coincidence

ض ي ف

ضافَ – يَضيفُ to stay as a guest
ضَيَّفَ – يُضَيِّفُ to take in as a guest, to receive hospitably, to entertain
أضافَ – يُضيفُ to add, join, or connect; to take in as a guest
إسْتَضافَ – يَسْتَضيفُ to invite (someone) as a guest
ضَيْفٌ (ضُيوفٌ) guest, visitor
ضِيافَةٌ accommodation, hospitality
حُسْنُ الضِّيافَةِ hospitality

مِضيافٌ hospitable; host
مَضافةٌ hostel, guesthouse
إضافةٌ addition, attachment; annexation; genitive construction
إضافيٌّ additional, supplementary
مُضيفٌ (مُضيفونَ) host, flight attendant

ط ر ز

طَرَّزَ – يُطرِّزُ to embroider, embellish, or garnish
طَرْزٌ (طُروزٌ) type, model, brand, sort
طِرازٌ (طُروزٌ / أطْرِزةٌ) type, model, class, brand; fashion, style; embroidery
على الطِّرازِ الحديثِ latest fashion
تَطْريزٌ embroidery

ط ف ئ

طَفَأَ – يَطفِئُ to be extinguished (fire or light)
أطْفَأَ – يُطْفِئُ to extinguish; to smother or stifle; to switch off
طَفَّايةٌ fire extinguisher; ashtray (in some dialects)
إطْفاءٌ extinguishing; firefighting
رِجالُ الإطْفاءِ firemen, fire department
إطْفائيٌّ fireman
إطْفائيَّةٌ fire department

ع ز ا / ع ز و

عَزا – يَعزو to charge, incriminate, or blame; to trace (back), ascribe (sth to)
عَزَّى – يُعَزِّي to comfort or console
عَزْوٌ tracing back; accusation
عَزاءٌ ceremony of mourning; solace; composure
تَعزِيةٌ (تَعازٍ) consolation, solace, condolence
مُعَزٍّ (مُعزونَ) comforter, condoler

ع ش ر

عاشَرَ – يُعاشِرُ to be on intimate terms
تَعاشَرَ – يَتَعاشَرُ to be on intimate terms, to live together
عُشْرٌ (أعْشارٌ) tenth part, tithe
عُشْرِيٌّ decimal

Culture, Religion, and Society

عِشْرَةٌ intimacy, companionship, relations
عَشيرةٌ (عَشائِرُ) tribe, kinsfolk, clan
يومُ عاشوراء Ashura, tenth day of Muharram
مُعاشَرَةٌ intimacy, companionship, association, social relations
آداب المُعاشَرةِ etiquette

ع ط و

عاطى – يُعاطي to give
أعطى – يُعطي to give, offer, grant, or bestow
تَعاطى – يَتَعاطى to pursue (activity); to take (medicine); to be busy or occupy oneself
عَطاءٌ (عَطاءاتٌ/أعطِيَةٌ) offer, tender; gift, present
عَطِيَّةٌ (عَطايا) gift, present
إعطاءٌ donation, presentation; granting
مُعطٍ donor

No root

عُنصُرٌ (عَناصِرُ) race, breed; origin; element (chemistry)
عُنصُريٌّ racial, ethnic; racist
التَّمييزُ العُنصُريُّ racial discrimination
الفَصلُ العُنصُريُّ apartheid
التَّطهيرُ العُنصُريُّ ethnic cleansing
عُنصُريَّةٌ racism

ع و د

عادَ – يَعودُ to return or come back; to refer or relate
عَوَّدَ – يُعَوِّدُ to accustom or habituate
تَعَوَّدَ – يَتَعَوَّدُ to be accustomed, to get used to, to habituate oneself
عُودٌ (عيدانٌ) wood, stick, branch, twig
عَوْدٌ/عَودَةٌ return, reversion, recurrence
الْعَودَةِ حَقُّ the right of return (for Palestinians)
عادَةٌ (عاداتٌ) habit, custom, usage, practice
عاداتٌ وتَقاليدُ customs and traditions
عادَةً usually
عادِيٌّ usual, customary, common

Culture, Religion, and Society

عِيادَةٌ (عِياداتٌ) clinic, office; consultation
تَعَوُّدٌ / تَعْوِيدٌ habituation
إعادَةٌ return; repetition; giving back; re-
عائِدٌ (عائِدونَ) returning; belonging (pl: people who return to their native country)
عائِدَةٌ (عَوائِدُ) benefit, profit, advantage, gain
مُتَعَوِّدٌ used to, accustomed to, habituated, conditioned (person)
مُعتادٌ used to, accustomed to, habituated, conditioned (object)
كَالْمُعتادِ as usual

ع ي ب

عابَ – يَعيبُ to be defective, blemished, or deficient; to frown upon
عَيَّبَ – يُعَيِّبُ to render faulty; to blame or find fault
عَيبٌ (عُيوبٌ) fault, shortcoming; shame, disgrace
مَعيبٌ / مَعْيوبٌ defective, deficient, faulty

غ ج ر

غَجَّرَ – يُغَجِّرُ to scold; to curse or swear
غَجَرِيَّةٌ gypsy
غَجَرِيٌّ (غَجَرٌ) gypsy
تَغجيرٌ scolding, cursing; abusive language

ف أ ل

تَفاءَلَ – يَتَفاءَلُ to be hopeful or optimistic
فَأْلٌ (فُؤُولٌ) good omen, auspice, sign
تَفاؤُلٌ optimism
مُتَفائِلٌ optimist

ف ج أ

فَجَأَ – يَفْجَأُ to come suddenly; to attack or confront suddenly
فاجَأَ – يُفاجِئُ to come suddenly, to attack or confront suddenly
فَجْأَةً suddenly, unexpectedly
مُفاجَأَةٌ (مُفاجَآتٌ) surprise
مُفاجِئٌ surprising

Culture, Religion, and Society 331

ف خ م

فَخُمَ – يَفْخُمُ to be imposing, splendid, or magnificent
فَخَّمَ – يُفَخِّمُ to intensify; to honour or treat with respect
فَخْمٌ imposing, splendid, superb
فَخَامَةٌ honour, excellence, eminence

ف و ت

فَاتَ – يَفُوتُ to elapse; to pass away or vanish; to anticipate; to relinquish[3]
فَوَّتَ – يُفَوِّتُ to make (someone) escape; to cause (someone) to miss; to let (someone) pass
فَوْتٌ (أَفْوَاتٌ) distance, interval; difference
فَوَاتٌ passing; lapse (time)
فَائِتٌ past, elapsed (time)

ق ب ر

قَبَرَ – يَقْبُرُ to bury or inter
قَبْرٌ (قُبُورٌ) grave, tomb
مَقْبَرَةٌ / مَقْبُرٌ (مَقَابِرُ) tomb, burial ground, cemetery

ق ل د

قَلَّدَ – يُقَلِّدُ to adorn with a necklace; to imitate; to appoint (someone to office)
تَقَلَّدَ – يَتَقَلَّدُ to wear a necklace; to adorn; to take over (power, control)
قِلَادَةٌ (قَلَائِدُ) necklace (pl: poems)
تَقْلِيدٌ (تَقَالِيدُ) imitation, copying (pl: tradition, custom, convention)
تَقْلِيدِيٌّ traditional, customary
مُقَلَّدٌ imitation; imitated, forged, counterfeit
مُقَلِّدٌ copycat

ق ل ق

قَلِقَ – يَقْلَقُ to be disturbed, restless, agitated, or apprehensive
أَقْلَقَ – يُقْلِقُ to trouble, worry, alarm, or disquiet
قَلَقٌ worry, fear, apprehension
قَلِقٌ restless

ك ن و / ك ن ى

كَنَى – يَكْنِي to use metonymically; to allude to

كَنَّى – يُكَنِّي to call (someone) by an agnomen (*abu* or *umm* followed by name of oldest son)

تَكَنَّى – يَتَكَنَّى to call oneself or be known by the surname of

كُنْيَةٌ (كُنْيَاتٌ / كُنًى) surname, epithet, agnomen (*abu* or *umm* followed by name of oldest son)

كِنَايَةٌ metonymy; indirect expression, allusion

ل ق ب

لَقَّبَ – يُلَقِّبُ to refer to someone by surname, title, or honorific

تَلَقَّبَ – يَتَلَقَّبُ to be referred to by surname, title, or honorific

لَقَبٌ (أَلْقَابٌ) title, nickname, honorific

مُلَقَّبٌ surnamed, nicknamed

ل ه ف

لَهِفَ – يَلْهَفُ to sigh, lament, or deplore

تَلَهَّفَ – يَتَلَهَّفُ to be eager; to yearn; to sigh, regret, or deplore

لَهْفٌ / لَهْفَةٌ regret, sorrow, lamentation, anxiety

لَاهِفٌ / مَلْهُوفٌ worried, troubled, grieved, anxious

مُتَلَهِّفٌ yearning, longing

م د ن

مَدَّنَ – يُمَدِّنُ to found or build cities; to urbanise; to civilise; to refine

تَمَدَّنَ – يَتَمَدَّنُ to be or become civilised; to enjoy the comforts of civilisation

مَدَنِيٌّ (مَدَنِيُّونَ) a civilian; urban, city dweller

مَدِينَةٌ (مُدُنٌ) town, city

مَدَنِيٌّ urban, city dwelling; refined, polished; civil, civic; a civilian

تَمْدِينٌ civilisation; refining (manners, culture)

تَمَدُّنٌ civilisation, refinement of culture

مُتَمَدِّنٌ civilised, refined

No root

مُودَةٌ / مُوضَةٌ (مُودَاتٌ / مُوضَاتٌ) fashion, style; fashionable

أُسْبُوعُ الْمُودَةِ fashion week

م ي ز

مَازَ – يَمِيزُ to distinguish or separate
مَيَّزَ – يُمَيِّزُ to distinguish, honour, or favour; to segregate or discriminate
تَمَيَّزَ – يَتَمَيَّزُ to be separated or distinguished; to be honoured
مِيزَةٌ characteristic; peculiarity
تَمْيِيزٌ distinction, segregation, discrimination
التَّمْيِيزُ عَلَى أَسَاسِ الجِنسِ sexism
التمييزُ ضِدَّ كِبَارِ السِّنِّ ageism
اِمْتِيَازٌ (اِمتيازاتٌ) advantage, benefit; distinction, discrimination
مُمَيَّزٌ distinguished, favoured, privileged
مُتَمَيِّزٌ distinguished, prominent, outstanding
مُمتازٌ excellent

م ي ل

مَالَ – يَمِيلُ to bend, lean, turn, or incline
مَيَّلَ – يُمَيِّلُ to incline or bend; to make someone favourably disposed; to alienate
تَمَيَّلَ – يَتَمَيَّلُ to stagger, sway, or swing
اِسْتَمَالَ – يَسْتَمِيلُ to cause to incline, to tip or tilt; to win over or attract
مَيْلٌ (مُيولٌ) tendency, inclination; tilt, bend, slope; affection, attachment
مَائِلٌ inclining, leaning, sloping

ن ز ل

نَزَلَ – يَنزِلُ to alight, descend, or get off; to be revealed (of Quran); to stay or lodge
نَزَّلَ – يُنَزِّلُ to lower, let down, or unload; to lodge; to download
أَنزَلَ – يُنْزِلُ to bring or take down; to dismount; to reveal (of God); to bestow (of God)
تَنَازَلَ – يَتَنَازَلُ to give up, renounce, or abandon; to waive or surrender
مَنزِلٌ (مَنازِلُ) house, dwelling, apartment; lunar phase
نُزولٌ descending; descent, landing (plane); arrival; a stay
تَنزيلٌ (تَنزيلاتٌ) revelation, inspiration; sales; downloading
تَنَازُلٌ relenting; relinquishment, surrender
عَدَمُ التَّنَازُلِ relentlessness, intransigence

ن ش د

نَشَدَ – يَنشُدُ to seek or search; to implore

334 Culture, Religion, and Society

ناشَدَ – يُناشِدُ to implore
أَنشَدَ – يُنشِدُ to seek or search; to sing or recite
نَشيدٌ / أُنشودَةٌ (نَشائِدُ / أَناشيدُ) anthem, song, hymn, chant
النَّشيدُ الْوَطنِيُّ national anthem
مُناشَدَةٌ (مُناشَداتٌ) appeal, urgent request
إِنشادٌ recitation, recital

No root

نَمَطٌ (أَنماطٌ) fashion, manner, way; shape; stereotype
صورَةٌ نَمَطِيَّةٌ stereotype
تَنميطٌ stereotyping

ن ه ض

نَهَضَ – يَنهَضُ to rise or get up; to pursue; to espouse or support
ناهَضَ – يُناهِضُ to resist, oppose, or defy
أَنهَضَ – يُنهِضُ to rise or awaken; to stir up or excite
إِنتَهَضَ – يَنتَهِضُ to get or stand up
إِستَنهَضَ – يَستَنهِضُ to awaken or rouse; to animate; to encourage or incite
نَهضَةٌ (نَهضاتٌ) awakening, revival, renaissance; rise, boom
نُهوضٌ raising; promotion; activation
مُناهَضَةٌ resistance, opposition

ه ج ن

هَجُنَ – يَهجُنُ to be incorrect or faulty
هَجَّنَ – يُهَجِّنُ to censure scathingly, to disparage or excoriate
إِستَهجَنَ – يَستَهجِنُ to consider (sth) as bad; to disapprove, condemn, or reject
هُجنَةٌ fault, defect, shortcoming
هَجينٌ (هُجَناءُ) lowly, base, mean; hybrid
إِستِهجانٌ disapproval, disapprobation

و ص م

وَصَمَ – يَصِمُ to disgrace or tarnish (name or honour)
وَصمٌ / وَصمَةٌ a disgrace

و ك ب

وَكَبَ – يَكِبُ to walk, proceed, or advance slowly
واكَبَ – يُواكِبُ to accompany or escort
مَوْكِبٌ (مَواكِبُ) procession, parade, cortege
مُواكَبَةٌ military escort

ي ق ظ

يَقِظَ – يَيْقَظُ to be awake or vigilant; to wake
أَيْقَظَ – يوقِظُ to wake up or awaken; to arouse or provoke
اِسْتَيْقَظَ – يَسْتَيْقِظُ to wake up or awaken; to be watchful or vigilant
يَقِظٌ (أَيْقاظٌ) awake; watchful, alert, vigilant
تَيَقُّظٌ vigilance, caution, alertness
مُسْتَيْقِظٌ awake

Exercises

1) Give two derived nouns for each of the following roots:

   أ ل ه
   ج س د
   ح ج ب
   ر و ح
   س ج د

2) Find the roots of the following words:

   الإسْلامُ
   اِنْتِصارٌ
   شيطانٌ
   صَليبٌ
   عِبادَةٌ
   فاحِشَةٌ

3) Give the plural of the following words (some may have more than one plural form):

   اِحْتِفالٌ
   تَضْحِيَةٌ

ثَقافَةٌ
ساحِرَةٌ
شائِعَةٌ
عَذراءُ
قِسّيسٌ
كافِرٌ
مَتحَفٌ
هَدِيَّةٌ

4) Give the Arabic words for the following definitions:

   a   National holidays
   b   Cult of personality
   c   I ask for God's forgiveness.
   d   The Holy Quran
   e   Orthodox Judaism

5) Translate into English:

   ـ تُعَدُّ الثَّقافةُ الْعَرَبِيَّةُ الإسلامِيَّةُ مِن أهمِّ الثَّقافاتِ.
   ـ شَهرُ رمضانَ شَهرٌ مُباركٌ.

6) Translate these sentences into Arabic:

   a) There are over one billion Muslims in the world.
   b) The Copts are the largest group of Christians in the Middle East.
   c) The boy performed his ablutions before praying.
   d) London is a multicultural city.
   e) The Jews consider themselves to be God's chosen people.

Notes

1 Usually said on either of the two Muslim Eids.
2 Literally, 'The Night of Decree'. This is the night in the month of Ramadan on which the Quran was first revealed to the Prophet Muhammad.
3 This is also used in Levantine dialects to mean 'to enter'.

9 Earth, Nature, and the Environment
الأرضُ والطَّبيعَةُ والبيئَةُ

Animals الحَيَواناتُ

No root

أبو سيفٍ swordfish

No root

أرْنَبٌ (أرانِبُ) rabbit, hare
أرْنَبٌ هِنْديٌّ guinea pig

أ س د

اِسْتَأْسَدَ – يَسْتَأْسِدُ to display the courage of a lion
أسَدٌ (أسودٌ) lion

No root

البَندا panda

No root

الغُرَيْرُ badger

No root

الكُوالُ / دُبٌّ أُسْتُراليٌّ koala

No root

الهامِسْتَرُ hamster

DOI: 10.4324/9781003250890-10

338 *Earth, Nature, and the Environment*

أ و ز

إِوَزَّةٌ (إِوَزٌّ) goose

أ و ى

أَوَى – يَأْوِي to seek refuge or shelter; to house or accommodate
مَأْوىً (مَآوٍ) retreat, shelter; habitation, abode
ابْنُ آوى (بَناتُ آوى) jackal

No root

بَجَعَةٌ (بَجَعاتٌ/بَجَعٌ) swan; pelican

No root

بَرٌّ land, terra firma; mainland
بَرّاً outside; by land
بَرِّيٌّ terrestrial, of or relating to land
بَرِّيَّةٌ (بَرارِي) open country; desert
الحَياةُ البَرِّيَّةُ wildlife
البَرمائِياتُ amphibians

No root

بِطريقٌ (بَطاريقُ) penguin

No root

بَطَّةٌ (بَطٌّ) duck
بَطَّةُ السّاقِ the calf of the leg

No root

بَغْلٌ (بِغالٌ / أَبغالٌ) mule

No root

بُلْبُلٌ (بَلابِلُ) a finch

ب ه م

أَبهَمَ – يُبهِمُ to make obscure or unintelligible

Earth, Nature, and the Environment 339

بَهِيمٌ (بُهُمٌ) jet black
بَهِيمَةٌ (بَهَائِمُ) animal, beast; livestock, cattle
بَهِيمِيٌّ / بَهِيمِيَّةٌ bestial, animal related; brutality
إِبهامٌ (أَباهيمُ) thumb; big toe
مُبهَمٌ dark, obscure, vague
عَدَدٌ مُبهَمٌ abstract number

ب ي ط ر

بَيْطَرَ – يُبَيْطِرُ to practise veterinary science
بَيْطارٌ (بَياطِرَةٌ) / بَيْطَرِيٌّ / بيطريّونَ veterinarian, vet
الطِّبُّ البَيْطَرِيُّ / البَيْطَرَةُ veterinary science

No root

ثَعلبٌ (ثَعالِبُ) fox

ث و ر

ثَوْرٌ (ثيرانٌ) bull, ox; Taurus

ج ر د

جَرادَةٌ (جَرادٌ) locusts
جَرادُ البَحرِ crayfish, langoustine

No root

جُرَذٌ / جِرْذَوْنٌ (جُرذانٌ / جَراذينُ) large rat

No root

جَملٌ (جِمالٌ / أَجمالٌ) camel
جَملُ اليَهودِ chameleon

ح ب ر

حَبَّرَ – يُحَبِّرُ to embellish or refine; to compose in elegant style
حِبْرٌ ink
أُمُّ الحِبرِ / الحَبّارُ squid, cuttlefish
حُبارى (حُبارياتٌ) bustard

ح ش ر

حَشَرَ – يَحشُرُ to gather or assemble; to cram, pack, or squeeze
يَوْمُ الْحَشْرِ Day of Resurrection
حَشَرَةٌ (حَشَراتٌ) insect

No root

حَلَزونٌ (حَلَزوناتٌ) snail; spiral

ح ي و / ح ي ي

حَيَّ – يَحيا to live; to experience or witness; to be ashamed
أَحْيا – يُحْيي to enliven, animate, or revive; to celebrate
اِستَحى – يَستَحي to be ashamed or embarrassed
حَيٌّ (أَحْياءٌ) living, alive; active, energetic; organism; district
المادَّةُ الحَيَّةُ living matter
عِلمُ الأَحْياءِ / الأَحْياءُ biology
كيمياءٌ أَحيائِيَّةٌ bio-chemistry
إِحْيائِيٌّ (إِحْيائِيّونَ) biological; biologist
حَيَّةٌ (حَيّاتٌ) snake, viper
حَياءٌ shyness
قَليلُ الْحَياءِ shameless, impudent
حَياةٌ (حَيَواتٌ) life; liveliness
حَيَوِيٌّ lively, vigorous
حَيَوِيَّةٌ vitality, vigour (n); bio, vital, important (adj)
حَيَوانٌ (حَيَواناتٌ) animal, beast; living creatures
حَديقةُ الحَيَوانِ zoo
حَيَوانٌ أَليفٌ domesticated animal
عِلمُ الحَيَوانِ zoology
المَملَكةُ الحَيَوانِيَّةُ animal kingdom
جَمعِيَّةُ الرِّفقِ بِالحَيَوانِ RSPCA
حَيَواناتٌ ثَدِيَّةٌ mammals
الحَيَواناتُ المُتَغَيِّرَةُ الحَرارَةِ / الحَيَواناتُ ذَواتُ الدَّمِ البارِدِ cold-blooded animals
حَيَواناتٌ فَقرِيَّةٌ / الفَقارِياتُ vertebrates
حَيَواناتٌ طُفَيلِيَّةٌ / الطُّفَيلِياتُ parasites
حَيَواناتٌ هُلامِيَّةٌ / الرَّخَوِياتُ molluscs
تَحِيَّةٌ (تَحِيّاتٌ / تَحايا) greeting

Earth, Nature, and the Environment 341

No root

خَرتيتٌ / سيِّد قِشطَة hippopotamus

No root

خَفَشٌ day blindness
أَخفَشُ (خُفشٌ) poor sighted
خُفَّاشٌ (خَفافيشُ) bat

خ ل ب

خَلَبَ – يَخلُبُ to claw or clutch; to pounce; to coax; to charm
اِختَلَبَ – يَختَلِبُ to claw, clutch; to pounce; to enchant
خِلبٌ (أَخْلابٌ) claw, talon; fingernail
خَلّابٌ captivating, attractive; deceitful
مِخلَبٌ (مَخالِبُ) claw, talon

No root

خُنفُسٌ (خَنافِسُ) dung beetle, scarab

د ج ن

دَجَنَ – يَدجُنُ to be domesticated or tame; to be gloomy; to remain or stay
دَجَّنَ – يُدَجِّنُ to tame or domesticate
أَدجَنَ – يُدجِنُ to be murky, gloomy, or dark
دُجنَةٌ darkness, gloom
داجِنٌ tame, domesticated; dark, gloomy
حَيواناتٌ داجِنَةٌ domesticated animals
دَواجِنُ poultry

د و د

دَوَّدَ – يُدَوِّدُ to be or become worm-eaten
دودَةٌ / دودٌ (ديدانٌ) worm, maggot, caterpillar, larva
دودَةُ الحَريرِ / دودةُ القَزِّ silkworm
الدّودَةُ الوَحيدَةُ tapeworm
دودَةُ الأَرضِ earthworm
مُدَوَّدٌ worm-eaten

No root

رِيمٌ white antelope

ز أ ر

زَأَرَ – يَزْأَرُ to roar or bellow
زَئِيرٌ roaring, bellowing

ز ح ف

زَحَفَ – يَزْحَفُ to crawl or creep; to advance (army)
زَحْفٌ (زُحوفٌ) advance; march (army)
زَحَّافٌ creeping, crawling
زاحِفٌ (زواحِفُ) reptiles

ز ر ز ر

زَرْزَرَ – يُزَرْزِرُ to chirp
زُرْزُرٌ / زَرْزورٌ (زَرازيرُ) starling

No root

زِعْنِفَةٌ / زَعَنَفَةٌ (زَعانِفُ) riff-raff, mob; low, base, mean
زَعانِفُ fins (fish), flippers (whales, dolphins, etc.)

س ر ح

سَرَحَ – يَسْرَحُ to move away or leave; to graze freely
سَرْحانٌ wolf

No root

سَرَطانُ الْبَحرِ / سَلْطَعونٌ crab

No root

سُلْحَفاةٌ (سَلاحِفُ) tortoise, turtle
سُلْحَفاةٌ بَحرِيَّةٌ / سُلْحَفاةُ الْماءِ turtle

س م ك

سَمَكَ – يُسَمِّكُ to thicken

Earth, Nature, and the Environment   343

سُمْكٌ thickness
سَمَكٌ (أَسْماكٌ) fish
سَمَكُ السَّردينِ sardines
سَمَكَةُ البوري / سُلطان إبراهيم red mullet
سَمَكَةُ الأطروط / سَمَكَةُ التَّرْوْتَة trout
سَمَكَةُ التُّنِّ tuna
سَمَكَةُ السَّلْمونِ salmon
سَمَكَةُ القاروصِ / سَمَكَةُ الشَّبَصِ seabass
سَمَكَةُ القُدِّ cod
سَمَكَةُ القِرشِ shark
سَمَكَةُ الهَلْبوتِ halibut
سَمَكَةُ موسى plaice/sole
سَمَكُ الرّايِ اللَّسّاعِ / اللَّخَمَةُ stingray

ش ب ل

شَبَلَ – يَشْبُلُ to live and grow up in luxury
أَشْبَلَ – يُشْبِلُ to take care of or look after; to give birth to lion cubs
شِبْلٌ (أَشْبالٌ) lion cub

ص ه ل

صَهَلَ – يَصْهَلُ to whinny or neigh (horse)
صَهيلٌ neighing

No root

ضَرْغَمٌ / ضِرْغامٌ (ضَراغِمُ / ضَراغِمَةٌ) lion

No root

ضِفْدَعٌ (ضَفادِعُ) frog

ط ي ر

(Full treatment in Politics chapter)

طارَ – يَطيرُ to fly
طَيْرٌ / طائِرٌ (طُيورٌ) bird; omen

No root

ظَبْيٌ (ظِباءٌ) gazelle
ظَبْيَةٌ (ظَبِياتٌ) female gazelle
أَبُو ظَبِي Abu Dhabi

ع ج ل

عَجِلَ – يَعجِلُ to hurry, hasten, speed
عِجْلٌ (عُجُولٌ) calf
عِجْلُ البَحْرِ / فُقْمَةٌ seal

ع ش ش

عَشَّشَ – يُعَشِّشُ to nest or build a nest; to take root or settle in
عُشٌّ (عِشاشٌ / أَعشاشٌ) nest

No root

عُصفورٌ (عَصافيرُ) sparrow; any small bird
عُصفورُ الجَنَّةِ swallow
عُصفورٌ دَوْرِيٌّ house sparrow
عُصفورٌ مُغَنٍّ warbler
عُصفورٌ كَناري canary
عُصفورَةٌ female bird
العُصفوريَّةُ insane asylum

No root

عَقرَبٌ (عَقاربُ) scorpion; sting; hand (clock, watch)

No root

عَندَليبٌ (عَنادِلُ) nightingale

No root

عَنزٌ (عِنازٌ) goat
عَنزَةٌ (عَنزاتٌ) nanny goat

Earth, Nature, and the Environment   345

No root

عَنْكَبوتٌ (عَناكِبُ) spider
بَيْتُ الْعَنكبوتِ/نَسيجُ الْعَنكبوتِ spider web, cobweb

ف ح ل

(Full treatment in Health chapter)

فَحلٌ (فُحولٌ) stallion; male (of large animals); a star or celebrity; virile

ف ر س

فَرَسَ – يَفرِسُ to kill or tear (of a predatory animal)
اِفتَرَسَ – يَفتَرِسُ to kill prey; to ravish or rape (a woman)
فَرَسٌ (أَفراسٌ) horse, stallion, mare (this is both m and f)
فَرَسُ البَحرِ/فَرَسُ النَّهرِ hippopotamus
فُروسِيَّةٌ/فُروسَةٌ knighthood; valour
فِراسَةٌ perspicacity, acumen
فَريسَةٌ (فرائسُ) prey
فارِسٌ (فُرْسانٌ) knight, horseman (pl: cavalry) (also a boy's name in the singular)
مُفتَرِسٌ rapacious; ravenous (of an animal)

ف ر ش

فَرَشَ – يَفرُشُ to spread; to pave or cover
اِفتَرَشَ – يَفتَرِشُ to spread out or lie down; to sleep with (a woman)
فَرشٌ (فُروشٌ) furnishings, furniture; bedding (when laid out on the ground)
فَرشَةٌ (فَرشاتٌ) mattress, bed
فَراشٌ moths, butterflies
فَراشَةٌ moth, butterfly; a fickle or flighty person
يَرقةُ الفراشَةِ/يَسروعٌ caterpillar

No root

فَظٌّ (أفظاظٌ) walrus; rude, uncivil

No root

فيلٌ (فِيَلَةٌ) elephant
فيلُ البَحرِ walrus

No root

فَهْدٌ (فُهودٌ / أَفْهادٌ) cheetah, lynx, panther, leopard

No root

قُبَّرَةٌ (قُبَّرٌ) lark

No root

قِرْدٌ (قِرَدَةٌ / قُرودٌ) monkey, ape
قُرادٌ / قُرادَةٌ (قِردانٌ) tick

ق ر ض

(Full treatment in Work chapter)

قَراضَةٌ clothes moth
القَوارِضُ rodents

ق ر ن

(Full treatment in Family chapter)

قَرْنٌ (قُرونٌ) horn, tentacle
وَحيدُ القَرْنِ / أُمُّ القَرْنِ rhinoceros

No root

قَشْعَمٌ (قَشاعِمُ) lion
أُمُّ قَشْعَمٍ hyena; eagle (female); calamity, disaster

No root

قِطٌّ (قِطَطٌ) tomcat, cat
قِطَّةٌ female cat
قُطَيْطَةٌ kitten

No root

قِنْديلٌ (قَناديلُ) lamp, candlestick
قِنْديلُ البَحرِ jellyfish

Earth, Nature, and the Environment

No root

قُنْفُذٌ (قَنَافِذُ) hedgehog
قُنْفُذُ البَحرِ sea urchin

No root

قَوقَعٌ seashell
قَوقَعَةٌ (قَواقِعُ) snail; crustaceans

ل ق ل ق

لَقْلَقَ – يُلَقلِقُ to clatter (stork); to babble, chatter, or prattle
لَقْلَقٌ / لَقلاقٌ (لَقالِقُ) stork
لَقلَقَةٌ clatter (of a stork); babble, chatter, prattle; gossip

No root

مَعَزٌّ / ماعِزٌ (أَمعُزٌ / مَواعِزُ) goat

ن ب ح

نَبَحَ – يَنبَحُ to bark
نَبحٌ / نُباحٌ / نَبيحٌ barking

ن ج م

نَجَمَ – يَنجُمُ to appear or come into sight; to rise (star); to begin; to follow
تَنَجَّمَ – يَتَنَجَّمُ to observe the stars; to predict the future using the stars
نَجمٌ (نُجومٌ) star, lucky star, constellation; male film star; partial payment
نَجمُ البَحرِ starfish
نُجَيمَةٌ small star; starlet
مَنجَمٌ (مَناجِمُ) a mine; origin
مُنَجِّمٌ (مُنَجِّمونَ) astrologers
تَنجيمٌ astrology

ن س ر

تَنَسَّرَ – يَتَنَسَّرُ to be torn; to break or snap
اِستَنسَرَ – يَستَنسِرُ to become eagle-like
نَسرٌ (نُسورٌ / نُسورَةٌ) eagle, vulture

ن ع م

نَعَمَ – يَنْعُمُ to live in comfort and luxury; to be happy or delighted
نَعَّمَ – يُنَعِّمُ to smooth, soften, or pulverise; to pamper
نَعَمْ yes, indeed, certainly
نَعَمٌ (أَنعامٌ) grazing livestock
نِعمةٌ (نِعَمٌ / نِعماتٌ) benefit, blessing, favour
نُعْمانُ blood
نَعامٌ (نَعائِمُ) ostrich
نَعيمٌ comfort, ease, happiness
نُعومَةٌ softness, tenderness
ناعِمٌ soft

ن ق ر

نَقَرَ – يَنْقُرُ to dig or excavate; to pierce; to engrave or inscribe
نَقَّرَ – يُنَقِّرُ to peck; to investigate or examine
نَقّارٌ carver, engraver
نَقّارُ الْخَشبِ woodpecker
مِنقارٌ (مَناقيرُ) beak, bill (of bird)

ن م ر

تَنَمَّرَ – يَتَنَمَّرُ to become angry or furious; to turn into a tiger
نَمِرٌ (نُمورٌ / أنمارٌ) tiger
نُمْرَةٌ (نُمَرٌ) spot, speck; tag
مُنَمَّرٌ spotted, striped

ن م س

نَمَسَ – ينمِسُ to hide, conceal, or keep secret
نِمسٌ (نُموسٌ) mongoose, ferret, weasel
ناموسٌ (نَواميسُ) mosquito; sly; a confidant

ن ه ق

نَهَقَ – يَنهَقُ to bray (donkey)
نَهيقٌ braying

Earth, Nature, and the Environment 349

No root

نَوْرَسٌ / نَوْرَسُ الْبَحْرِ seagull

ن و ق

تَنَوَّقَ – يَتَنَوَّقُ to be squeamish; to be fastidious
نَاقَةٌ (نوقٌ / نَاقاتٌ) she-camel
نَيِّقٌ squeamish; fastidious

ه ر ر

هَرَّ – يَهِرُّ to growl, whimper, or whine
هِرٌّ (هِرَرَةٌ) tomcat, cat
هِرَّةٌ (هِرَرٌ) cat
هَرِيرٌ growling; whining, whimpering; spitting (of a cat)
هُرَيْرَةٌ kitten

و ح ش

أَوْحَشَ – يوحِشُ to be deserted; to oppress; to make someone feel lonely
تَوَحَّشَ – يَتَوَحَّشُ to be brutal; to be desolate; to be or become wild or savage
وَحْشٌ (وُحوشٌ) wild animal or beast; wild, untamed; lonely
الْوُحوشُ الضَّارِيَةُ predatory animals
وَحْشَةٌ / إيحاشٌ loneliness
وَحْشِيٌّ wild, untamed, brutish, cruel
تَوَحُّشٌ savagery, brutality
مُتَوَحِّشٌ wild (animal); savage, barbaric

و ل و ل

وَلْوَلَ – يُوَلْوِلُ to howl; to wail
وَلْوَلَةٌ (وَلاوِلُ) wailing; wails

ي ر ع

يَرَعَ – يَيْرَعُ to be a coward
يَرَاعٌ firefly, glowworm; cowardly; cane, reed; pen

No root

يَرَقانٌ larvae; jaundice; mildew
يَرَقانُ الضَّفادِعِ tadpoles

Weather and Climate الطَّقسُ والمُناخُ

ب ر ق

بَرَقَ – يَبرُقُ to strike (of lightning); to light up or flash; to shine or sparkle
أَبرقَ – يُبرِقُ to strike (of lightning); to light up or flash; to cable or telegraph
بَرقٌ (بُروقٌ) lightning flash; a telegraph

ج ف ف

جَفَّ – يَجِفُّ to become dry or dry out
جَفَّفَ – يُجَفِّفُ to dry or make dry
جَفافٌ drought; dryness
تَجفيفٌ drying; dehydration
مُجَفَّفٌ dried, dehydrated

No root

جَوٌّ (أَجواءٌ) sky, atmosphere, air, weather
جَوّاً by air
جَوِّيٌّ air, atmospheric, aerial, aero-
غِلافٌ جَوِّيٌّ atmosphere
الضَّغطُ الْجَوِّيُّ atmospheric pressure
التَّوَقُّعاتُ الْجَوِّيَّةُ weather forecast
الأَحوالُ الْجَوِّيَّةُ atmospheric conditions

خ ر ف

خَرِفَ – يَخرَفُ to be senile; to talk foolishly; to spend the autumn
خَرَفٌ feeble-mindedness, senility
الْخَريفُ autumn
خَريفِيٌّ autumnal
خَروفٌ (خِرفانٌ) young sheep, lamb
خُرافَةٌ (خُرافاتٌ) superstition; fable, fairy tale
خُرافِيٌّ fabulous; legendary

Earth, Nature, and the Environment 351

ر ب ع

رَبَعَ – يَرْبَعُ to sit, stay, or live; to gallop (horse); to approach (of spring)
رَبَّعَ – يُرَبِّعُ to quadruple; to square (a number)
رَبْعٌ (رُبوعٌ) home, residence; region, area; group of people
رُبْعٌ (أرباعٌ) a quarter
رَبيعٌ spring
أربَعَةٌ four
يَومُ الأربِعاءِ Wednesday
مُرَبَّعٌ (مُرَبَّعاتٌ) square

ر ذ ذ

رَذَّ – يَرَذُّ to drizzle
رَذاذٌ drizzle

ر ط ب

رَطَبَ – يَرطُبُ to be moist, damp, or humid
رَطْبٌ moist, damp, humid; juicy
رُطوبَةٌ humidity, moisture, dampness
مُعَدَّلُ الرُّطوبَةِ humidity levels
راطِبٌ / رَطيبٌ / رَطِبٌ moist, damp, humid, wet
مُرطِّباتٌ refreshments, soft drinks

ر ع د

رَعَدَ – يَرعَدُ to thunder
رَعْدٌ (رُعودٌ) thunder
رَعّادٌ a stingray or electric ray

س ح ب

سَحَبَ – يَسحَبُ to withdraw; to pull out; to drag along
اِنسَحَبَ – يَنسَحِبُ to pull out or retreat; to fall back
سَحْبٌ withdrawal (troops, money, rights, etc.)
سَحابٌ clouds
سَحابَةٌ (سُحُبٌ / سحائِبُ) clouds
سَحابَةُ رَمادٍ ash cloud
سَحّابٌ zip

352 Earth, Nature, and the Environment

مَسْحوبُ الهَواءِ air vacuum
اِنْسِحابٌ withdrawal, retreat; evacuation

س ر ب

سَرَبَ – يَسرُبُ to flow, run out, or leak
تَسَرَّبَ – يَتَسَرَّبُ to flow; to escape, to sneak or steal away; to penetrate
اِنْسرَبَ – يَنْسرِبُ to hide in or crawl into its lair (animal)
تَسَرُّبُ المَعلوماتِ / تَسريباتٌ leaked information
سِرْبٌ (أَسرابٌ) group; herd, flock, swarm; squadron
سِرْبٌ مِن النَّحْلِ swarm of bees
سَرَبٌ (أَسرابٌ) burrow, lair, den; underground passage
سُرْبَةٌ (سُرَبٌ) herd, flock, swarm
سَرابٌ mirage, phantom
مَسرَبٌ (مَسارِبُ) river bed; drain, sewer; lane, motorway

ش ت و

شَتا – يَشتو to pass the winter; to become cold; to hibernate
شَتَّى – يُشَتّي to rain; to pass the winter; to hibernate
شِتاءٌ winter; rainy season

ش م س

شَمَسَ – يَشمُسُ to be sunny; to be headstrong
شَمَّسَ – يُشَمِّسُ to expose (sth) to the sun; to lay (sth) out in the sun to dry
أَشمَسَ – يُشمِسُ to be sunny
تَشَمَّسَ – يَتَشَمَّسُ to sunbathe
شَمسٌ (شُموسٌ) sun
شُروقُ الشَّمسِ sunrise
غُروبُ الشَّمسِ sunset
دَوَّارُ الشَّمسِ sunflower
شَمسِيٌّ solar/sun-
الحُروفُ الشَّمسيَّةُ the sun letters (in Arabic grammar)
طاقةٌ شَمسيَّةٌ solar power
أَلواحُ الطّاقةِ الشَّمسيَّةِ solar panels
المَجموعةُ الشَّمسيَّةُ the solar system

Earth, Nature, and the Environment 353

شَمسِيَّةٌ (شَمسِيّاتٌ) umbrella, parasol
مُشمِسٌ sunny

ص ق ع

صَقَعَ – يَصقَعُ to crow (cock)
صَقَعَ – يُصقَعُ to be icy or ice-cold
صَقعٌ (أَصقاعٌ) area, region, district
صَقعَةٌ frost; severe cold[1]
صَقيعٌ frost, ice

ص ي ف

صَيَّفَ – يُصَيِّفُ to spend the summer
صَيفٌ (أَصيافٌ) summer
صَيفِيٌّ summery
مَصيَفٌ / مُصطافٌ (مَصايفُ / مُصطافونَ) summer resort

ض ب ب

ضَبَّ – يَضُبُّ to take hold; to keep under lock and key, or to guard carefully
أَضَبَّ – يُضِبُّ to be foggy
ضَبٌّ (ضِبابٌ / ضُبّانٌ) lizard
ضَبابٌ fog, mist

ط ق س

طَقَّسَ – يُطَقِّسُ to introduce into one of the orders of the Christian church
تَطَقَّسَ – يَتَطَقَّسُ to perform a rite or ritual
طَقسٌ (طُقوسٌ) weather, climate (pl: rites, rituals, religious customs)
تَنَبُّؤاتُ الطَّقسِ weather forecast
طُقوسٌ دينِيَّةٌ religious rituals

غ ي م

غامَ – يَغيمُ to become cloudy or overcast (of sky); to become blurred
غَيَّمَ – يُغَيِّمُ to cloud over or become cloudy; to billow or waft (smoke)
غَيمٌ (غُيومٌ) clouds, mist, fog
غائِمٌ foggy, overcast, cloudy
مُتَغَيِّمٌ / مُغَيِّمٌ clouded, overcast

ف ص ل

(Full treatment in Law chapter)

فَصْلٌ (فُصولٌ) season; semester, term; class; separation
فُصولُ السَّنَةِ seasons of the year

ق ح ط

قَحَطَ – يَقْحَطُ to be withheld (also of rain)
أَقْحَطَ – يُقْحِطُ to be rainless
قَحْطٌ drought, famine; scarcity

ق ح ل

قَحِلَ – يَقْحَلُ to be or become dry or arid; to wither or dry up
قَحْلٌ/قُحولَةٌ dryness, aridity
قاحِلٌ/قَحِلٌ barren; dry, arid

ق و س

قَوِسَ – يَقْوَسُ to be bent, curved, or crooked
قَوَّسَ – يُقَوِّسُ to bend or curve; to shoot (an arrow)
قَوْسٌ (أَقْواسٌ) arch, arc; a violin or bow
قَوْسُ قُزَحٍ rainbow

م ط ر

مَطَرَ – يَمْطُرُ to rain or pour out; to shower or douse
أَمْطَرَ – يُمْطِرُ to rain or cause to rain; to shower (someone with things)
مَطَرٌ (أَمْطارٌ) rain
أَمْطارٌ حِمْضِيَّةٌ acid rain
أَمْطارٌ سَوداءُ black rain
مَطْرَةٌ (مَطْراتٌ) downpour (rain)
مَطِرٌ/ماطِرٌ/مُمطِرٌ rainy
أَمْطارٌ مَوسِمِيَّةٌ monsoon rain
مَواسِمُ مُمطِرَةٌ rainy seasons

No root

مُناخ (مُناخاتٌ) climate

Earth, Nature, and the Environment 355

تَغْيُّرٌ مُناخِيٌّ climate change
مُكافَحَةُ تَغَيُّرِ المُناخِ combatting climate change
الاخْتِلالُ المُناخِيُّ climate change

م و ج

ماجَ – يَموجُ to heave, swell, or roll; to be excited
تَمَوَّجَ – يَتَمَوَّجُ to rise in waves or undulate; to be rippled
مَوْجٌ (أَمْواجٌ) waves, ripples; billows
مَوْجَةٌ (مَوجاتٌ) sea; waves, ripples, undulation; vibration
مَوْجَةُ حَرٍّ heat wave
تَمَوُّجٌ (تَمَوُّجاتٌ) oscillation, vibration, undulation
تَمَوُّجاتٌ صَوْتِيَّةٌ sound waves
مائِجٌ surging, tumultuous, stormy, high (sea)

ن س م

نَسَمَ – يَنسِمُ to blow gently
نَسَمٌ (أَنسامٌ) breath
نَسَمَةٌ (نَسَماتٌ) breath, breeze; person, soul (also a girl's name in the singular)
نَسيمٌ (نِسامٌ/نَسائِمُ) breeze, fresh air (also a boy's name in the singular)

ه ط ل

هَطَلَ – يَهطِلُ to rain heavily or pour down
تَهاطَلَ – يَتَهاطَلُ to rain heavily or pour down
هِطْلٌ/هَيْطَلٌ (هَياطِلَةٌ/هياطِلُ) wolf
هُطولٌ heavy rain, downpour

ه و ى

(Full treatment in Education chapter)

هُوَّةٌ (هُوىً/هُوّاتٌ) abyss, chasm, hole; pit, ditch
هَواءٌ (أَهْوِيَةٌ/أَهْواءٌ) air, atmosphere; weather, climate; a draft of air, wind
طَواحينُ الهَواءِ windmill
هَوائِيٌّ airy, breezy; atmospheric
هَوّايَةٌ (هَوّاياتٌ) fan, ventilator
تَهوِيَةٌ airing, ventilation

و ب ل

وَبَلَ – يَبِلُ to pour down (rain)
وَبُلَ – يَوْبُلُ to be unhealthy or noxious (climate, air)
وَبلٌ downpour
وابلٌ hail
وَبيلٌ unhealthy, unwholesome (climate), hurtful, noxious; disastrous

و س م

وَسَمَ – يَسِمُ to brand, stamp, or mark; to stigmatise
وَسَّمَ – يُوَسِّمُ to distinguish
سِمَةٌ (سِماتٌ) sign, mark, characteristic; features, facial expression
وَسمٌ (وُسومٌ) brand, mark; characteristic; coat of arms; tag (internet)
وِسامٌ (أَوْسِمَةٌ) badge, medal; decoration (also a boy's name in the singular)
وَسيمٌ (وُسَماءُ) handsome, graceful, beautiful
مَوسِمٌ (مَواسِمُ) season; festival

الكَوارِثُ الطَّبيعيَّةُ Natural Disasters

No root

بُركانٌ (بَراكينُ) volcanoes
بُركانِيٌّ volcanic

No root

تسونامي tsunami

ز ل ز ل

زَلْزَلَ – يُزَلْزِلُ to shake or convulse; to cause to tremble
تَزَلْزَلَ – يَتَزَلْزَلُ to quake (earth); to be shaken
زِلزالٌ/زَلْزَلَةٌ (زَلازِلُ) earthquake; convulsion; shock, concussion

No root

زَوْبَعَةٌ (زَوابِعُ) storm, hurricane

ط ب ع

طَبَعَ – يَطْبَعُ to impress, print, stamp, or seal

Earth, Nature, and the Environment 357

طَبَّعَ – يُطَبِّعُ to tame, domesticate, or train
تَطَبَّعَ – يَتَطَبَّعُ to assume another's characteristics or traits
طَبْعٌ (طِباعٌ) characteristic; nature, disposition; print, stamp
طَبْعاً naturally
طَبْعَةٌ (طَبَعاتٌ) edition, issue; printing
طَبَّاعٌ / طابِعٌ printer
طِباعَةٌ printing
طَبيعَةٌ (طَبائِعُ) nature, constitution, character
الطَّبيعَةُ nature
بِطبيعةِ الْحالِ naturally
فَوْقَ الطَّبيعةِ supernatural
ما وراءَ الطَّبيعةِ metaphysics
طَبيعيٌّ natural, innate, relating to nature
الإِنتِقاءُ الطَّبيعيُّ natural selection
مَوارِدُ طَبيعِيَّةٌ natural resources
مَطْبَعَةٌ (مَطابِعُ) printing press; publishing house
طابَعٌ (طَوابِعُ) character; stamp, seal, imprint
مَطبوعٌ (مَطبوعاتٌ) printed materials, newspapers and magazines; printed (adj)
اِنطِباعٌ (اِنطِباعاتٌ) impression

ع ص ر

عَصَرَ – يَعصِرُ to press or squeeze (fruits, olives etc.); to wring or compress
عاصَرَ – يُعاصِرُ to be a contemporary
اِنعصَرَ – يَنعصِرُ to be squeezed or pressed
عَصْرٌ pressing, squeezing; wringing
عَصْرٌ (عُصورٌ) time, age, period; afternoon
عَصْريٌّ contemporary, modern, recent
عَصيرٌ juice
إِعصارٌ (أَعاصيرُ) whirlwind, hurricane, typhoon, tornado, cyclone
مُعاصِرٌ (مُعاصِرونَ) contemporary

ع ص ف

عَصَفَ – يَعصِفُ to storm, rage, or blow violently
عَصْفٌ storming, blowing
عاصِفٌ blowing violently (also a boy's name)
ريحٌ عاصِفٌ violent wind, gale

358 Earth, Nature, and the Environment

عاصِفَةٌ (عَواصِفُ) hurricane, tempest, gale, storm
عَواصِفُ رَعدِيَّةٌ thunderstorms
عَواصِفُ رَملِيَّةٌ sandstorms

No root

على مقياسِ ريختَر / بِمقياسِ ريختَر on the Richter scale

ك ر ث

إكتَرَثَ – يَكتَرِثُ to take care or heed
كُرَّاثٌ leek (food)
إكتِراثٌ attention, care, heed, concern
قِلَّةُ الإكتِراثِ indifference
كارِثٌ oppressive, depressing, grievous, painful
كارِثَةٌ (كَوارِثُ) disaster, catastrophe
الكَوارِثُ الطَّبيعيَّةُ natural disasters
كارِثَةٌ بيئيَّةٌ environmental disaster

ن و ع

ناءَ – يَنوعُ to collapse, fall, or sink down; to oppress someone grievously
نَوعٌ (أنواعٌ) tempest, storm, gale, hurricane; disaster
الأنواعُ الطَّبيعيَّةُ natural disasters
مُناوَأةٌ resistance, opposition, struggle; insubordination

ه ز ز

هَزَّ – يَهُزُّ to shake, rock, swing, or make tremble
اِهتَزَّ – يَهتَزُّ to tremble, quake, or quiver; to be moved
هَزَّةٌ (هَزَّاتٌ) tremor, shake, vibration; motion; agitation, convulsion
هَزَّةٌ أرضيَّةٌ earth tremor, seismic shock
اِهتِزازٌ shock, tremor; trembling, shaking
مَوجةُ اِهتِزازٍ shock wave

ه و ر

(Full treatment in Health chapter)

اِنهيارٌ a crash, fall, or downfall; a collapse or breakdown

Earth, Nature, and the Environment 359

اِنهيارٌ أَرضِيٌّ avalanche
اِنهيارٌ طينيٌّ mudslide

Natural Resources and Energy المَوارِدُ الطَّبيعِيَّةُ والطَّاقَةُ

No root

إعادَةُ التَّدوير recycling

No root

تَيَّارٌ (تَيَّاراتٌ) flow, stream, course, current

ج ذ ب

جَذَبَ – يَجذِبُ to pull, draw, attract, or appeal to
تَجاذَبَ – يَتَجاذَبُ to pull back and forth; to contend; to attract each other
جَذبٌ attraction, gravitation; appeal, lure
جَذَّابٌ / جاذِبٌ attractive; charming, captivating
اِنجِذابٌ attraction; tendency
جاذِبِيَّةٌ attraction, gravitation; charm, fascination
الْجاذِبِيَّةُ الأَرضِيَّةُ gravity
مَجذوبٌ (مَجاذيبُ) possessed (by demons); insane (pl: maniac, madman, idiot)

ج ر ب

جَرِبَ – يَجرَبُ to be mangy; to fade (colour)
جَرَّبَ – يُجَرِّبُ to test, to try, or sample; to rehearse
جَرَبٌ itch, scabies
أَجرَبُ (جُربٌ) mangy
جُرابٌ (جُراباتٌ) socks
تَجرِبةٌ (تَجارِبُ) trial, test, experiment; attempt, practice
حَقلُ تَجارُبٍ field of experiment or guinea pig
تَجريبِيٌّ experimental
مُجَرَّبٌ tried, tested

ج ز أ

جَزَأَ – يَجزَأُ to be content
تَجَزَّأَ – يَتَجَزَّأُ to divide; to be separated or partitioned off

جُزْءٌ (أَجْزاءٌ) part, portion, component, division; section (of the Quran)
جُزْئِيٌّ partial; minor, trivial
جُزْئِيّاً partly
جُزَيْءٌ (جُزَيْئاتٌ) particle, molecule
تَجْزِئَةٌ division, partition

ح ط ب

حَطَبَ – يَحطِبُ to gather firewood
حَطَبٌ (أَحطابٌ) firewood

ح ف ز

حَفَزَ – يَحفِزُ to pierce or stab; to incite or urge
تَحَفَّزَ – يَتَحَفَّزُ to get ready or prepare oneself; to pay attention
اِحتَفَزَ – يَحتَفِزُ to be ready
تَحَفُّزٌ readiness, preparedness
حافِزٌ (حَوافِزُ) drive, incentive
مُتَحَفِّزٌ (لِ) ready, prepared (for)
عامِلٌ مُحَفِّزٌ external factor; catalyst

No root

خامٌ (خاماتٌ) raw materials; raw, unprocessed, unskilled
المَوادُّ الخامُ raw materials

خ ش ب

خَشَّبَ – يُخَشِّبُ to become wood-like; to line with wood
تَخَشَّبَ – يَتَخَشَّبُ to become wood-like; to become hard, stiff, or rigid
خَشَبٌ (أَخْشابٌ) wood, timber, lumber
خَشَبَةٌ (خَشَباتٌ/أَخْشابٌ) a piece or plank of wood
تَخَشُّبٌ stiffness, rigor, rigidity
الخَشَبُ المَيِّتُ dead wood

خ ص ب

(Full treatment in Health chapter)

خَصَبَ – يَخصِبُ to be fertile

Earth, Nature, and the Environment 361

خَصَّبَ – يُخَصِّبُ to enrich; to fertilise or make fertile
خَصِبٌ / خَصِيبٌ fertile
تَخْصِيبُ الْيُورانيومِ uranium enrichment
يورانيوم مُخَصَّبٌ جِداً highly enriched uranium

د م ج

دَمَجَ – يدمِجُ to be incorporated
دَمَّجَ – يُدَمِّجُ to write shorthand
اِندَمَجَ – يَندَمِجُ to be inserted or incorporated; to be annexed; to merge or be absorbed
تَدميجٌ shorthand
اِندِماجٌ fusion, merging; assimilation, insertion
اِندِماجٌ نَوَوِيٌّ nuclear fission

ذ ر ر

ذَرَّ – يَذُرُّ to scatter, sprinkle, or spread
ذَرٌّ atoms; specks; sprinkling
ذَرَّةٌ (ذَرَّاتٌ) atom; tiny particle, speck
ذَرِّيٌّ atomic
قُنْبُلَةٌ ذَرِّيَّةٌ atomic bomb
طاقَةٌ ذَرِّيَّةٌ atomic energy
ذُرِّيَّةٌ (ذُرِّيَّاتٌ) descendants, children

ش ع ع

شَعَّ – يَشِعُّ to radiate; to diffuse or spread
أَشَعَّ – يُشِعُّ to radiate or emit rays; to spread or diffuse
شُعاعٌ (أَشِعَّةٌ) rays, beams
الأَشِعَّةُ radiology
أَشِعَّةٌ سِينِيَّةٌ / أَشِعَّةُ إكس X-rays
الأَشِعَّةُ فَوقَ البَنَفسَجِيَّةِ ultra-violet rays
الأَشِعَّةُ تَحتَ الحَمراءِ infrared rays
إِشعاعٌ (إشعاعاتٌ) radiation; radioactive
ذو نَشاطٍ إشْعاعِيٍّ radioactive
تَسَرُّبٌ إشعاعِيٌّ radioactive fallout
مُشِعٌّ radioactive

ص ف و

صفا – يَصفو to be or become clear, unpolluted, or pure
صَفَّى – يُصَفِّي to purify or filter; to settle, pay or liquidate (accounts)
صافى – يُصافي to be sincere or deal honestly
اِصطَفى – يَصطَفى to choose or select
صَفوانٌ stone, rock
صِفوةٌ sincere friend, best friend
صَفاءٌ clearness, clarity, purity; serenity, happiness (also a girl's name)
صَفِيٌّ (أَصفِياءُ) clear, serene, pure (pl: good friends)
مِصفاةٌ (مَصافٍ) strainer, filter, sieve; refinery, purification plant
مِصفاةُ النَّفطِ oil refinery
تَصفِيَةٌ (تَصفِياتٌ) purification, filtration; settlement, liquidation (accounts)
تَصفِيَةٌ نِهائِيَّةٌ final settlement
تَصفِيَةُ الحِساباتِ settlement of accounts
تَصافٍ (بَينَ) compromise (between), peaceful settlement; good will
صافٍ / الصّافي net
مُصَفًّى purified, pure, clear, limpid
مُصْطَفى chosen, selected (also a boy's name)
المُصْطَفى epithet of Prophet Muhammad

ط و ق

طاقَ – يَطوقُ to be able or capable; to bear, stand, or sustain
طَوَّقَ – يُطَوِّقُ to put a collar or necklace on someone; to surround or enclose
أَطاقَ – يُطيقُ to be able or capable; to bear, stand, or sustain; to master
طَوقٌ (أَطْواقٌ) ability, faculty, power (pl: necklace, headband, collar)
طاقَةٌ (طاقاتٌ) energy, power, capacity; ability
مُطاقٌ bearable
طاقَةُ الرِّياحِ wind power
طاقَةٌ بَديلَةٌ alternative energy
كِفايَةُ الطّاقَةِ energy efficiency
طاقَةٌ مُتجدِّدةٌ / طاقَةٌ قابِلَةٌ للتَّجديدِ renewable energy
طاقَةٌ غَيرُ مُتجدِّدةٍ non-renewable energy
الطّاقَةُ النَّوَوِيَّةُ nuclear power

No root

عَدَنٌ Eden, Paradise; Aden (city in Yemen)

Earth, Nature, and the Environment

مَعدِنٌ (مَعادِنُ) mineral; metal; mine; source
مَعادِنُ ثَمينَةٌ / مَعادِنُ نَفيسَةٌ precious metals
عِلْمُ الْمَعادِنِ mineralogy
مَعدَنِيٌّ metallic; mineral (adj)
ماءٌ مَعدَنِيٌّ mineral water

ف ح م

فَحَمَ – يَفحُمُ to be or become black; to be unable to answer
فَحَّمَ – يُفَحِّمُ to blacken (with charcoal); to carbonise
فَحْمٌ coal
فَحْمَةٌ (فَحْمات) lump of coal
فَحْمَةٌ blackness
أَسْوَدُ فاحِمٌ pitch-black

ك ت ل

كَتَلَ – يَكتِلُ to agglomerate or gather into a mass
تَكَتَّلَ – يَتَكَتَّلُ to be heaped up; to cluster or gather in a mass; to unite in a bloc
كُتْلَةٌ (كُتَلٌ) clot, lump
كُتْلَةٌ ذَرِّيَّةٌ atomic mass

ك ه ر ب

كَهْرَبَ – يُكَهْرِبُ to electrify or ionise
تَكَهْرَبَ – يَتَكَهْرَبُ to be electrocuted or ionised
كَهْرَبَةٌ / كَهْرِباءٌ electricity
كَهْرَبٌ (كَهارِبُ) electron
مَحَطَّةُ تَوْليدِ الْكَهْرَباءِ power station
كَهْرَبائِيٌّ electric, electrician
تَيَّارٌ كَهْرَبائِيٌّ electric current
شَبَكَةُ الطَّاقةِ الْكَهْرَبائِيَّةِ power grid
مُكَهْرَبٌ electrically charged, electrified, ionised

No root

كيمياءٌ chemistry
الكيمياءُ chemistry, alchemy
كيماوِيٌّ / كيمائِيٌّ chemical; chemist

الْكيمياءُ الْحَيَوِيَّةُ bio-chemistry
كيماوِيّاتٌ chemicals

م غ ط س

مَغْطَسَ – يُمَغْطِسُ to magnetise
مَغْطَسَةٌ magnetism

م غ ن ط

مَغْنَطَ – يُمَغْنِطُ to magnetise
مَغْنَطيسٌ / مَغْناطيسٌ magnet

ن ب ط

نَبَطَ – يَنْبُطُ to well or gush out
اِسْتَنْبَطَ – يَسْتَنْبِطُ to find or discover (oil, water); to invent or devise
نَبْطٌ depth, core, heart
اِسْتِنْباطٌ discovery, invention

ن ض ب

نَضَبَ – يَنْضَبُ to be absorbed into the ground; to dry up; to be depleted
أَنْضَبَ – يُنْضِبُ to exhaust or drain; to deplete or dry up
ناضِبٌ (نُضَّبٌ) dried up, arid; barren, sterile
اليورانيومُ المَنْضَبُ depleted uranium

No root

نَفْطٌ / النَّفْطُ / البِترولُ oil, petroleum, naphtha
بِئْرُ نَفْطٍ oil well
نَفْطٌ خامٌ crude oil
إنتاجُ النَّفْطِ oil production
تَكريرُ النَّفْطِ oil refining
حُقولٌ نَفْطِيَّةٌ oil fields

ن ف و / ن ف ى

نَفَى – يَنْفي to deny, reject, or negate; to expel, banish, or exile
نافى – يُنافي to hunt, chase, or pursue; to contradict or be inconsistent
اِنْتَفى – يَنْتَفي to be banished or exiled

Earth, Nature, and the Environment 365

نَفْيٌ exile, banishment, expatriation
حَرفُ النَفْي negation particle (grammar)
نُفايَةٌ (نُفاياتٌ) refuse, waste, garbage
نُفاياتٌ مُشِعَّةٌ radioactive waste
النُفاياتُ النَوَوِيَّةُ nuclear waste

ن و ى

نَوى – يَنوي to intend or plan; to resolve or determine
نَوَّى – يُنَوِّي to miaow
اِنتَوى – يَنتَوي to propose or intend
نَوىً distance, remoteness; destination
نَواةٌ (نَوَيَاتٌ) nucleus, atomic nucleus; core, stone, pit
نَوَوِيٌّ atomic, nuclear
تَفاعُلٌ نَوَوِيٌّ nuclear reaction
مُفاعِلٌ نَوَوِيٌّ nuclear reactor
رادِعٌ نَوَوِيٌّ nuclear deterrent
اِنصِهارٌ نَوَوِيٌّ nuclear meltdown
إِشْعاعٌ نَوَوِيٌّ nuclear radiation
كارثَةٌ نَوَوِيَّةٌ nuclear disaster
مَحَطَّةُ الطّاقةِ النَوَوِيَّةِ nuclear power station
أَسلِحَةٌ نَوَوِيَّةٌ nuclear weapons
مَنطِقةٌ خالِيَةٌ مِن الأَسلِحَةِ النَوَوِيَّةِ nuclear-free zone
اِنتِشارُ الأَسلِحَةِ النَوَوِيَّةِ nuclear proliferation
نِيَّةٌ (نِيَّاتٌ/نَوايا) intention, purpose, plan
حُسْنُ النِيَّةِ good intention, honesty
سوءُ النِيَّةِ bad intention, malice

و ق د

وَقَدَ – يَقِدُ to ignite or burn
أَوقَدَ – يُوقِدُ to kindle, ignite, or light
اِستَوقَدَ – يَستَوقِدُ to kindle, light, or ignite
وَقَدٌ fuel; fire, combustion
وِقادٌ/وَقودٌ/وَقيدٌ fuel
مَوقِدٌ (مَواقِدُ) fireplace, stove
إيقادٌ kindling, ignition
الوَقودُ الأُحفوريُّ fossil fuel

366 *Earth, Nature, and the Environment*

و ل د

(Full treatment in Family chapter)

تَوْلِيدٌ generating (power, electricity); procreation; midwifery

مَحطةُ تَوليدٍ power station

مَحطةُ تَوليدِ القُوَّةِ الكَهْرِبائِيّةِ electric power station

تَوَلُّدٌ / إِستيلادٌ generation, production

مُوَلِّدٌ (مُولِّداتٌ) generating, producing; generative; obstetrician (pl: generator)

The World and Beyond العالَمُ والفَضاءُ

No root

أَرضٌ (أَراضٍ) earth; land, country, region

أَرضِيٌّ terrestrial

أ ق ل م

أَقْلَمَ – يُؤَقْلِمُ to acclimatise, adapt, or adjust

تَأَقْلَمَ – يَتَأَقْلَمُ to acclimatise (oneself)

إِقليمٌ (أَقاليمُ) area, region, province; administrative district

إِقليميٌّ climatic; territorial; regional, local

No root

المِجَرَّةُ galaxy, constellation of stars

ب أ ر

بَأَرَ – يَبْأَرُ to dig a well

بِئْرٌ (آبارٌ) well, spring

بُؤْرَةٌ (بُؤَرٌ) abyss; pit; site

ب ح ر

بَحَرَ – يَبْحَرُ to travel by sea or make a voyage

أَبْحَرَ – يُبْحِرُ to travel by sea; to go on board; to go downstream

تَبَحَّرَ – يَتَبَحَّرُ to delve or penetrate deeply; to study thoroughly

بَحرٌ (بِحارٌ) sea, large river; a noble or great man

Earth, Nature, and the Environment 367

سَطْحُ الْبَحرِ sea level
بَحراً by sea
الْبَحرين the Bahrain islands
بَحريٌّ marine, nautical
طُحلُبٌ بَحريٌّ seaweed
الْبَحريَّةُ the navy
بُحَيْرَة (بُحيراتٌ) lake
مُتَبَحِّرٌ profound; erudite; well informed
بَحرُ الْعَرَبِ Arabian Sea
الْبَحرُ الأَبْيضُ الْمُتَوَسِّطُ the Mediterranean
بَحرُ الشَّمالِ the North Sea
بَحرُ الْبَلْطيقِ the Baltic
الْبَحرُ الأَسْوَدُ the Black Sea
الْبَحرُ الأَحمَرُ the Red Sea
الْبَحرُ الْمَيِّتُ the Dead Sea

ب ع ث

(Full treatment in Politics chapter)

الِانبِعاثاتُ emissions
اِنبِعاثاتٌ كَربونِيَّةٌ carbon emissions
الِانبِعاثاتُ الغازِيَّةُ gas emissions

ب ق ي

بَقِيَ – يَبقى to remain or stay; to maintain or keep up
أَبْقى – يُبْقي to make (someone) stay; to retain, preserve, or maintain
بَقِيَّةٌ (بَقايا) remainder, residue
بَقاءٌ survival, continuation; immortality, eternal life

ب و ء

باءَ – يَبوءُ to come again or return; to yield
تَبَوَّأَ – يَتَبَوَّأُ to settle down or occupy
بيئَةٌ (بيئاتٌ) environment; home, habitat, domicile
الْبيئَةُ the environment
عِلمُ الْبيئَةِ ecology

368 Earth, Nature, and the Environment

صَديقٌ لِلْبيئَةِ eco-friendly
مِن أنصارِ الْبيئَةِ environmentalist
الْمحافَظَةُ على الْبيئَةِ preservation of the environment
التَّنَوُّعُ الْبيئيُّ ecological diversity
النِّظامُ الْبيئيُّ ecosystem
البيئاتُ الْبَحريَّةُ marine biology

No root

تِبْنٌ straw
دربُ التّبانةِ Milky Way

ت ر ب

تَرِبَ – يَتْرَبُ to be dusty or covered in dust
تارَبَ – يُتارِبُ to be someone's comrade
تِرْبٌ (أَتْرابٌ) contemporary; friend, companion
تُرْبَةٌ / تُرابٌ (تُرَبٌ / أَتربةٌ) earth, dirt, dust, ground, soil

No root

جَبَلٌ (جِبالٌ / أَجبالٌ) mountain, mountain range

No root

جَدْوَلٌ (جَداولُ) little stream, creek, brook; timetable

ج ر ف

جَرَفَ – يَجرُفُ to sweep or wash away; to tear away or remove
اِنْجَرفَ – يَنْجَرِفُ to be swept or carried away
تَجريفٌ / تآكُل التُّربةِ soil erosion
جُرْفٌ (جُروفٌ / أَجرافٌ) shore; cliff, precipice
جُرْفٌ جَليديٌّ avalanche
جَرَّافَةٌ (جَرَّافاتٌ) rake; tractor
جارِفٌ torrential (of water), stormy, violent (of emotions)

ج ز ر

جَزَرَ – يَجزُرُ to massacre, slaughter, or kill; to sink; to drop (of water)

Earth, Nature, and the Environment 369

جَزْرٌ slaughter, butchering; ebb (of the sea)
الْمَدُّ وَالْجَزْرُ ebb and flow
جَزِيرَةٌ (جُزْرٌ) island
شِبْهُ جَزِيرَةٍ peninsula
جَزَائِرِيٌّ (جَزَائِرِيّونَ) Algerian
مَجْزَرٌ (مَجَازِرُ) slaughterhouse, abattoir
مَجْزَرَةٌ (مَجَازِرُ) massacre, carnage, butchery
جَزَّارٌ (جَزَّارُونَ) butcher

ح س ن

حَسُنَ – يَحسُنُ to be handsome or beautiful; to be suitable or proper
تَحَسَّنَ – يَتَحَسَّنُ to improve; to become more beautiful or handsome
اِستَحسَنَ – يَستَحسِنُ to approve or condone; to admire (sth)
حُسْنٌ beauty, handsomeness, excellence
حَسَنٌ (حِسَانٌ) beautiful, handsome, lovely
أَحسَنُ better, nicer
حَسَنَةٌ (حَسَناتٌ) good deed; charity, alms (pl: advantages)
حَسُّونٌ (حَساسِينُ) goldfinch
مَحْسَنَةٌ (مَحَاسِنُ) something good; advantage
تَحسِينٌ beautification; improvement, amelioration
تَحسِينٌ وِرَاثِيٌّ genetic modification
إِحسَانٌ charity, alms-giving
تَحَسُّنٌ improvement, amelioration
مُستَحسَنٌ approved; pleasant, agreeable

ح و ط

حَاطَ – يَحِيطُ to guard, protect, or watch; to attend; to surround
حَوَّطَ – يُحَوِّطُ to build a wall; to surround
تَحَوَّطَ – يَتَحَوَّطُ to guard or protect; to be careful or cautious
اِحتَاطَ – يَحتَاطُ to be cautious or on one's guard; to surround; to guard or protect
حِيطَةٌ caution, circumspection
إِحَاطَةٌ understanding, knowledge; encirclement
تَحَوُّطٌ provision, precaution
اِحتِيَاطٌ (اِحتِيَاطَاتٌ) caution, prudence, care; precautionary measures
اِحتِيَاطِيٌّ precautionary, preventive; reserve funds; military reserves
حَائِطٌ (حِيطَانٌ / حَوَائِطُ) wall

مُحيطٌ (مُحيطاتٌ) ocean; circumference (of circle); milieu
الْمُحيطُ الْهادي / الْمُحيطُ الْهادِئُ Pacific Ocean
الْمُحيطُ الْهِنديُّ Indian Ocean
الْمُحيطُ الْأَطْلَسيُّ Atlantic Ocean
الْمُحيطُ الْمُتَجَمِّدُ الشَّماليُّ Arctic Ocean
الْمُحيطُ الْمُتَجَمِّدُ الْجَنوبِيُّ Antarctic Ocean

خ س ف

خَسَفَ – يَخسِفُ to be eclipsed (of moon); to sink; to disappear
اِنْخَسَفَ – يَنْخَسِفُ to sink or go down
خَسْفٌ baseness, disgrace; causing to sink
خُسوفٌ lunar eclipse
خُسوفُ الْقَمَرِ moon eclipse

خ ض م

خَضَمَ – يَخضِمُ to bite or munch on
خِضَمٌّ sea, ocean (n); vast (said of the sea) (adj)

ذ ر و / ذ ر ى

ذَرى – يَذري to disperse or scatter; to carry off
تَذَرَّى – يَتَذَرَّى to be fanned; to climb or scale; to take refuge
ذُرَةٌ corn, maize
ذُرْوَةٌ (ذُرُواتٌ / ذُرَىً) summit, top, peak; climax

ر و د

رادَ – يَرودُ to walk about; to look; to search or prowl
راوَدَ – يُراوِدُ to entice; to approach or accost
أرادَ – يُريدُ to want, wish, or have in mind; to desire; to be bound (place)
اِرْتادَ – يَرتادُ to return (to a place); to explore
رَوْدٌ / رِيادَةٌ exploration
إرادَةٌ (إراداتٌ) will, desire; decree
إراديٌّ intentional
رائِدٌ (رُوَّادٌ) astronaut; visitor; explorer; leader (also a boy's name in the singular)
مُرادٌ wanted, desired; intended (also a boy's name)

Earth, Nature, and the Environment 371

ز ه ر

زَهَرَ – يَزْهَرُ to shine, give light, or be radiant
اِزْدَهَرَ – يَزْدَهِرُ to blossom, flourish, or prosper
زَهْرٌ (زُهورٌ / أَزْهارٌ) flowers, blossoms
زَهْرَةٌ (زَهَراتٌ) flower, blossom; splendour, beauty
زُهْرَةٌ brilliancy, light, brightness
الزُّهَرَةُ planet Venus
مَزْهَرِيَّةٌ flowerpot, vase
اِزْدِهارٌ boom (economic); flourishing
مُزْهِرٌ in bloom; luminous, bright

س م و

سَما – يَسْمو to be high, elevated, or tall; to exceed
سامى – يُسامي to excel
تَسامى – يَتَسامى to vie with one another for glory; to be high or elevated
سُمُوٌّ height, altitude; eminence
سَماءٌ (سَمَواتٌ) heaven, sky, firmament
سَمائِيٌّ / سَماوِيٌّ heavenly, celestial; open air, outdoor
أَسْمى higher, above, more exalted (also a girl's name)
سامٍ (سُماةٌ) high, exalted, elevated

س ي ل

سالَ – يَسيلُ to flow or stream; to be or become liquid
سَيَّلَ – يُسَيِّلُ to make flow or cause to stream; to liquefy
سَيْلٌ (سُيولٌ) flood, inundation, torrential stream
سُيولَةٌ liquidity
سائِلٌ (سَوائِلُ) fluid, liquid

No root

صَحْراءُ (صَحارٍ / صَحارى / صَحراواتٌ) desert
صَحْراوِيٌّ desolate; (of or relating to the) desert
أَراضٍ صَحْراوِيَّةٌ desert areas

ص ن ف

صَنَّفَ – يُصَنِّفُ to classify, sort, or categorise; to compile or write

372 *Earth, Nature, and the Environment*

صِنفٌ (أَصنافٌ / صُنوفٌ) type, species, genus; article
تَصنيفٌ (تَصانيفُ) classification, categorisation; compilation; literary work
تَصنيفةٌ assortment, selection

غ د ر

غَدَرَ – يَغدُرُ to deceive or betray
غادَرَ – يُغادِرُ to leave or depart
غَدْرٌ treachery, betrayal; treason
غَديرٌ (غُدرانٌ / غُدُرٌ) pond, pool; stream, brook (also a girl's name in the singular)
غَدّارٌ / غادِرٌ treacherous, deceitful, false

غ و ص

غاصَ – يَغوصُ to plunge or submerge; to dive
غَوّاصٌ (غَوّاصونَ) diver, pearl diver
غَوّاصةٌ (غَوّاصاتٌ) submarines

ف ض و / ف ض ي

فَضا – يَفضو to be or become spacious
فَضّى – يُفضّي to empty, void, or vacate
فَضاءٌ outer space; vast and unlimited space
رائدُ الفَضاءِ spaceman, astronaut
سَفينةُ الفَضاءِ / مَركَبةٌ فَضائيّةٌ spaceship
كائِناتٌ فَضائيّةٌ UFOs
فاضٍ empty

ف ي ض

فاضَ – يَفيضُ to overflow, flood, or inundate; to flow or stream
أفاضَ – يُفيضُ to pour forth; to be verbose; to dwell
فَيْضٌ (فُيوضٌ) inundation, deluge; abundance; streams
فَيّاضٌ overflowing, bountiful, liberal
فَيَضانٌ (فَيَضاناتٌ) flood, inundation
فائِضٌ (فَوائِضُ) abundant, plentiful (pl: interest (on money))

ق ط ب

قَطَبَ – يَقطِبُ to gather or collect; to frown or scowl

Earth, Nature, and the Environment

قَطَّبَ – يُقَطِّبُ to frown
اِستَقطَبَ – يَستَقطِبُ to polarise
قُطبٌ (أَقطابٌ) pole, axis, pivot; leader
القُطبُ الشَّماليُّ the North Pole
القُطبُ الجَنوبيُّ the South Pole
القارَّةُ القُطبِيَّةُ الجَنوبِيَّةُ Antarctica
قُطبِيٌّ polar
الدُّبُّ القُطبِيُّ polar bear
اِستِقطابٌ polarisation

ق ط ر

قَطَرَ – يَقطُرُ to drip or trickle
قَطَّرَ – يُقَطِّرُ to let drip; to dribble; to filter; to form a train of camels
تَقاطَرَ – يَتَقاطَرُ to come in successive groups; to crowd or flock
قَطرَةٌ (قَطَراتٌ) drops
قُطرٌ (أَقطارٌ) region, district; country, land; diameter (of a circle)
قِطارٌ (قِطاراتٌ) train; a train or caravan of camels; single file (of soldiers)

ق م ر

قَمَرَ – يَقمُرُ to gamble; to defeat in gambling
قامَرَ – يُقامِرُ to gamble, stake, bet, or speculate
أَقمَرَ – يُقمِرُ to be moonlit (night)
قَمَرٌ (أَقمارٌ) moon; satellite
قِمارٌ / مُقامَرَةٌ gambling; bet, wager
لَعِبُ القِمارِ gambling

ق م م

قَمَّ – يَقُمُّ to sweep
قِمَّةٌ (قِمَمٌ) summit, top, peak
قِمَّةُ مَجموعةِ العِشرينَ G20 Summit
قُمامَةٌ rubbish, refuse

No root

قَنالٌ canal
قَنالُ السُّوَيسِ Suez Canal

ق ن و / ق ن ى

قَنا – يَقنو to acquire or appropriate; to possess or own; to adhere to
قَنَّى – يُقَنِّي to dig a canal; to acquire
قَناةٌ (قَنَواتٌ) stream, canal, channel
قَنَواتٌ دُبلوماسِيَّةٌ diplomatic channels

ك س ف

كَسَفَ – يَكسِفُ to be or become dark or gloomy; to be eclipsed; to reprimand or shame
اِنكَسَفَ – يَنكَسِفُ to be eclipsed; to be shamed or ashamed; to blush
كَسْفٌ darkening, eclipse
كُسوفٌ eclipse, solar eclipse
كاسِفٌ dejected, downcast, sad, gloomy
كُسوفُ الشَّمسِ solar eclipse

No root

كَوكَبٌ (كَواكِبُ) star; a planet
كَوكَبَةٌ (كَواكِبُ) star; group, troop, squadron
كَوكَبِيٌّ star shaped; stellar, astral

ك و ن

كانَ – يَكونُ to be or to exist; to happen, occur, or take place
كَوَّنَ – يُكَوِّنُ to make, create, or originate; to bring forth; to shape
تَكَوَّنَ – يَتَكَوَّنُ to be created or formed; to consist of
كَوْنٌ (أَكوانٌ) being, existence; an event
الكَوْنُ the universe, the cosmos
كِيانٌ being, essence, substance
مَكانٌ (أَمْكِنةٌ / أَماكِنُ) place, site, location
مَكانةٌ (مَكاناتٌ) place, location, position; office; influence
تَكوينٌ (تَكاوينُ) forming, shaping; origination (pl: rock formations)
تَكَوُّنٌ genesis, birth, origin
كائِنٌ (كائِناتٌ) being, creature
كائِنٌ حَيٌّ living creature
مُكَوِّنٌ creator; shaper

ل و ث

لاثَ – يَلوثُ to pollute, tarnish, or sully; to hesitate
لَوَّثَ – يُلَوِّثُ to pollute, tarnish, or sully; to hesitate
تَلَوَّثَ – يَتَلَوَّثُ to be stained, tarnished, or polluted
مُلَوَّثٌ stained, tarnished, polluted
تَلَوُّثٌ pollution

No root

مَرجانٌ small pearls; coral
مَرجانيٌّ coral; coral-red
الشُّعابُ المَرجانيَّةُ coral reefs
جَزيرةٌ مَرجانيَّةٌ atoll

م و ه

ماءٌ (مِياهٌ) water, liquid, fluid
ماءٌ عَذبٌ / ماءٌ فُراتٌ fresh or potable water
ماءٌ غازيٌّ carbonated water
مِياهٌ إقليميَّةٌ territorial waters
مِياهٌ جَوفيَّةٌ groundwater
مِياهٌ ساحِليَّةٌ coastal waters
مِياهٌ عَميقَةٌ deep waters
مِياهٌ سَطحيَّةٌ rivers
نَقصُ المِياهِ water shortage
تَنقيَةُ المِياهِ water purification
تَحليَةُ المِياهِ water desalination
مائيٌّ aquatic, relating to water

ن ق ع

نَقَعَ – يَنقَعُ to stagnate or be stagnant; to quench; to infuse or brew
أنقَعَ – يُنقِعُ to soak; to quench (thirst)
اِستَنقَعَ – يَستَنقِعُ to stagnate or be stagnant; to be swamp-like (ground)
نَقعٌ (أنقُعٌ / نُقوعٌ) soaking, steeping, infusing (pl: stagnant water, swamps, bogs)
مُستَنقَعٌ (مُستَنقَعاتٌ) marsh, swamp
حُمّى المُستَنقَعاتِ malaria

ن ه ر

نَهَرَ – يَنْهَرُ to stream forth; to scold or reject; to drive away
اِنْتَهَرَ – يَنْتَهِرُ to scold; to drive away
نَهْرٌ (أَنْهُرٌ / أَنهارٌ / نُهورٌ) river, stream
نَهْرُ النّيلِ the Nile
نَهْرُ دِجْلَةَ Tigris River
نَهْرُ الأردنِّ Jordan River
نَهارٌ (أَنْهُرٌ / نُهُرٌ) daytime; day

ن و ع

نَوَّعَ – يُنَوِّعُ to sort or classify; to compose; to diversify; to change or modify
تَنَوَّعَ – يَتَنَوَّعُ to be diverse in kind or form; to be complex
نَوْعٌ (أنواعٌ) species, sort, kind; classification
تَنْويعٌ diversity; change, alteration, modification
تَنَوُّعٌ diversity, variety, multiplicity; change
مُنَوَّعٌ / مُتَنَوِّعٌ different, diverse, various; complex

ه ج ن

هَجُنَ – يَهْجُنُ to be incorrect or faulty
هَجَّنَ – يُهَجِّنُ to censure or disparage
اِسْتَهْجَنَ – يَسْتَهْجِنُ to consider (sth) bad; to disapprove or condemn
هُجْنَةٌ fault, defect; baseness, meanness
هَجَّانٌ (هَجَّانَةٌ) camel rider
هَجينٌ (هُجُنٌ) low, base, mean
هَجينةٌ (هجائِنُ) hybrid; racing camel
اِسْتِهْجانٌ disapproval

ه ض ب

هَضَبَ – يَهْضِبُ to be long-winded or verbose
هَضَبَةٌ (هِضابٌ) hill, mountain, elevation

ه ل ه ل

هَلَّ – يَهِلُّ to appear or come up; to show (of crescent moon); to begin
هَلَّلَ – يُهَلِّلُ to say 'la illah illa allah'; to rejoice or applaud

Earth, Nature, and the Environment

تَهَلَّلَ – يَتَهَلَّلُ to be radiant or glow; to be delighted
انْهَلَّ – يَنْهَلُّ to pour down; to undertake
هِلالٌ (أَهِلَّةٌ / أَهاليلُ) new moon, half moon, crescent
الهِلالُ الأَحمَرُ the Red Crescent
هِلالِيٌّ crescent shaped, lunar
تَهليلٌ (تَهاليلُ) utterance of formula 'la illaha illa allah'; rejoicing, cheering
تَهَلُّلٌ joy, jubilation, exultation

No root

واحٌ / واحَةٌ (واحاتٌ) oasis

No root

وادٍ (أَودِيَةٌ) valley

و ح ل

وَحِلَ – يَوْحَلُ to get stuck in the mud; to be stuck or stranded; to be in a fix
وَحَّلَ – يُوَحِّلُ to become muddy
تَوَحَّلَ – يَتَوَحَّلُ to be or become dirty or muddy
وَحْلٌ (وُحولٌ) mud, mire
مُوَحَّلٌ / وَحِلٌ muddy, dirty

ي ب س

يَبِسَ – يَيْبَسُ to be or become dry
يَبَّسَ – يُيَبِّسُ to dry
يَبْسٌ dry, arid
اليَبَسُ / اليابِسَةُ dry land; land, terra firma
يُبوسَةٌ dryness (also of speech and writing)
يابِسٌ dry, arid, rigid, hard

Exercises

1) Give two derived nouns for each of the following roots:

ح ب ر
ح ي ي
خ ر ف

378 Earth, Nature, and the Environment

ف ر ش
ن ج م
و ح ش

2) Find the roots of these words:

أَسَدٌ
اِنْسِحابٌ
تَلَوُّثٌ
جاذِبِيَّةٌ
حَطَبٌ
رُطوبَةٌ
طَبيعَةٌ
كَهرَبَةٌ
هَواءٌ

3) Give the plural of the following words (some may have more than one plural):

اِبنُ آوى
بيئَةٌ
تَجربةٌ
جَزيرَةٌ
زَهرَةٌ
ضَبٌّ
عاصِفَةٌ
قَمَرٌ
نَسيمٌ

4) Give the present tense of the following verbs:

اِفتَرَسَ to kill prey
دَوَّدَ to be or become worm-eaten
زَرْزَرَ to chirp
شَتَّى to rain; to pass the winter; to hibernate
طارَ to fly
نَبَحَ to bark

5) Translate these sentences into Arabic:
   a) Climate change is a global problem.
   b) The weather forecast: sunny and humid.

c) Pollution is a direct result of human behaviour.
d) Russia increases the price of petrol.

6) Translate these sentences into English:

- مَوْجَةُ حَرٍّ مُقبلةٌ على القارَة الأوروبيَّة الأسبوعَ المُقبلَ.
- يدرسُ أخي الطِّبُّ البَيْطريُّ في جامِعَةِ "كامبريدج".
- طاقَةُ الرّياحِ هِيَ نوعٌ من أنواعِ الطّاقَةِ المُتَجدِّدَةِ.
- إعصارٌ في ألمانيا تَسبب في انهيارِ سقوفِ المَباني.
- هل كارِثَةٌ نَووِيَّةٌ مُحتملةٌ إذا تعرضَتْ أوكرانيا لِهجومٍ من روسيا؟

Note

1 This is used in the dialects to mean 'cold'.

10 Information Technology
تَقنِيَّةُ المَعلوماتِ

No root

أَداةٌ (أَدَواتٌ) tool, instrument; apparatus, device
أَدَواتُ اللُّغةِ language tools

No root

اسم (أَسماءٌ / أَسامٍ) name; reputation; noun (grammar)
الاسمُ الكامِلُ full name
الاسمُ المُستَعارُ alias

No root

إِدراجُ السِّلَعِ عَلى الإِنتَرنِت online listing
اِحتِيالٌ عَبرَ الإِنتَرنِت phishing, online fraud
الإِنتَرنِت the internet
أَمنُ الإِنتَرنِت internet security
تَجَسُّسٌ عَبرَ الإِنتَرنِت online spying
تَسَوُّقٌ عَلى الإِنتَرنِت internet shopping
تَغطِيةُ الإِنتَرنِت internet coverage
تَهدِيدٌ عَلى الإِنتَرنِت cyberthreat
جِيلُ الإِنتَرنِت net generation
عالَمُ الاِنتَرنِت cyberspace, internet space
كامِيرا الإِنتَرنِت webcam
مَتجَرٌ عَلى الإِنتَرنِت online shop
مُحتالُ الإِنتَرنِت internet scammer
مُزايَدَةٌ عَلى الإِنتَرنِت online bidding
مُطارَدةٌ عَبرَ الإِنتَرنِت cyberstalking
مَقهى الإِنتَرنِت internet café

Information Technology 381

مُنتَدى الإنتَرنِت discussion forum
ميم الإنتَرنِت internet meme
نِسبَة الحُضورِ والمُشارَكةِ على الإنتَرنِت online presence
نَشاطُ الإنتَرنِت internet activism
هُجومٌ عَبرَ الإنتَرنِت cyberattack

No root

إلِكترونيٌّ electronic (loanword), e-
اِستِمارةُ طَلَبٍ إلِكترونيَّةٌ online application
بِطاقاتُ التَّهنِئَةِ الإلِكترونيَّةِ e-cards
تِجارةٌ إلِكترونيَّةٌ e-commerce, e-business
تَجَسُّسٌ إلِكترونيٌّ online spying
تَسويقٌ إلِكترونيٌّ e-marketing
تَنَمُّر إلِكترونيٌّ cyberbullying
خِدماتُ الدَّفعِ الإلِكترونيَّةُ الآمِنةُ secure online payment service
خِدماتٌ إلِكترونيَّةٌ e-services
دَفعٌ إلِكترونيٌّ e-payment
كِتابٌ إلِكترونيٌّ e-book
مُجتَمَعٌ إلِكترونيٌّ online community
مَزادٌ إلِكترونيٌّ online auction
مَوقِعٌ لِلتِجارَةِ الإلِكترونيَّةِ e-commerce site

أ م ر

(Full treatment in Politics chapter)

مُؤتَمَرٌ (مُؤتَمَراتٌ) conference, convention, congress
عَقدُ مُؤتَمَراتٍ عَبرَ الإنتَرنِت web conferencing
عَقدُ مُؤتَمَراتِ البَياناتِ data conferencing
عَقدُ مُؤتَمَراتٍ بِالفيديو videoconferencing

ب ح ث

(Full treatment in Education chapter)

بَحَثَ – يَبحَثُ to search
الباحوثُ/مُحَرِّكُ البَحثِ/مَوقِعُ مُحَرِّكِ البَحثِ web search engine
مُحَرِّكُ البَحثِ الأَمثَلِ search engine optimisation (SEO)
آخِرُ نَتائِجِ البَحثِ recent searches

382 Information Technology

ب ر د

(Same root letters as 'feeling cold, getting a cold' but different root)

أَبْرَدَ – يُبرِدُ to send by mail; to mail
بَريدٌ post, mail
ساعي الْبَريدِ postman
بَريدٌ صَوْتيٌّ voicemail
قائِمَةُ الْبَريدِ mailing list
بَريدٌ مُرْسَلٌ sent mail
صُنْدوقُ الْبَريدِ الوارِدِ inbox
صُنْدوقُ الْبَريدِ الصَّادِرِ outbox
إرسال البَريدِ المُزْعِجِ / إرسال البَريدِ غَيرَ المَرغوب فيه spamming
مُرْسِلُ الرَّسائِلِ غَيْرِ المَرْغوبةِ spammer
بَريدٌ إلِكترونيٌّ email
حِسابُ بَريدٍ إلِكترونيّ email account
عُنْوانُ الْبَريدِ الإلِكترونيّ email address

No root

(A verb that has been formed through the process of verbing)

بَرمَجَ – يُبَرمِجُ to programme
بَرنامَجٌ (بَرامِجُ) a programme or schedule
بَرنامَجُ الْحاسوبِ software
مُطَوِّرُ الْبَرامِجِ software developer
بَرنامَجُ حِصانٍ طِروادةَ Trojan
بَرامِجُ مُضادَةٌ لِلْفَيروساتِ antivirus software
بَرمَجَةٌ programming
بَرمَجِيّات تَطْبيقيَّةٌ application software
بَرمَجِيَّاتٌ خَبيئَةٌ malicious software, malware
بَرمَجِيّاتُ تَجَسُّسٍ spyware
مُبَرمَجٌ programmed

ب و ب

بَوَّبَ – يُبَوِّبُ to divide into sections; to arrange or classify
بابٌ (أَبوابٌ / بيبانٌ) door, gate, entrance
بَوّابةٌ (بَوّاباتٌ) large gate, portal

Information Technology 383

بَوَّابةُ الإنتَرنِت web portal
عَلامَةُ تَبويبٍ tab

ب ي ن

(Full treatment in Media chapter)

بَيانٌ (بَياناتٌ) data; clarity; announcement
إدارةُ الْبَياناتِ data management
تَخزينُ الْبَياناتِ data storage
قاعِدةُ الْبَياناتِ database
مُعالَجَةُ الْبَياناتِ data processing
مُعَدَّلُ نَقلِ الْبَياناتِ / باند ويدث internet bandwidth
باند ويدث مَفتوحٌ unlimited bandwidth

ت ب ع

تَبِعَ – يَتْبَعُ to follow or succeed; to trail or pursue; to observe
تابَعَ – يُتابِعُ to follow up; to agree; to pursue or chase
تَتابَعَ – يَتَتابَعُ to be consecutive or successive
اِتَّبَعَ – يَتَّبِعُ to follow or come after; to prosecute
تَبَعٌ (أَتْباعٌ) succession; subordinate (pl: followers)
تَبَعِيَّةٌ (تَبَعِيّاتٌ) subordination; dependency, reliance; citizenship
التّابِعِيَّةُ following (online)
إلْغاءُ الْمُتابَعةِ unfollowing (online)
مَتْبوعٌ / مُتَّبَعٌ followed; succeeded
مُتابِعٌ (مُتابِعونَ) follower (on a blog, site)

ج ر ى

(Full treatment in Politics chapter)

جَرى – يَجري to occur or take place; to flow or stream; to hurry
جارٍ / جاري الـ... in progress, in the process of
جاري التَّحْقيقِ verifying
جاري إعادةِ التَّوْجيهِ redirecting
جاري الإرْسالِ sending
جاري الإتِّصالِ connecting
جاري الْحَذفِ deleting

ج م ع

(Full treatment in Education chapter)

الإنتَرنتُ الاجتِماعيُّ / الويب الاجتِماعيُّ the web, the social web
المُيولُ الاجتِماعيَّةُ / الاتّجاهاتُ الاجتِماعيَّةُ social trends
إعلامٌ اجتِماعيٌّ social media
إعلامٌ إلكترونيٌّ electronic media

ج ه ز

جَهَزَ – يَجْهَزُ to finish (someone) off
جَهَّزَ – يُجَهِّزُ to arrange or prepare; to supply, provide, or equip
جِهازٌ (أَجهِزَةٌ) device, equipment, apparatus
جِهازُ خَرجٍ output device
نُقطةٌ ساخِنةٌ للأَجهِزةِ mobile hotspot

ج و ل

(Full treatment in Politics chapter)

تَجَوَّلَ – يَتَجَوَّلُ to surf the web; to roam, patrol, or wander
تَجَوُّلٌ عَبرَ الشَّبَكةِ العالَميَّةِ surfing the net
جَوْلَةٌ (جَوْلاتٌ) circuit; patrol; trip, tour
جَوْلَةٌ افتِراضيَّةٌ virtual tour
جَوَّالٌ (جَوَّالاتٌ) mobile phones
الإنتَرنِتُ الجَوَّالُ the mobile internet
مُتَصَفِّحُ الإنتَرنِتِ عَبرَ الجَوَّالِ mobile browser
تَطبيقاتُ الجَوَّالِ mobile applications, mobile apps
مَجالٌ (مَجالاتٌ) domain, field; theories; room, space
اسمُ المَجالِ domain name

ح ج ب

(Full treatment in Culture chapter)

مَحجوبٌ concealed; appear offline; blocked
رابِطٌ مَحجوبٌ blocked link
مُستَخدِمٌ مَحجوبٌ blocked user

ح د ث

حَدَّثَ – يُحَدِّثُ to upgrade or update (system or software); to tell or relate
تَحديثٌ (تَحديثاتٌ) update
جاري التَّحديثِ updating
تَحديثُ النِّظامِ system upgrade

ح س ب

(Full treatment in Work chapter)

حاسوبٌ إلِكترونيٌّ / كُمْبيوتَرٌ computer
حاسوبٌ مَكتَبِيٌّ desktop computer
حاسوبٌ دَفتَريٌّ notebook
حاسوبٌ مَحمولٌ / حاسوبٌ نَقّالٌ laptop
حاسوبٌ لِتَصَفُّح الإنترَنِت netbook
حاسوبٌ لَوْحِيٌّ tablet PC
عَتادُ الْحاسوبِ computer hardware
عالِمُ الكمبيوترِ / عالِمُ الْحاسوبِ computer scientist
فَأرَةُ الْحاسوبِ (computer) mouse
فيروسُ الْحاسوبِ computer virus
ذاكِرَةُ الْحاسوبِ computer memory

ح ف ظ

(Full treatment in Politics chapter)

حَفِظَ – يَحْفَظُ to save
الْحِفْظ بِاسْم ... to save as ...
حِفْظُ التَغْييراتِ save changes

ح م ل

(Full treatment in Health chapter)

حَمَلَ – يُحَمِّلُ to upload (a file); to load (software); to load or burden
تَحميلٌ uploading (a file); loading, burdening
تَحميلُ الأغاني music upload
جاري التَّحميلِ loading
تَحميلاتٌ uploads

خ د م

(Full treatment in Work chapter)

server قاعدةُ بياناتٍ لِلإنتَرنِت / خادِمٌ / خادومٌ / سيرْفَر
proxy server حاسوبُ خِدمةِ بروكسي
internet service provider مُزَوِّدُ خِدمةِ الاتِّصالِ بِالإنتَرنِت
secure server خادِمٌ آمِنٌ
user; employee مُستَخدِمٌ (مُستَخدِمونَ)
user account حِسابُ المُستَخدِمِ
username اِسمُ المُستَخدِمِ
user interface واجِهةُ الاِستِخدامِ

خ ر ق

(Full treatment in Politics chapter)

hacking; breakthrough, penetration اِختِراقٌ (اِختِراقاتٌ)
computer hacking, internet piracy اِختِراقُ أَجهِزةِ الحاسوبِ / تَهكيرٌ / قَرصَنةُ الإنتَرنِت
hacktivist ناشِطُ اِختِراقِ أَجهِزةِ الحاسوبِ
hacktivist قُرصانٌ (قَراصِنةٌ / قَراصينُ)
hacktivism نَشاطُ اِختِراقِ أَجهِزةِ الحاسوبِ

خ ز ن

(Full treatment in Work chapter)

storage; store تَخزينٌ
storage device وَسيلةُ تَخزينٍ / جِهازُ تَخزينٍ
web storage تَخزينٌ عَلى الإنتَرنِت
buffering تَخزينٌ مُؤَقَّتٌ لِلبَياناتِ
cloud storage تَخزينٌ سَحابِيٌّ

خ ص ر

(Full treatment in Health chapter)

shortcut; summarisation اِختِصارٌ (اِختِصاراتٌ)

خ ف ى

to hide or conceal خَفى – يَخفي

Information Technology

خَفِيٌّ / مَخفِيٌّ hidden, concealed; secret, unknown
إخفاءٌ hide; hiding, concealment

No root

(A verb that has been formed through the process of verbing)

دَرْدَشَ – يُدَرْدِشُ to chat
دَرْدَشَةٌ idle talk, chatter
دَرْدَشَةُ الإنتَرنِت chat
غُرْفةُ دَرْدَشة chatroom
دَرْدَشةٌ مَرْئيَّةٌ video chat

د ف ع

(Full treatment in Work chapter)

دَفعٌ بِرِفقٍ to nudge or push (on social media)
دَفعَةٌ (دَفعاتٌ) a push or nudge (on social media)

د و ل

(Full treatment in Politics chapter)

تَداوُلٌ access
مُحاوَلَةُ تَداوُلٍ access attempt
رَمزُ التَّداوُلِ / كود التَّداوُلِ access code

د و ن

دَوَّنَ – يُدَوِّنُ to blog; to record, register, or write down; to book (something)
تَدَوَّنَ – يَتَدَوَّنُ to be recorded or written down
ديوانٌ (دواوينُ) an anthology; account books; governmental offices
تَدوينٌ blogging; recording, writing down
مَوْقِعُ تَدوينٍ blogging site
تَدوينٌ مَرْئيٌّ / تَدوينُ فيديو video blogging, vlogging
تَدوينَةٌ (تَدويناتٌ) blog post
تَدويناتٌ ذاتُ عَلاقةٍ related posts
مُدَوِّنٌ (مُدَوِّنونَ) blogger
مُدَوَّنَةٌ (مُدَوَّناتٌ) a record or note; body of laws (pl: writings)
مُدَوَّنَةٌ مَرئيَّةٌ / مُدَوَّنةُ فيديو video blog, vlog
مُدَوَّنَةٌ صَوْتيَّةٌ podcast (literally audio blog)

ر ب ط

رَبَطَ – يَربِطُ to bind or tie up; to fasten or attach
اِرتَبَطَ – يَرتَبِطُ to be linked or connected; to bind or commit oneself; to be tied
رَبْطٌ connecting, binding, fastening
اِرتِباطٌ connection, link; commitment
رابِطَةٌ/رابِطٌ (رَوابِطُ) link; internet link; union, league
رابِطٌ مُمَوَّلٌ sponsored link
رَوابِطُ مُفيدَةٌ useful links
مُرتَبِطٌ (بِـ) connected, linked (with)

ر ج ع

(Full treatment in Education chapter)

اِستِرجاعٌ recovery, retrieval; withdrawal
اِستِرجاعُ مُشتَرَياتِ الموبايل restoring mobile purchases
عَلامَةٌ مَرجِعِيَّةٌ bookmark

ر د د

(Full treatment in Politics chapter)

اِرتَدَّ – يَرتَدُّ to bounce (emails)
رَدٌّ (رُدودٌ) answer, reply; rejection
رَدُّ الفِعلِ reaction; feedback
رُدودُ فِعلٍ مُحايِدَةٍ neutral feedback
رُدودُ فِعلٍ إيجابِيَّةٍ positive feedback
رُدودُ فِعلٍ سَلبِيَّةٍ negative feedback

ر س ل

(Full treatment in Media chapter)

إرسالٌ submitting, sending
مُرسِلٌ (مُرسِلونَ) sender (person); transmitter
مُرسَلٌ إليهِ recipient
صِياغةُ رِسالَةٍ/كِتابةُ رِسالةٍ composing a message
رِسالةٌ نَصِّيَّةٌ text message

رِسالَةٌ مَرْئِيَّةٌ video message
رِسالَةٌ صَوْتِيَّةٌ voice message
خِدْمَةُ الرِّسالَةِ الْقَصيرَة short message service (SMS)
مُراسَلَةٌ فَوْرِيَّةٌ instant messaging (IM)

ر ق ب

(Full treatment in Media chapter)

الرِّقابَةُ على الإِنْتَرِنِت internet censorship
مُراقَبَةُ الدُّخولِ / مُراقَبَةُ التَّداوُلِ access control

ر ق م

رَقَمَ – يَرقُمُ to write; to imprint or mark; to number
رَقَّمَ – يُرَقِّمُ to digitise; to number; to rule
رَقَمٌ (أَرقامٌ) numeral, number
رَقَميٌّ digital
كِتابٌ رَقَميٌّ digital book
ظِلٌّ رَقَميٌّ digital footprint (literally digital shadow)
صورَةٌ رَقَمِيَّةٌ digital image
بَصمَةٌ رَقَمِيَّةٌ internet identity (literally digital fingerprint)
شَبَكَةٌ رَقَمِيَّةٌ digital network
إِشارَةٌ رَقَمِيَّةٌ digital signal
قُوَّةُ الإِشارَةِ الرَّقَمِيَّةِ signal strength

ر م ز

رَمَزَ – يَرمِزُ to make a sign; to wink or nod; to point
رَمزٌ (رُموزٌ) a sign, nod, or wink; symbol; hint, allusion
رُموزُ المَشاعِرِ emoticons
رُموزُ الحاسوبِ computer code
حَلُّ الرُّموزَ to decode
رَمزِيٌّ symbolic; in code (also a boy's name)
كَلِمَةٌ رَمزِيَّةٌ code word
رِسالَةٌ رَمزِيَّةٌ encoded message
رَمْزِيّاتٌ cipher, code

Information Technology

ر و د

(Full treatment in Earth chapter)

رائِدٌ (رُوَّادٌ) surfer or reader (online); visitor, scout, explorer

س ج ل

(Full treatment in Education chapter)

سِجِلٌّ (سِجِلَّاتٌ) list, register; records
سِجِلُ العَلاقاتِ الشَّخصِيَّةِ online contacts
تَسْجيلٌ sign-up (for mailing list or website)
دُخولٌ/تَسْجيلُ الدُّخولِ log in, sign in
خُروجٌ/تَسْجيلُ الخُروجِ sign off, log off

س ح ب

(Full treatment in Earth chapter)

سَحَبَ – يَسحَبُ to drag (a file); to pull or drag; to withdraw
السَّحبُ والإسقاطُ/إسحَبْ وأَسقِطْ drag and drop

س ل ك

سَلَكَ – يَسلُكُ to follow or travel (a road); to behave; to thread (a needle)
أَسلَكَ – يُسلِكُ to insert; to thread a needle
سِلكٌ (أَسلاكٌ) wire, thread, string; line
سِلْكِيٌّ by wire; wire (adj)
لا سِلْكِيٌّ wireless, radio (noun, adj)
قَناةٌ لاسِلْكِيَّةٌ radio channel
اِتِّصالاتٌ لاسِلْكِيَّةٌ wireless or radio communications
بَثٌّ لاسِلْكِيٌّ فائِقُ الدِّقَّةِ والسُّرعةِ/وايْ فايْ Wi-Fi

س و د

سَوَّدَ – يُسَوِّدُ to draft; to scribble; to make black
سَوادٌ black or dark
أَسْوَدُ (سودٌ) black
تَسويدٌ rough draft
مُسْوَدَّةٌ (مُسْوَدّاتٌ) draft; rough copy

ش ب ك

شَبَكَ – يَشْبِكُ to entangle; to fasten or attach
تَشَبَّكَ – يَتَشَبَّكُ to be entwined; to be or become complicated
اِشْتَبَكَ – يَشْتَبِكُ to be or become entangled; to be complicated; to merge or fuse
مَوْقِعُ تَشْبِيكٍ اِجْتِماعِيٍّ social networking site
شَبَكَةٌ (شَبَكاتٌ / شِبَكٌ) net, snare; network
شَبَكَةُ الْمَعْلوماتِ الإِلِكْتِرونِيَّةِ / شَبَكَةُ الإِنْتَرْنِتِ internet
شَبَكَةُ الإِنْتَرْنِتِ العالَمِيَّةِ / الشَّبَكَةُ العالَمِيَّةُ World Wide Web (www)
عَلى الشَّبَكَةِ online
خارِجُ الشَّبَكَةِ offline
الشَّبَكِيَّةُ the retina (eye)
شُبّاكٌ (شَبابيكُ) network; window

ش خ ص

(Full treatment in Education chapter)

مَوْقِعٌ شَخْصِيٌّ personal site
صَفْحَةٌ شَخْصِيَّةٌ personal profile
شَبَكَةٌ شَخْصِيَّةٌ personal network

ش ر ط

(Full treatment in Politics chapter)

شَريطٌ (شَرائِطُ / أَشْرِطَةٌ) strip, band, ribbon; tape, film
شَريطُ الأَدَواتِ toolbar
شَريطُ الْمَهامِّ task bar

ش ر ك

(Full treatment in Work chapter)

اِشْتَرَكَ – يَشْتَرِكُ to subscribe
اِشْتِراكٌ (اِشْتِراكاتٌ) subscription; partnership, collaboration
إِلْغاءُ الاِشْتِراكِ unsubscribe
شَرِكَةٌ إِلِكْتِرونِيَّةٌ online company
مُشارِكٌ / مُشْتَرَكٌ (مُشارِكونَ / مُشْتَرَكونَ) subscriber (to a blog)
مُشارَكَةٌ partnership, collaboration, cooperation

ش غ ل

(Full treatment in Work chapter)

شَغَّلَ – يُشَغِّلْ to load (software); to engage; to work or produce
تَشْغِيلٌ loading; computer processing; employment

No root

(A verb that has been formed through the process of verbing)

شَفَّرَ – يُشَفِّرْ to encrypt or encode
شِفْرٌ / شِفْرَةٌ / شِيفْرَةٌ cipher, code
حَلُّ الشِّفرةِ to decode
تَشْفِيرٌ encryption
فَكُّ التَّشْفِيرِ decryption
كَلِمَةُ سِرٍّ مُشَفَّرَةٍ encrypted password

ش ه د

(Full treatment in Law chapter)

مُشاهَدَةٌ (مُشاهَداتٌ) watching things online; seeing, viewing
عَدَدُ مُشاهَداتِ الصَّفْحةِ page views

ش و ش

شَوَّشَ – يُشَوِّشْ to muddle or confuse; to disturb
تَشَوَّشَ – يَتَشَوَّشْ to be confused; to be disturbed; to be ill
شاشَةٌ (شاشاتٌ) screen; cloth
اسْمُ الشَّاشَةِ screen name, username
لَقْطَةُ شاشةٍ screenshot
شاشَةُ لَمْسٍ touchscreen

ص ف ح

(Full treatment in Education chapter)

تَصَفَّحَ – يَتَصَفَّحْ to browse; to leaf or thumb through (book); to scrutinise
صَفْحَةٌ (صَفحاتٌ) page, sheet; surface, exterior
صَفْحَةٌ إِلِكْترونِيَّةٌ webpage
الصَّفْحَةُ الرَّئيسِيَّةُ homepage

تَصَفُّحٌ browsing; examination, scrutiny
تَصَفُّحُ شَبكةِ الإنتَرنِت surfing, browsing the net
تَصَفُّحُ المَعْلوماتِ أَثْناءَ التَّجوالِ data roaming
سِجِلُّ المُتَصفِّح/كوكي cookie (web)
مُتَصَفِّحُ الويب web browser
سِجِلُّ المُتَصَفِّح browser history

ص ي د

صادَ – يَصيدُ to catch or ensnare; to hunt
تَصَيَّدَ – يَتَصَيَّدُ to troll (online); to hunt for prey
إصطادَ – يَصْطادُ to catch in a trap; to hunt
صَيْدٌ hunting; hunt
صَيْدُ السَّمكِ fishing
صَيّادٌ (صَيّادونَ) hunter, fisher
صَيّادُ السَّمَكِ fishermen
مِصيَدَةٌ (مَصايدُ) trap, snare, net; fishing grounds
تَصَيُّدٌ trolling (online); catching
تَصَيُّدٌ عَبْرَ الإنتَرنِتِ phishing
مُتَصَيِّدٌ (مُتَصَيِّدونَ) phisher

ض ر ب

(Full treatment in Work chapter)

ضَربَةٌ (ضَرباتٌ) hits (internet); a knock or punch
عَدَدُ ضَرباتِ الصَّفْحةِ page hits

ض ي ف

(Full treatment in Culture chapter)

إستَضافَ – يَستَضيفُ to host (websites)
إستِضافةُ مَواقِعَ web hosting
مُستَضيفُ مَواقِعَ web host

ط ب ق

طَبَّقَ – يُطَبِّقُ to apply or implement; to cause, to coincide; to cover
تَطْبيقٌ (تَطْبيقاتٌ) application, app; adaptation

Information Technology

تَطْبيقُ الْويب web application
مُطَوِّرُ التَّطْبيقاتِ application developer
مَتْجَرُ التَّطْبيقاتِ application store, app store

ع ب ر

(Full treatment in Media chapter)

تَعْبيرٌ (تَعْبيراتٌ) expression, phrase, term
تَعبيراتٌ اِنْفِعاليَّةٌ emoticons

ع ر ض

(Full treatment in Politics chapter)

عَرْضُ شَرائِحٍ slideshow

ع ل ق

(Full treatment in Media chapter)

عَلَّقَ – يُعَلِّقُ to comment; to remark or state; to tie
تَعْليقاتٌ حَوْلُ البائِعِ seller feedback

ع ل م

(Full treatment in Education chapter)

أُعلومةٌ (أعلومات/ أعاليمٌ) tag
مَعلوماتٌ knowledge; information, data
مَعلوماتٌ خاصَّةٌ personal information
أَمْنُ المَعلوماتِ information security
مَعلوماتِيَّةٌ/ تِكنولوجيا المَعلوماتِ information technology (IT)
الوَعْيُ المَعْلوماتِيُّ digital literacy
فَضاءٌ مَعلوماتِيٌّ cyberspace

غ ر د

غَرِدَ – يَغرَدُ to sing; to twitter (a bird); to tweet (online)
غَرَّدَ – يُغَرِّدُ to sing; to twitter (a bird); to tweet (online)
غَرَدٌ/ غَريدٌ/ تَغريدٌ song, singing; twittering

Information Technology

تَغريدَةٌ (تَغريداتٌ) a tweet
إعادةُ التَّغريدِ retweeting
مُغَرِّدٌ (مُغَرِّدونَ) singing, twittering; Twitter users, tweeters
أرسَلَ رسالةً باسْتِخدام تويتَر to tweet
تويتَر Twitter
رسالةُ تويتَر Twitter message
تابِعونا عَلى التِويتَر follow us on Twitter

غ ل ق

غَلَقَ – يَغلِقُ to shut, close, or lock
إغلاقٌ collapse; closing, shutting
مُغلَقٌ closed, shut, blocked; obscure

غ م ز

غَمَزَ – يَغمِزُ to wink; to blink; to signal
تَغامَزَ – يَتَغامَزُ to wink at one another
غَمزَةٌ (غَمَزاتٌ) signal, sign, wink, hint

ف ع ل

(Full treatment in Politics chapter)

تَفعيلٌ activation
تَفعيلُ الحِسابِ activating an account
تَفاعُلِيٌّ interactive

No root

فيديو video
مِلَفُّ فيديو video file
مَقْطَعُ فيديو / فيديو كْليب video clip
نِظامُ لُعْبةِ الفيديو video game console

No root

فيسْبوك Facebook
حَمْلةُ فيسْبوك Facebook campaign
تابِعونا على الفيسْبوك follow us on Facebook

ق ر ص

قُرصٌ (أَقراصٌ) a round, flat loaf of bread; a plate; a disc
قُرصٌ صَلبٌ hard drive
وَحدَةُ تَشْغيلِ الأَقراصِ disc drive

ق ط ع

(Full treatment in Work chapter)

اِنقَطَعَ – يَنقَطِعُ to log off; to be cut off
اِنقطاعٌ logged-off

ك ل م

(Full treatment in Media chapter)

كَلِمَةٌ (كَلِماتٌ) word, speech, utterance, remark
كَلِمَةُ المُرور / كَلِمَةُ السِّرّ password
قُوَّةُ كَلِمَةِ السِّرّ / قُوَّةُ كَلِمَةِ المُرور password strength

ل ف ف

مِلَفٌّ (مِلَفّاتٌ) file
صيغَةُ المِلَفِّ file type
مُشارَكةُ المِلَفّاتِ file sharing
مِلَفّاتٌ مُرْفَقَةٌ attachments
مِلَفّاتُ الارتِباطِ internet cookies

ل و ح

(Full treatment in Education chapter)

لَوحَةٌ (لَوحاتٌ) board; blackboard
لَوحَةُ المَفاتيحِ keyboard
اِختِصاراتُ لَوحَةِ المَفاتيحِ keyboard shortcuts
لَوحَةٌ لَمسيَّةٌ touchpad
لَوحَةُ التَّحَكُّمِ control panel

م س ح

ماسِحٌ ضَوئيٌّ / ماسِحَةٌ scanner
مَسحُ العَينِ retina scan

ن ب ه

(Full treatment in Family chapter)

تَنْبِيهَاتٌ notifications
تَشْغِيلُ التَّنْبِيهَاتِ notifications on
إيقافُ تَشْغِيلِ التَّنْبِيهَاتِ notifications off

ن ز ل

(Full treatment in Culture chapter)

نَزَّلَ – يُنَزِّلُ to download (a file); to unload; to lower; to diminish
تَنْزِيلٌ downloading
جاري التَّنْزِيلِ downloading
تَنْزِيلُ الأَغاني music download
مِلَفٌّ قابِلٌ لِلتَّنْزِيلِ downloadable file
تَنْزِيلاتٌ downloads

ن س خ

نَسَخَ – يَنْسَخُ to copy or transcribe; to cancel (contract); to repeal (law); to abolish
تَناسَخَ – يَتَناسَخُ to follow successively
إِسْتَنْسَخَ – يَسْتَنْسِخُ to copy or transcribe
نَسْخٌ copying, transcription; abolition, cancellation
نَسْخٌ اِحْتِياطِيٌّ backup (data)
نُسْخَةٌ (نُسَخٌ) copy; transcript
نُسْخَةٌ نَصِّيَّةٌ text version
نُسْخَةٌ كَربونِيَّةٌ carbon copy (CC)
نُسْخَةٌ كَربونِيَّةٌ مَخْفِيَّةٌ blind carbon copy (BCC)
الإِسْتِنْساخُ cloning

ن س ق

نَسَقَ – يَنْسُقُ to format (computer); to arrange or set up
نَسَّقَ – يُنَسِّقُ to place in order, arrange, or set up
تَنَسَّقَ – يَتَنَسَّقُ to be well ordered or arranged; to be disposed
نَسْقٌ / نَسَقٌ order, arrangement; sequence, system, method
تَنْسِيقٌ setting up (computer); ordering, arrangement
تَناسُقٌ arrangement, order; symmetry

398   Information Technology

ن ط ق

(Full treatment in Law chapter)

نِطاقٌ فَرعِيٌّ subdomain
اِسمُ النِّطاقِ domain name

ن ظ م

(Full treatment in Politics chapter)

نِظامٌ (أَنظِمةٌ / نُظُمٌ) system; method; order
فَشَلُ النِّظامِ system failure
نِظامُ العَدِّ الثُّنائيِّ binary code

ن ف ذ

(Full treatment in Work chapter)

نَفَذَ – يَنفُذُ to pierce; to arrive or reach; to open (a door or window)
نافِذةٌ (نَوافِذُ) window
نافِذةٌ مُنبَثِقةٌ (نَوافِذُ مُنبَثِقةٌ) pop-up window
نَوافِذُ إعلانيّةٌ مُنبَثِقةٌ pop-up ads
مانِعُ النَّوافِذِ المُنبَثِقةِ pop-up blocker

ن ق ر

(Full treatment in Earth chapter)

نَقَرَ – يَنقُرُ to tap or click (an icon); to dig, bore, or pierce
بِنقرةٍ واحدةٍ with one click

ن ق ل

(Full treatment in Media chapter)

اِنتَقِلْ إلى scroll
اِنتَقِلْ إلى أَعلى scroll up
اِنتَقِلْ إلى أَسفَل scroll down

ن ك ز

نَكَزَ – يَنكُزُ to poke (online)

Information Technology

و ج ه

(Full treatment in Media chapter)

تَوجيهُ الأَبَوَيْن parental guidance
التَّوجيهُ routing

و س ط

(Full treatment in Law chapter)

واسِطَةٌ / وَسيطَةٌ (وَسائِطُ) the means; a medium
وَسائِطُ مُتَعَدِّدَةٌ / وَسائِطُ سَمْعِيَّةٌ وبَصَرِيَّةٌ multimedia
وَسائِطُ مُتَعَدِّدَةٌ تَفاعُلِيَّةٌ interactive multimedia

و س ل

(Full treatment in Media chapter)

وَسيلَةٌ (وَسائِلُ) the means; medium; device
وَسائِلُ الإيضاحِ السَّمعِيَّةُ والبَصَرِيَّةُ audiovisual aids

و ص ل

وَصَلَ – يَصِلُ to connect, link, join, unite, or combine
واصَلَ – يُواصِلُ to be connected; to continue or persist
تَواصَلَ – يَتَواصَلُ to be interconnected
اِتَّصَلَ – يَتَّصِلُ to connect (online); to log on; to be attached or connected; to unite
صِلَةٌ (صِلاتٌ) link, bond, connection; relation; kinship
وَصْلٌ (أَوْصالٌ) union, combination; relation, link, connection
وُصْلَةٌ / وَصْلَةٌ (وُصْلاتٌ / وَصْلاتٌ) connection; fastening, link, attachment
وُصْلَةُ بياناتٍ data link
وُصولٌ arrival; receipt; voucher
الوصولُ المَفتوحُ open access
الموصِلُ Mosul (in Iraq)
مُواصَلَةٌ (مُواصَلاتٌ) connection; continuity (pl: lines of communication[1])
إيصالٌ (إيصالاتٌ) joining, connecting; communication; transport
تَواصُلٌ continuity; continuance
التَّواصُلُ الاِجتِماعِيُّ social networking
شبكةُ التَّواصُلِ الاِجتِماعِيِّ social network

Information Technology

مَوْقِعُ تَواصُلٍ اِجْتِماعِيّ social networking site
اِتِّصالٌ (اِتِّصالاتٌ) contact, liaison; connectedness (pl: telecommunications)
اِتِّصالٌ عَنْ بُعْدٍ remote logon
اِتِّصالٌ فَوْرِيٌّ instant messaging
سُرْعةُ الاِتِّصالِ connection speed
الاِتِّصالاتُ البَعيدَةُ telecommunications
تَقَنِياتُ المَعلوماتِ والاِتِّصالاتِ IT and communications
مُتَّصِلٌ online; uninterrupted
غَيْرُ مُتَّصِلٍ offline

و ق ع

(Full treatment in Politics chapter)

مَوْقِعٌ (مَواقِعُ) website, site; position
مَوْقِعٌ إباحِيٌّ porn site
مَوْقِعٌ إخبارِيٌّ news site
مَوْقِعُ تَعارُفٍ dating site
مَوْقِعُ تَبادُلِ المَرئِيّاتِ video sharing site
مَوْقِعُ تَمويلٍ جَماعِيّ crowdfunding site
مَوْقِعٌ مَحظورٌ blocked site
مَوْقِعُ مُشارَكةِ الأَغاني music sharing site
مَوْقِعُ مُشارَكةِ الصُّوَرِ photo sharing site
عُنوانُ مَوْقِعِ الإنتَرنِتِ website address
نِظامُ تَحديدِ المَوْقِعِ العالَمِيّ Global Positioning System (GPS)
مُصَمِّمُ المَواقِعِ website designer
تَصميمُ المَواقِعِ الإلِكترونِيَّةِ website design

مُصطَلَحاتٌ مُفيدَةٌ Useful Terms

(These terms are largely calques or loanwords)

إِسْ إِمْ إِسْ SMS
أَسْئِلَةٌ شائِعةٌ frequently asked questions (FAQS)
اِستِكشافُ الأَخْطاءِ وإصْلاحُها troubleshooting
إشعاراتٌ notifications
الإعداداتُ settings
الأَندرويْد Android

Information Technology

البروفايل profile
التَّرامُنْ syncing
الجيلُ الثالِثُ / ثري جي 3G
الجيلُ الرّابِعُ / فور جي 4G
الجيلُ الخامِسُ / فايْف جي 5G
الخِياراتُ options
الدَّعْمُ الفَنِّيُّ technical support
المُلاحَظاتُ والإقتِراحاتُ feedback and suggestions
المُواصَفاتُ specifications
أَيْقونةٌ (أَيْقوناتٌ) icon
بايْت byte
تَأْثيراتٌ خاصَّةٌ special effects
البْلوتوث Bluetooth
ثُلاثِيُّ الأَبعادِ three-dimensional, 3D
جِدارٌ ناريٌّ / جِدارُ الْحِمايَةِ firewall
جيجا بايْت gigabyte
حَلَقَةٌ link
خوارزميَّةٌ / خوارزمٌ algorithm
سَمّاعَةُ الرَّأسِ headphones
صيغةٌ (صِيَغٌ) format
فلاش USB flash drive "يو اِس بي"
كود code
كيلو بايْت kilobyte
مُستقبِلٌ receiver
مُعطَيَةٌ (مُعطيَاتٌ) data
مَهْووسٌ بِالتِّكْنولوجيا / غيك geek
موبايلٌ (موبايلاتٌ) mobiles
ميغا بايْت megabyte
هاتِفٌ ذَكِيٌّ smartphone
هاشتاجٌ / كَلِمَةٌ مِفتاحِيَّةٌ (هاشتاجاتٌ / كَلِماتٌ مِفتاحِيَّةٌ) hashtag

Exercises

1) Give the roots of the following words:

إرسالٌ
بَيانٌ

تَحديثٌ
جِهازٌ
شاشَةٌ
مُؤتَمَرٌ

2) Give the plural of the following words:

اِختِصارٌ
بابٌ
جَوْلَةٌ
سِلكٌ
شَبَكَةٌ
مُتابِعٌ
نافِذَةٌ
وَسيلَةٌ

3) Translate these sentences into Arabic:

   a) She is the most famous blogger online.
   b) Most people do their shopping online.
   c) There are some areas that have no internet coverage.
   d) Cyberattacks are very common nowadays.

4) Translate the following into English:

   ـ بَعضُ الباحثينَ يَرَوْنَ أنَّ الإنتَرنِت يُؤدي إلى عُزلَةِ الطِفلِ اجتِماعِيّاً.
   ـ مِن مَحاسِنِ الإنتَرنِتِ استخدامُه لِلتَّواصُلِ مَعَ الأصدِقاءِ.
   ـ تَستَخدِمُ الحكوماتُ الإنتَرنِتَ لِلتَجَسُّسِ على المُواطِنينَ.
   ـ ما هُوَ التَنَمُّرُ الإلكترونيُّ؟

Note

1 In some dialects this is also used to mean 'transportation'.

Answer Key

Chapter 1: Family

1)

سِلفٌ / سُلفَةٌ   ابنٌ / بِنتٌ
عائلَةٌ / عائلَةٌ   خَليفَةٌ / اخْتِلافٌ
وَلَدٌ / وِلادَةٌ   رَمَلٌ / أَرمَلَةٌ

2)

ن س ب   ع ز ب
أ ه ل   س ل ف
                   خ ل ف

3)

شَبابٌ   شَجاعَةٌ
بُغضٌ   كَريمٌ
زَواجٌ   جَشَعٌ

4)

بُخلٌ   حُبٌّ
             حَزينٌ

5)

وُلِدتُ في هذا اليومِ.   استَلفَ المالَ مِنْ صَديقِهِ.
                         تَرَمَّلَ الرَّجُلُ بَعدَ سَنتينِ مِن الزَّواجِ.

404 *Answer Key*

6)

بِساطاتٌ / بُسُطٌ / أَبسِطَةٌ	قُرونٌ
تُعساءُ	مُساعِدونَ
حِزاماتٌ / أحزِمةٌ	أهرامٌ / أهراماتٌ
خُبُثٌ / خُبَثاءُ	

7)

شاعِرٌ	ظَرْفٌ
عشيقٌ	نَعامٌ
كَرْمٌ	

8)

- لَقد كانَ زَوْجها رجُلاً مَكّاراً.
- اِنفصَلَت عن زَوْجها بِسببِ بُخلِهِ.
- لَقد فَرِحَت أُمُّها كثيراً لأن اِبنتها ولدت توأماً؟
- غَضِبتُ عندما سمعتُ الأخبارَ المُخجِلة.

9)

- The boy found his parents and was very happy.
- My sister lives in Germany with her husband.
- She is a beautiful and generous woman but her husband is an unpleasant and spiteful man.

Chapter 2: Health

1)

بدَنٌ / بَدانَةٌ	سَمَعٌ / سَمّاعَةٌ
جِلدٌ / جَليدٌ	عَصَبٌ / عِصابةٌ
رِجلٌ / رَجُلٌ	قَلبٌ / اِنقِلابٌ

2)

ر ه ق	ج ن س
ص و ب	ح م م
ك ئ ب	ض ر ر
ه و ر	ع ق ر
ب ر د	ج ن ن

Answer Key   405

3)

حَنجَرَةٌ	قَلْبٌ
أَعْمى	عُضالٌ
سَقيمٌ	أَلَمٌ

4)

جُنينَاتٌ / جَنائِنُ	ضَمائِرُ
حُقَنٌ	مُسَهِّلاتٌ
أَزمِنَةٌ	أَوبِئَةٌ
سُمومٌ / سِمامٌ	

5)

- جَرَحتْ رجلها وَهِيَ تَلعبُ كُرةَ القدمِ.
- هُوَ يُعاني من الصُّداع الشَّديد.
- ماتَتْ ابنتُهُم.
- لَقد طَلَّقَتْ زَوْجَها عِندما اِكتَشَفتْ أَنَّهُ عَقيمٌ.

6)

- Sara visited the doctor because she feels pain in her back/because her back hurts.
- Their father died after two days in the hospital.
- I feel intense pain in my shoulder when I use the computer.
- Obesity has become a big problem in the Gulf States.
- After the examination, the doctor informed her that the cancer had spread throughout his body.

Chapter 3: Education

1)

بِدايَةٌ / مَبْدَأٌ	سَكَنٌ / سِكّينٌ
جُملَةٌ / جَمالٌ	عِلمٌ / عالَمٌ
دَرسٌ / دِراسةٌ	

2)

ب د أ	غ ي ب
م ح ن	ر ج ع
ع ل م	ف ر د
ذ ك ر	ن ج ح
ص د ق	

406   Answer Key

3)

اِجْتِماعٌ	صَفْحَةٌ
أُسْلوبٌ	صَفٌّ
بَيْتٌ	لَوْحَةٌ
تَخَيُّلٌ	مَدْرَسَةٌ
حِكايَةٌ	

4)

- يَجِبُ على الطلاّبِ التسجيلِ للحصولِ على بطاقةٍ شخصيّةٍ في بِدايَةِ العامِ الدَّراسيِّ.
- لا أدري أَيْنَ المُدَرِّسَ.
- إمْتِحان الدُّخول في شهر مارس، ولكن الإمْتِحان النهائيّ في شهر يوليو.
- أُختي نابغة.
- أهملوا واجباتِهم.

5)

- The student refused to study.
- My sister studies comparative literature at the University of Paris.
- The writer became very famous.
- He is a careless boy.
- The girl translated the lecture for the new Arab student.
- Smoking is not allowed on the university campus.

6)

بَراعَةٌ	نابِغَةٌ
تِلميذٌ	جَهْلٌ

Chapter 4: Politics

1)

أُمٌّ / أُمَّةٌ	رأسٌ / رَأسمالٌ
حَرٌّ / حُرِّيَّةٌ	عَرضٌ / عَريضةٌ
دُبٌّ / دَبّابَةٌ	غَرْبٌ / غُرَبةٌ

2)

ج ب ر	ط ر ف
خ ر ق	ح ر ب
أ م ر	ح ص ن

Answer Key 407

ح ك م	س ل م
د و ل	س و س

3)

إمارةٌ	قُوَّةٌ
جاسوسٌ	مَرْكَزٌ
حَرَكَةٌ	مُفاوَضةٌ
سَفارةٌ	مَمْلَكةٌ
شَرْطٌ	نائبٌ
عَمَليَّةٌ	

4)

يَستَلِمُ	يَشْرُدُ
يَستغرِبُ	يُصَوِّتُ
يُعينُ	يُقَرِّرُ
يَتَطَوَّرُ	يَقعُدُ
يَثورُ	يُنازِعُ
يُحارِبُ	

5)

- The Russian president meets with the French president to discuss the war in Ukraine.
- What is the purpose of normalisation between the Emirates and Israel?
- Could the Emirati position be considered a betrayal of their Palestinian brothers and sisters?
- The British minister of health resigned after breaking the rules in the fight against Coronavirus.

6)

- إسرائيلُ تقتلُ صحفيّينِ في خلالِ شهرٍ واحدٍ.
- لقد أعلنتْ الأممُ المتحدة انَّ الوضعَ في اليَمَنِ كارثي.
- أصبحتْ المَمْلَكةُ المُتحدةُ دَوْلَةً بوليسيَّةً.

7)

سَطا	تَحَزَّبَ
نَظَمَ	جاهَدَ
عارَضَ	

Chapter 5: Work

1)

شُغْلٌ / شَغِيلٌ   أَجْرٌ / إيجارٌ
نَفَذٌ / مَنفَذٌ   بَديلٌ / بَدلةٌ
دَوامٌ / دَوَامَةٌ

2)

ر خ ص   ه ل ك
ض ر ب   ع و ض
ح س ب   خ س ر
ن ف ع   د ع م

3)

أَشْغالٌ   أُسُسٌ / أَساساتٌ
غَراماتٌ   اِستثماراتٌ
فُلوسٌ   أَغانٍ / أُغنيّاتٌ
أَمْوالٌ   أَحْرُفٌ / حُروفٌ
مَصْروفاتٌ / مَصاريفُ   رَواتِبُ

4)

باعَ   صَنَعَ
دارَ   طَرَدَ
ساوَمَ   عَمِلَ
اِشتَرَى   كَسَبَ

5)

- كانَ المحامي مهنيّاً جِدّاً، ولكنَّ أُجورَهُ كانتْ عاليةً جِدّاً.
- لقد انخفضَ مُعدَّلُ البَطالَةِ في دبي.
- اشتَكَت إلى مُديرِها بسببِ ساعاتِ الدَّوامِ الطَويلةِ.
- يَحتاجُ كُلُّ شخصٍ إلى تأشيرةِ عملٍ.
- إنَّ خِبرةُ العملِ شيء أساسيٌّ هذِهِ الأيامِ.

6)

- London has become the biggest market for Islamic finance.
- The Bank of England raises the interest rate for the fourth time this year.
- Jordan relies completely on imported energy.
- Lebanon's government declares the country and the central bank bankrupt.

7)

صادِراتٌ   تَوْظيفٌ
زِيادةٌ

Chapter 6: Media

1)

عالَمٌ / إعلامٌ   خَبَرٌ / خَبيرٌ
رُسولٌ / رِسالةٌ

2)

ع و م   س ب ع
ق ص ص   و ز ع
ص د ر   ج د د
ق و ل   ش ه ر
        ط ب ع

3)

قُبلاتٌ / قُبَلٌ   إعلاناتٌ
كُتُبٌ   تَعليماتٌ / تَعاليمُ
وَسائِلُ   خاتِماتٌ / خَواتِمُ

4)

يُقابِلُ   يُعلِنُ
يَكتُبُ   يُحَرِّرُ
يُواجِهُ   يَصدُرُ

5)

- قامَ الصَّحفيُّ بِنَشْرِ كِتابِهِ الأوَّل.
- قَدَّمَ رئيسُ الوزراءِ بَياناً مُقتَضَباً.
- تَحَدَّثَ الرئيسُ عن المَزاعِمِ في التلفاز.
- أكَّدَ المُراسِلُ على حِياديته.
- يَملِكُ صديقي أكبرَ وَكالةِ أنباءٍ في إنجلترا.

6)

- The latest world news.
- Journalists are essential in maintaining democracy.

- What is the role of journalists today?
- The media play an important role in our time.
- The British press agency mentioned that the prime minister has resigned.

Chapter 7: Law

1)

جَدَلٌ / مُجادِلٌ	عَقْلٌ / اِعتِقالٌ
حِرامٌ / حَرامِيٌّ	ثِقَةٌ / وَثيقَةٌ
شارِعٌ / مَشروعٌ	

2)

ع ق ل	س ج ن
ف ر ض	ش ر ع
ب ر ر	ك ف ل
ج ن ح	و ر ط
ج و ب	س م ح
ح ر م	

3)

إجابَةٌ	زَعيمٌ
إشارَةٌ	فَقيهٌ
شَجَرٌ	قاضٍ
تَحْقيقٌ	مُجادَلَةٌ
جِنايَةٌ	مُحامٍ
حَقٌّ	وَصِيَّةٌ
دَعْوَةٌ	

4)

يَبتَزُّ	يخدَعُ
يَتَّهِمُ	يَرشو
يَسْتَغِشُّ	يَعْقِدُ
يَنتَقِمُ	يَفسَخُ
يُجَرِّمُ	يُوَكِّلُ

Answer Key 411

5)

- لقد نَدِمَ الرَجُلُ على تَصرّفِهِ.
- رَفَعَ صديقي دَعْوى عَلى الشرطة بِسبب التَمييز.
- مَمْنوع الخروج خِلال حَظْرُ التَجوُّلِ.
- اتَّهَمَ بِالتَحايُلِ.
- هَرَبَ السَّجين.
- جاري من ذوي السوابِقُ.

6)

- There has been an unprecedented increase in murder rates in America.
- Knife crimes in Britain have reached an all-time high.
- London has become the capital of thefts in Britain.

7)

أَثْبَتَ	حَرَّمَ
مُذنِبٌ	شَكَّ
حَقيقةٌ	

Chapter 8: Culture

1)

إلَهٌ / إلاهةٌ	ريحٌ / روحٌ
جَسَدٌ / تَجسيدٌ	سَجّادَةٌ / مَسجِدٌ
حِجابٌ / حاجِبٌ	

2)

س ل م	ص ل ب
ن ص ر	ع ب د
ش ي ط ن	ف ح ش

3)

إحتِفالاتٌ	عَذارى / عَذراواتٌ
تَضحِياتٌ	قِسّيسونَ
ثَقافاتٌ	كافِرونَ / كُفّارٌ
ساحِراتٌ / سَواحِرُ	مَتاحِفُ
شائِعاتٌ	هَدايا

412 Answer Key

4)

الْقُرآنُ الْكَريمُ	الْأَعيادُ الْوَطَنِيَّةُ
الْيَهوديَّةُ الْأَرْثوذوكْسِيَّةُ	عِبادَةُ الشَّخصِ
	أَستغفِرُ اللهَ

5)

- The Arabic Islamic culture is considered one of the most important.
- Ramadan is a blessed month.

6)

- هُناكَ ما يزيدُ على بَليونِ مُسلمٍ في العالَمِ.
- الْأَقباطُ أكبرُ مَجموعةٍ مسيحيَّةٍ في الشَّرقِ الْأَوسطِ.
- تَوضَّأَ الْوَلَدُ قَبْلَ الصَّلاةِ.
- لندنُ مَدينةٌ مُتداخِلةُ الثَّقافاتِ.
- يَعتبِرُ الْيَهودُ أنفسَهُمْ شَعبَ اللهِ الْمُختارَ.

Chapter 9: Earth

1)

فَرشٌ / فَراشٌ	جِبرٌ / حُباري
نَجمٌ / مَنْجَمٌ	حَيٌّ / حَيَّةٌ
وَحشٌ / إيحاشٌ	خَرَفٌ / خَروفٌ

2)

ر ط ب	أ س د
ط ب ع	س ح ب
ك ه ر ب	ل و ث
ه و ى	ج ذ ب
	ح ط ب

3)

ضبابٌ / ضُبّانٌ	بَناتُ آوى
عَواصِفُ	بيناتٌ
أقمارٌ	تَجاربُ
نِسامٌ / نَسائمُ	جُزُرٌ
	زَهراتٌ

Answer Key 413

4)

يَفتَرِسُ	يُشَتّي
يُدَوِّدُ	يَطيرُ
يُزَرْزِرُ	يَنبَحُ

5)

- الاختِلالُ المُناخِيُّ مشكِلَةٌ عالميَّةٌ.
- التَوَقُّعاتُ الْجَوِّيَّةُ: الطقسُ مُشمِسٌ وفيه رطوبةٌ.
- التلَوُّثُ نتيجةٌ مُباشرةٌ للسلوكِ البشريَّةِ.
- تَرفَعُ روسيا أسعارَ البترولِ.

6)

- A heatwave is heading to the European continent this coming week.
- My brother studies veterinary science at Cambridge University.
- Wind power is a type of renewable energy.
- A hurricane in Germany destroys the roofs of buildings.
- Is a nuclear disaster possible if Ukraine is subject to a Russian attack?

Chapter 10: Technology

1)

ر س ل	ج ه ز
ب ي ن	ش و ش
ح د ث	أ م ر

2)

إختِصاراتٌ	شَبَكاتٌ / شَبَكٌ
أبوابٌ / بيبان	مُتابِعونَ
جَوْلاتٌ	نَوافِذُ
أسلاكٌ	وَسائِلُ

3)

- هِيَ أشهرُ مُدوَّنةٍ على الإنترنتِ.
- مَعظَمُ النّاسِ يَتَسَوَّقونَ على الإنترنتِ.
- هُناك بعضُ المناطِقِ من غيرِ تَغطيةِ للإنترنتِ.
- أصبحَ الهُجومُ عَبْرَ الإنترنتِ شائعاً جِدّاً هذهِ الأيامِ.

4)

- Some researchers believe that the internet leads to social isolation in children.
- One of the positives of the internet is its use to communicate with friends.
- Governments use the internet to spy on their citizens.
- What is cyberbullying?

Index

accountancy 209
acid 40, 354
agriculture 193
aid 23, 180–182
alcohol 47, 61
animals 11, 73, 114, 163, 236, 257, 273, 337–350, 352
Arab 103, 130, 245
Arabic 104–105, 108, 110, 117, 124; grammar 1–7, 68, 81, 107, 172, 246, 352
Arabisation 2
atheism 305, 314

bank 192, 208, 216, 247, 408
bankruptcy 220, 408
blogging 2, 383, 387, 391, 402
body 4, 26, 38–39, 43, 68, 72, 218, 269, 298, 405
borrowings 105, 218
British Broadcasting Corporation (BBC) 207
budget 217, 224
business 110, 113, 136, 187, 192, 196, 198–199, 216, 240, 381

calques 2, 400
censorship 250–251, 389
Christianity 296, 298, 316–317
clause 85, 108, 133, 138, 228, 244, 247, 268
climate 120, 350, 353–356, 378
commerce 106, 196, 198, 206, 381
communication 228, 287, 390, 399–400
computer 2, 209, 236, 385–386, 389, 392, 397, 405
constitution 57, 129, 130, 300, 313, 357
convictions 280, 284
court 167, 255, 257–260

crime 30, 42, 99, 161, 254, 255, 270–271, 285, 293, 411
crisis 58, 142, 212, 222
culture 90, 94, 98, 207, 294, 319, 322–323, 332, 412
cure 72–74, 287
currency 136, 192

data 88, 259, 381, 383, 393–394, 397, 399, 401
death 72, 77–78, 126, 175, 277, 290, 324
debt 78, 84, 212–213, 219, 324
defence 75, 78, 144, 147, 157, 212, 257, 259
deficit 206, 217
deposit 150, 204, 207, 209, 212, 224
derivation 1–6, 13, 15, 99, 105, 224
development 181
dictionary 2, 103, 105
digital 389, 394
disability 76, 190
displacement 180
DNA 40
drugs 56, 117

earth 169, 208, 308, 337, 356, 358, 366, 368, 412
Easter 313
economics 88, 110, 187, 208
education 81, 83, 85–86, 88, 90, 94, 230, 287, 322, 405
elections 178–180, 239
electronic 2, 238, 381, 384
emotions 16, 24, 26, 51, 59, 94, 109, 368
employment 187–189, 192–193, 196, 226, 257, 392
energy 16, 93, 359, 361–362, 408, 413
engineering 195

environment 337, 358, 367–368
European Union 143

Facebook 395
family 9, 10, 14–15, 129, 159, 403
finance 208, 222, 408
freedom 128, 160, 236, 241

government 46, 121, 125, 129–130, 167, 387, 408, 414

hacking 152, 386
health 33, 38, 74, 77, 165, 179, 212, 284, 287, 356, 404, 407
history 109, 110, 393
horoscopes 321
human 9, 67, 69, 77, 111, 163, 187, 188, 207, 257, 379

illness 39, 58, 61–62, 66–69, 71, 73, 261, 284, 320
industry 203
information technology 380
internet 2, 356, 380–381, 383–384, 386, 388–389, 391, 393, 396, 402, 414
investment 208
Islam 91, 130, 165, 174, 184, 256, 260, 263, 268, 276, 296, 304–306, 308, 327, 408, 412

journalism 110, 186, 227, 229–230, 253, 409–410
Judaism 318, 336
justice 144, 180, 221, 262, 264, 266, 270

language 1, 2, 48, 100, 104–106, 110, 114, 117, 124, 218, 247, 312, 321, 330, 380; *see also* Arabic
law 89, 106, 113, 129–130, 142, 161, 226, 254–260, 265, 268, 276, 306, 387, 397, 410
lexicon 103–105
linguistics 2, 110
loanwords 2, 7, 211, 245, 381, 400
love 19, 22, 26–27, 34–35, 60, 106, 120–121, 169, 205, 242, 369

media 110, 227, 252, 384, 399, 410; social media 384
medicine 73, 75, 260, 329
member of parliament (MP) 127, 136, 143
Middle East 267, 336
mind 57, 280
modernisation 146

money 45, 52, 130, 192, 209, 213–216, 220, 222, 241, 314, 351, 372
monopoly 147, 199
multimedia 399

nature 108, 117, 237, 300, 313, 315, 337, 357
network 166, 389, 391, 399–400
news 227–228, 230, 234–235, 251, 253, 400
non-governmental organisation (NGO) 129
North Atlantic Treaty Organisation (NATO) 142
nouns 3, 5–7, 101
nuclear 361–362, 365, 413

offense 274, 285
opinion 26, 218, 241, 244, 263

parliament 126–127, 136, 142–143, 199, 245
party 133, 136–137, 146, 155, 186, 192, 307, 309
peace 25, 32, 101, 136, 147, 149, 159, 165, 167, 176, 269, 306, 320, 362
politics 125, 406
pollution 375, 379
press 229–230, 234, 244, 245, 410
profession 105, 188, 194, 203, 259
programming 382
publishing 235, 237–238, 357

radiation 20, 361, 365
Ramadan 304, 311, 313, 336, 412
refugee 180–182
religion 1, 31, 131, 212, 294, 302, 311
rights 256–257, 291, 351
roots 1–2, 6, 7

school 5, 81–83, 233
security 149, 151–152, 154–155, 217, 244, 281, 306, 380, 394
sex 40, 49, 51–52, 54, 96–97, 187
society 97, 160, 294, 319
sociology 88, 97
statistics 88, 209
Stock Exchange, the 201
subjects 107, 109–110
synonym 7, 42, 124

tax 216–217, 219, 222
television 2, 227, 253
terrorism 153
trade 106, 110, 136, 188, 192, 195–198, 201, 203, 217
tradition 268, 287, 306, 320, 329, 331

treaty 142, 145, 260
Twitter 394–395

United Nations (UN) 126, 207

verb 1, 3, 4–5, 7, 85, 96, 101, 138, 202, 224, 235, 245

war 10, 161, 166, 271, 407
weapons 163, 165, 365; weapons of mass destruction (WMD) 163
weather 120, 214, 350, 353, 355, 378
website 145, 390, 393, 400
wireless 390
world 88, 208, 230, 302, 366

Printed in the United States
by Baker & Taylor Publisher Services